THE MAVERICKS

Lessons Learned from the West's Winning Entrepreneurs

Paul Grescoe

McGraw-Hill
Ryerson

Toronto • Montréal • New York • Burr Ridge • Bangkok • Bogotá • Caracas
Lisbon • London • Madrid • Mexico City • Milan • New Delhi • Seoul
Singapore • Sydney • Taipei

McGraw-Hill
Ryerson Limited

A Subsidiary of The McGraw·Hill Companies

ISBN: 0-07-560437-X

1234567890 TRI 99
Printed and bound in Canada.

Canadian Cataloguing in Publication Data

Grescoe, Paul, 1939 –
   The mavericks: lessons from the west's winning entrepreneurs

Includes index.
ISBN 0-07-560437-X

1. Entrepreneurship—Canada, Western. 2. Success in business—Canada, Western.
3. Businesspeople—Canada, Western—Biography. I. Title.

HC112.5.A2G73   1999   338'.04'0922712   C99-931879-9

Publisher: **Joan Homewood**
Editorial Co-ordinator: **Catherine Leek**
Production Co-ordinator: **Susanne Penny**
Editor: **Michael Carroll**
Electronic Page Design and Composition: **Kim Monteforte / Heidy Lawrance Associates**
Cover Design: **Keith Chang / Silverpoint Graphics Group Inc.**

To some dear if disparate west-coast friends:
Carsten and Laurence, whose only talk of business
is about the books they write so beautifully;
Gray, once a faithful partner in an honest-to-god business;
Wayne, who works the other side of the street so well;
Mark, a fellow veteran of the freelance wars;
Rob, who helps support my writing habit;
and Chuck, for his wit and warmth of friendship.
In their own ways, Mavericks all.

Contents

INTRODUCTION: The Making of the Mavericks 1

PART 1: The Empire Makers 23

1 Marathon Man 29
Gary Charlwood, Century 21 Canada, and Uniglobe Travel (International)

2 The Entertainer 57
Tim Gamble, Peace Arch Entertainment Group

PART 2: The Palate Pleasers 83

3 Hot Dogger 89
Yves Potvin, Yves Veggie Cuisine

4 The Passionate Vintner 115
Harry McWatters, Sumac Ridge Estate Winery, and Hawthorne Mountain Vineyards

PART 3: The Tourism Impresarios 143

5 Mr. Submarine 149
Dennis Hurd, Atlantis Submarines

6 The Railroader 177
Peter Armstrong, Great Canadian Railtour Company

PART 4: The Manufacturing Magicians 205

7 Boondocks Warriors 209
Brad and Lori Field, Pacific Safety Products

8 The Hucksters 233
Jim and Bruna Scharf, Jim Scharf Holdings

PART 5: The High-Tech Entrepreneurs 255

9 The Pathfinders 261
Ed and Shirley Fitzhenry, Pacific Navigation Systems

10 The Gamesman 285
Chuck Loewen, Online Business Systems

PART 6: The Gender Pioneers 305

11 The Healer 311
Dr. Julia Levy, QLT PhotoTherapeutics

12 The Samurai's Daughter 333
Kazuko Komatsu, Pacific Western Brewing

INDEX 357

Acknowledgements

Thanks to all those Mavericks who by definition are hellishly busy and preoccupied with today's detail yet gave me so much of their time, their history, and their thoughtfulness. Thanks also to two of them who so generously took me for a ride—Peter Armstrong of Great Canadian Railtour and Dennis Hurd of Atlantis Submarines—and to all the spouses and business partners of the featured Mavericks, in hope they understand why I had to focus primarily on individuals for this book.

And many thank-yous to:

John Schreiner of *The Financial Post*, who gave me vital background on the wineries of B.C. and whose various books on the subject proved invaluable in my research; Bonnie Irving of *B.C. Business Magazine*, who published condensations that helped with the cashflow; and Ellen Godfrey, Brian Daisley, Murray Atherton, and Sherrill MacLaren, who tipped me off to Julia Levy, Yves Potvin, Peter Armstrong, and Audra Hollingshead, respectively.

The unsung publicists and corporate-communication specialists who facilitated my research and access, people such as Stephen Lewis, Louise Gallagher, and the indefatigable Tina Baird.

Kim Sinclair, my fellow islomane, who so diligently transcribed most of the interviews, in the process meeting a lot of interesting characters in her adopted country.

My publisher, Joan Homewood, who had faith in the project from the start, and my editor, Michael Carroll, who again brought his usual skill and care to the book.

My agent, Carolyn Swayze, who seems to be evolving into our family agent, and who does her job so well, with dispatch, determination, and sensitivity.

And finally to my wife, Audrey, not only for giving me the idea in the first place but also for giving me the space, time, and support, which she always does with such grace.

Introduction

The Making of
The Mavericks

If there is any one entrepreneur who person-
ifies a province of western Canada—as
K. C. Irving did in New Brunswick, Pierre
Péladeau did in Quebec, and Conrad Black still does in Ontario—he
would be Jimmy Pattison. The Saskatchewan-born, British Columbia-
bred chief executive officer and sole owner of The Jim Pattison Group,
Canada's third-largest private company, choreographs dozens of wildly
diverse divisions operating throughout North America and around the
world. Yet the bantam tycoon with the Jack Nicholson smile is inextrica-
bly entwined with the progress of British Columbia. The province's residents shop at his supermarkets, eat his canned seafood, take home a
mind-boggling array of products wrapped in his packaging, purchase and
lease vehicles at his car dealerships, drive by his billboards and neon signs,
listen to his radio stations, read the magazines and books he distributes,
and even subscribe to his glossy quarterly that celebrates his adopted
province. Nearly a decade and a half ago, I came to know the flamboyant
though circumspect businessman when I collaborated with him on his
autobiography. (And, as fair warning about what follows, let me note that
I continue to do corporate-communications work for him today.) In the
course of researching his life and career, I came across a series of little
truisms that had guided him over the decades. Some of them sounded outright corny, most were borrowed shamelessly from other sources, but all
expressed a kernel of business wisdom that he had reaped the traditional
hard way—by committing pretty basic entrepreneurial blunders. As he
learned from these almost-inevitable, financially traumatic errors, Pattison
often translated his mistakes into lessonlike advice to pass on to the executives of his companies, whether they wanted to hear it or not.

Recognizing the potential appeal of these aphorisms and the stories behind them, I persuaded him to present a sampling as a final chapter of his book, a coda of counsel that might inspire or enhearten embyronic or struggling entrepreneurs. The sayings ranged from the vaguely sarcastic and gender-improper ("There's no limit to what a man can do or where he can go if he doesn't mind who gets the credit") to the wonderfully pragmatic ("Nothing will ever be attempted if all possible objections must first be overcome"). What made these lines more than the overworked platitudes they can be—what transformed them into meaningful, thought-exciting maxims—was the real-world experience Pattison recorded to underscore their absolute relevance to creating and building any business anywhere. Even today, in his seventh decade, Pattison continues to preach his gospel, retailing minor commandments of capitalism. In an interview with *The Financial Post*'s Diane Francis a couple of years ago, he talked about his long-past days as a salesman peddling pots and pans door-to-door, when he discovered that "people like dealing with happy people, so I increased my productivity by whistling and being happy."

Whistling aside, as a fellow westerner and sometime entrepreneur, I could relate many of his axioms to my own limited experience. I had had entrepreneurial instincts since my late teens, when some friends and I hired the fellow who did the CBC radio guide in Winnipeg and we published Canada's very first newsstand television-listings magazine. *Preview* survived only a few issues, but it did predate *TV Guide*'s appearance in this country, and had the distinction of employing as an ad salesman a struggling young actor named Len Cariou, who went on to star with Elizabeth Taylor and Diana Rigg in the Oscar-winning *A Little Night Music*. Long after, when Pattison told me his mother's personal philosophy—"Not failure, but low aim is crime"—I realized it was one that I had unconsciously shared as a boy publisher. And again, a couple of decades ago, my aim was equally high when considering the scary takeover of a failed city magazine in Vancouver. My wife and I, having virtually no investment money of our own, enlisted a couple of partners, and the lone periodical turned into a viable concern that eventually published three city magazines in the West, a men's magazine in Quebec, and an airline magazine in the United States.

One of Pattison's own pet phrases sounds arrogant and even fiscally suicidal: "Maybe in error, never in doubt." But it expresses his belief in decisiveness, his disbelief in dithering. It also reflects the superficially reckless attitude that later led me into another partnership, this time in corporate communications. For whatever reason, I never had any doubt that my colleague and I could quickly create a successful business from a standing start. And after the first ten days of cold-calling, our client list included the Canadian pavilion at Expo 86, British Columbia's largest public company (MacMillan Bloedel), and its largest private enterprise (yes, the selfsame Jim Pattison Group). The first few years were good ones, but I began to doubt and saw the error of my ways: my first love was the writing of books. That was when I fell back on another Jimmyism to tell my partner I was going solo. "You gotta wanna," Pattison had pointed out—you have got to want to succeed in what you are doing this minute—and, in analyzing my business career, I knew I no longer did.

Earlier I had collaborated on a book about western Canadian entrepreneurs, *The Money Rustlers: Self-Made Millionaires of the New West.* * My fascination with the breed deepened with my research and writing about the quintessential new western self-made multimillionaire that Pattison had become. After I left business for books, this interest found fresh focus with my more recent chronicle of the Bonnycastles, husband, wife, son, and daughter, a western family that had constructed an extraordinary publishing empire on mass-market love stories. It was while crossing the country to promote *The Merchants of Venus: Inside Harlequin and the Empire of Romance* that I began to field comments from interviewers encouraging me to do a sequel to *The Money Rustlers.* In the dozen years since that book, a whole new crop of candidates had surfaced. They were in many ways a more grown-up, less callow group of risk takers than their predecessors had represented, and they were flourishing in the context of a much more economically mature West. Through it all, they maintained their distinctiveness from their eastern counterparts: more laid-back and personal and often more outspoken and open-minded. My cheerleaders thought the field was fertile for an update featuring some exemplars of the region's most compelling entrepreneurs, whose personalities,

---

* My collaborator was David Cruise, assisted by his wife, Alison Griffiths. They have since written other bestselling books with business themes: *Fleecing the Lamb: The Inside Story of the Vancouver Stock Exchange, Lords of the Line,* and *Net Worth: Exploding the Myths of Pro Hockey.*

philosophies, and business backgrounds remained largely unexamined even if their companies' fortunes were not.

It was tempting to repeat the old formula. But I was saved from self-imitation by a suggestion from my wife, the writer Audrey Grescoe, who pointed out that the times, and the economy, demand more than another collection of straight business biographies. Corporate restructuring and government downsizing have forced thousands of Canadians to become their own bosses. Fortunately we are more and more enamoured of starting our own companies, or at least encouraging our children to. A 1998 survey of entrepreneurial attitudes in five countries—Canada, the United States, Germany, Britain, and Finland—showed that 89 percent of Canadians said they would approve of their sons and daughters opening a business (Americans were the next most approving at 85 percent, the British the least at 68). Already more than two million of us are self-employed, and small business generates most of our jobs. Business historian Michael Bliss says entrepreneurship is transforming our country —and "this is the way we have to grow if we are to compete in the world."

The fact is, my wife argued, what most of our embryonic and growing entrepreneurs need now is good advice on how to run their businesses and how to spot consumer trends and interpret demographic realities. That was when I recalled Pattison and his habit of wedding cautionary and motivational words with working examples drawn from everyday commerce. *The Mavericks: Lessons from the West's Winning Entrepreneurs* follows that lead: combining the stories of successful businesspeople with wise counsel that comes out of their own experience and is related mostly in their own words. And who better to give guidance and talk about trends than successful risk takers from western Canada, where creating an enterprise far from the financial citadels and denser population pools of Ontario and Quebec can be just that much tougher (and sometimes, paraxodically, that much easier)? One consequence of this smaller consumer base for products and services is that western companies tend to reach out more readily to the larger national and international marketplaces. It is no coincidence that all of the entrepreneurs I would come to interview, however modestly they began, have had to court foreign customers as a means of growth, if not survival.

There are many other reasons to focus on the experiences of self-starting businesspeople in Manitoba, Saskatchewan, Alberta, and British

Columbia. As the Center for Strategic and International Studies in Washington, D.C., pointed out in a paper in 1998, this half of the country is increasingly setting the national policy-making agenda. The author, political scientist David Rovinsky of Pennsylvania's Bloomsburg University, wrote: "Western Canada has definitely come to be the motor of Canadian political thought in the 1990s." You don't have to be a political-science major to know that the more conservative thought processes in place have prompted a friendlier attitude on the part of the four provincial governments toward business and industry. Even the New Democratic administration of British Columbia, hungry for new jobs, has had to make gestures of conciliation to the province's executives and entrepreneurs.*

Three years ago, when I first started entertaining the idea of this book, Alberta and British Columbia had replaced Ontario's Golden Triangle as Canada's job-creation engine. While our westernmost province is now mired in a mild recession (although the banks are predicting the economy will rebound this year), Alberta continues to gush prosperity as an expanding "have" province, despite low commodity prices. Calgary trails only Toronto as home to major head offices. In *Report on Business* magazine's 1998 survey of Canada's fastest-growing cities, both Calgary and Edmonton loomed large. A study earlier that year showed much-smaller Medicine Hat, Alberta, led 61 cities in job growth over the past two years, and among the list's top five centres, four were western: Nanaimo, British Columbia, and Medicine Hat, Red Deer, and Calgary, Alberta. Meanwhile the West's other two provinces are thriving. In 1997, three years after its NDP government brought down the first balanced budget in 13 years, Saskatchewan became the best place in Canada for young people to find jobs, followed by Alberta and Manitoba. Skilled workers of all ages are in particularly short supply in Manitoba, which in 1998 was one of Canada's most quickly increasing economies, with the lowest unemployment rate, 5.2 percent.

---

* Glen Clark's government has a long way to go in terms of redeeming itself: small businesses consider it the least effective among Canada's four wealthiest provinces. A survey by Hart & Associates Management Consultants of Toronto in 1998 showed that on a ten-point scale British Columbia rated only 3.2 in effectiveness while Alberta led the field at 4.4 (Ontario and Quebec were 3.5 each). Kitchener, Ontario (4.0), topped all cities, followed by Calgary, Vancouver, Montreal, and Toronto.

Luckily the one resource the western provinces are not short of is Mavericks.

The Mavericks

Maverick (noun): an unbranded range animal; an independent individual who does not go along with a group.

Selecting the entrepreneurs for this book was both a simple and a difficult task. The West is abrim with winners who will wear no one else's insignia, who refuse to ride with the herd—who take pride in being Mavericks. Given the disarming openness of most of their breed, there was no lack of people who would be frank about discussing the hard-won lessons they have learned in real-life situations.* The problem was to cull just a few who in their individualism and energy and reflectiveness could represent their kind. My criteria were simply that they had to have been intimately involved in conceiving businesses, that they continue to run independently owned operations, and that their companies are currently viable—that is, not deeply mired in debt or facing bankruptcy —and promise even more success in coming years.

---

*One exception was Milton Wong, Vancouver's water-walking money manager who turned a $40-million nest egg into $3.5 billion in assets in less than seven years. The eighth of nine children of a Chinatown tailor, he subsequently saw his high-riding investment-counselling firm, M. K. Wong & Associates, virtually collapse in the wake of Black Monday, the 1987 market crash. He recovered, hiring a cohort of young, computer-clever fact sifters to detect and dissect technologically sophisticated small-capitalization oil and gas ventures, among other hot prospects. Their stocks became part of the New Economy Growth Fund, which in its first six months alone had a return of 122 percent. A recipient of an Order of Canada, Wong represents an astonishingly high level of humanity in the business world. He has been the key fund raiser for various charitable causes; the spark plug behind the Laurier Institute, a national nonprofit organization promoting multiculturalism; and the organizing chairman who called in all his cards to make a success of the 1997 World Chinese Entrepreneurs Convention in Vancouver, the first such gathering outside Asia. Both *Canadian Business* and *B.C. Business* magazines have named him Socially Responsible Entrepreneur of the Year. While I very much wanted to spend time with this thoughtful investment counsellor, Wong demurred for personal reasons he declined to explain, other than the wish to protect his family's privacy. My ego was salved by the fact that his company has since been acquired by the Hongkong Bank of Canada, which makes him ineligible as an independent Maverick.

6

I finally chose 15 men and women whose personal stories proved to be as fascinating as the thoughtfulness they inspired.

The Empire Makers

Gary Charlwood is the German-born, London-raised coconstructor of Century 21 Canada, the country's largest real-estate operation. Later, he created Vancouver-based Uniglobe Travel (International), the world's third-largest travel organization.

Tim Gamble, whose Peace Arch Entertainment Group produces television commercials, corporate and educational videos, made-for-TV movies, and television series with Francis Ford Coppola and other major American producers, owns two studios and a Vancouver heritage building, and has partnered with Sugar Entertainment, a successful film company.

The Palate Pleasers

Yves Potvin is a Quebec chef who embraced the West Coast lifestyle and invented the tofu wiener for health-wise consumers, making Yves Veggie Cuisine the leading refrigerated meat-alternative brand on the continent. In 1999 he christened the first in a chain of fast-food restaurants featuring his products.

Harry McWatters, president of Sumac Ridge Estate Winery and Hawthorne Mountain Vineyards in British Columbia's Okanagan Valley, was lured by the mystique of the grape to leave a high-paying job to sell modest hybrid wines, and then cofounded his own company to make award-winning whites, varietal reds, and sparkling and ice wines that have fans as far away as Taiwan.

The Tourism Impresarios

Dennis Hurd is the professional engineer who founded Atlantis Submarines of Vancouver, which built and operates the world's biggest fleet of tourist submarines and has recently diversified to become the biggest single tourist operator in both Hawaii and the Caribbean.

Peter Armstrong is a former hotel doorman who launched his own tourist-bus companies in British Columbia. Then he bid against industry giants to buy VIA Rail's failing Rocky Mountaineer train service through the western peaks, transforming it into Canada's first profitable passenger rail line in 40 years.

The Manufacturing Masters

Brad and Lori Field are the husband-and-wife team that parlayed a skiing backpack into Pacific Safety Products, a $10-million-a-year public company in the relative backwater of Kelowna, British Columbia. The firm makes bulletproof vests and other body armour for American paramedics, Bosnian peacekeepers, and Japanese cops.

Jim and Bruna Scharf, the Perdue, Saskatchewan, farmers who did innovative deals with TV stations to run pervasive commercials about their patented E-Zeewrap 1000 plastic-wrap dispenser, built their company into a multimillion-dollar kitchen-gadget manufacturer and then concocted an instant-cooking lentil product for Mexicans and Spanish-speaking Americans.

The High-Tech Innovators

Edward and Shirley Fitzhenry, husband and wife, are the founding chairman and (until recently) senior vice president of Calgary's Pelorus Navigation Systems, designers and installers of trailblazing Earth-satellite navigational and meteorological systems in 150-plus airports on six continents, and new partners of U.S. heavyweight Honeywell Inc.

Charles "Chuck" Loewen's information-technology consultancy, Online Business Services of Winnipeg, has been named one of the 50 best-managed companies in Canada and ranks consistently among the fastest-growing as it expands from its Winnipeg base across the West and into the United States—all of which Loewen handles like a great game.

The Gender Pioneers

Julia Levy, once an ivory-tower microbiologist, went on to cocreate Vancouver's QLT PhotoTherapeutics and assumed the reins as CEO to help make it one of the continent's 25 top biotechnology companies.

Now QLT is on the verge of launching a blockbuster drug that works with lasers to treat an otherwise incurable eye condition of the elderly.

Kazuko Komatsu is a former schoolteacher who recovered from cancer treatment and the loss of her memory to walk log booms and fly into fishing grounds on behalf of buyers back home in Japan before becoming the only female owner of a substantial North American brewery, Pacific Western Brewing Company of Prince George, British Columbia.

The Also-Rans

Many obvious names that appeared on my initial roster of Mavericks failed to make the cut. At the time I compiled the list, they were in full sail and appeared to be contenders for inclusion in the book. As I continued my research, or as conditions changed in the West, or their own situations evolved, they no longer qualified.

The most conspicuous these past couple of years has been *Ray Loewen* of The Loewen Group, the world's second-largest funeral-home and cemetery operator, once worth almost $3 billion. By 1995 the Mennonite from Steinbach, Manitoba, was Canada's 17th-richest man, whose lifestyle included a 33.5-metre yacht. Surely he could be forgiven for believing that this entrepreneurial achievement had rendered him impervious to the humiliating possibility of filing for bankruptcy protection. Yet there he was in November of that year, hunkered down in his Vancouver headquarters, suffering from a bad hip and facing a half-billion-dollar judgement from a Mississippi court for malicious breach of contract, common-law fraud, bad-faith dealing, and attempted monopolization—the largest such damage award in U.S. history. He became all the more intriguing by surviving that case (by paying a mere $175 million), avoiding bankruptcy, and then fighting off a hostile takeover attempt by the rival Service Corp. International. But as the months passed it became clear that Loewen was taking on water. His vice presidents rebelled and started giving him orders, he let go his public-relations staff, and the sharks began closing in as the company's stock took a dive. By the time I was making my final selection, newspaper headlines spoke of a "deathwatch" and The Loewen Group was sinking fast; its founder resigned ignominiously in October 1998.

For another reason entirely, I also sidestepped *Hassan Khosrowshahi*, the founding chairman of the Inwest Investments real-estate realm and Future Shop, which has about 100 stores in Canada and the United States peddling $1.25 billion worth of electronic products a year. His has been a remarkable riches-to-rags-to-riches story: an immigrant who had to flee Iran, abandoning the $2-billion family business (petrochemicals, fertilizers, manufacturing for Cadbury's), and resettled in Vancouver, where he started from nothing with a little office-equipment shop in the early 1980s. Soon realizing he needed administrative strength, Khosrowshahi smuggled an executive out of Iran to help build the company. He has since parted company with his longtime friend and partner and named himself president and CEO, as Future Shop Canada wages a bitter marketing fight with western-based A&B Sound, complete with lawsuits and industrial espionage. A good story, but while his socialite wife appears in the gossip columns, the elusive "Mr. K" is relentlessly media-shy. Someone so privacy-conscious, so self-contained, I decided, would be a poor bet for a book that demands open and honest communication about the mistakes that entrepreneurs make along the way. I might also have been influenced by the fact that in 1998, Khosrowshahi dumped a dozen marketing people as Future Shop's earnings declined by 20 percent and later closed five of his 28 money-draining stores in the northwestern United States.

The one prospective Maverick I was sorry to lose, midway through my research, is *David Graves*, who founded Winnipeg's Broadband Networks Inc. He is a textbook study of the mid-career executive who tires of being shuffled from city to city and becoming a victim of downsizing. The electrical engineer's revenge was to identify an embryonic technology—wireless communications networks delivering data, voice, video, and Internet across licensed airwave frequencies—and then design and manufacture microwave radio equipment that enhances the capacity of wireless networks. He floated the company for a ridiculously modest investment in 1993, attracting venture capital from Cadillac Fairview cofounder Ephraim Diamond, and began building Broadband into a world leader in the field. Only four years later he sold it for an astonishing $586 million to Northern Telecom, where he was once on staff. Graves brought more than technological smarts from his work with Nortel, Alberta's NovAtel, and Hughes Electronics: he had an innate capacity to inspire his 240 employees in Winnipeg and Dallas; the corporate vision statement said quite simply, "We will be the best in the world." Although it was announced that he would continue to run Broadband, it was no surprise when David Graves resigned soon after, with about $160 million in his pocket, and dropped out of sight.

The Maverick Mindset

The 15 Mavericks profiled on the following pages are as dissimilar in their interests, opinions, and characters as any group of entrepreneurs can be. They are unpretentious and arrogant, gregarious and guarded, direct and disingenuous. They are neither saints nor sinners, although Julia Levy and Kazuko Komatsu have seraphic reputations as employers (offering their staff bonuses or profit-sharing as well as other perks) and Peter Armstrong and Yves Potvin do confess to venial sins in their early careers (Armstrong actively flouting transportation-industry rules and Potvin looking the other way in an under-the-table deal that backfired badly). Yet many of them share similar characteristics and casts of mind, some of which spring from the settings where they do business— from the West itself.

In fact, one immediately apparent touchstone is the Mavericks' profound sense of place. Walter Good is a professor of marketing at the University of Manitoba and the author of *Building a Dream*, a book for entrepreneurial hopefuls. Observing western risk takers at work, he tells me, "They tend to be sons of the soil, very loyal to the area where they got their start." He points to deeply ensconced Winnipeg families like the Establishment Richardsons (grain, securities, real estate) and the more *nouveau* Aspers (CanWest Global TV) who have the flexibility and the finances to move to more sizable and salubrious cities, yet stay put. A subphenomenon of Good's province is the Mennonite entrepreneurs who have established enormous businesses in small towns such as Steinbach and Morden. "These are companies that could have gone anywhere in the country, in the world," Good says, "but they have a real sense of their roots. Peter Enns with Triple E down in Winkler, the motor-home and trailer development [Canada's largest RV manufacturer]. Friesen, one of the most successful printers—to build a multi-million-dollar business out of a town like Altona and continue to stay

11

really demonstrates tremendous community commitment."* Good sees an inordinate number of successful western entrepreneurs staying put: "They support and try to build their local community with [charitable] contributions and investments. They're really proud of their origins. I don't think you get that sort of commitment elsewhere."

Elsewhere, of course, means the East—more particularly Toronto, the Canadian financial capital. In *The Money Rustlers,* we described a state of mind that "includes a regional bias that at times expresses itself as virulent antipathy towards Ontario, sometimes to the detriment of the entrepreneurs or their businesses." Today the Mavericks, more self-assured and at ease with their successes—and less dependent on the financiers and occasionally even the markets of eastern Canada—view the rest of the country with more equanimity, and less outright dislike. Most of them no longer need the East as a whipping boy, conveniently at hand when they encounter problems. At worst they now treat it with disdain, at best with a quiet amusement about how seriously those stuffy, effete easterners tend to take themselves.

Roy Hurd, father of Vancouver submarine builder Dennis, lives in Toronto. He remembers getting a phone call one day to report that his son was coming to town to meet potential shareholders. The caller was a Toronto broker concerned about Dennis's penchant for wearing rough wool sweaters and no tie. "Do you think you could get him to put on a suit?" the man asked.

"You don't know much about the West Coast, do you?" Roy replied. "No, I don't think he's going to wear a suit."

---

*Mennonites began immigrating to southern Manitoba from Russia in 1874 and now number about 60,000 in the province. Descended from Anabaptist Christians of the early 16th-century Reformation, and speaking Low German, they had been on the move across Europe, escaping persecution for their pacifist religious beliefs. In the 19th century, a German-speaking agent for Canada, which wanted the West populated to preclude an American takeover, described them as "hardworking, sober, moral, and intelligent people. ... I found prosperous merchants, manufacturers, and mechanics." Most of them settled in as farmers, but in 1914 a Friesen in Steinbach, Manitoba, was the first Ford car dealer in western Canada and the town eventually became the province's "automobile city." Another success story has been the DeFehr family's Palliser Furniture, which employs 3,000, mostly in Winnipeg, and is now run by Art DeFehr, who graduated from Harvard Business School. The employees of Friesen Printers, which started as a school-yearbook printing house, typify the Mennonites' hard-work ethic: president David Friesen says the company has "absolutely no problem with absenteeism."

Accountant Ken Bolton, an adviser to Yves Veggie Cuisine of Delta, British Columbia, finds on his eastern visits far fewer companies that adopt casual-clothes Fridays. "Here, I don't have anybody in my clientele that doesn't," he insists. Certainly he himself is relaxed enough about his professional image to hand out calling cards promising a passel of distinctive services, among them "cows branded" and "saloons emptied." Not long ago Bolton discussed other differences between the two halves of Canada with seven other accountants, three of whom have practised in the East, and summed up the consensus for me: "We are very definitely more casual in the West. There, everything is confirmed in writing. Here, I can make a deal on the telephone and understand that the individual knows there's a deal. ... There's a lifestyle difference. Our personal time in the West is of greater import, with more emphasis on one's self and one's family. That time after five or six o'clock is very important, whereas in the East it's okay to work till 8:00 or 8:30. ... There's another distinction. In high tech, we are more creative. *They're* still doing it the way they were yesterday. They're not as flexible. We have the ability to attract more new things because we're more open-minded."

Smug as all that sounds, there truly is a sense of possibility in the West. There is still room to start a winery, assemble an entertainment empire, build a body-armour factory in the boondocks and develop it into an enterprise strong enough to swallow its major eastern competitor. (And so many of the Mavericks have launched themselves on a relative pittance of capital investment—as little as $10,000 cash—which they raised by resorting to such clichés of entrepreneuralism as mortgaging their houses or hitting up friends and relatives.) Sandy Altner is an ex-New Yorker, president of The Management Exchange Inc., a small-business consulting and training agency in Winnipeg. "I have always felt that Winnipeg was like a new frontier," she has said. "There were many things that were happening elsewhere that Winnipeggers weren't aware of yet, things that were too new to accept immediately. ... Winnipeg is not a perfect place, but it allows us to change it, slowly, to have an effect and a voice, to be part of the evolution toward what it absolutely must become in the new, global economy."

Farther west, the feeling of frontier—and the resulting elbow room—intensifies. Julia Levy of QLT PhotoTherapeutics, the biotech company, is speaking especially of the West Coast when she says, "In my gut I know that we're different, that it's partly an atmosphere of freedom and an atmosphere of tolerance. I think of Toronto as the three-piece-suit place where everybody is a prototypical Canadian, [doing] kind of stodgy, conservative business. Whereas here you're sort of loonier, willing to enjoy life, enjoy the risk—say, 'Hey, this is not a dress rehearsal. Let's try something.'"*

Levy also believes western executives are more plain-spoken and out-spoken. She tells the story of Maria Klawe, then University of British Columbia vice president of student and academic services, who was in Ottawa with her at a science-career day sponsored by the Royal Society of Canada. Among the only three westerners at an awards dinner that night, they sat together at a table of civil servants, most of them women. A Montreal radio-station representative rose to accept a prize. "He had these wretched slides, and the first one was *Man* and his World. There were rumblings at the table and then the guy went from bad to worse. He was just incredibly insensitive about the changing mores of the world: 'What we really want to do is engender the same thrill that the young *boy* has at Christmas when *he* gets *his* first chemistry set.' Maria is the same kind of rabble-rouser that I am and she said, 'What about the young *girl?*' Everybody in the room heard her. He chose to ignore it." Klawe posed the question again; again he brushed it off. "I could see the women at our table: 'Who are these people? Ill-mannered slobs!'" After the dinner, Klawe pursued the man, who said, "You ruined my evening. I have a daughter—I'm not insensitive." An Ontario woman sharing the same table was upset by the outspokenness and refused to join the westerners for a drink afterward. However, the next day she sought them out to say, "You know, I went to my room and I started thinking about this. You were right. I actually went out and looked for you." As Levy says of Klawe's uninhibited candour, "That's a western thing."

---

*In fact, British Columbia has a generally younger population than the national average, which might help explain the fact that risk-taking appears more popular in this province. An Angus Reid survey for Royal Bank of Canada showed that about 23 percent of the 1,000 polled were self-employed, as opposed to the average of 19 percent in the rest of the country; and 40 percent of British Columbians said they were very likely or somewhat likely to be self-employed in the coming year, compared to the Canadian average of 30 percent.

The Newest West

Since *The Money Rustlers*, western Canada has ripened into a more self-confident and more economically rounded region. In the past decade and a half, the collective psyche here has become more accepting of businesses beyond the basic industries (mostly centred around resources) and of the disparate kinds of entrepreneurs emerging to operate them. In the earlier book, for instance, we could find nobody typical to represent Saskatchewan nor were there any profiles of women. The agricultural province has had a well-chronicled history of cooperatives and government entrepreneurship, rather than one of publicly traded companies and other Maverick-style private enterprise outside of farming. Today, however, it is becoming a hothouse of entrepreneurial activity, although the national media still clings to the old image, as witness this amusing letter to *Profit* magazine from Brad J. Wall, director of business development in Swift Current:

> *We are proud of the ranking of our own Batco Manufacturing as one of Canada's hottest startups. ... We were somewhat disappointed, however, by the story's lead line: "Swift Current, Sask., is not normally considered a hub of entrepreneurship." Many cities with the entrepreneurial character of Swift Current would bristle at this affront and counter with some good old vitriolic Western indignation. Instead, we've chosen to offer the cost of a hotel room and a meal to allow you to discover this hub of entrepreneurship.*
>
> *We will arrange for you to meet with countless entrepreneurs such as the principals of Urban Forest Recyclers, who manufacture one of every two egg cartons on the continent, or the folks from National Hardware who employ 300 people to manufacture nuts and bolts. We could also introduce you to the purest entrepreneurs in the world: farmers. Those who face the volatility of world markets, unpredictable weather and the scourge of vermin while they execute annual multi-million-dollar operating plans could provide some insight into our entrepreneurial spirit.*
>
> *You should act quickly. What with all the entrepreneurial activity in our community, it is difficult to get accommodation.*

Although a good if offbeat example of Saskatchewan risk takers figure in this book—grain farmers and gadget manufacturers Jim and
Bruna Scharf—they are only two of many men and women from that
province whose stories and lessons could be recounted. As for women
entrepreneurs leading their own companies, they form the final chapter,
"The Gender Pioneers," where their contributions are discussed in
detail. Another symptom of their growing pervasiveness is the fact that,
of the dozen businesses I have portrayed, half have husbands and wives
working together in varying degrees of involvement.

One of the women featured is Kazuko Komatsu, president of Pacific
Western Brewing, who came from Japan in the mid-1970s while her
nation was flexing its economic muscles and investing in North America.
Throughout the 1990s the Asian influence pervaded western Canada,
especially British Columbia, as Japanese, Taiwanese, and Hong Kong
and mainland Chinese not only brought money but also sent their children to school or settled here themselves. About 40 percent of the
150,000 residents of the Greater Vancouver city of Richmond are ethnic Chinese immigrants and almost half the students in its schools take
English as a second language. In mid-decade the great wave from Hong
Kong alone made up about 20 percent of Canadian immigrants. While
well-heeled Chinese investors such as Li Ka-Shing and his son, Victor,
got the exposure, they were atypical of the real Asian impact on the
West (and, after living in Vancouver for a while, the younger Li has
returned to Hong Kong). A 1997 Asia Pacific Foundation of Canada
report on Chinese-Canadian entrepreneurs pointed out, "Media and
economic analysts usually emphasize the wealth of Chinese immigrants
and their high, and conspicuous, levels of investment in Vancouver.
Certainly recent Chinese immigration has impacted developments in
the city, but to focus exclusively on the richest Chinese-Canadians does
not do justice to the majority, many of whom lead quite ordinary middle-
class lives." Surprisingly the foundation's study found that the Chinese-
Canadian entrepreneurs surveyed, even those catering to their own
ethnic market, followed Canadian business practices. "Though their
Chinese identity is extremely important, especially in family life, it does
not influence their behaviour in business."

At decade's end, as the economic flu spreads in Asia, immigrant investment in western Canada is waning—both in numbers and levels of

wealth—although the effects differ depending on the province. In an article for the *Vancouver Sun* in 1998, Garrett Lambert, a University of Victoria business professor, confirmed that the West was no longer attracting as many millionaires: "The latest arrivals can support themselves during their start-up years, but most need to generate new income for the longer term either through entrepreneurship or employment. That's one of the reasons Alberta's share of the immigration flow started to rise about four years ago." Alberta's burgeoning economy and relatively low tax rates are seductive compared with British Columbia's stagnation and high corporation capital tax. With the Asian downturn, British Columbia has plunged to number ten from number one in economic growth among the provinces.

Generation E

If the West must now rely less on Asian immigrants to spice its entrepreneurial stew, it can find comfort in the fact that a younger generation of risk takers is surfacing. Realizing that their world offers no employment guarantees, they are increasingly schooling themselves to fend for themselves.

And if anything will help a province like British Columbia out of the deep end, it could be a real commitment to official government policy encouraging such entrepreneurship. In one baby step over the past few years, the B.C. Ministry of Small Business, Tourism and Culture has been funding a program called You BET!—Youth Business and Entrepreneurship Training. It offers workshops throughout the province introducing 15- to 29-year-olds to the small-business world: identifying opportunities, conducting feasibility studies, and developing business plans. They can then be matched with local business mentors who monitor their progress. Dave Tanchak and his colleagues at Resonant Communications, a Web site design house in Burnaby, took 12 days' training in market research, writing a business plan, and exploring financing options. Without that, he says, "we'd probably still be floundering around with research and paperwork." Since the workshop in 1996, Resonant has been creating sites for a variety of government, public-relations, and financial clients. Nicole and Jeremy Page used the training program to get their environmentally oriented retail store, Ecotropolis, up and running in Vancouver. And 23-year-old Karla Denby, a former office temp, attended the workshops and then opened her own personnel agency in Prince George.

The B.C. Institute of Technology (BCIT) in Burnaby has a Venture Development Centre that offers Venture, a business incubator providing professional counsel and office space for hopeful entrepreneurs, and a 12-week BCIT Entrepreneurial Skills Training Course (BEST), funded by Human Resources Development Canada, to prepare younger people to become self-employed. This year the college has a new course called Lift-Off, twice as long as BEST, with high-involvement workshops and four months of training and ongoing support for mature workers thinking of going out on their own. The relatively high cost—$8,000—may be picked up by companies as part of severance packages for downsized employees. BCIT is hoping the older students will mix with and mentor the less-experienced Venture participants.

Throughout the four provinces, the federal government's Western Economic Diversification Canada uses its $25-million annual budget to foster small- and medium-size businesses.* Part of its mandate is the Western Youth Entrepreneur Program, which funds loans, loan guarantees, and equity investments up to $25,000 for businesses owned and operated by 18- to 29-year-olds in rural areas. It is a belated attempt to reverse a trend of at least six decades that has seen much of the cream of a young crop desert agricultural communities. Saskatchewan especially has suffered those losses, and its education system is responding with new programs geared to producing self-employed graduates who might decide to stay home. Since 1993, high-school students can take a course called Entrepreneur 30 that highlights problem-solving and decision-making in business, not to mention life (Manitoba has a similar option in Grade 11). The University of Saskatchewan's College of Commerce has revised its curriculum to create a more holistic approach—a synthesis

---

*And in 1997 the federal Business Development Bank, partnering with the Bank of Montreal and the Canadian Imperial Bank of Commerce, created a Canada-wide $30-million fund for entrepreneurs aged 18 through 34 to set up new businesses. The Young Entrepreneur Financing Program provides management counselling, mentoring, and up to $25,000 in loans.

of material from four specialties—that will better prepare students for the crosscurrents they will experience in the messy world of private enterprise, particularly if they become solo-sailing entrepreneurs. Next door in Alberta, the University of Calgary offers an innovative master of business administration in enterprise development to foster entre-preneurship in start-up companies or intrapreneurship within large cor-porations. The program matches teams of first-year M.B.A students with local companies for project work. The following year each student does four consulting projects with owner-managers to get frontline experience and acquire mentors.

Alberta, which begets Mavericks the way its ranches breed cattle, tried to take the educational process one absurd step farther when a group of Calgary parents approached the government in 1998 to open the Charter School of Commerce. A sort of half-pint Harvard Business School for budding Bob Blairs and Ron Southerns, it would enroll pupils as young as eight, the boys to wear white shirts and ties, the girls no more than two earrings at a time, with both genders urged to carry briefcases instead of backpacks. The curriculum, based on a Florida model, would have the kids studying résumés and other business documents as liter-ature and real-estate and stock-market prospectuses as math. The Calgary Board of Education rejected the concept, and while the provin-cial education minister voiced his approval, more conservative minds in his department seem to have squelched the school (among many resul-tant wry letters to the editor was Torontonian David Ross's to the *Globe and Mail*: "What this program will create, if the Alberta government approves it, are the sort of one-dimensional bores that other people will cross the street to avoid having to talk to").

A far saner approach in both that province and Manitoba has been Canada's first summer entrepreneurship camps, which opened in 1998. In Alberta teenagers spent a week on a Cypress Hills ranch doing mildly risk-taking physical activities and mind-stretching exercises such as learn-ing how to prepare a business plan and promote a product. The Youth Entrepreneurship Camp, funded by Western Economic Development, attracted mostly middle-class teens. Manitoba's version—two weeks on the University of Manitoba campus—was designed for promising kids aged 14 to 18 who were considered at risk in the community. Based on U.S. programs run by the National Foundation for Teaching

19

Entrepreneurship, it was organized by the university's Asper Centre for Entrepreneurship. Walter Good, to whom the centre reports, says, "We've never had as strong a response from the community. If we wanted, we could have raised $100,000." As it was, a large sum came from an anonymous businessman with interests in Winnipeg, and local companies donated all the food and sponsored campgoers' attendance. An American instructor taught everything from feasibility studies to marketing. The teens took field trips to the Commodities Exchange, the Nygard International women's wear factory, and even Costco, where they were given cash to buy supplies (one magnate-in-the-making did nice business selling his peers soft drinks). The armed forces ran team-building exercises; the police chief, aboriginal leaders, and social-service people offered straight-talk advice. Some of the most useful presentations came from local entrepreneurs, including Randy Cunningham, a major McDonald's franchisee; others acted as mentors, among them Kathy Drysdale of Pro Image, an audiovisual sales and rental firm.

"There's an extensive pool of very active young entrepreneurs that's developed in Winnipeg," says Good. Many of them have been members of the Young Leaders Committee sponsored by Winnipeg 2000, the city's economic-development initiative. The committee, formed in 1994 to support youthful enterprise, published a fund-raising book a year later with capsule biographies and words of counsel from 44 local businesspeople. *Anatomy of an Entrepreneur*, a handsome 212-page volume illustrated with Leonardo da Vinci drawings, was a revealing X ray of a rising generation of western risk takers. They included Douglas Martin, publisher of *What! A Magazine*, Canada's largest-circulation teen publication; Clark Johannson, a partner in Carlyle Computer Products, which at the time had annual revenues of $30 million from seven Canadian branches; and Dulcie Price, whose Optimum Agra Services helped farmers market their grain and oilseed production. Collectively the youngest of the contributors were richly representative of the unbranded, free-ranging entrepreneurial winners the West (and Canada) absolutely require to continue prospering, not simply surviving, into the next century. I was heartened that in their opinions and insights—as the following samples attest—they were all sounding a lot like healthy new Mavericks.

Tamara Fast, the entrepreneurial 30-year-old general manager of Chemcrest Architectural Products, a family business that sells almost

$10 million worth of polyurethane round-top windows and millwork, says: "Recruiting people that have a different perspective than the owner is ... important—their views bring balance and creativity to the decision-making process. Sometimes those differences in opinion and style make life a little challenging, but the occasional friction is worth the diversity. Ensuring that the people working with you have the autonomy and authority to make things happen is important. If you are confident that you are working with good people, then trust them to do their jobs and get things done."

Ash Modha, a youthful Ugandan exile whose Mondetta Clothing Company sells logoed sportswear around the world, maintains: "We were very confident that as soon as our product was on retail shelves, it would check out immediately. ... [In 1987] we decided it was time for us to create our own opportunity. For the next month, the Mondetta team, together with about 20 to 30 of our friends, would phone the same ten retailers in Winnipeg, Saskatoon, Regina and Vancouver asking if they carried the brand name Mondetta. ... Of the ten stores we phoned, nine ended up buying our line [and continued to be among the company's best customers]."

And 30-year-old *Darcy Stoddart* of Tuxedo Affairs Catering Company, a commercial kitchen and pastry shop she started in her parents' basement and recently sold as a successful going concern, says: "I ... catered a downtown barbecue in the rain, but I was still smiling. This attitude is a must. Everything in life is contagious and if you are positive, upbeat, and enthusiastic you will make everyone around you feel comfortable, especially your customers."

Whistlin' Jimmy Pattison, a Maverick four decades older than Darcy, couldn't have expressed it better.

The
Empire
Makers

If one definition of *empire* is "an extensive enterprise under single domination or control," then consider SMED International of Calgary. Mogens Smed is the Danish-born, Alberta-raised founder, president, chief executive officer—and enlightened emperor—of this manufacturer of sophisticated, high-end office and furniture systems. Note: systems, not merely chairs and desks. In 1998, the company moved into the largest factory west of the Great Lakes, a $79.5-million, 71,245-square-metre facility that Smed calls "the most efficient and first fully intelligent office building in the world," with a gym and a health centre run by four full-time nurses. His publicly traded company is doing $183 million a year in business, 70 percent of it in the United States, with clients such as Bank of America and Walt Disney, *The New Yorker* and Calvin Klein.

Like the disparate pair of Mavericks profiled in detail over the next two chapters—Gary Charlwood of Century 21 Canada and Uniglobe Travel (International) and Tim Gamble of the Peace Arch Entertainment Group—Mogens Smed is an Empire Maker. A visionary like those two, as freewheeling, audacious, and ambitious, he could be quoting them when he says: "We don't play by the rules." He has never been hobbled by the usual constraints of Canadian business—for instance, that you must advertise, direct-mail, or telemarket, or compete vigorously with your mighty American rivals by targeting the retail market. SMED does none of those things; the corporate motto is: "Our only competition is conventional thinking." Nor has its CEO been held back by his location in the comparative boondocks of western Canada. He has showrooms on three continents and sells in more than 40 countries. "Calgary is the best place in the world to manufacture," he likes to say, referring to the reasonable cost of its utilities, corporate taxes, and even shop labour (in the past decade, the workforce has risen to 1,800 from 350). And Calgary's proximity to the Rocky Mountain foothills has given him an ideal setting for Falkridge, his flagstone-faced marketing retreat that looks like a posh resort, sitting on grounds graced with waterfalls and a 20-metre-tall gazebo that can accommodate 500 clients.

Just into his fifties, this son of a fine cabinetmaker has no modesty about where he is going. Within the next half-dozen years, Smed predicts, annual sales will reach $1 billion. As an indication of how well SMED International is already doing, the 20 percent of his personal shares that he gave his employees when the company went public in 1996 has soared in value to $24 million from $9 million.

I offer this snapshot of Mogens Smed's success story in burgeoning Alberta just to counterpoint the fuller accounts that follow about two flourishing Empire Makers who epitomize the breed in the recession-bound province to the west. In good times and bad, western Canada is a place to make empires. For one thing, it is still possible for an individual to create an extensive enterprise out of whole cloth here, where not everything that needs doing has been done, and where new ideas are as welcome as rain on drought-stricken fields. And from the beginning of European settlement, as the chroniclers of our popular history have let us know, the West has been erected on pillars of empire. Peter C. Newman recounts how the wilderness caesars of the Hudson's Bay Company—the world's oldest incorporated joint-stock merchandising venture—once controlled and milked 40 percent of what became the Dominion of Canada, most of it the land stretching across the left-hand side of our map. Pierre Berton documents the profit-driven syndicate of national dreamers who in the late 1800s propelled the Canadian Pacific Railway across our western expanses to the last spike in British Columbia. And in the process they created a conglomerate that reached well beyond transportation to capitalize on communications, land development, tourism, mining and metallurgy, weapons manufacturing, and world trade.

The tycoons who led these early invasions were European, American, and eastern Canadian carpetbaggers. During the 20th century, most of western Canada's empires—perhaps with the major exception of those in the petroleum industry—have been built on the entrepreneurial feats of indigenous individuals and families. These men and women either sprang from the four westernmost provinces or moved there and made them their own. In Manitoba, for example, the Richardson dynasty began its royal-like ascension as grain merchants at the turn of the century and moved into commodity and stockbroking, shipping, farming and ranching, property development, oil and gas pipelines—and politics. "The Richardsons," Diane Francis points out in *Controlling Interest: Who Owns Canada?*, "are among those rare families who wholly own a corporation in the billion-plus league." As the century ends, another kind of imperial power has been emanating from Winnipeg, the province's capital. The Asper family has fashioned a broadcasting barony that now includes not only the immensely profitable Global Television Network in Canada but also major broadcasting companies in the Republic of Ireland, Northern Ireland, New Zealand, and Australia—where its initial $52-million investment mushroomed to $1.4 billion last year before the government ordered it to reduce its stake in the private national network. Founder Izzy Asper's three children—David, Gail, and Leonard—work in senior positions at CanWest Global Communications in Winnipeg, where they can heed their father's advice: "Never do a little deal."

The other provinces have had their archetypical entrepreneurs-as-emperors. Saskatchewan's Fred Hill and his scion have been pervasive in insurance, development, resources, and television. Alberta's Ron Southern heads an industrial behemoth whose grasp has ranged from petroleum exploration to electrical power generation, construction-camp housing to prefab hospitals, commercial real estate to an internationally celebrated equestrian centre. And, of course, British Columbia's Jimmy Pattison has grown a multinational with 20,000 employees, annual sales of $4 billion, and assets of $2.2 billion—a vast dominion he enjoys describing in superlatives: "Canada's largest western-based food-store chain," "North America's third-largest wholesale news-distribution company," "the world's largest custom electric-sign company."

For their part, Gary Charlwood and Tim Gamble demonstrate significantly different ways of making empires. One method is not as concerned with broad global reach but more with diversity of the base to build on; if a single pillar crumbles, there are enough others to support the enterprise. Until recently that has been the case with Tim Gamble, who has depended mainly on North American markets for the motley TV, film, and multimedia offerings of his Peace Arch Entertainment Group and who seems almost equally focused on having a real-estate stronghold in Vancouver. Another style of empire-building is to home in on a basic product or service and take it to the world—the formula of Gary Charlwood of Uniglobe Travel (International). While he also chairs Century 21 Canada, that real-estate giant is constrained by its very name, reflecting its mandate, to be uninational. Charlwood, like his son Martin—Uniglobe's president—has always had much wider business horizons. "Whereas I love and respect Century 21," Marty says, "it's still Canada and I wanted the world." Yet despite the fact that Gary Charlwood and his two sons control companies that seem quite dissimilar in focus, both depend on the same basic product: franchising.

There are other differences between these two Empire Makers. At 58, twice-wed Gary Charlwood has a succession plan in place to turn the family business over to his sons; Tim Gamble, in his early forties, has never been married. Charlwood recently went public with one of his companies, Uniglobe Travel Online, which represents but a small part of his business; Gamble has always looked over the shoulder of his Banana Republic shirts to see how the shareholders of publicly traded Peace Arch are viewing him. Charlwood, the Marathon Man, has seemed on a steady race to success; Gamble, the Entertainer, has, from time time, dropped some of his juggling balls.

Inevitably there are similarities, too. Both came as adults to British Columbia from elsewhere (Charlwood from England, Gamble from Ontario) and refuse to relocate from their adopted province. Both are relentlessly athletic: the older man runs marathons, the younger plays hockey. And both are endlessly positive—former partner Reg Worthington, recalling Gamble's "No problem" catchphrase, says, "These two words would be Tim's standard response to any question posed to him during our partnership."

At this writing, their optimism is well placed. Gamble's Peace Arch recently sold American rights to the first 22 episodes of its television series *First Wave*—coproduced by Francis Ford Coppola—to The Sci-Fi Channel. The deal is worth as much as $5.5 million, not including a commitment to buy another 44 episodes. Charlwood's Century 21 is on an accelerating growth curve, after a downturn earlier in the decade. His Uniglobe Travel has been expanding into the electronic-commerce and cruise-ship markets and is poised to become a major tour wholesaler in the leisure field it had once shunned in favour of corporate accounts. Uniglobe is also embarking on a slick new style of fast-forwarding its core business. Starting in the United States, it is approaching key travel-agency owners to become representatives of those many areas where the company still has no presence and would take a long time to establish one on its own. These area developers, knowledgeable about the local industry, must first become Uniglobe franchisees. Which they do, for a very seductive reason: the incentive they receive as paid mentors—as opposed to master licensees—to recruit more franchisees and initially reap half the resulting revenues.

The goal is nothing less than to double the number of Uniglobe locations over the next five years—a typically aggressive target for entrepreneurial emperors. After a quarter century of peddling franchises, an unflagging Gary Charlwood, Empire Maker, can still muster all the enthusiasm to say (and to mean it): "I'm incredibly excited."

Chapter One

Marathon Man

U. Gary Charlwood, Century 21 Canada and Uniglobe Travel (International)

When Peter Thomas levelled the shotgun at him, Gary Charlwood didn't blink. Thomas thought the gun was fully loaded, but Charlwood knew better. The spoils at the centre of this duel of wills and nerve were the considerable assets of Century 21 Canada. In 1988 the Vancouver-based franchise organization, with its familiar gold-jacketed sales force of "neighbourhood professionals," was the largest real-estate company in the country. Thomas chaired it from a distance, but Charlwood ran it as president and CEO as well as operating Uniglobe Travel (International), his own successful worldwide franchise chain of travel agencies. The weapon Thomas wielded was the buy-sell provision, the shotgun clause in the agreement detailing their partnership, then a dozen years old. Wanting to take the company public, he offered to buy out his partner's 25-percent shareholding. Charlwood weighed the deal for a month, then refused it point-blank. By selling his shares into a public company controlled by Thomas, he would be surrendering all the safeguards in the existing corporate arrangement that gave him powers well beyond his minority-partner status. Instead he reversed the shotgun, triggering the required counterbid on the same terms he had been offered—which would give Thomas a hefty $23 million for his 72 percent of the privately held company.

But the two Mavericks wound up in court when the Century 21 chairman balked at this counteroffer. Demanding proof that his president could actually come up with such a massive sum, he declined to hand over his shares. Gary Charlwood, reacting like a steel-eyed Clint Eastwood, called his bluff. He sued, won the costly lawsuit in the British Columbia Supreme Court, and paid the purchase price and $2 million in interest within the agreed-upon year. Later, Thomas would admit he had taken bad legal advice in letting the case go to court: "If I had to do it over again, I would have handed the shares over to Gary and closed."

He should have known not to challenge U. (for Uwe) Gary Charlwood. Just looking at the man—his muscled, middle-aged body as lean as a rifle barrel, his cropped drill-sergeant's hairstyle, the thick moustache that bisects his bullet head—you would suspect he likes to run long and hard ahead of the pack. And Peter Thomas had a track record as a sprinter, an entrepreneurial salesman who loved the art of the deal but loathed the idea of administering the companies he acquired. He had had another partner in a previous business, Vancouver property flipper Nelson Skalbania, whose financial empire imploded for the first time in 1981. It dragged down Thomas and left him with $30 million in debt. Faced with bankruptcy, he had only one nest egg: his piece of Century 21 Canada, which over the next seven years, as the real-estate market improved, Charlwood would nurture into a highly profitable enterprise. If Thomas is a 100-metre man, Charlwood is a long-distance racer who runs his companies the way he has competed in four major marathons: steadily, relentlessly, seldom breaking stride, his eye forever on the finish line. Along the way he has learned some lessons—about the exigencies of family business, entrepreneurial style, the consequences of candour, the lack of due diligence, and negative energy—that have universal application.

"I am never again going to talk about this issue," Charlwood tells me one afternoon during a series of interviews at his home-office eyrie high up on the flanks of the West Vancouver mountains. The issue is his corporate divorce from Thomas, which he has reluctantly but openly discussed, responding to the details I read him from his former partner's 1991 autobiography. *Never Fight with a Pig: A Survival Guide for Entrepreneurs* has a line on the copyright page that carefully notes: "The title of this book does not constitute a direct or indirect reference to anyone in the book." Charlwood claims never to have read the memoir disguised as an inspirational guide and makes it clear, in his cultivated mid-Atlantic accent, that he has no interest in rehashing Thomas's take on a relationship that ended in an unnecessary lawsuit. "The next person that comes to me, I'm going to say: 'No comment—that was a long time ago.'"

The well-read, well-conditioned executive has more compelling books on his crowded desk, among them *8 Weeks to Optimum Health* and *The Columbia Encyclopedia of Nutrition,* and on his shelves, where E. Annie Proulx's Newfoundland novel *The Shipping News* stands next to *Shifting Gears,* Nuala Beck's business guidebook. The little white cat doll and *Sesame Street* puppet in the office are explained when four-year-old Bianca comes pirouetting in to say that she will be practising her ballet in her dad's exercise room next door. She dances beside his pricey Pacemaster treadmill, at the ready for those rainy days when he can't do his weekly 32 kilometres of outdoor runs. The tennis court and swimming pool help keep him trim, too. They share 1.2 hectares—behind a formidable iron gate and a chain-link fence—with the long, white-pillared house that looks out over a gasp-inspiring vista of Lions Gate Bridge, sea-rimmed Stanley Park, and Vancouver's skyscraping downtown. This is home to Charlwood and his second family: his daughter and his wife of ten years, Maria Isabel, who once danced with a modern Cuban ballet company and has the graceful form of a Latin willow (her husband speaks reasonable Spanish as well as fluent German and French).

On one wall of Charlwood's home office hangs a framed photo of him in racing gear for one of his three runnings of the Honolulu marathon. "In the month before the marathon, you've got to do several 20-milers just to get the feel of it," he says, "and a 20-miler will take me three hours. Some of my training runs were in Chicago in November, in a balaclava. But that's a very confidence-forming experience. You come back when you've been running in the pouring rain with icicles on your face and your hands are cold and other people are saying, 'Oh, how could you do that?' It's a great feeling."

Such stamina has sustained him in the hazard-full decade since he bought out his partner. Century 21 Real Estate Canada Ltd. has weathered a long dramatic downturn in the market and an assault by a new wave of undercutting competitors that forced it to slash two-thirds of its corporate staff. In the past three years, it has reinvented itself to become the fastest-growing franchise realty company in Canada, vying for the number-two spot in volume behind the current industry leader, Re/Max. Century 21's sales force has rebounded to about 6,000 in 290 franchises grossing $8 billion in annual sales. Regina-born Don Lawby, a former banker and general manager of a small B.C. travel-agency group, has been president and chief operating officer since Charlwood gained control of the company in 1989. "Much of the industry looked at us as dinosaurs—the gold-jacket team back in the eighties," Lawby admits. "It took us a long time to turn it." Of his relationship with his chairman, he says, "Gary and I are very good friends. We've fought a lot over business. I'm not a yes man and he didn't want that. He's the boss, but I'm not afraid of him. ... He's committed to his people—to a fault. There may have been times when he should have got rid of me. He cares, and it's not a show."

Uniglobe Travel (International) Inc. also has about 6,000 people, but they are spread through 16 countries in 1,100 agencies that generate sales of $2.7 billion a year. Uniglobe is the largest single-brand franchisor of travel agencies in the world. Among global travel companies, it is third in size only to the immense American Express, which absorbed the corporate-travel division of Britain's Thomas Cook Group in 1994, and Carlson/Wagonlit, another British power, which recently merged with Cook. Both competitors target the larger corporate accounts, while Uniglobe focuses on the small- to medium-size ones, ranging from $20,000 to $2 million in annual travel expenditures; only recently has it pursued the leisure-travel market. Over the years, the Canadian company has been a leader in the fight against the major airlines as they capped and then cut commissions to travel agents. It won one battle of brinkmanship in 1992 against American Airlines cuts, saving its franchisees $500,000 in commissions, and responded to the industry-wide capping four years later with a successful campaign to net Uniglobe agents 110 percent of their previous margins within 110 days of the caps. When the airlines slashed commissions again in 1997, Charlwood finally urged his franchisees to start charging clients transaction fees, which about 80 percent of the North American ones now do.

Charlwood has 51 percent of the Canadian offshoot of U.S.-based Century 21 and in late 1998 paid off all the money he had borrowed to buy out Peter Thomas, leaving the company debt-free. His major partners are Sun Life Assurance of Canada and the Independent Order of Foresters. The IOF fund is also a significant shareholder in Uniglobe, but Charlwood retains 70-percent control. He is chairman of both his companies. And in 1999, as if he didn't have enough races to run, he chaired the International Franchise Association—the first non-American to head the world body based in Washington, D.C., which in 1991 named him Entrepreneur of the Year. With this high-profile position, he stepped into the spotlight he had long avoided, unlike Peter Thomas who has sought it out (Charlwood gets one line in a profile of Thomas in the second volume of Peter C. Newman's comprehensive trilogy, *The Canadian Establishment*, and nary a mention in the latest, *Titans*).

In his late fifties, Charlwood hasn't stopped running, on racecourses or off. In some marathons, he has had the company of his two sons. Christopher, now 34, and Martin, 32, began running with their father in 1985 during a nostalgic journey back to his childhood homes in Europe. He was trying to learn more about his adoptive father in England and the German birth father he barely knew, a U-boat sailor in the Second World War. It was during this trip that he proposed the idea of a family business dynasty, in which his sons would come into his companies and someday take them over. It seemed inevitable: they had been sitting in on corporate board meetings since their early teens.

When Christopher and Martin turned 21, he gave them gold rings, which all three still wear, with the initials of their first names backing on to the *C* of Charlwood framed by waves symbolizing the sea voyage Gary took to the New World at 25. He also gave them a 15-percent share in the Charlwood Pacific Group, the corporate umbrella for the real-estate and travel companies and their spin-offs.* Chris is the founding president of one subsidiary, Cobalt Real Estate Corporation, which has managed eight development projects totalling $56 million in Vancouver and Seattle, one of them for Microsoft cofounder Paul Allen. Marty is president and COO of Uniglobe and its new Internet arm, Uniglobe Travel Online. After a rocky launch, the Web site—the first publicly traded company of the group—is now specializing in the cruise-ship packages sold by a subsidiary. In 1997 Uniglobe bought

---

* This generosity made both sons concerned observers and participants during the negotiations with Peter Thomas, their father's ex-partner. They attended the court case, many of the lawyers' meetings, and the pivotal closing. As Martin recalls: "In 1989, when we bought Peter Thomas out for 26 million bucks and change [including a two-year management contract based on profits], Chris and I were in the law office till three o'clock in the morning, intricately involved with all the details. That was an M.B.A. of sorts."

Pacific Northwest CruiseShipsCenters Inc. of Vancouver, which was based just down the block. Chairman Michael Drever had used the Uniglobe model to build the cruise-only company into 43 western Canadian franchises generating $60 million a year in sales and has since expanded it in the United States as a boutique add-on in 72 existing Uniglobe agencies. All three Charlwood males backed the CruiseShipCenters acquisition, but when it came to moving on to the Internet and financing the online division with a stock-market offering, the usually pacesetting father had to be pulled down the track by his two sons.

Some people think his boys look like twins, with their smooth good looks and forms as whippet-sleek as their dad's. But in personality Marty is as eager and engaging as the Old Man, while his older brother is laconic and quietly thoughtful, the backroom strategist of the pair. "This is the second generation. I convinced Dad that we had to get into the Internet," Chris says. "Marty's done all the hard work." The act of going public for the first time—especially on the volatile Vancouver Stock Exchange—was equally upsetting to the senior Charlwood. "If we'd done it privately," Chris points out, "we would've had to give up a big piece of the company with a joint-venture partner, and funding it ourselves was not an option at the time"—because Uniglobe had recently done an expensive buyback of the master licences held by large franchisees in the United States. "There was nervousness on my father's side."

Gary Charlwood's confidence in his sons, despite their youth, overrode his fears. He tells two stories that illustrate his respect for them as individuals. In early 1997, when Uniglobe's president, Michael Levy, was resigning to go home and run the British operation, the company's board of directors urged their chairman to appoint Martin as successor. While the son was then executive vice president, his father was reluctant to kick him upstairs. "In his young life," he told the board, "I don't want him to be into the 16-hour day."

Martin, hearing his father's concern, responded, "Dad, I think you really ought to ask me. Let me balance it."

And, Gary Charlwood says now, he does balance it. Martin has even had the same girlfriend for the past year, although he doesn't see much of her.

"Martin will defer to Christopher on issues," their father continues. "Christopher is a very good leader, but he likes private things." In 1998 Chris phoned from Australia and said: "Dad, I've got some news for you. I'm getting married."

"Good. When?"

"Tomorrow."

Typical, his dad says: "He likes things to be real low-key and, God bless him, he should have the right to be that way."

Such concern manifested itself tangibly when it came to considering the far-away future of the businesses Charlwood has been constructing over the past quarter century. Luckily he had children who were actively, happily involved in them and who he was confident would be good stewards when he eventually passed on the baton. His advice to any entrepreneurs in similar cirumstances who are anxious about the companies they have founded is straightforward.

In a family business, plan early for orderly succession—consider a family trust for emotional security as well as tax purposes

Family firms account for 70 percent or more of all businesses in Canada (and employ 60-plus percent of the workforce). Yet an astonishing 70 percent of them are either liquidated or sold after their founders depart the scene, either through death or retirement. And half of the 180,000-plus Canadian family-owned operations with annual sales exceeding $500,000 now have principals aged 51 to 70. There are a few devices, such as estate plans, to ensure harmonious succession in such tightly held enterprises. Yet many families are loath to even discuss the possibility of an owner's impending demise and its consequences. More than three years ago, Gary Charlwood—recognizing the potential for problems, even though he was only 54 and his sons were on either side of 30—began planning a family trust through his Charlwood Pacific Group. "Which means that the entire family still participates in the growth of the businesses as time goes by, and in 21 years—which is the limit of the trust—I can take everything back to myself and then pay taxes, or [my children] will give me a side payment for the rest of my years"—and the businesses will become theirs. In the meantime, the senior Charlwood holds voting control as the so-called protector of the trust, owning 70 percent compared to his sons' combined 30. Agreeing to such an arrangement today obviously prevents dissension tomorrow, which pleases the young Charlwoods. "From a tax perspective, it's absolutely a must," Martin says. "I totally credit my dad for taking a potentially thorny issue and—tackling it almost like a saint—looking at what's going to happen to what he built over the years and making sure that everyone's dealt with fairly."

At the risk of practising Psychiatry 101, I have wondered if the care and handling Charlwood has devoted to his offspring has anything to do with the fractured families he sprang from himself. He was born Uwe Heinrich Gustav Schremer in 1941 in Schöningen near what became the East German border. His father was one of the so-called Sea Wolves, the submariners in the deadly U-boat fleet that fought the Battle of the Atlantic. His pretty, outgoing mother was among the many young women conscripted to help the Nazi war effort in vital seaports. Her only child has few memories of her but speaks lovingly of her parents who, during the war, raised him in Kiel on the Baltic Sea. At one point they fled with him just before a bomb destroyed their apartment. Uwe's father died in service and in late 1946 his mother met and married a soldier in the British occupation force. Albert Charlwood took her back to England and a year later brought her son to live with them in London and attend school, knowing not a word of English. Yet the boy thrived, fighting off bullies, taking up soccer and cricket, and becoming a protégé of a kindly English teacher who helped him lead the class in his adopted language. Among the school buddies he won over was Roger Moore, who grew up to be a management consultant for British Airways and other sizable corporations and a current director of the Charlwood Pacific Group.

Uwe spent his summers with his grandparents in Germany. At 15, infatuated with jazz, he stayed home instead and saved up to buy himself a drum set. He had delivered heating paraffin and groceries, been a stockboy for Woolworth's, and now began hauling fridges and stoves for an appliance reconditioning shop. His stepfather, a post-office employee, was no entrepreneurial role model. Uwe, graduating from Selhurst Grammar School with a university scholarship in hand, took a year off to become a management trainee with Royal Mail Lines, one of the world's oldest shipping companies. Wearing a bowler hat and a dark suit, stamping bills of lading and running errands, he thought none of the people there looked happy and knew the job wasn't what he wanted.

Hearing about jobs at the Butlin chain of family holiday camps that were flourishing after the war, he fled the corporate world to be a summer sports coach, at six pounds a week, and soon became one of the glamorous Butlin Redcoats charged with special duties. One day a manager who misinterpreted Uwe's slim musical background told him to fill in as a warm-up singer to entertain the holidayers—and for the occasion renamed him the more easily pronounced "Gary." As a solo act, the boy crooner was wretched, but the manager became a mentor, teaching him to perform. After that first summer, Gary—as he started calling himself—studied German literature and economics at the University of Southampton until learning that his parents were about to divorce. He returned to London to be with his mother and that winter, already disenchanted with college, found one of the few jobs for a Redcoat at Butlin's headquarters in Clacton. His mentor was working there, and when the 18-year-old began seriously considering a career with the company, he strongly advised against it.

Seeking another line of work, Charlwood answered an ad in a London newspaper for a German-speaking tour guide with the Swiss Travel Service in Austria. In landing the position at Fuschl am See, a popular alpine-lake resort area near Salzburg, he was taking his first tentative steps to becoming an entrepreneur. The only instructions he received were to divert the 44 British tourists arriving by bus each week. How he did it was up to him. Next door to his hotel he found Sepp Sterlinger, six years older and the owner of an old bus, who agreed to pay Charlwood a ten-percent commission if he convinced the vacationers to take tours. But the first arrivals had just been on a "bloody" bus from London most of one long day and were a bit "chuffed" about getting aboard another one the next morning; the embryonic tour guide had few takers. That was when he realized a classic principle of enterprising salesmanship.

Disarm your clients with directness and honesty

"If indeed you must be candid," the Lebanese poet Kahlil Gibran wrote, "be candid beautifully." When a second group of holidayers arrived at his Austrian resort, Gary Charlwood approached them with a psychologically beautiful bit of candour: "I know what it must have been like for you to travel all of those hours in a coach, and probably the last thing you could imagine is doing that again. So what I've arranged for tomorrow is just a real casual tour, which I think you're going to love. It is absolutely spectacular." This time—having heard his disarming acknowledgement of their weariness, but not wanting to miss out on anything spectacular—his clients filled the bus. On later tours taking them into towns to souvenir-hunt, he would point them to a particular shop by bluntly stating: "I recommend that you go there for a very key reason. I get ten percent of whatever you buy." And charmed by his cheeky directness, they cheerfully bought from the shops he had made deals with. A few years later Charlwood would translate this principle of frankness into the real-estate world by telling a prospective house buyer: "I never work with any more than six or eight clients a month. So I'm trying to determine for myself whether you ought to be one of those clients. Because when that happens, I promise you I will sleep, eat, drink your needs. But I just assume that whenever you see something you like, you're not going to call the salesperson who's listing it because then I'm wasting my time." That dazzlingly direct approach usually guaranteed him absolute client loyalty. Decades later his son Chris says, "One thing I've taken from my dad is to be as up-front and honest as possible about your business."

Halfway through his third season, Gary Charlwood became area manager for the Belgium Travel Service in Ostend, supervising a team that organized entertainment and bus tours throughout Europe. That season he met an auburn Austrian beauty named Uta, an Alpine ski instructor about to be divorced. She joined him in Belgium and they were soon married and expecting a child. The prospect of family reinforced a feeling he had about leaving Europe for life in the New World, specifically

Australia, Uta urged him to move to Vienna first to get to know her family. He worked there in planning development for the Austrian Travel Agency, sang in a cathedral choir, and in 1965 became a father to Christopher. When their second child was imminent, Charlwood became more determined to move to Australia. And then a trade attaché he had befriended at the Canadian embassy argued that Canada offered him more opportunities. He had his Australian papers and was a month away from departing when the persuasive attaché sped up the immigration process and soon had the 25-year-old husband and father on a ship to Montreal with $2,000 in savings (his family followed later).

Charlwood had written ahead to several travel agencies in cities from Montreal westward. Offered a job with each one, he didn't accept any until he reached Vancouver, his preferred resting place. He spent only a few weeks as sales manager of the Hagen's agency group before joining Air Canada, which promised to make him their German sales representative. The position never materialized and after four months as a reservations agent, he moved to Western Airlines, which was newly arrived in Vancouver. Over the next few years, with his experience on this side of the travel industry he laid the foundation for what would one day become Uniglobe. He spent five years with Western, the last couple in Los Angeles, where he began as a brash young assistant manager who eventually took heed of his superior's advice: "Don't go in there and be a know-it-all." His final assignment was the running of an innovative program he had created using recent college graduates as onboard customer-relations representatives for business passengers. It wasn't until talk of a merger between Western and Continental Airlines panicked his much-older bosses about their futures that he began to doubt the business he was in. That, and the threat of continuing earthquakes, were enough to convince him to sell the beautiful old house he had bought in Pasadena and bring his family back to Vancouver.

He returned in 1970 to be consumer affairs director for Canadian Pacific Airlines. It was a good job, but veteran employees felt the same insecurity as their Western counterparts, which by year's end further encouraged him to consider another career. Before moving to Los Angeles, Charlwood had studied for his realtor's licence as a possible escape hatch from a salaried position. He had had a hard time qualifying to buy his first house, even though it was a bargain in Vancouver, and then had to stretch to buy the pricier one in California. The possibility of

39

unlimited income from a commissioned job now appealed to him. So, despite an offer from the airline to make him a regional vice president for eastern Canada and South America, Charlwood finally decided to ignite his latent entrepreneurialism and chance the rocket ride of real estate.

"The reason I went into real estate," he recalls, "is that you have a multimillion-dollar inventory you don't have to pay for." He had a choice of working for a company that specialized in shopping-centre developments and a conventional one—Malcolm Boot Realty—that sold recently opened houses in North Vancouver. Boot and his co-owner, both salesmen looking for someone with Charlwood's managerial ability, promised to make him a future partner. The neophyte figured his $3,000 in savings, much of it from moonlighting as a drummer in his own band, would last the estimated three months he had to survive before completing a sale. He spent the first month in his ten-year-old Mercedes driving around to every open house on the North Shore, taking extensive notes, and accompanying the firm's top salespeople on their rounds, watching how they worked, with the unswerving attention of a salmon-hungry eagle scanning the sea. Within six weeks he sold a friend's house. Trying to get the jump on other agents, he routinely went to the office late at night to see the new-listings sheet just delivered by courier and then early the next morning phoned the listing agents about seeing their properties before the first open house was held. By now he had some of his own hopeful buyers, having qualified his prospective clients by telling them he acted for only a half dozen or so at a time—and would they commit to him? Once they did, he called them about any of the relevant new properties he had seen in advance and, drama dripping from his voice, asked if they would visit the houses with him immediately. "I'll pick you up in ten minutes," he would say. Charlwood was discovering some home truths that he would adapt in the later stages of his entrepreneurial career.

Actively develop your own style of doing business and then nurture it—despite the conventional wisdom of your industry.

"I broke rules," Gary Charlwood says now. "The standard rule was that you never take the husband or the wife out by themselves. I mean, we teach that in our [Century 21 training] schools. And it's a good idea. But I did it because I recognized that the husband was at work and the wife usually made a decision on this, anyway, so I would ignore the rule." He would tell the husband he was showing the house to the wife that morning and wanted to pick him up at his office in the afternoon well before the other husbands would show up after work. "And by the time the whole world woke up to what was happening, I would have an offer." Another rule that Century 21 recommends is to focus on getting listings: knock on doors if you must to maintain 20 or 30 properties in your portfolio. "In my case," Charlwood says of his young self, "I concentrated on the buyer, and that was against everything that any real-estate salesperson would ever tell you. I felt it was my edge because everybody was looking for listings." And a third convention he ignored was to focus on his area, the North Shore, to such an extent that he would actively discourage listings from other areas at a time when "salespeople, hungry for a dollar, would take a listing anywhere." All of his tactics were creating a personal business style, which a realtor who became a close friend had advised him is always unique in character: "It's something that nobody else can do. It's not duplicatable."

In his first 15 months, Charlwood sold more real estate than anyone else in British Columbia— a remarkable 118 houses. Today the leading Century 21 realtor may sell as many as 290 houses in a year but might have four or five licensed sales assistants, while Malcolm Boot Realty back then had a single receptionist supporting 30 salespeople. In one day, Charlwood sold five houses, sending some of his waiting clients to a White Spot restaurant for lunch on him while he dealt with the assembly line of sales. With his annual income four times what his salary as consumer-affairs director at Canadian Pacific had been, he managed to put $50,000 in the bank. But when he asked Malcolm Boot about becoming a partner, the owner went back on his word.

On a vacation in the Okanagan Valley (where he saw his pear shape in the mirror and decided to start running), Charlwood noticed a newspaper ad from North Vancouver's Hunt Realty. It sought a managing partner to acquire a $50,000 half-interest in the six-employee firm. In 1972 Charlwood used his savings to buy in and choreographed Hunt's move from cramped offices beside a pizza joint to smart new premises. Within a year the realtor grew from 90th in sales volume to 11th in the Greater Vancouver area. Its expanded staff of 40 now included chief financial officer Michael Levy, a chartered accountant fresh from England; Levy continues with Uniglobe to this day. So successful was the firm that Toronto-based A. E. LePage, on its way to becoming the world's second-largest real-estate group, then offered to buy Hunt Realty—without Charlwood's partner, Hilar Billing, in place. Although that deal never materialized, Charlwood eventually did pay just about what he had invested to buy out his co-owner, whose own development project outside of Vancouver was going badly. The new sole owner of Hunt Realty discovered just how badly when investors Peter and Jeffrey Barnett—the twin brothers who would go on to open Vancouver's Elephant and Castle Pub & Restaurant chain—asked for their money back, as the partner had promised them. Charlwood was forced to repay them about $50,000.

Despite that setback, Charlwood had become a walking legend in the Vancouver real-estate industry. It was 1974 and he was about to field a phone call that would begin the most momentous chapter in his saga.

Born in England, Peter Thomas came to Canada as a child when his father started a trucking business in northern Alberta. Thomas had a seven-year career in the Canadian army, two years' labour in the oil patch, and finally a job as a mutual-fund salesman and then sales manager with the Principal Group of Edmonton.* In 1968 he went out on his own to start real-estate syndicating—selling properties in limited and general partnerships—and also realized the joys of the flip, the buying and quick selling of a property to snag handsome profits, sometimes in deals with Vancouver's notorious Nelson Skalbania. Thomas joined the Young Presidents Organization, and in 1974, at age 36, was at a YPO Hawaiian conference when he first

---

*The Principal Group was Donald Cormie's umbrella corporation of mostly financial companies. It was chronicled in *The Money Rustlers* before its calamitous decline and fall in 1987.

heard about a two-year-old franchise real-estate company. A Californian named Art Bartlett was offering advertising, hiring and training services, and a national-brand image to small real-estate brokers in return for a franchise fee and an ongoing piece of their commissions. At this point fewer than 500 brokers in the United States had agreed to come aboard and wear the gold blazers that became mobile billboards identifying them as the so-called neighbourhood professionals of Century 21 Real Estate. Thomas hopped a plane to Los Angeles the same day he learned of the concept and persuaded Bartlett to give him the master franchise rights to all of Canada—for a token $5,000 down and $95,000 in future earnings over the next ten years, as well as the promise to sell 120 franchises over the next three years. Spelled out on the back of a napkin, the deal was to be leveraged, with no capital risk.

Now that Thomas had a business, he had to find someone to run it. In *Never Fight with a Pig*, he writes: "I looked around for the best real-estate agent in town for the job of selecting prospective brokers and managing the franchises. I wanted a hard worker who could demonstrate a high rate of success, and who would know the best local dealers to bring into the system. After making a few phone calls, I knew that the person for the job was a man named Uwe (Gary) Charlwood."

The man in question was unimpressed. Charlwood had once considered buying a franchise operation: while at Western Airlines, waiting impatiently for his immigration papers to the United States he looked into the possibility of acquiring a Denny's restaurant but decided it was too dear. In 1975 he was attempting to buy Malcolm Boot Realty from his former boss; the idea of becoming a partner with this Edmonton fellow he had never heard of was less than exciting. "I had just got out of a partnership," Charlwood says, "and I thought, 'Do I really want one in which I'm not totally in control?' I did a search on Peter, and the word was that he is a pretty nice guy, effervescent, full of piss and vinegar, but maybe a little bit blue-suede-shoeish—a guy that talks and doesn't deliver. But we had several dinners together and I liked him." Not well enough, though, to become his partner. However, when the deal to take over Boot Realty fell through and Thomas asked Charlwood to meet Art Bartlett at a regional Century 21 meeting in Houston, he went. By now, 1976, the Canadian operation already had a president—"a *real* blue-suede-shoer," in Charlwood's mind—and when he mentioned his opinion of the man, Thomas again invited him to run the company.

"Peter, there is no way that a company can have two people running it, and the only way that I'd be interested in doing this is if we were equal partners and if I was the boss," Charlwood said.

Thomas offered him virtual autonomy in operating Century 21 Canada but only a ten-percent share—not enough of a financial enticement for Charlwood.

Meanwhile the B.C. Securities Commission ordered the fledgling company to suspend operations during an investigation. Competing realtors had stated publicly that the franchise-marketing system was akin to selling securities without a licence. Thomas laid off his few employees and over the next six months tried to solve the crisis. His memory is that he called the well-connected Jimmy Pattison, who put him in touch with Vancouver securities lawyer Michael Butler, who approached the Securities Commission. In one of many contradictions of his ex-partner's account, Charlwood says it was his call to his local lawyer, Tom Collingwood, that led him to Jack Giles of Farris Vaughan Wills & Murphy, who then convinced the commission that Century 21 wasn't peddling securities. Thomas writes that when all this happened, the company's executive vice president was Charlwood, who counters that at this time he still wasn't working for Thomas and had simply arranged his lawyer's intervention as a favour.

They became partners in 1977, after Charlwood had bought the first Canadian franchise for $7,500 and continuing royalties of six percent. In assuming the presidency, he got 25 percent of Century 21 Canada. From the standpoint of controls he had built into their contract, he says he was much more than a minority partner: "There was very little Peter was able to do without my approval." One clause in their agreement stated that the two men had to be described as cofounders. Thomas confesses that "I knew that having me around was driving Gary crazy, so soon after the business was in full swing I moved out of the offices and into my own corporate headquarters. It might have been good for staff morale, but it didn't do much for our working relationship, which was polite but cool."

While Thomas paints himself as the hard-driving entrepreneur, he describes his partner as "a hardworking, take-charge administrator who looked after the details." It's a distinction that still riles Charlwood, who considers himself just as much of an entrepreneur, as he has since proved in conceiving and propelling Uniglobe. Taking the helm of Century 21, he sold Hunt Realty, hired its CFO, Mike Levy, as his financial man, and assembled a team of four crack salesmen to begin pitching franchises in Greater Vancouver. He says, "We got kicked in the face for a long, long time," as local realtors refused to buy into what many saw as this aggressively American concept of franchising.* To sell it, the Canadians were using the parent company's ploy of inviting a couple of dozen realtors to a group breakfast. That didn't work, so Charlwood sent his salespeople to meet the prospective franchisees individually in their own offices; he followed up to close the deals. Within the first sales quarter, 32 realtors had agreed to pay the master Canadian franchisor six-percent royalties and about $300 a month in advertising fees (now approaching $800)** in return for the services and the brand name of what was growing into the world's largest real-estate organization. One of the new sales associates was the general manager of a realty firm in the Okanagan Valley; by 1978 Don Lawby became a training consultant in Century 21's Vancouver head office, en route to becoming president a decade later.

Two of the original sales team moved into Alberta and Saskatchewan to hawk franchises, with their boss closing the sales and another company rep coming in to help the existing real-estate firms reposition themselves as franchise operations. Part of the appeal for franchisees was what Charlwood describes as "the sense of belonging to something that was exclusionary." As well as being

---

*Century 21 wasn't the first such franchise operation in Canadian real estate. Similar concepts had surfaced in some provinces, where U.S.-based Realty World had already sold some franchises. However, with its high-impact advertising spilling over the border from American TV stations, as it does today, Century 21 was probably the most high-profile of the companies peddling the concept.

**The first TV commercial, which was timed to appear around the company's Impact Opening Day in 1976, had a couple of Natives deciding to move and one of them opening the flap of their teepee to reveal a Century 21 sign. It used the line "My heart soars like an eagle," which was a well-known line from a book by Vancouver's Chief Dan George, the actor who appeared in the film *Little Big Man*. "And then I got a phone call from his legal representative," Charlwood says, "and so we had to change the ad and we apologized."

identified with a well-advertised North American brand name, they became members of a Broker Council, electing their own slate of officers who would convene annually with the head office to plot the future. In 1978 Century 21 breached the borders of Ontario and the company began expanding with the speed of a four-minute miler; within two years there were 425 franchisees in Canada doing $2 billion worth of business. Charlwood recollects being in Toronto, where he would then live one of out every three weeks: "I recall one day running there and thinking to myself, 'Do you realize that this month we don't have to have a single franchise sale because we actually are breaking even and making money on royalty revenue?' That was the watershed."

While Thomas stayed out of the way most of the time, he occasionally intruded, as he did one day to announce that Century 21 Canada was going to buy a corporate plane. No, it wasn't, Charlwood replied.

"Goddamn it, we're going to buy a plane," his partner remembers insisting.

"Absolutely not, Peter. It doesn't make financial sense." When Thomas blustered, Charlwood said, "Well, do whatever you want, issue the shotgun, but we're not buying the plane."

The shotgun would come later, but Thomas would soon have to become more involved in the company, however briefly. His reluctant stewardship happened not long after Charlwood created Uniglobe Travel (International) in 1980. The idea followed an approach Thomas had earlier made to Century 21 in the United States to suggest it buy back the wildly successful Canadian master franchise. While the two partners entertained the possibility, which they finally decided against, Charlwood wondered what he would do with the many millions of dollars he would reap from his shares. "Well, I would want to work," he mused. "I like building things. I have now built something national. I'd like to build something international. And I know about the travel industry."

He had a knowledgeable contact at Century 21's California headquarters: Ray Townsend, one of the spark plugs behind the parent company (who has since become a vice president of global sales and marketing for Uniglobe). Townsend helped organize a high-level research study of the North American travel industry to determine how well franchised agencies would succeed. Suppliers such as the airlines and car-rental agencies said many travel agents weren't well-informed or professional, implying that they might benefit from the training and business practices of an umbrella organization. There was a Canadian precedent for such a company—in fact, the owner of AATCO Worldwide Travel in Toronto had approached Charlwood in 1978, asking for advice on franchising travel agencies. He received it, along with the caution that his adviser was considering the same idea.

Two years later Charlwood launched Uniglobe Travel, modelling it on the Century 21 franchising model, even to the identifying blazers— teal blue rather than gold. He chose the name from a list that included Travel Ink and Foreign Intrigue before tests with travellers at airports showed a preference for the one-world theme. The market niche was the small- to medium-size corporate-travel account, averaging no higher than $100,000 per year, while competitors Amex and Carlson/Wagonlit concentrated on *Fortune* 500 companies. At the time, Charlwood was running Century 21 Canada, a fact that bothered Thomas, who complains that his partner used the real-estate company's staff and facilities for the start-up: "After consultation with lawyers, I decided not to take legal action. By mutual agreement, Century 21 acquired a ten-percent interest in Uniglobe. But the relationship was never the same."

To run Uniglobe, Charlwood hired the owner of a successful Saskatoon travel agency who also got about ten percent of the company. He didn't last. "I think he was being bombarded by his peers in the travel industry saying this is an American concept and franchising is going to ruin the industry," Charlwood now says—just as realtors had said about Century 21. Within a few months, when it was obvious the man was ill-suited for the position, Charlwood stepped in to replace him. That was when he recruited Thomas to be a hands-on operator of their real-estate company for the first time. Both men now agree that during Thomas's half year in charge of Century 21, he was like a jogger who had stumbled into a long-distance race. When Charlwood returned to be vice chairman and CEO, he was replaced at Uniglobe by Century 21's Mike Levy, who was an investor in the new company.

The first franchisee to commit was a travel-agency manager based in Cranbrook, British Columbia, a dynamic woman named Laurie

Radloff. In those early years, it cost $7,850 for an established agency to become a franchisee and $30,350 to open a new turnkey operation.* Eventually Radloff would sell the Uniglobe agency she started and become president of the company's sublicensed western Canadian region, which she now owns with several partners and has expanded to 86 franchise locations. (Frank Dennis, a former senior vice president for the Kellogg cereal makers, would later run the eastern region, which now has about the same number of outlets.) The selling of such master agreements gave the umbrella company good local representation and the financial strength arising from a series of regional power blocs.

Uniglobe's first explosive expansion happened in Ontario in late 1981 when it acquired the 35 agencies of Toronto's AATCO Worldwide Travel, the Canadian industry's pioneer in franchising. The owner, whom Charlwood had advised about the franchise business three years earlier, approached Uniglobe about buying him out: "It was the first acquisition we'd ever done and we didn't do it well." It proved to be a painful exercise in learning, which can be summed up in a single admonition.

Never stint on the due diligence that you must always do when making acquisitions

"The lesson is so elementary," Gary Charlwood says. "We didn't do due diligence." The deal to buy the AATCO franchise group was attractive because it would mean major overnight growth. "But we should have allowed a two-week interview process with their franchisees and we would have understood that there was distrust between them and the franchisor. We didn't know that this was what you ought to do. I knew [the owner], we were going to go into Toronto, so why not start there with a bang? Not only did we pay to buy the company, but we denied ourselves the revenue of the 35 franchise sales, as well"—a turnkey

---

*The current fee for a new turnkey franchise for eastern Canada is $41,500 and the minimum cash required by a franchisee is $140,000; for the western region, $54,000 and $160,000. Royalties to be paid to the parent company range from five to ten percent and advertising fees are $747 to $790 a month. In return, franchisees receive financial, realty, computer, accounting, and administration services as well as ongoing training and agency development—and the collective clout, marketing presence, and buying power that they could never get as independent agents.

start-up costing four times what an existing one then did. But the money wasn't the primary problem. Due diligence—the care that a reasonable person exercises in researching a potential acquisition—would have uncovered the poisoned atmosphere between the franchisor and his franchisees. It was so venomous, Charlwood says, that they had their own lawyer in the audience when Uniglobe announced the purchase— although he left when the new owners refused to continue the meeting in his presence. "We would never do an acquisition again that way," Charlwood says. "From that time forward, I began employing the services of my advisers extensively. My hit team here will not just consist of my internal people. I insist on an appointed lawyer and an appointed [accounting] representative and we go in and study the books and look at the contract. We didn't do that and, when I think of it now, how incredibly stupid!"

Uniglobe also grew rapidly through the 1980s in the United States. The expansion there began naturally with Charlwood's Century 21 connections. He still goes to quarterly regional meetings of the American real-estate company's directors and vacations with them. And when they heard about his initial success with Uniglobe, some of them asked to buy the rights for certain states or regions. As early as 1982, he had sold three regions: the northeastern states, Ohio, and southern California— the latter bought by Ray Townsend, who had helped him research the feasibility of a franchise travel organization. All these first three franchisees were involved in Century 21, with Townsend as the independent advertising genius behind the original concept. Eventually Uniglobe became the biggest Canadian-based franchisor south of the border, operating from Los Angeles, Washington, D.C., and 11 service centres in between.

At the time of all this growth, Charlwood was a bachelor once more. He and Uta had divorced during the hectic early stages of his partnership with Peter Thomas. Now he was a weekend dad to his two sons. Yet Martin says he remained a strong presence, even coaching their soccer teams: "He'd be working 18 hours a day, six days a week, and he'd still make time to show up at a soccer game. ... Even if he was busy in the office, we knew how to get hold of him."

Chris remembers: "We did all the fun stuff with him—the trips and gifts and going out for dinners. And Mom gets the weekdays, which is the tough times. He heard the stories thirdhand of the problems and his solution was to try to be strict, but if you're going to be strict, you need to spend more time, so the strict stuff backfired—with me, anyway. That caused a strained relationship in the teens, and after it became closer." Today Chris characterizes his father as "a very worldly man, very open-minded, very unbiased, very fair."

Back then he brought his teenage sons into his boardrooms, where they began to appreciate the drama of big business, eventually hanging around all day during directors' meetings. It was no surprise that they both became fascinated with their father's world. Martin even dismissed his dad's encouragement to go to New York City to study the acting he enjoyed. Instead he majored in psychology at the University of British Columbia, following his older brother, who got his arts degree there. Each pursued his entrepreneurial instincts in the summer; one season Chris made $30,000 from his driveway-resurfacing business.

They had both reached their 21st birthdays and received their 15-percent shares of the Charlwood Pacific Group when Charlwood and Thomas went through their final divorce throes in the late 1980s. The young men watched in fascination as the co-owners of Century 21 called each other on their buy-sell agreement, facing down the shotgun clause until Thomas's final intransigence delivered them to the B.C. Supreme Court in 1989.

For Charlwood, finding the $26 million he agreed to pay his partner was as arduous as running a marathon in bare feet. The Independent Order of Foresters was already an investor; now he needed another player with deep pockets to help him come up with the money by the legal deadline. One possibility was Metropolitan Life, the current owner of the parent Century 21 in the United States. Met Life expressed interest but was in no hurry to conclude a deal; sitting back, it let the Canadian franchise holder twist in the wind while he desperately sought funding. "I very clearly felt that I was being strung along," Charlwood says, "and then suddenly I realized I had got myself into some very dangerous water. Because being strung along to the point at which I couldn't recover from the timing gave them all the controls—and I would have to cut a deal with them at any cost." A second option was a Canadian venture-capital company, but he felt its terms were excessive. His project team of legal and accounting consultants flushed out Sun Life Assurance of Canada as a potential partner. In a phone call to this second insurance company on the scene, he said, "Look, I just do not have time to waste on going through another month of discussions." Sun Life's negotiators assured him they could do a deal with dispatch. "So then we moved heaven and earth to clear our debts and they did huge due dilegence and we completed the transaction—24 hours ahead of schedule."*

Sun Life has since recommended a research company specializing in incentive-based sales organizations, which interviewed a cross section of the Canadian real-estate industry for Century 21. The so-called Project 2000 that resulted from this research has reshaped the organization, reducing its income dramatically but making it much more appealing to franchisees. Since instituting a fee-for-service structure instead of the flat six-percent royalty it charged them before 1994, the company has seen its national market share climb by about one-third to 12 percent. "We'll leave this century with 350 offices," says president Don Lawby, "and at the end of 2001 we'll be at 450."

Of course, Charlwood prefers to dwell on this recent recovery of Century 21 rather than its decline during the early 1990s and more particularly those dark days previously when he and Thomas held the shotgun at each other's head. In this, his attitude is typical of the successfully self-employed—one that is almost a prerequiste for anybody enrolling in Entrepreneurial Risk-taking 101.

Don't allow the negatives of life to litter your path

Walter Good, a marketing professor at the University of Manitoba, says: "My anecdotal evidence supports the fact that entrepreneurs consciously do try to avoid negative energy. They have to maintain that positive thought process. Their attitude

---

* Peter Thomas took the cash—"my go-to-hell money"—and began rebuilding his Samoth Capital Corporation as a merchant banker focused on real-estate lending, investing in distressed hotels, master-planned communities, and multifamily projects. At last count it owned 28 hotels and maintained a portfolio of properties throughout the United States. In the 1998 Canadian Entrepreneur of the Year Awards sponsored by Ernst & Young, he was named the Pacific regional winner.

toward failure is that it's a learning process—you take the positive out of it and learn from it."

He points to a study done for Babson College in Wellesley, Massachusetts, an independent school of management education. Of 21 inductees into its Academy of Distinguished Entrepreneurs (including McDonald's Ray Kroc and The Body Shop's Anita Roddick), all mentioned three learnable attributes and behaviours they considered crucial to their success. The first—followed by "taking personal initiative" and "having great perseverance"—was "responding positively to all challenges and learning from mistakes." Good paraphrases their response as: "Put it behind me. Move on." Gary Charlwood, in discussing his rocky relationship with Peter Thomas, says: "I always like to communicate on the high road. ... If someone said to me at the end of my life, 'Was it positive that you met Peter?' I would say, 'Absolutely'—and he would say the same thing. My statement about [his being] an effervescent, bubbly kind of guy still stands. He is great company—for a couple of hours." That last aside is about as much negative energy as Charlwood allows himself. (He would likely agree with Oscar Wilde, who said: "Always forgive your enemies; nothing annoys them so much.") Dealing with setbacks, he inevitably stresses the positive. He offers the example in real estate of a dramatic rise in interest rates that affects Century 21 franchisees. His response: "Look, we can't change this. So we can mope or go around complaining—or we can say, 'Hell, how do we deal with these circumstances?'" As his son Martin says, "Gary's view is always: Look forward, not back."

Of the two younger Charlwoods, Christopher was the one intrigued by real estate early on. In his midteens, he began looking for a nice home for his father, who was then bacheloring it in a penthouse. Chris was 23 when he finally found the West Vancouver house on 1.2 hectares where Gary Charlwood moved a decade ago. Coincidentally, the very same day, Gary married Maria Isabel Sebazco, the Cuban dancer he had met through mutual friends in Miami. Stoph, as his brother calls him, was briefly sidetracked by the travel business. After their graduation, Charlwood let his sons take over a Uniglobe agency in downtown Vancouver—perhaps the worst-performing franchise in western Canada—which he had bought for his girlfriend of the time. It was losing $100,000 a year on $900,000 in sales. Reporting to master franchisee Laurie Radloff, they got it to a break-even point by the second year, when it was generating about $2.5 million annually. Chris then left it to his brother to run and sell soon after. The buyer had an M.B.A. and a master's in law; Marty says he earned his own M.B.A. negotiating over four months to emerge with a deal that earned the Charlwood boys a decent profit.

The first time Chris came to his father to ask for investment funds to buy some property with partners, Charlwood advised him to start by learning more about the industry. His son sold apartment blocks for Century 21 for six months before founding the company that became Cobalt Real Estate—"what I consider my own start-up business." Its first project was the renovation of a 26-apartment building bought with money from the Charlwood Pacific Group and four former classmates whose family owned the local Earl's restaurant chain. That investment made $1.5 million within 18 months. Martin, meanwhile, advanced through various roles at Uniglobe, from coordinating an ill-fated Premier Vacations leisure division to more fruitfully selling master-licensing agreements outside North America. In 1993 he pioneered these franchise sales in the Benelux countries and followed up on years of negotiation his father had initiated with Japan, where the master licensee was the mammoth trading company C. Itoh, which also had rights to Century 21.

Uniglobe's first overseas venture had been in England three years earlier, with mixed results. The master licensees—who paid about $1 million, with a third down—were part of the British travel establishment and wanted to do things their way. "They ran off the rails," Charlwood says, "and then they did the worst thing of all—they delved into the advertising fund, which is a fiduciary fund they hold on behalf of the franchisee. It was a very serious offence and we terminated the region." That was when Mike Levy, then president of Uniglobe Travel (International) and about a five-percent shareholder, asked to go home after all his years in Canada and run the British region. At the same time, the board of directors suggested that Martin Charlwood had proved himself as executive vice president and should be bumped upstairs as Levy's successor.

The young Charlwood says: "We set ourselves a goal in the early to mid-1990s that within ten years we would shift from a mix of 90-percent corporate, ten-percent leisure, to a more balanced mix of 50 percent of each. And we did that because leisure, by and large, is more lucrative to sell, with higher margins, and there's the demographic support—there's more people looking for more vacation experiences and having more disposable income in their hands than ever before. To help speed up that process, we began thinking about acquisitions that could bring in some of that concept and some of the expertise, and that's when we came across CruiseShipCenters and Mike Drever"—who came aboard in 1997.

That was two years after Uniglobe began investigating the idea of an "electronic travel agency" and, at Chris's suggestion, formed a subisidary called Uniglobe Travel Online. The Charlwoods were concerned even then, before the World Wide Web had really surfaced in the public consciousness, that suppliers such as airlines would soon be bypassing travel agencies and going directly to the consumer. "Christopher and I believed that the ongoing growth of Uniglobe was going to be limited unless we had an Internet solution," Martin says. It took some false starts, trying to be all things to the traveller, before the publicly traded UTO focused on the cruise market and learned how to reward Uniglobe's franchisees at the same time. Now they can go to the Web site and purchase the CruiseShipCenters' wholesale cruise products for their clients. That decision took UTO from $250,000 in sales in the last quarter of 1997 to $3 million in the third quarter of 1998. And this was before it concluded a deal to woo the general public to its home page to buy cruise packages. In late 1998, it formed a marketing partnership with Microsoft Expedia to be on the e-commerce company's Web site, which receives 100 or more times the hits than UTO's does. "The Expedia deal has caused a tenfold increase in activity to our Web site," Martin noted not long after. "We can't even hire enough people to handle the business."

The next leap, he says, will be to act as a tour wholesaler—for example, buying up blocs of cruise-ship cabins or onshore packages at a deep discount and then using Uniglobe's wide network of franchisees to sell them. Christopher has his own plans for the travel company, too, hoping to develop boutique hotels in the cruise centres of Vancouver and Miami that the Web site and the agencies can fill. They agree with their father that Uniglobe might well double in size over the next five years. But they will both be pleased when his term as volunteer chairman of the International Franchise Association ends in 1999 and the Marathon Man returns to run the same business tracks as his sons. "It's been a huge drain. It's caused our businesses to suffer a bit short-term," Chris says. "In the long term, it's probably going to pay off in droves because he's forging great relationships and has got some great ideas from a whole bunch of very intelligent businesspeople."

"There's hardly a week goes by that I don't hear a completely new and untried idea for franchising," Gary Charlwood told me. But some ideas are much more intriguing than others.

TrendWatch

"The franchising sector is consistently growing by ten to 12 per cent a year and we anticipate this continuing," said Gary Charlwood in his role as International Franchise Association chairman. "And a major portion of the recent growth has come from franchising that offers the flexibility of operating from home. There's a major explosion in home-based franchises." Among them: commercial and domestic cleaning companies, food deliveries, business-form and advertising-product distributors, home-office business counsellors, home-furnishing suppliers—all of them run by franchisees from their residences. As Gary Charlwood pointed out (sitting in his own office at home where he does a lot of work), the investment required is low, operators get a tax break by locating in their homes, and women in particular—who represent such a high percentage of the increasing number of entrepreneurs in this country—can work effectively amid domestic surroundings. "Downsizing is not a temporary phenomenon," Charlwood told a franchising convention in Madrid in 1998, "but a permanent part of the business world today as big business finds it cheaper to outsource the mail, food services, copying, and travel, payroll, and maintenance services. The human-resources departments of *Fortune* 500 companies are actually becoming outsource specialists—and creative franchisors worldwide are filling the void. As you can imagine, all this bodes well for the future of franchising."

Chapter Two

The Entertainer

Tim Gamble, Peace Arch Entertainment Group

Central casting could have sent him to play the role of Hollywood producer. Larry Sugar is sporting a silver bracelet, a diamond stud in one ear, black denim jeans, and a white shirt emblazoned with a whimsical imprint of spectacles on a string. In a corner of his office at one of the Vancouver production studios of the Vidatron Entertainment Group (renamed Peace Arch a year later) perches a canvas director's chair bearing his name. Otherwise the decor runs to cattle horns, a saddle, and paperback cowboy novels framed like a piece of art—funky reminders of his successful western series, *Dead Man's Gun*, which is about to start shooting a second season for the Showtime cable network in the United States and CHUM Television in Canada.

But this afternoon in March 1998, his kinetic mind is on two other projects. He is gearing up to produce *So Weird*, the pilot of a half-hour prime-time series for the Disney Channel, and his publicist needs some background. "I kinda describe it as *Harriet the Spy* meets *Poltergeist*," he tells her, conjuring up a high concept that she will pass on intact to the media. Sugar's phone rings. It's a call from Francis Ford Coppola's American Zoetrope office in Los Angeles. The creator of *The Godfather* trilogy and *Apocalypse Now* is an executive producer on the other project looming in Sugar's immediate future: a raunchy hourlong science-fiction series called *First Wave*. Zoetrope is phoning about a potential producer. "You got it," Sugar reassures the caller, briskly summing up the conversation. "Just close the deal." He turns his attention back to me: "There's been amazing growth. I was doing about $11 million a year for the three years before. Now I'll do"—he adds it up—"$70 million U.S. Think so. The series alone are $44 million—*First Wave* and *Dead Man's Gun*. Then the pilot and two family films. And a mini-series we anticipate doing based on an Anne Rice book, *Servant of the Bones.* And I believe we'll be able to announce the first series commitment for '99. *Another* series—totally B.C."*

Across the Burrard Street Bridge, in a heritage warehouse building in the gentrified Yaletown district of downtown Vancouver, Tim Gamble has been on the phone much of the morning. He is trying to track down $3 million to help sweeten Sugar's life. Gamble is a decade younger than his partner's 52 years, but they share similar black caterpillar eyebrows and silvered hair, although Sugar's is a mass of curls. And where the older man has a paunch despite daily gym workouts following a couple of recent heart attacks, the Hollywood-handsome Gamble, with pale blue electric eyes, is as thin as the hockey sticks he has wielded since boyhood. This leanness reflects his regular stints as a compact centre on a team with 20-year-olds in a college league, where he suffered his only recent health problem, a badly separated shoulder. Sugar, recently divorced, is building a home in Santa Fe, New Mexico, and has renovated a Victorian gem in Vancouver adorned with stained glass and his collection of such modern-art masters as Milton Avery and Andy Warhol (and reportedly a Rembrandt, too). The never-married Gamble lives in the same pleasant but unspectacular False Creek condo he has since his less-affluent days; his one indulgence may be a black Saab 900SE convertible.

There are other significant differences between the partners, not least their personalities. Sugar's is American-brash, exciting, excited, expressive of his quarter-century career as a top executive with film and television giants—Warner Bros. International, 20th Century Fox, CBS Productions. Gamble's is Canadian-quiet, yet charismatic, hewn from 15 years of pioneering Canada's first publicly traded film and video business—working with partners who were as absent of experience as he was, and slowly guiding it, full of detours and disasters, in a domestic setting not always conducive to growth.

---

*In fact, revenues for Vidatron's fiscal 1998, which ended in August, totalled $32.5 million, an increase of 36 percent from 1997—with the television division contributing a little more than a half of that growth. Net earnings of $1.8 million, or 27 cents a share, contrasted with the previous year's loss of $1.2 million, or 26 cents a share. As the year ended, neither the Anne Rice miniseries nor the other "totally B.C." series Larry Sugar was touting had yet come to pass.

"How do you *not* like Tim?" Sugar says. "Tim's like Sara Lee. He's a nice person and he likes people. It's impossible not to like Tim." Well, in fact, he has made some enemies, principally among former colleagues, but even they are wont to describe the ingratiating Gamble as "the world's greatest schmoozer."

Linking the two unlikely partners is the most fully integrated entertainment company in western Canada. The understated Peace Arch Entertainment Group—as it was named in mid-1999—develops, produces, and distributes its own film, television, video and interactive programming. Its subsidiary, The Eyes, is one of the West's major producers of video, and other short-form programs for corporate clients, from a film with a jazz score and dazzling digital effects for General Paint to multimedia touch-screen programs in interactive kiosks for BC Hydro and municipal governments. The subsidiary also offers production services for North American broadcast programming and produces TV commercials. A sister company, Aviator Pictures, is Peace Arch's main commercial maker, for weighty brand names such as Tide and Rice-A-Roni (in 1998 it won one of the Television Bureau of Canada's gold Bessies for a poultry company's spot called "Dead Chicken," which showed two elderly Chinese women snapping a live hen's neck so they could board a bus without carrying a live animal). A spin-off company, Toolshed, makes music videos for Canadian bands, among them Dream Warriors, Delerium, and Juno winners Rascalz, whose rap video led its category in the MuchMusic Awards on the Canadian cable channel.

Much of this activity takes place in the redbrick, big-beamed building that Peace Arch owns in Yaletown. The cornerstone of its shrewd investments in real estate, the turn-of-the-century manufacturing and warehousing relic has been officially declared a civic heritage building. The company is refurbishing the solid three-story structure, adding two floors, and stratifying it into retail and office units. Purchased for $1.8 million, it will be worth $10 million, according to a bank appraisal. Equally impressive, Peace Arch also has its own studios to shoot its own films and TV series as well as to lease to visiting producers. In February 1998, it bought and quickly converted a venerable 5,109-square-metre industrial behemoth that sprawls over a half hectare of land along the south shore of False Creek. The site is near the original 2,229-square-metre Vidatron Studio, where some episodes of *Millennium* and *The X-Files* were shot.

What further distinguishes Peace Arch from most competitors in the local industry is the fact that it generally creates product that it co-owns. The others are usually for-hire companies servicing the American movie and TV producers who squat in British Columbia to take advantage of the lower Canadian dollar and our generous government tax credits. What makes Peace Arch an even more rarified specimen in the current hothouse of the B.C. film world is that the Canadian-owned company has actually reversed this bootlicking trend. In 1997 it acquired a company that was, for all intents and purposes, American: Sugar Entertainment, the production business of the plugged-in Larry Sugar, who only recently had become a landed Canadian immigrant.

Suddenly Tim Gamble and his lawyer partner, CEO Cam White, were doing the family movies-of-the-week they had dreamed of producing a couple of years earlier. These were part of a series called *Contemporary Classics* that Sugar had launched for Showtime and Hallmark Entertainment. *The Prisoner of Zenda, Inc.* and *Ronnie and Julie* are modern adaptations of the hoary old Anthony Hope novel and the William Shakespeare play, the latter movie featuring Vancouver's Joshua Jackson, who has starred in Disney's *The Mighty Ducks* and the hit coming-of-age TV series, *Dawson's Creek*. Yet for all the glamour of movies, the revitalized Peace Arch is more tightly focused on cash-flow-fuelling television series, inspired by its second-season sale of *Dead Man's Gun* and its partnership with Hollywood heavyweight Coppola in *First Wave*.

The merger of the two entertainment companies created a synergistic hybrid that Peter Mitchell, director of the B.C. Film Commission, has described as a quickly emerging mainstream player in the indigenous film industry. He ranked it at the top with Pacific Motion Pictures, a local private company financed by Tony Allard, the scion of the Western International Communications-Allarcom broadcasting fortune.* "I would see Peace Arch and PMP as being market leaders," Mitchell says. "I think Peace Arch is a much more diversified operation

---

* Pacific Motion Pictures was acquired in 1998 by Vancouver's Rainmaker Entertainment Group, a major one-stop postproduction shop for mostly Hollywood features. Rainmaker had recently signed a deal with Vidatron to give Larry Sugar's productions volume discounts and priority scheduling in return for an exclusive on its services.

than the vast majority of production-services companies. They have a more solid base with real assets."

With Larry Sugar onboard, Vidatron's revenues leaped in 1997 by nearly 500 percent to $24 million and by 36 percent a year later. In the six months ending February 1999, revenues increased by 86 percent—to $30.2 million—over the same period in 1998. Yet so low-profile is its president, Tim Gamble, that few people knew of him or his company in November 1997 when a brief article on the *Vancouver Sun* business pages reported that British Columbia's Securities Fraud Office had charged him for the late filing of his personal trades in the corporate stock. This lack of recognition had prevailed in spite of his long apprenticeship in the Canadian video and multimedia arena and his friendships with such entertainment icons as actor Martin Sheen *(Apocalypse Now, The American President)* and television producer David Wolper *(Roots)*, with whom he plays golf in film-industry tournaments four times a year. The unwelcome newspaper publicity—over what turned out to be a misdemeanour born of his characteristic procrastination—briefly propelled him into the consciousness of the public, which then promptly forgot about him.

Based on past performance, Gamble would prefer such anonymity. It was only within the last year that he had reluctantly put a publicist under contract, the well-connected Tina Baird, and then only for two days a week. For someone in the business of communications, the head of a public company dependent on investors, he had long disregarded a cardinal truism that so many busy entrepreneurs ignore.

Trumpet your legitimate successes intelligently in an organized campaign of public relations

"I've always thought this is a business where action speaks louder than words, and I wanted our action to be doing the talking." Tim Gamble says. "Being a little understated isn't so bad." But Gamble's partners and publicist think otherwise. "Larry says he wouldn't think of working without a publicist at his hip," says Tina Baird of Baird McClelland Inc. Peace Arch CEO Cam White believes that a public company runs two different businesses: "You run the business that you're in and you run the business of being public. And both of them have to achieve critical mass. In terms of being public, you have to constantly get your name out there." Peace Arch, he feels, had only lately begun to do a good job of publicizing itself, which was one reason why—despite recent successes—its stock was still undervalued. Pushed, Gamble agrees: "Certainly you have a responsibility to your shareholders to provide some visibility for the company." And he acknowledges that his past reluctance to proclaim even small triumphs, such as industry awards, may have had internal consequences, as well: "I've always underestimated the benefit publicity had to employees and the company's morale."

Peace Arch's contracting of a publicist in its hometown and an investor-relations consultant in Miami has begun to pay off, as it did last March, when the media overreported the relocation of *The X-Files* production team to Los Angeles after five years' filming in Vancouver. The front-page story in the *Vancouver Sun* reassuringly pointed out that the television series was just one of 20 to shoot in the Lower Mainland during 1997—and they were among 167 productions, including feature films and TV movies and pilots, that had contributed $630 million to the B.C. economy.* The *Sun* then underscored the company's role as a prominent player in the industry by observing: "Among the new series waiting to go before the cameras is Vidatron Entertainment's large-budget science-fiction extravaganza *First Wave*—which, ironically enough, was created and developed by a former *X-Files* script writer, Chris Brancato."

It was *First Wave* for which Gamble had been trying to raise $3 million that spring morning in 1998. This was the final ten percent of the budget for the 22-part, first-season series. He had been hoping for just that amount from the Canada Television and Cable Production Fund, a federal initiative. In fact, in a November 1997 investment newsletter, Yorkton Securities mentioned such a possibility in underlining its recommendation to buy Vidatron stock. But the Cable Production Fund changed its rules to insist that the underlying material of a program had to be created by a Canadian—not an American like Brancato.

As Gamble would later confess in an e-mail to a former partner, Reg Worthington, now working in Singapore: "The last couple of months

---

* *The X-Files* did, however, contribute about 300 jobs and $35 million in direct spending (a reported $2 million U.S. an episode) since it went on the air in 1993.

have been real stressful for me. We begin shooting *First Wave* on Monday and last week one of our funding sources fell out. As usual our blessed government decided to change the rules to one of the programs that we had set up to qualify for—two weeks before our first day of principal photography. It cost us $100,000 US an episode. They simply changed the rule to eliminate any project that was based on any material that wasn't created by a Canadian. No grandfathering either. This business really isn't easy. Why did you allow us to get into it? I'm sure it is all your fault."

If it was anyone's fault, it was more Tim Gamble's. His mother, Kathleen, likes to show off a photograph of the four-year-old Tim and his elder brother, Mark, in Mississauga, outside Toronto, where the Gamble family lived. They are both swinging golf clubs. "His brother has his eye on the ball," she points out, "and Tim has his eye on the camera." Typical of him? "Oh, I think so." There is more than one layer to her remark. The youngest of her three sons seemed not only predestined to get involved with cameras, but he was also an entertainer, a schmoozer, who liked to be surrounded by friends and be part of team sports, where he could perform. "As soon as he could walk, he was on skates," she says. "He was a natural," says her husband, John, as we head upstairs in the late-model house in White Rock, British Columbia, that Tim bought for them a few years ago. There, in a room where Tim and his longtime girlfriend (Jennifer Perrault, a striking blond investment dealer with Nesbitt Burns) have since stayed over many weekends, is a little shrine to his boyhood: a dozen hockey trophies, dating from his Minor A Atom days (1966: Leadership, Ability, Character) to his late teens at Trinity Western College in Langley, British Columbia (1976: Most Valuable Player).

It was during those years that he learned a technique he would someday wield consciously as an entrepreneur.

Envision your goals in as tangible a way as you can—and then believe in your vision

"This is something I never would have admitted to ten years ago," Tim Gamble says, "but in sports the difference between somebody who's average and somebody who's exceptional is the ability to visualize what's going on around them. And to then plan and make decisions and visualize where they want to be in the future. I remember as a kid literally lying on the couch watching television and saying I'd love to produce commercials, videos, or television shows. But I never admitted it to anyone because I really never believed it was possible. At the same time, I also remember playing hockey, [and beforehand] lying in bed visualizing what I was going to do when I got the puck. I really believe in visualization as a very important part of planting the seeds for where you're going to be. And whether you're doing it consciously or subconsciously, you have to have a vision. Vision creates an action. As someone once said, 'If you sow a vision, then it reaps an action, and you sow an action and you reap a habit, and if you sow a habit you reap a reality or result.' I only came to trust visualization when I realized you saw the results of it. If you really do have a vision, things will fall into a place where you open yourself up to opportunities. I remember sitting with Cam [White] about four or five years ago, saying, 'You know, we really should produce children's family films. Vancouver's a great place to do them. We can do them with a fairly below-the-line budget, relatively economically.' And then the next thing you know, you have a relationship with Larry Sugar and you've done them. Step back a bit to consider where you want to be in five years and all of a sudden opportunities come up—it's amazing."

Gamble's parents, now aged 85 and married for 56 years, recall that he was always interested in business. His father was a salaryman, a lithographer for a Toronto printing company, and his mother taught school. They were intensely religious, to the point where they mortgaged their home to help finance a breakaway Associated Gospel Church. None of the family liked confrontation, Gamble's mother remembers; that trait would come back to haunt their son in his business career. "The absolute perfect family. Storybook," he says of his childhood environment. Neither of his parents' careers interested him, but he heeded his mother's advice and took an education degree as a fallback. Moving west to study at the religiously oriented Trinity Western, Gamble finished his degree at the University of British

Columbia. He funded his schooling by setting chokers in the West Coast woods and teaching tennis; he and a partner took the doubles trophy at the provincial Summer Games.

Always interested in real estate, too, Gamble had his parents' financial help in putting a down payment on a beat-up cottage in White Rock, which he rented out (one tenant was an unwed mother, whose presence discouraged him from flipping the property). Graduating in 1980, he began to substitute as a teacher, all the while recognizing that he would really rather be an entrepreneur. When his middle brother, J.D., an environmentally conscious chemist, decided to sell his business—making some of the first biodegradable floor waxes—Gamble considered buying it until his mother reminded him he knew nothing about chemicals. Instead, he planned to acquire Canadian rights to a line of disposable toothbrushes, with toothpaste in their handles, designed by a Salt Lake City inventor. A Vancouver real-estate boom had boosted the value of his little cottage, bought for $28,000, to $100,000. He took out a $50,000 mortgage to buy about 100,000 brushes. But for the first and only time in his life, Gamble was too ill to get on a plane and make the deal.

The following week he was due in Rio de Janeiro to visit Mark, an engineer building nuclear power plants for Westinghouse. Trying to help guide the baby of the family, the much-older brother said: "Tim, whenever we have a part come down here that needs to be installed in a special way, rather than sending an engineer down, we send a video-tape now. You know what? You should get into the video business." The world's first videotape had been introduced in 1952, but more than a quarter century later videocassette recorders were only beginning to be an important corporate-communications tool. Tim Gamble had never even held a video camera in his hand.

Back home, toothbrushes forgotten, he looked in the Vancouver phone book and found virtually no competition in video productions. He approached Reg Worthington, a charter-bus driver whom he had met on the tennis courts. "He was the closest thing I knew to somebody who understood video—because he was a musician," Gamble recalls. "He played guitar and piano in a Christian rock band, but he was very, very talented and had an instinct and an appreciation for being in the video business." Another friend, Craig Sawchuk, was interested in photography and helped explain the basics of video equipment to them. Among their earliest jobs was a video for a local builder of steel structures, which they taped with a borrowed camera that didn't work during their first shoot. While they pretended to be taping, Gamble distracted the client. All to no avail: the company ran into financial problems and didn't pay for any of the footage.

Looking for work, the friends recognized that a holiday-tour company might be able to use videos of its destinations. They picked a name from the Yellow Pages and Gamble called Wellington Lee, the president of Silver Wings Holidays.

Displaying classic *chutzpah* from the start, the hopeful entrepreneur got through after several tries by telling Lee's secretary that it was a personal call. He then fast-talked him about the need for a video that displayed hotel prices in Nevada and featured the services Silver Wings could offer travel agents.

"Great idea," Lee said. "Can I come out and see something you've done?"

"You can't do that because I'd have to make my bed," Gamble replied. He and his friends were working from his parents' home. "It had a lot of advantages," Worthington remembers. "Close to home, built-in maid and food service, already furnished."

"Well," Lee wondered, "can you bring something in to show me?"

Sure they could—although they had no demo reel to show. Worthington now says: "We duped the local Sony representative into cutting a pretty-pictures reel from a camera test one of their guys had done." With that and a borrowed three-quarter-inch video recorder from a local cable station, Gamble and Worthington made their presentation on a Friday afternoon. Lee, impressed by their enthusiasm, said a heavy snowfall had just blanketed Lake Tahoe; could they be on a plane with him Sunday morning to film it? Gamble—just as his friend was about to stall for time—said, "*No problem.*"

Worthington didn't know then that the two-word response would be his partner's standard reply to any challenge posed to him over the next dozen years.

Using Gamble's second-mortage money, they spent that afternoon buying new video-production equipment. "We practised how to use it all day Saturday. I had my litle notes—plug this cord in here, shoot this way—and met Wellington Lee and the president of Pacific Western Airlines at the airport. So Reg and and Lee went through customs and I was left behind with all these big cases of equipment." When U.S. Immigration asked him why he was travelling south, Gamble innocently said he was going down to work. Sequestered in a room for further questioning, he panicked as the clock advanced past flight time. Eventually the PWA president, whose airline was cross-promoting with Silver Wings, had him sprung. He ran through the airport, got on the charter plane, sat beside his friend, and said, "Here we go."

The adventure had just begun. Arriving in Reno, they set up the camera on a borrowed tripod to videotape holidayers disembarking from the plane. Suddenly one of the telescopic legs collapsed and the expensive JVC KY2000 tumbled to the tarmac and broke. "Set it back up. Fake it. Keep shooting," Gamble told Worthington. The next morning he found an electronics engineer at the University of Nevada who repaired the exotic camera.

The two naïve young friends went straight from there to tape some casino action. "As usual Tim's damn-the-torpedoes attitude had us in a restricted area of a parkade overlooking Circus Circus," Worthington recalls. "We were getting some wonderful footage when a black Mercedes pulled up and the people inside asked us to join them." Gamble picks up the story: "Two big bodyguards. The next thing I know, I'm sitting in the manager's office and he's saying, 'What are you doing videotaping my casino?'" He schmoozed the man into letting him shoot without showing gamblers' faces.

From such a shaky start in 1981—the video was shelved after their first-ever client viewing—was born Medco Productions Inc. (for Marketing and Educational Company). By now their colleagues included Craig Sawchuk and his cousin Murray Duncan, friends and fellow teachers subbing in classrooms as they learned the video business. Four years later, when the company first went public, Gamble's initial cash investment was to give him a much larger piece than the others got through sweat equity. "The first year we made $20,000," Duncan says. Some of Medco's earliest work was for tourist attractions in the Okanagan Valley, where the producers could at least get in the door to pitch potential clients. "Nobody would see us here in Vancouver. When we went up there, we were a Vancouver production company."

67

Over the first couple of years, they did develop some local clients, mining companies among them, and a few solid prospects.* Worthington was pursuing his passion for commercials and the others were producing industrial and training tapes. But within a single week three of their clients—including Finning Tractor, which wanted a heavy-equipment video—cancelled $80,000 worth of business. Interest rates had been escalating throughout North America (the U.S. prime had reached 21.5 percent, the highest since the American Civil War), causing corporations to cut back. It was time to regroup and decide what business Medco Productions should be in. It was then that Gamble recognized a piece of wisdom that many other entrepreneurs had won the hard way.

Whenever practical, be less dependent on clients' whims and more driven by sustainable products that you create yourself

"From the very beginning, we did service work for corporate clients—corporate videos and then television commercials and music videos," Tim Gamble says. "But we were always reinvesting that money into product development. We always wanted to become less client-focused and more product-driven. So wherever possible, we've always tried to take clients and turn them into partners to develop product." The crash of their embryonic business had forced the video producers to rethink things. "Had the interest rates not gone from 12 percent to 22 percent, we'd probably be out of business now. It forced us then to think that, 'Jeez, we've got all this investment in equipment. We can't be dependent on clients. We've got to create a product that we can sell all around the world.'"

---

* "I remember finally getting a paycheque and spending half of it on a new Donnay tennis racket," Reg Worthington says. "Tim was ready to disown me as a partner and a friend. I have to admit, in retrospect, it wasn't too bright a move. We were going without meals and getting Care packages from our loving and devoted girlfriends at the time. Tim and I like to socialize—a lot. Give us a beach, a bar, a nightclub, anywhere the action was, we wanted to be part of it. ... I don't think we were exactly killing ourselves on the work front in those days."

The product that proved the point was born of their own experience. They had taught themselves how to operate a video camera professionally; perhaps they could create a video that showed others how to use one for personal use. He and Worthington spent the summer of 1983 and about $45,000 piecing together a 40-minute tape and an accompanying booklet, which taught the basics of focusing a camera and the finer points of composition and continuity. The final production—*Home Video: Shoot Like a Pro*—had a professional actor and actress speak the lines of a simply written script that reflected Gamble's teacher training. A camera manufacturer would be the most obvious target to distribute such a product, so Gamble approached Sony Corporation in Toronto, which wasn't interested. Undaunted, he cold-called Sony's American president, Eli Stern, who invited the charming Canadian to New York City. Stern sent him on a shuttle bus to see the manager of Sony's Betamax merchandising division in New Jersey. Waiting around for six hours, Gamble schmoozed the man's secretary into compiling a written proposal that he could present to her boss. She tracked down figures for the good-looking 26-year-old and even typed the final presentation. Sony initially agreed to buy one tape for each of its 3,000 North American dealers, netting Medco $21,000.

Craig Sawchuk, focused on educational videos, took over the ongoing sales of the Sony product, convincing the company to insert a card with each camera that offered the buyer a special price for the instructional tape. Ultimately the video sold more than 100,000 copies and Sawchuk created a similar product for Pentax 35-millimetre cameras—funnelling a steady cash flow into the still-struggling production company. In the years to come, the company would repeat the process with other clients. BC Hydro funded *ElectroJuice*—an imaginative electrical-safety video warning high-school students away from power lines—which Peace Arch has sold to hydro companies across the continent. The Canadian division of Merck Pharmaceuticals, for whom it did multimedia work, financed *HeartSafe*—a heart-care video that cardiologists have routinely prescribed for their patients—hosted by Martin Sheen, who had suffered a heart attack while filming *Apocalypse Now*. Both projects offered more than a continuing stream of income: one young viewer credited *ElectroJuice* (a gold-medal winner at the New York Film Festival) for the knowledge he used to save a friend from electrocution, and *HeartSafe* was named best patient-education video of the year in the United States.

Medco became Vidatron in 1985, when it went looking for more capital to develop its products.* A Vancouver promoter who had a privately owned porcelain-enamel factory in Seattle convinced Gamble and his colleagues to join forces and go public on the Vancouver Stock Exchange. The multimedia company—the first of its kind in Canada to become publicly traded—did add some pizzazz to the initial public offering, but there was no rationale to the new venture and within two years the partners amicably exchanged shares and went private again as separate entities. The stock had never performed with any vigour.

By now Vidatron was consulting Cam White, a partner in a securities and corporate-law firm, whose clients included the flamboyant VSE promoter Murray Pezim. In 1987 White was shepherding the capital-hungry Vidatron through its second run at going public at a time when the exchange was booming. Then the October Crash crippled the markets throughout North America. When the company did make its initial public offering the following January, during a subsequent mini-crash, it raised only half a million dollars. "It was legally public," White says, "but it was capitalized like a private company and probably would have had 200 to 300 shareholders."

Vidatron had built up two dozen full-time staff, about the same number it has today, who were producing corporate videos, TV commercials and—for a few months—a daily live five-minute television show, *VSE Today,* which was fed across the continent. "One thing that Vidatron became noted for—both good and bad for us—was quality," says Murray Duncan. "We were never known as the least expensive." One of Gamble's deals was the acquisition of Finning Tractors' training division. "With it," Worthington says, "we also got their management team. I recall one of them putting new tires for his car and trinkets for his boat on his expense account. I wasn't happy, but felt powerless to turn this big locomotive around." When he

---

* It was about that time I met Tim Gamble, who was making a video for a client for whom my corporate-communications firm was doing print publicity. Bonita Thompson, then head of the B.C. International Commercial Arbitration Centre in Vancouver, recalls being impressed by his charm and sheer energy as he and Reg Worthington "tossed ideas around like Ping-Pong balls" and produced a sophisticated video production for a global target market.

threatened to leave the company, Gamble—tears welling in his eyes—convinced Worthington to stay as head of a new commercial-production boutique called Hot Shots. At one point it was Vidatron's most profitable division.

Meanwhile Gamble would lead the company into other new fields. He was attracted to a fledgling Vancouver film house, Northern Lights Media, a subsidiary of Meta Communications, a public company on the Toronto exchange. By buying Northern Lights from the financially troubled Meta, Vidatron acquired a movie-in-progress, *The Outside Chance of Maximilian Glick,* a warm, fuzzy Canadian film that sank after limited distribution.

The acquisition had forced the company into assuming a convertible debenture floated by promoter Don Busby, one of the company's original seed-stock investors. "We got had on that transaction," recalls Duncan. "If you think they can dance in *Riverdance,* you should have seen us." Gamble prefers to downplay the incident: "Don Busby had a convertible debenture that we ended up having to pay back, and we did. There wasn't any particular problem."

There certainly were problems, however, with a series of limited partnerships Vidatron took on. With no demand for venture shares, particularly entertainment stocks, the company was seeking mechanisms to give investors a tax benefit. One idea was a partnership modelled on the so-called mining flow-through, in which investors in mining plays not only got a tax benefit but could then convert both the benefit and their investment into equity. "We probably did three or four limited partnerships," Gamble says, admitting that they led to a major dilution of shares for the original investors. "There's a lot of errors over the years. A lot we invested in didn't pan out. But the reality was that it was very different times ... we had never worked for anybody else and never had the experience of working with somebody who was in our industry. We were definitely pioneering the whole industry in terms of going public, in the types of financing structures we were looking at. ... It took up an incredible amount of mind space and time just worrying about the finances of the company."

But acquiring Northern Lights, despite the financial problems it triggered, had given Gamble a taste for feature films. "Tim was off in Europe all the time, allegedly trying to get these movie deals together," says Sawchuk. One consummated deal began with Martin Sheen's agent mentioning that the veteran actor wanted to make his directorial debut with a drama about blacks and whites in an army prison. Gamble's friend, Frank Giustra, was the head of Vancouver's Yorkton Securities and the financier of the International Movie Group, a global distributor of modest films run by Hollywood producer Peter Strauss. At Gamble's suggestion, the Movie Group agreed to back the picture— in return for worldwide distribution rights while selling the American rights to Republic Pictures. *Cadence,* released in 1991, was a Sheen family production, with Martin directing and appearing in it along with sons Charlie Sheen and Ramon Estevez. The picture garnered luke-warm and even hostile reviews ("A sluggish comedy of race relations from the sappy Sheens," the *Washington Post* said of the politically cor-rect drama).*

Gamble shared executive-producer credits with Giustra and Strauss; a production photo from the film still hangs in his modest office. While *Cadence* was financially successful for the Movie Group and Republic, Vidatron discovered a hard truth: "We learned that as a producer, in order to get that thing made, you had to give it away, pre-sell it," Gamble says. "And by preselling it, it left you with no rights. And so we really ended up only just earning our fee. Now, we'd earned a nice fee, but *they* were the ones who made money." He resolved "to get more involved in distribution, projects we could distribute our-selves, and then control the rights in certain areas. Really, the reason to be in production is at the end of the day to be holding distribution

---

*Frank Giustra resurfaced in the B.C. film business in 1997 as chair and CEO of Lions Gate Entertainment, which roared to life the following year as it partnered with Peter Guber, former head of Sony Pictures Entertainment, to create a production company called Mandalay Pictures. Mandalay announced it would develop and produce 20 feature films budgeted at more than $800 million over five years. But its first public venture—the filming of Bret Easton Ellis's *American Psycho* to feature Leonardo DiCaprio—encoun-tered bad press when the *Titanic* star said he hadn't signed any deal, despite Lions Gate's suggestions in the media. Giustra had already annoyed *Vancouver Sun* columnist Malcolm Parry, who criticized him for hype and evasion which, Parry claimed, "is received skepti-cally even on Howe Street, where other promoters might deem it to be a digestive byprod-uct found abundantly in cattle-grazing areas." As a distributor, however, Lions Gate got a high profile when two films it put into general release—*Affliction* and *Gods and Monsters*—won Oscars at the 1999 Academy Awards.

rights. In the film business, if you're not the distributor, there's not much likelihood that you'll see more than the initial advance."

There were to be no more feature films over the next few years. Northern Lights faded to black and the underfunded Vidatron scrambled as it continued to lose money, once getting stuck for more than $50,000 when a small ad agency went bankrupt. That was one of the times it was forced to ask for its suppliers' patience. Its landlord reacted by padlocking the office doors. Gamble reacted by taking up an offer from an investor to give Vidatron half equity in his Yaletown building in return for some company stock; half a year later, in 1994, it owned the heritage structure it is now developing. Vidatron bought Image Media Services, western Canada's largest distributor of educational videos, CD-ROMs, and software, and then sold it a couple of years later ("We didn't have the skills to micromanage it," Gamble explains). Pilot Software, an eastern Canadian distributor of educational software, followed the same scenario. A better fit was The Eyes Multimedia Productions, a competitor in film, video, and TV programming, which then spawned the Toolshed music-video division.

All of this juggling affected the bottom line as well as the staff's morale. One lesson that Gamble hadn't mastered yet could be simply expressed but was often damnably difficult to practise.

Focus on your corporate and personal strengths and don't be easily distracted

"We did some things successfully, but we tended to lose focus," Murray Duncan says, reflecting on his years with Vidatron, which ended in 1994. "Now we're in the motion-picture business. No, we're in the health-care business. We originally started doing educational videos, but we never capitalized on our strengths." His cousin Craig Sawchuk concurs: "We were leadership-deficient. There was no consensus on the direction we were going. Tim Gamble was kind of the de facto leader, but he has the attention span of an Irish setter." In Vidatron's 1994 annual report, Gamble himself acknowledged this lack of focus: "Two years ago we sat down to define what our business was and where it was going. What we were clear about was our

73

ability to conceive, develop, and produce innovative, award-winning programming, both for clients and our own product library. What our analysis told us was that, in our enthusiasm to tackle any opportunity to produce quality programming, we often did not focus on the jobs and products which made the biggest and most consistent contribution to our bottom line."

By 1994 three of Vidatron's original four partners had gone. Reg Worthington—disaffected by the lurching progress of the parent company—had lit out for work in Singapore, well before his TV-commercial division, Hot Shots, folded (Gamble later resurrected it as Aviator Pictures). Craig Sawchuk and his American wife had been running a Seattle office to distribute educational videos such as *HeartSafe* and *Home Video: Shoot Like a Pro*. Cash flows were ebbing and the Sawchuks were frustrated with the Vancouver head office because they wanted to move well beyond their simple distribution role into video production. They eagerly took a buyout and reestablished Seattle as an independent operation, retaining an ongoing relationship with Sony. While faring well financially, they claim that Vidatron left their American suppliers holding the bag for about $60,000; Vidatron's CFO, Juliet Jones, counterclaims that the company did, in fact, send them money earmarked to repay those debts. "One of the most important things is to know when to cut your losses, starting with Craig Sawchuk and the U.S. company," Jones says. Murray Duncan was asked to leave when his services were no longer felt necessary for Vidatron's new direction. This was, Duncan points out, a month after the company had borrowed $100,000 from him to cover the payroll. He wasn't renominated as a director in 1997 and has since launched a lawsuit against Vidatron, charging that the options in his severance agreement weren't paid out in a timely fashion.*

Tim Gamble seemed congenitally incapable of confronting his partners about their future with the company: "I tend to shield people, protect people from what I think might be confrontation, protect myself

---

*Duncan landed on his feet as director of corporate communications for Vancouver's Intrinsync Software, which has excited a lot of stock watchers as it develops, makes, and supports software tools and components for the development of Microsoft Windows-embedded systems. Intrinsync's young president, a graduate of Motorola's wireless-data division, is an electrical engineer named Derek Spratt.

from getting into confrontative situations." Helping Gamble make the tough decisions was Cam White, who had left his law firm and moved into the former Hot Shots office to freelance as a lawyer. In 1994 the soft-voiced redhead became CEO of Vidatron, a company then at a crossroads. "Using a tennis analogy, it was sort of in no-man's-land," White says. "You either had to go to the net or drop back. You either had to really focus on going out there and building a big company or pulling back to a tiny core, maybe even go private again." He recalls going for a walk with Gamble and agreeing that there was a void in the Vancouver marketplace to be filled by a fully integrated film and television company—based on the successful eastern Canadian models of Alliance Communications, Atlantis Communications, and Cinar Films.*

Vidatron's timing was impeccable. That year a record 85 television series, TV movies, and feature films would generate $400 million directly and about $1.2 billion in spin-offs for the B.C. economy. Most of the investment came from American studios, which were originally lured to the province by the shrunken Canadian dollar, its proximity to Los Angeles, and the photogenic and versatile backdrops.** Now they were digging in because of the solid infrastructure of the local creative and technical crews. Major series, including *MacGyver, The Commish,* and *The X-Files,* were shooting in the massive North Shore and Bridge studios. Of the dozen or so prospering homegrown production companies, the closest to what Gamble and White were considering was Pacific Motion Pictures. Matthew O'Connor and Tom Rowe had produced $150 million worth of movies in the past three years. But PMP acted as a one-stop service company for the Americans, and only with

---

*In 1998 Atlantis and Alliance merged and Cinar, a Montreal-based animation production company, reported a one-year return of 83 percent, all of which helped to spur new interest in Canadian show-business stocks. Roger Dent, head of research at Yorkton Securities, pointing to better-quality senior management in domestic film companies, has been quoted as saying, "People have realized they are real businesses and they can make money." Of course, Yorkton's vice president, Nelson Smith, is a director of Vidatron.

**As the *New York Times* would report in 1996, "Some of the busiest locations are Riverview, an old mental hospital just outside the city that has been converted and reconverted for filming since [producer Stephen J.] Cannell first used it for *Wiseguy*; Lonsdale Quay in North Vancouver, the site of numerous police raids and mob hits; and Stanley Park, a forest near the center of the city that is regularly used for funerals, car chases and the seclusion of military compounds."

the recent injection of Allard money was it starting to take the financial risk of funding its own productions.

Not until 1996 did Gamble and White identify a specific opportunity for a strategic acquisition that would catapult them into full-time international film and television. Larry Sugar had come to town. He arrived in early 1995 to start filming *Contemporary Classics*, a series of TV movies with a teen sports theme that updated old chestnuts like *Robin Hood*. Showtime had asked him to shoot them in British Columbia, for all the usual reasons. Having left his soul in the warmth of his new domicile in Santa Fe, New Mexico, Sugar was in grey, damp Vancouver reluctantly—until May, which had 22 straight days of sunshine. Smitten, he began entertaining the notion of landed-immigrant status. His mother had been a Canadian, after all, and he had lived in Toronto as a youngster before moving south with his family to attend prep school and study law at the University of Southern California. His first job, in 1971, was director of legal and corporate affairs for the international division of Warner Bros., the half-century-old studio that had recently been taken over by a conglomerate. The senior vice president he assisted for three years became a mentor.

His career since read like a Hollywood roll call: in charge of business affairs, production, and copyright infringement at 20th Century Fox (where he wrote the FBI warning about video piracy); independent distributor with his wife, Bonnie, representing Fox, Warner, The Ladd Company, and Orion to market films outside North America; president of Lorimar International in the early 1980s ("the best years in the business"), quitting when Lorimar refused to buy *Kiss of the Spider Woman*; a vice president of CBS Productions ("the most amazing job of my career"), handling global distribution and acquisition and meeting heads of state, including the emperor of Japan and Queen Elizabeth II (four times); a brief time-out, while his wife was ill with cancer, when he produced two forgettable films; executive vice president of Weintraub Entertainment ("not a good experience—Jerry Weintraub is one of the last great living movie moguls, with all that entails"); and finally president of Republic Pictures International ("*Repulsive* Pictures. A terrible mistake. Russell Goldsmith is not a risk taker").

In between Weintraub and Republic, he had launched Sugar Entertainment, which would produce several films by preselling them in the United States and international markets. He was executive producer on *Shattered,* starring Tom Berenger (an "expertly intricate new thriller," the *Washington Post* said); *Stephen King's Graveyard Shift* ("will pass quickly into that great video graveyard in the suburbs"), and *Boxing Helena* ("Confidential to Kim Basinger: That $8.5 million you paid to get out of *Boxing Helena* was worth every penny"). Sugar has written an unpublished manuscript, *Boxing Hollywood,* about the court case that clouded this last picture.

"It was always difficult," he says. "It was always a hustle." Which is one reason he was open to an alliance when Gamble and White came calling. His marriage ended, Sugar had decided to stay on in Canada—"I'm not as unique in L.A."—and by becoming a Canadian took advantage of the tax and funding benefits the federal and provincial governments offered domestic producers. He was simply seeking a studio facility—"not a partner, because I didn't want a partner." Werner Aellen, a dean of Vancouver filmmakers, was the link between him and Vidatron, whose offices Aellen had worked out of for years. Gamble and White had an ongoing desire to buy a building to house a studio and, based on Sugar's interest, found a suitable space in a former restaurant-supply warehouse in an industrial area near False Creek. They signed him up as a major tenant and six months later—having become a distributor of his family films, like the ones they had considered doing themselves—they approached him about becoming partners.

For $260,000 cash and 20 percent of Vidatron, Sugar sold his company to Gamble and White. As he explains. "I wasn't as comfortable being a solo entrepreneur in Vancouver as I would have been in Santa Fe or L.A., where I knew everybody and knew the territory. I didn't know anybody or anything here, other than my crew. I didn't have a bank contact. I didn't have accountants. Everything was new and different for me. This was a company that had been around a long time, and that much I knew—mom-and-pop or not. A small public company. Honest guys. I think it's a good fit. Because I get to do what I really love doing, man, which is making product. Even directing and writing. And I don't have to worry about all the other stuff that normally as an independent is also my domain—finding the money, setting up the banking. I always come in [on the financing] because my background would demand that I do it. For part of the financing, but I'm not alone in setting it all up." Financing such as finding the last $3 million for *First Wave*, as Gamble was then attempting? I ask. "He'd like me to do it, but"—Sugar shouts across False Creek to the corporate headquarters—"you're doing it, Tim! All alone!" (Gamble finally did it by arranging the private placement of 800,000 of the company's common shares with British Columbia's Working Opportunities Fund.)

First Wave—a cross between science fiction and *The Fugitive*—revolves around the one man who can save Earth from a hostile takeover by aliens posing as humans. The deal to get the series on the small screen was a perfect example of how Sugar's background and contacts have propelled Peace Arch into the major leagues. His lawyer knew the agent who represents film and TV writer Chris Brancato, the show's creator. One of Sugar's old friends is Brian Harris, managing director of Pearson Television International, the distribution arm of London-based Pearson Television, a leading producer of TV programming around the world. Pearson was partnering in the project with Brancato and the American Zoetrope studio of Francis Ford Coppola, the executive producer on the series. Initially these partners signed with Vancouver's Everest Entertainment which, unlike its competitor, Vidatron (as it was then known), had agreed to produce the series without having a Canadian buyer in hand to make it more profitable. When Everest couldn't make the vital Canadian sale, the partners came back to Vidatron, which then sold domestic broadcast rights to CHUM Television, operator of Toronto's Citytv, the MuchMusic and Bravo! channels, and Space: The Imagination Station, where *First Wave* airs in Canada. In late 1998 The Sci-Fi Channel in the United States bought rights to 66 episodes while channels in seven other countries, including England and Australia, have picked up the series.

The science-fiction series was shooting in one studio at the same time Sugar was producing the second 22-episode batch of *Dead Man's Gun* in the other. This anthology series follows the progress of a gun in the lives of western characters, played by a variety of medium-echelon stars, including Henry "The Fonz" Winkler, who is executive producer. Then there was the Disney series pilot, *So Weird*, starring Mackenzie Phillips, going into its second 26-episode season, and the *Contemporary Classics* teen movies, *Treasured Island* and *Out of*

Time (based on Rip Van Winkle).★ Vidatron was coproducer, with Vancouver's Greedy Productions, of a weekly half-hour TV series about the video-game industry; *Electric Playground* premiered to good reviews across the continent and went into its second season of syndication on 25 stations in 1998. And in a whole new venture, The Eyes was making two Canadian documentaries, *Citizen Shame,* an exposé of child poverty, and *In Harm's Way,* about youth and violence, for fall showings on Vancouver's VTV.

Oh, and Tim Gamble was working on a video fund-raising documentary for the Elizabeth Fry Foundation, which he agreed to do after being fined $1,100 for the late filing of his corporate director's insider reports two years earlier. Trying to save money, he had always completed those reports himself, rather than pay a professional or have his own financial people do them. The lesson to be learned was a cliché, no less true for being trite.

In vital areas like regulatory reporting and income-tax filing, don't be penny-wise and pound-foolish

"There's a great lesson here," Tim Gamble admits sheepishly. "As a director of a public company, you're required to file insider reports within ten days of the end of every month. And it costs you $50 a month for every month that you're late. What happened was that I was late six, nine months, so my file got passed over to the RCMP. It was upsetting for me, embarrassing. I just got behind. The lesson is probably not to be penny-wise and pound-foolish. I honestly looked after myself last. I am as late with my insider reports as I am with my income tax. It's just a personal trait. As opposed to spending the $100, $200 a month to have someone do it. For the last two years I

★ Obviously none of these reek of Canadiana, which is typical of so much made-in-Canada movies. As John Haslett Cuff has noted in the *Globe and Mail,* "The result is that even after a dozen years of sustained growth in the television industry (Canada is now the second-largest exporter of television to the world—if a distant second to the United States), it is still a Sisyphean task to raise money to produce television that has a distinctively Canadian flavour."

have had somebody doing it and they've been on time. Especially now it's really important to have them in on time. [A few years ago] people didn't have access to insider reports. Now they publish them on the Internet, so they're much more accessible."

His procrastination and the brief bout of bad publicity it generated came at a time when Vidatron was applying to go on the Toronto Stock Exchange. "So the only thing I cared about was that our company get listed on the TSE because that was most important to shareholders," he says. "We disclosed it, I told the Toronto Stock Exchange that I had this issue, and never heard anything about it." And despite his blunder, The Vidatron Entertainment Group appeared to be on a roll, suggesting to patient shareholders reasonable returns on their investment. Even unhappy former partners Murray Duncan and Craig Sawchuk, who remained shareholders, saw the marriage between the company and Sugar Entertainment as one made in Hollywood, if not in heaven. ("It was a wonderful piece of timing," Duncan said.) In 1997 Vidatron raised $6 million in a private placement from several Canadian mutual funds, opened up a $10-million revolving line of credit, and went on the TSE. In 1998 it completed $5 million in equity financing with the B.C. government's Working Opportunity Fund and the Royal Bank Capital Corporation, putting the bank division's western vice president, Darrell Elliott, on its board. The major Vancouver law firm of Campney & Murphy featured Vidatron in an investment seminar as one of ten B.C.-based, publicly traded companies that represented "some of Canada's most exciting growth stories." The business media were firmly aboard, too. *The Financial Post* described Vidatron as "a once-struggling mish-mash of entertainment companies, reborn as a hot TV production house." By mid-1999 the company had filed with the U.S. Securities and Exchange Commission for the sale of 2 million limited voting shares in a public offering—and it was ensuing legal complications south of the border that prompted Vidatron to change its name to Peace Arch (for a monument at a border crossing from British Columbia to Washington state).

Nearly two decades ago Tim Gamble had identified and shrewdly capitalized on a momentous trend: the rise of video and its effective use in corporate and educational storytelling. But his will-'o-the-wisp mind and his concern for keeping a public company afloat had distracted him from homing in on his core business. Can a man with a history of hop-scotching, whose most telling failure has been an inability to focus, now exploit a new trend in the entertainment industry? Gamble believes he has seen the light and knows exactly where his company has to concentrate its efforts.

TrendWatch

"My passion really lies in television," Tim Gamble now says. "Typically in the movie business, as a producer you're a long ways away from the cash register. But in the television business you're dealing directly with the broadcasters that really have the wherewithal to pay. There's an incredible appetite for programming, and it's expanding globally. [In Canada alone during 1998 six new cable channels went on the air and two dozen others expanded]. And really there's no better place in the world to produce it and manufacture it than B.C., for all sorts of good reasons: Canadian-European coproduction treaties, the obvious proximity to Los Angeles, the same time zone." Not to mention the province's recent 20-percent tax credit for eligible film-labour costs for B.C.-based production companies, a further 11-percent labour credit for both Canadian and foreign producers to match Ontario, and Premier Glen Clark's unprecedented visit to Los Angeles in spring 1998 to woo more moviemakers to British Columbia. "And it's just beginning. Especially for a company that's in the business of providing consistency in terms of earnings and revenues and so on, the television business makes the most sense. For individuals, though, there are so many opportunities, whether it's multimedia, music, documentaries, feature films—that whole industry is just exploding. Especially in Vancouver. The industry here will be worth a billion dollars by 1999. The only real limit you have is whether you can dream and believe in it." Like that boy back in Ontario lying on the couch and watching television, dreaming one day of producing commercials, videos, and television shows.

The Palate Pleasers

Bread and meat. Historically the West has put two of the most basic staples on the plates of Canada and the world (we export nearly three-quarters of our wheat and more than half of our beef and cattle). And not just any loaves and steaks. Saskatchewan hard red spring wheat has a universal reputation for its peerless milling and baking qualities; Alberta beef from barley-fed cattle has the favoured white-fat colouring and a tenderness superior to most international rivals. Our grain farms and ranches have not only fed us well, they have also furnished fundamental nourishment to the western economy, particularly the Prairie provinces. Yet as another kind of economy—that of scale—is increasingly dictated by the demands of global competition, farmers and ranchers have become fewer in number while agribusiness operations have become gargantuan. As possibilities for rural entrepreneurs shrink in these traditional entrepreneurial industries of western Canada, aging agriculturalists sell out and retire to Victoria and Kelowna. Their young flee to the big cities to find work in the company of others or lifetime careers as future risk-taking Mavericks. In much of Saskatchewan, for instance, towns and villages that once had their own hockey clubs now have to scramble for enough youthful bodies to form regional teams.

All of which accentuates the importance of two tangible developments that are slowly reshaping the West. One is a diversification into new kinds of farms harvesting anything from ginseng to specialty salad components, as well as the coming of age of one specific crop: grapes. The transubstantiation that turns green and red grapes into still and sparkling wines has given British Columbia a newly successful and necessary resource-based industry. Meanwhile another financially significant development is affecting the West: a willingness to fashion fresh types of foods that had never before been key ingredients in the economic stew.

Winemaker Harry McWatters and meat-analogue manufacturer Yves Potvin personify these trends as Palate Pleasers. McWatters is the founder of the estate wineries Sumac Ridge and Hawthorne Mountain Vineyards amid British Columbia's Okanagan Valley. He has some discerning and eager palates to please: the province has the continent's highest per-capita consumption of wine.* And the fact is, the 50-plus wineries that form the West Coast industry are finally producing some extraordinary vintages, even by world standards, ever since adopting the Vintners Quality Alliance criteria in 1990. Michael Goldberg, a commerce professor at the University of British Columbia, points out that "B.C. used to grow low-quality grapes for the global cheap-wine market, but free trade and countries like Chile ended that for us. And luckily so. Forced to adapt, we've developed distinctive wines that fetch higher prices." The whites have been celebrated for much of the past decade, but only recently did the red wines begin to match them. Robin Mines, host of the Women's Television Network series *Canadian Wine Cellar*, wrote in the September 1998 *Winetidings* magazine that the reds used to be considered fit only for sangria and sauces: "The strong, new 1995s changed our minds in a big hurry and recent plantings of Cabernet Sauvignon, Cabernet Franc, and Merlot in the desert-like conditions of the South Okanagan Valley have everyone as excited as kids with a new computer game."

---

* *Winetidings* magazine, an industry journal, estimates B.C. consumption at 20 litres per capita each year, although Statistics Canada says the province's wine drinkers led the nation with 14.3 litres per capita in 1997, Quebec's following with 12.9. Wine consumption is highest in the four largest provinces, with Ontario and Alberta lagging a little below the national average of 10.6, and lowest in the six smallest provinces—Newfoundland at the bottom with 3.6 (its drinkers are tops in downing beer: 89.5 litres per capita).

The rising popularity of the reds has created a shortage of premium grapes, which vintners are meeting by developing new vineyards in the province, where an estimated 142 more hectares were added in 1998 to the existing 1,024. Vincor International Inc., an interloper from Niagara Falls, Ontario, has leased and optioned 810 hectares on Osoyoos Indian Band land in the South Okanagan to dramatically boost British Columbia's supply of good vinifera-style wine grapes over the next decade. While grapes have been grown in the southern area since the late 1800s, commercial production began in the 1930s, and the Osoyoos Indians themselves have been harvesting the fruit there since the 1970s. Farther north, on the eastern flanks of Okanagan Lake, a rose grower named Jesse Willard Hughes pioneered vines of a hybrid of the native labrusca varieties in 1926 and sold the grapes to Victoria's Growers Wines. The climate of the entire valley falls comfortably within the North Temperate Zone, where most of the world's best vineyards are found, and the southern stretches have weather conditions similar to Bordeaux.

While the very corporate Vincor is Canada's largest vintner (under the brands Inniskillin, Jackson-Triggs, and Sawmill Creek), most wineries in British Columbia are no more than medium-size and often family businesses where couples and sometimes their kids work together, like the McWatters at Sumac Ridge and Hawthorne Mountain. Many are much smaller, like Peachland's Hainle Vineyards (rhyming with "finely," which is how its wines are made). German-born Tilman Hainle and his Saskatchewan lawyer wife, Sandra, were the first in Canada to have their vineyard and winemaking certified organic. That followed father Walter Hainle's pioneering Canadian production in 1973 of ice wine, the luscious dessert libation from late-harvest grapes frozen on the vine. Today the ice wines fermented in the Okanagan are adjudged exceptional around the globe, even in the Hainles' old home of Germany, where these sweet wines have long been a tradition.

This sort of international reach is also becoming more common among the West's Palate Pleasers in the food-processing arena. Two intriguing stories illustrate the trend. Walter Makowecki, founding chairman of Edmonton's Heritage Foods, was visiting Expo 67 in Montreal when he inquired at a Soviet Union pavilion about a machine that would make perogies, the Polish name Canadians use for the traditional handmade, dough-wrapped, mashed-potato dumplings of his Ukrainian ancestors.* It took another five years before the farmboy-turned-businessman had located suitable equipment in Ukraine and began mass-producing a line of Canadian-style frozen perogies marketed under the label Cheemo (Canada's official toast, which translates as a friendly greeting from the Inuit language). Now believed to be the world's biggest perogy producer, selling $10 million of the dumplings throughout Canada in 1998, Heritage has recently taken coals to Newcastle. In a joint venture with the old-country company that made the original machines, Makowecki and son Joe, the current president, have invested about $500,000 to open a perogy plant in Sumy, northeastern Ukraine. And while the business is struggling there because of the chaotic free-market distribution systems, lack of indigenous capital, and electricity shortages that limit production to four hours a day, Walter Makowecki says, "I think it'll survive." That kind of entrepreneurial optimism is what led the Alberta government magazine *Venture* to name him recently one of the province's 50 most influential businesspeople. "Not bad for an old stubble jumper," he allows.**

The other tale has a nice twist, too. In 1997 the Scots who run McIntosh of Dyee, a food processor specializing in meat pies, were trying to break into the North American market when they met with Tom Poole of Sepp's Gourmet Foods of Langley, British Columbia. This prepared-foods producer and distributor was an amalgamation of eight

---

*In Ukrainian perogies are known as *vereneyky*, dumplings that are boiled, or *pyrohy*, those that are baked. Heritage makes eight million of them a week from 100,000-plus kilograms of Alberta potatoes and flour. Another perogy entrepreneur is Winnipegger William Konyk, who began selling Ukrainian food at Vancouver's Pacific National Exhibition and eventually developed a restaurant chain impolitically called Hunky Bill's House of Perogies, which he franchised at $10,000 a location. He once sponsored a perogy-eating contest in which first prize was a week in Winnipeg in January and the second prize two weeks.

**Another western Palate Pleaser who has gone international in an intriguing way is former bank-loans officer Anne Chong Hill of Richmond, British Columbia. In 1998 the public company she and her husband started a decade earlier, Global Commerce Development Inc., opened the first of what they intend to be scores of Annie's Food Kiosks in mainland China. In a joint venture with Beijing Trolley Bus Company, the kiosks at the capital's bus terminals (labelled with the maple leaf) will serve steamed dark-meat chicken, hash browns, and french fries—all made from Canadian products supplied by Maple Leaf Foods International.

companies that had grown in eight years to $21 million in annual sales from $1.2 million. McIntosh, with sales in Britain more than double Sepp's in Canada, was hoping to buy such a smaller compatible operation over here. But when the private company couldn't raise enough quick cash, the publicly traded Sepp's proposed that it take over McIntosh instead. Offering equity shares and some cash, the fast-moving Poole, a former lawyer with an M.B.A., did just that in March 1998 ("*Now* is a good time to do almost anything"). Combined sales for 1998 hovered around $75 million, with Sepp's expanded line presenting a smorgasbord that ranges from vegetarian burger patties for the health-food market to a variety of chilled (rather than frozen) take-home meals for the time-challenged consumer.

Those two types of products are also marketed by Yves Veggie Cuisine of Delta, British Columbia, the trendsetting creation of former Québécois chef Yves Potvin, whose arrival in lifestyle-heavy Vancouver transformed him a decade and a half ago. Potvin specializes in meat alternatives—tofu and vegetable wieners, burgers, deli slices—a market niche that in the past five years has doubled in size across the continent. And early in 1999 he revisited his past by opening the first two in a series of Yves mini-restaurants focused on bring-home as much as dine-in meals. British Columbia already has Canada's highest number of restaurants per capita, but Potvin is banking on two other facts: eight of ten Canadians use quick-service eateries, and one of the hottest trends in dining today is the convenient, ready-made, take-out meal.

Ideally—or so fellow Palate Pleaser Harry McWatters would hope—a meal to be washed down with a glass of his western-crafted wine.

Chapter Three

Hot Dogger

Yves Potvin, Yves Veggie Cuisine

Ideas, Yves Potvin insists, are a dime a dozen. It is what you do with them that can turn them into gold. Still, there is something sweet about conjuring up a concept, of being in precisely the right place at exactly the right time, and seeing an idea for a business spring full-blown from your own mind, your own circumstances, your own experience. For Potvin, trained as a classical chef in Quebec, the idea that came to mind in his 28th year seemed somewhat down-market, a little déclassé (and even, perhaps, a little silly). Yet it would prove to be truly, madly revolutionary. And the circumstances that spawned it were a strange combination: a copy of *Time* magazine and a James Dean movie, a certain childhood food passion, and his decision as an adult to live on the less-fettered, more lifestyle-defined West Coast of Canada.

In the fall of 1983, Potvin left his home in Quebec, a girlfriend, and a career as a restaurateur—chef, partner in a café, and then manager of a new restaurant—to cycle across the country and redefine himself in Vancouver. Working there as a saucier in a bistro, he quickly realized anew that being a chef left him no life to live; he needed a change of vocation. One evening the following spring, he was watching a video, *East of Eden,* the 1953 film classic of John Steinbeck's saga of a California farm family, Potvin was struck by how the most astute of the farmers had invested in bean futures and sold the crops for a hefty profit when the First World War broke out. The right place, the right time. As for beans—he remembered reading an article in *Time* about how Tofuti, an ice-cream substitute made from the soybean curd the Japanese call tofu, was becoming popular with fat-wary North Americans.

"So the big question for me was—what's my right place and my right time? What's my spot in life? I believe that everybody has a space," he tells me, philosophizing at home while his wife breast-feeds their new baby girl. He certainly seems to be in the right space now as a late-blooming father, married only since 1995 to the Chinese-Canadian Sylvia, a former advertising woman a dozen years younger. He must have been a highly eligible bachelor, with his dimpled, plump-cheeked, heart-shaped face, pale blue but penetrating eyes, and his penchant for elegant clothes, among them the silky mock turtlenecks he buys in batches at Saint Croix stores in San Francisco.

His accent still heavily, charmingly Québécois, he often speaks in the present tense, sometimes dropping the *s* from his nouns like crumbs from a cake. "I start analyzing myself as I would a balance sheet—not knowing what a balance sheet was," he says about that crossroads 15 years ago. "My assets are—I'm a health-conscious person. I'm a trained French chef. Therefore I know how to make food taste good. And I know I have perseverance because I prove it with my bicycle trip. I'm full of energy. I've run business before. I have, I believe, good social skill. And I want to start something. Well, what does society need?" He had observed the baby boomers around him jogging or at least watching Jane Fonda exercising on TV: "They are going to want to have a healthy lifestyle to benefit from the material possession they have." *Bien sûr*, Weight Watchers was already producing dinners for dieters, but what if he could create a healthy fast food for the average person who was simply trying to avoid culinary excess? "Hey," he says he told himself, "you know, the guy did tofu ice cream. What if I can come out with a tofu wiener?"

As a kid, raised in a meat-and-potatoes family, he had loved hot dogs. Per capita, Quebeckers had perhaps loved them more than most Canadians—until the scandal that erupted in the 1960s when Mafia-controlled meat packers were found to be stuffing wieners and sausages with parts from sick and long-dead animals. Searching the market now, Potvin could find no sign of a lean, wholesome wiener, though he did learn that North Americans were consuming 50 million hot dogs a day. "And that was the flash of intuition. If I can come out with a veggie dog, something made from vegetable [and low in fat and cholesterol], there has to be a market. I was excited because it seemed like I'd found my spark—as crazy as the idea was."

Crazy—like a fox that had found its way into the henhouse. Although he would have to survive at least two dark passages (the

Sting and the Embarrassing Burger), Vancouver-based Yves Veggie Cuisine is, less than a decade and a half later, the leading refrigerated meat-alternative brand on the continent. In Canada it is the front-runner in the entire field of refrigerated *and* frozen products. Over the past four years, despite virtually no advertising, the private company's sales have been increasing by 40 to 50 percent a year. In 1998 they hovered around $33 million—in a single month equalling more than the total of Potvin's first seven years in business. Today the recently redesigned corporate logo—a colourful caricature of a chef in red beret and white neckerchief embracing a basket of vegetables—is becoming familiar to shoppers in produce sections throughout North America, the United Kingdom (where the recent mad-cow scare helped the launch), and even such offbeat locales as the Bahamas and the Middle East.

The gamut of fresh (not frozen) products, made from soy and other vegetables, includes variously successful mimics of patties, burgers, ground round, deli slices, pepperoni, back bacon, breakfast links, and a line based on the mock meat that started it all: veggie wieners, jumbo veggie dogs, and chili dogs. Cholesterol- and fat-free (except for one percent fat in the historic tofu wiener), they are high in protein, nutrients, and fibre. These so-called meat analogues have been anointed by no less than the Center for Science in the Public Interest as worthy choices for families seeking taste and convenience along with good nutrition. Testers for the influential American consumer group found, in fact, that the Veggie Burger Burger "tastes so much like a real burger that some of our vegetarians wouldn't take a second bite."

Not every food critic agrees, but over the years the company has had some important fans.* In 1990 San Francisco Giants general manager

---

*The *Boston Herald* called the burgers "a bit rubbery" with "a slightly fake taste"; two among a *San Francisco Chronicle* panel of nonvegetarian testers said "it tasted like charcoal-lighter fluid"; and, as for Yves Veggie Wieners, 25 New York-based samplers for *Self Magazine* ranked them among the worst of 15 brands—"My dog wouldn't eat this," one said. A more palatable critique has come from the *Toronto Star*'s Marion Kane, who wrote: "One of the best meatless products I've found are the amazingly low-fat, low-cal, tasty, tofu-based wieners, patties and imitation deli meats made by Yves Veggie Cuisine." And a recent *Vancouver Sun* panel couldn't distinguish between Veggie Ground Round and real meat in a beef enchilada, stating "for flavour, the scores were identical." As for me, I eat Potvin's products from time to time and enjoy most of them.

Al Rosen, recovering from a heart attack, chose Potvin's tofu wiener as the lone low-fat hot dog sold at Candlestick Park. Three years later, as Yves Veggie Cuisine won a Manning Foundation Award for excellence in Canadian innovation, high-profile vegetarian Linda McCartney made the company the official supplier of Veggie Dogs for husband Paul's North American concert tour (and later of meatless pepperoni for her brand of vegetarian pizzas in the United Kingdom). The following year, in 1994, at the SIAL d'Or in Paris, the food world's Olympics, Yves Veggie Pepperoni was named best new deli product among entries from 18 nations. And in the past few years the domestic grocery industry has given Veggie Burger Burger, Veggie Pepperoni, and Veggie Ground Round Canadian Grand Prix New Product Awards in the veggie lifestyle category.

Yves Potvin's genius as a marketer is most evident in how he is transforming his first good little idea into a fully realized food realm. In the fall of 1998, he introduced "ready meals" to his supermarket trade: prepared portions of entrées in sauces with a long shelf life, such as chili and a meatball-like stew. A natural extension of his product line, *n'est-ce pas?* But then he took the concept one brilliant stride further in 1998 by stepping back into the restaurant business he had abandoned in 1983. It is a calculated gamble, given the high failure rate in that field. The first two Vancouver restaurants of what he hopes will be his own continent-wide chain of veggie fast-food locations are featuring all his products, including dishes with much shorter shelf lives such as lasagna and shepherd's pie, which use his soy-protein Ground Round. The pilot Yves on Fourth and Yves on Eleventh opened in 1999 on the same busy blocks as ubiquitous Starbuck's coffee shops, which served as an inspiration for Potvin's chain (he and Starbucks share the same Seattle graphic-design firm). Among the flattering reviews, Yves on Fourth received was this from Angela Murrills in *The Georgia Straight*: "This is tasty food you can feel smug about eating. Are we talking a winning formula here or what? ... Why not all over town in a couple of years? ... And, after that, the world."

This could be the icing on the cake of his kingdom, as the restaurants complete the circle of sales outlets where he can reach his market. Here customers can either dine in—on his hot dogs and burgers, soup, sandwiches stuffed with his deli meats, and lasagna and chilis—

or take the ready meals home. Here, too, they can get recipes and ingredients to re-create the dishes themselves or cents-off coupons to use the next time they buy his products at Safeway. And at the supermarket, potential customers can pick up a coupon to get a break on their next meal at a Veggie Express—where they might be willing to risk sampling their first-ever tofu hot dog. This is Potvin's version of vertical integration and illustrates one of his core beliefs.

Your hush-hush good idea doesn't guarantee success on its own—you might have to dare to expose it and develop it intelligently in full public view

Yves Potvin wasn't the only one to conceive a meat-substitute wiener. A few months after founding his company, he attended a California trade show where he met a man from St. Louis who had created a similar "light-link" tofu product. Upset at first, Potvin persevered. And what happened to his competitor? "He went out of business because he was creative, but he was not an entrepreneur. He didn't evolve to become a business person." At first Potvin had hoarded his concept, not even letting his employees know the recipe for his tofu wiener, which meant he had to do all the laborious mixing of ingredients himself. "In the beginning, most people who have an idea are so afraid to share it with everybody. They're afraid that people will steal the idea from them. But it's what you do with it [that matters]. For years I was paranoid that somebody would come and steal my recipe. Well, it is a fact that somebody can steal a recipe, but the strength of the company is the brand name and the distribution and the broker network and the people we have [working for us]." In the years since, Potvin hasn't been afraid to signal his intention of introducing new product lines—on the theory that discussing the ideas with others will lead to innovations he hasn't conceived of himself.

Yves Potvin's own evolution—from home cook to trained chef to restaurant manager to entrepreneur to business executive—begins in Waterloo, Quebec, where he was born in 1956, the fourth of five children. Neither parent had much to do with food other than growing vegetables in a big garden in the Eastern Townships village. Yves was a creative kid, dabbling in soapstone sculpture and stained glass, developing photographs in his own darkroom, while picking up English playing defence with anglophones on Juvenile and Junior B hockey teams. After high school, he did a two-year architectural design program in Sherbrooke. But it wasn't until he took the following summer off to work as a landscaper that a young woman suggested he should be a professional cook—she had probably tasted his formidable spaghetti sauce. Appreciating the mystique of the white-hatted chef, thinking he might express his creativity through food, and seeing the vocation as a passport to travel the world, Potvin studied for two years at the Ste-Hyacinthe School of Cooking. He found work as a saucier at a resort in Mont Tremblant and then as a chef at a French-style restaurant in Sherbrooke.

The world beyond Quebec beckoning, he visited a friend in Texas and went on to Guatemala, where he studied Spanish and tested children's health at a Catholic mission. Several months later he returned home to a waiting girlfriend and a partnership with three others in an informal, 50-seat French restaurant. Of his $5,000 investment, $1,000 was his own and the rest came from a brother and a sister. With live music after hours and a menu of light cuisine, the place was packed, yet the two men and two women made little profit. "The main thing I learned was it doesn't matter how successful you are if you don't have the financial background," Potvin says now. "You know, it's not how many cases you sell, it's what price you sell them and what you do with your expense—what is the bottom line?" In the laboratory of his first restaurant, he also came to know that "you can make it happen if you work hard enough and if you are smart enough—but other people don't have those same values. ... I had difficulty when people were not pulling their weight. Especially if they are partners."

Leaving with little more than he had invested, he opened a restaurant in Lennoxville for a supportive Montreal Jewish investor. John Max tended the books and Potvin the kitchen, hiring and managing the staff and designing a menu heavy on organic foods and light on rich sauces. (Thinking of serving gourmet hot dogs in the summer, he sought a source of good real-meat wieners and learned about the questionable ingredients they contained.) Although his overseeing of Le Café was a success, he left after a year.

"Yves," Max had told him, "you work so hard, it's like the restaurant was yours."

"Well, I don't make that difference, whether it's mine or not mine." And that, he understood, is what many entrepreneurs soon comprehend: if you are going to work hard, it might as well be for yourself.

It was 1983 and Yves Potvin, in his late twenties, was at a life-shaping junction. Sculpting intrigued him, but he didn't think he could support himself with art. While his longtime girlfriend wanted to settle down, he didn't; his parents' marriage had broken up and he wasn't sure this young woman would be the perfect wife he imagined for himself. Besides, he hadn't travelled enough. One morning he woke up after dreaming about Vancouver and asked himself, "Why not move there?" Expo 86 was on the horizon and he knew how Expo 67 had transformed Montreal. Not only that, why not cycle to Vancouver, camp along the way, see his country and its people from the ground? It, too, was a crazy idea—he had never tented and hadn't ridden a bike since childhood—but he embraced unusual ideas. ("Yves," Claude, his older brother, said, not understanding, "I'll give you the airfare.")

Yves dressed up in a tuxedo to cook a farewell dinner for his girlfriend. And after two months' training, he took 55 days on a 12-speed Norco racer to cross Canada. En route, he had time to start sorting out his life and analyzing his family—warmhearted mother, dominant father—and understand that he had been in danger of repeating that pattern with his girlfriend. This realization helped steer him away from marriage until he was 39. "Take the time to think about what you like, what you don't like," he advises now. "Take the time off and think."

Arriving in Vancouver, fitter and more at peace, he moved into a co-op, ran his first marathon, and took a job in the kitchen at Le Chef et Sa Femme, a popular bistro. It was there he came to the conclusion that working in a restaurant—especially someone else's—wasn't his life's dream. But it was also there, with the owner's blessing, that he began to experiment with the prototypical tofu wiener. This was not—to make a culinary comparison—a piece of cake.

Meat analogues were nothing new: by the early 20th century, John Harvey Kellogg, who ran a Seventh-Day Adventist Sanatorium in

Battle Creek, Michigan, had developed several of them, along with the flaked cereals for which he became famous.* The difference was Potvin's belief that he could transform bland tofu into a tasty meat substitute. Soybean curd, usually considered a staple of Japan, was only introduced in that country in 1212 from China, where this high-quality protein source has been consumed for more than 2,000 years. Potvin liked the idea of crossing Asian and western foodstuffs; all he had to do was figure out how to make it work. He first bought a book that showed him how to create a cheeselike curd from soya milk. It took him a couple of months to find someone to build a wooden form that would shape the tofu like a wiener. Unfortunately the first versions had the taste and texture of nothing more than wiener-shaped tofu. Grinding the curd, he then used a grease gun to stuff it into sausage casings and cooked it in the oven in a double boiler. Well, that helped—the heat broke down the protein so that it took the right shape. He experimented further with a variety of ingredients, some of which he tracked down in books for butchers: wheat starch, bread crumbs, a passel of spices to beef up the flavour of tofu, and gluten to add bite. Still, the stuff refused to bind well and have the feel of a regular wiener. Three months later he was walking around at night, discouraged, telling himself, *I've tried everything. I don't think I can make a wiener from vegetables.*

Yvonne Jones, a consultant at the B.C. Research Council, believed in his idea and passed him on to a protein specialist, Dr. Nakai at the University of British Columbia. The food chemist told him he needed an emulsifier to bind the product and suggested albumin, egg white. Although Potvin wanted to keep the wiener strictly vegetarian, he relented. After working with the scientist and some of his students for a few weeks to improve the texture, he decided to carry on himself when the issue of paying the university arose. At various points he further spiced up the flavour with liquid smoke and wood chips, using a

---

*As Canadian Scott Mowbray notes in *The Food Fight: Truth, Myth and the Food-Health Connection* (Random House, 1992), such foods were being served in North American health-food restaurants in the first decade of this century: "Around 1907, for example, the Pure Food Vegetarian Café, located in Vancouver, B.C., offered its diners cereal coffee, graham-flour bread, nut cream toast, nut butter sandwiches, malted nut gruel, and assorted meat substitutes with names such as nuttolene, nut bromose, and protose."

$300 meat smoker he bought at The Bay. He introduced rice syrup and honey as a sweetener and beet powder for colouring. Slowly the taste, appearance, and mouth-feel of the tofu wiener started to resemble its fleshy cousin.

He told no one but the research woman and the chemist exactly what he was attempting. The tofu suppliers and the butchers he consulted thought he was making a soy pâté. Only when he was ready to make batches of wieners did he tell the representative of a Chicago manufacturer of cellulose casing about his experiment; the rep, intrigued, dropped off a whole case of his product at no charge.

By August 1984—having tried the tofu wiener on a few friends— Potvin felt confident enough to raise funding to launch production. He had only $10,000 of his own money. The landlady of the house where he lived in the attic had an accountant daughter who told him about a colleague—"this crazy accountant, probably the only guy who can help you." Ken Bolton was then, as he is now, larger than life. Literally: double-chinned and a deep voice booming out of a beer-keg chest. And figuratively: his business card has a list of 18 services he allegedly performs, from "wars fought" to "crocodiles controlled," along with a list of products and services he supposedly understands, from firewood to yacht charters. The raffish CA represents several high-growth, entrepreneurial companies (five of them currently winners of Canadian Awards of Excellence for business). "I heard many times that Ken, because of his stature and his voice, could intimidate people," Potvin says. "And I remember going in his office and seeing the big furniture and the big view and everything. And you kinda make an assumption that probably, because of his figure and his chain-smoking, he doesn't know what the hell I am trying to do. And so he was intimidating me and it took a couple of years for me to get over that."

Bolton had some reservations about the young French Canadian with the aggressively accented English who came to see him about starting a company: "He's got ten grand, an inability to communicate, and a poor product." But the accountant was shrewd enough to realize that, if the concept worked, it would be "the hula hoop of the food industry." He took Potvin on as a client—even after tasting his product one day in November: "I was with my secretary. Yves had come over to work on three-year budgets for financing from the Bank of Montreal.

Very proudly he gave us a package of his tofu wieners. He had just left and we decided to try them. We got ourselves some ketchup and mustard, put them in the microwave oven. We tasted it—and my secretary's words to me were, 'We better keep ahead of this client in our billings.' The product was not good. It tasted like dirty socks. Poor colour. It lacked texture." Potvin—"typically unwilling to give up"—reassured him it was going to get better.

However, the tofu wiener's creator would need an additional $30,000 to launch the project. When Potvin was reluctant to borrow that much, Bolton said he would help him find the money. Preparing a business plan raised issues his client couldn't answer, such as how much he hoped to sell in the first three years. Potvin hired a local marketing consultant, experienced in the health-food industry, who bore an appropriate name. Michael Weiner of New Age Marketing, who had worked with the Best Foods division of CPC International in New York City, was enthusiastic about the homemade product's potential and arranged field research in a natural-food store and a regular supermarket.* Extrapolating the data—roughly a quarter of the tasters said they would buy it—the optimistic Potvin decided he would have $1 million in sales by the third year. When the first two bankers he saw weren't impressed, his accountant arranged for a $20,000 Small Business Improvement loan from the Bank of Montreal guaranteed by the federal Industry, Trade, and Commerce Ministry. With another $10,000 to find, Potvin again approached his brother and sister in Quebec. Claude, a head buyer for Kinney Shoes' women's division, and Francine, a former model who organized fashion shows in Montreal, each lent him $5,000.

Ready to manufacture on a larger scale, Potvin found 46 square metres on the fourth floor of a building along the gritty reaches of downtown East Hastings. The irony was that it was above a store called Save-On Meats, which among other items sold horsemeat. (Bolton, seeing the location, wondered to himself, *Wow, what am I getting into?*) Providentially the space came equipped with an oven and a machine

---

* Micheal Weiner worked with Yves Potvin over the next four years, introducing him to Health Valley Natural Foods, the largest such wholesaler in the United States, which gave him 32 distributors down south. Potvin later had another aptly named person in his life, an executive assistant named Kathy Helps.

used to stuff meat into casings. Another stuffer built to produce sausages one at a time was a virtual antique, full of rat droppings when Potvin found it. Meanwhile Weiner arranged for him to make a presentation to LifeStream,* a flourishing Vancouver natural-foods chain where he had been marketing director. The store executives tried the handmade samples and agreed to order professionally produced tofu wieners.

Now that he had a product, Potvin needed a package design, a logo, and a brand name. Among the contenders were Renaissance Foods and Natural Deli, but Weiner suggested naming it for its creator: Yves Fine Foods. When Potvin protested that his first name was hard to pronounce for anglophones, his consultant pointed out the high profile and classy quality of fashion designer Yves St. Laurent. The Frenchness, he said, lent the food product a certain—how should we call it?—gourmet cachet.

Once Potvin incorporated in January 1985, he was left with $5,000 and an order from LifeStream for 91 kilograms of tofu wieners, which he promised to deliver within a month. All on his own the first day, he overloaded the oven with all the wieners, expecting them to be ready within two hours. For a long time, they seemed to be barely cooking. Six hours later, they suddenly started burning and exploding. A ski-bum friend showed up to help overnight, and after 36 straight hours Potvin managed to produce only 77 kilograms—having tossed out slightly more than that amount of blackened, burst failures.

The good news was that LifeStream immediately ordered the same quantity again and a store in Seattle asked for 20 cases, too. By month's end, Yves Fine Foods had earned $2,000. When that wasn't enough to finance further production, Potvin convinced his first customer to pay within seven days and then hit up his brother for another $5,000 loan. Revenues began doubling, month by month, and Potvin began hiring. He took a bookkeeping course to handle the cash flow and, getting cocky, replaced $125-an-hour Ken Bolton with a couple of accountants who charged one-third that rate. By year's end, while

---

*In a paradigm of the corporatizing of the health-food business, LifeStream Natural Foods itself would become so successful a chain that it would be bought in 1991 by Nabob Foods of Burnaby, British Columbia—owned by Swiss billionaire Andreas Jacobs—which in turn would be bought two years later by Kraft General Foods Canada, a unit of the multinational Philip Morris Cos. Inc.

the business had generated $235,000, it lost about $4,000 and its owner had taken a salary of only a few thousand dollars while starting to repay his siblings. When his new accountant wouldn't bother to explain the financial situation—"It's your first year. You did very well"—a penitent Potvin asked Bolton if he would take him back as a client. "This guy might be $125 an hour, but at least he is teaching me something," he recalls. "The other guy is $40 and he doesn't show me anything. And I need to learn."

Less admirably perhaps, he was learning how to beat the system. A city health inspector came by to point out what Potvin had long known: the premises were zoned for retail, not manufacturing, and he would require a zoning permit to keep operating there. He went to city hall one day to find all the staff in the zoning department off on a break. Taking advantage of their absence, he showed a cashier his approved health permit and asked her if he could pay for his licence to operate. "Are things okay for zoning?" she wondered. "Yeah," he replied, "everything's fine." He got his licence.

Potvin had more trouble giving up his exclusive knowledge of the wiener recipe. He was taking orders and delivering product in a Volkswagen van and trying to mix batches of tofu and his still-secret ingredients. Finally he revealed the recipe to a male employee. "That was one of the toughest things to do. You give him the golden goose—because if this guy stole the recipe, I am gone." At night the entrepreneurial chef was also conceiving another product, deli slices, but failed to keep good notes of his experiments with different ingredients. "I came out with a fantastic product—almost as good as we have now—and I could never duplicate it, even after I go over all my notes. But my notes are all full of oil and scratch[es] and I say, 'What have I done? I must have done something.' And it is never the same taste."

Within that first year he had expanded to eastern Canada and had a staff of seven. Quebec distributors saw his product at a Vancouver health-food trade show, then an Ontario company began ordering, and soon he had a half-dozen major accounts. At first he had relied for help on two Québécois friends living in Whistler. With production booming, he needed full-time employees but couldn't afford them even at minimum wage. Again he went down an avenue that many entrepreneurs neglect.

Explore—or have your advisers research—the wide range of government programs that can support your fledgling business financially

Yves Potvin has called upon various government schemes to help keep his company alive and well, from finding federal funds to attend industry trade shows to using a provincial low-interest loan to buy $100,000 worth of capital equipment. While some of these programs no longer exist, new ones have surfaced. "Certainly," says accountant Ken Bolton, "enterpreneurs should be talking to their local governments about the need for those monies even if current funding isn't available. And they should be canvassing the federal government for grants and forgivable or repayable loans because they often have credit thresholds that are not as onerous as conventional financing." Potvin, in his first borrowing from a bank, had already capitalized on a federal-government loan guarantee. Other early approaches to bankers ended in failure; he couldn't get a line of credit for the first four years of operation. But in his first year, he heard about a federal Industry, Trade, and Commerce ministry scheme that paid a significant percentage of the salaries of new employees. He used it to hire unemployed political refugees, Salvadorans and Guatemalans, with whom he could speak in Spanish, and he even helped pay for night-school classes in English. (One refugee from El Salvador who started with him as a cleaner is now his production manager; another from Guatemala is special-projects manager.) In Potvin's first few months, as well as being chef, order taker, and delivery man, he was the head mechanic when his old machinery broke down. A flashlight in one hand, he would swear with frustration while extracting a bolt to replace a part in the middle of the night. Enough incidents like that convinced him to upgrade his equipment. This time he got a grant from Ottawa to finance a study that would recommend replacement equipment and the size and kind of facility he needed.

In 1986 Potvin was feeling as squeezed in his mini-factory as a wiener stuffed into a casing. Learning that the Federal Industrial Development Bank offered funds to companies that wanted to evaluate their growth needs, he commissioned a consultant to do such a study. "The guy did a pretty good job and said, 'You're going to need $250,000 worth of equipment and, to increase capacity, about 3,000 or 4,000 square feet.' I said, 'Holy cow!'"

Knowing the skeptical banks would be reluctant to advance him all the money for the move, Potvin returned to his brother and sister. By now he had some profile in his home province, having appeared on Quebec television. "My Dad figured, well, if TV has it, it must be good." Potvin says. Bringing Bolton along to negotiate, he asked his older siblings to invest $50,000 apiece. This time, in return, they wanted half the shares of the company. The accountant convinced them to accept 20 percent each. Yves Potvin convinced his bank to lend him another $150,000.

The grand total wasn't enough both to relocate and buy replacement machinery, such as meat cutters, at the usual prices. Potvin knew a slightly shady if likable used-equipment broker in nearby Langley. He had already dealt with Wally Ludwig and now asked him to look for machines at bargain prices. It was late 1986, well into Yves Fine Foods' second year in business, and its founder was about to embark on a bizarre adventure.

Potvin had just located a much larger space on East Georgia Street in the city's downtown industrial area, where he could afford to buy. Weeks passed and Wally, as Potvin came to know him too intimately, had found nothing for him. Then one day the broker called to say there had been a bankruptcy in Winnipeg and he had just the equipment his client needed. He offered details and even photographs of each piece. The whole package was supposed to be auctioned, but Ludwig had a deal with the auctioneer and could get it under the table for only about $80,000. Of course, he needed a quarter of that as a deposit—in cash.

Potvin said his accountant wouldn't like that—in fact, he hadn't told Bolton about his dealings with the broker—but he would give Ludwig a cheque for $5,000. Fine; he'd give his friend Yves a promissory note.

After two tense months, as the move to new quarters neared and Potvin advanced Ludwig a further $15,000, the broker reported a big problem: another company was bidding, after all, and offering more for the machinery. "If we want this deal, we're going to have to go a little higher," Ludwig said confidentially. His client dutifully, if reluctantly, gave him a cheque for $20,000.

Potvin was calling Ludwig every week now, only to hear that the deal was almost done. That wasn't good enough, "I'm going to move in February amd I need my machinery!" Potvin told Ludwig. Finally, at the end of January 1987, the broker called to say the machines would arrive by truck the following week. They didn't. "They had an accident along the way," he explained. "You know the big snowstorm—well, they got caught in it, but the machinery is okay."

Too late: Potvin had to move his old machines into the new location. Long days later the replacement equipment was in a warehouse in Vancouver, Ludwig said, but a trustee had locked it up and its new owner couldn't see it yet. Something snapped in Potvin. He called a local tofu supplier and asked him to do a credit check on Ludwig. The report that came back, the man from the credit bureau said, was five pages long. "Mr. Ludwig has quite a history. On a scale of zero to 100, he's a 99—and the best is zero. He has been in court for fraud five times." Ol' Wally, it turned out, owed hundreds of thousands of dollars, not to mention Potvin's $40,000 for nonexistent machinery.

An abashed Potvin confessed to Bolton what he had done. The accountant sent him to the RCMP, who said, "You got hit by Wally? Well, he's good. He's got a lot of people in town. He screwed his lawyer *and* his accountant."

Bolton told his client not to waste his time trying to collect from the fraud artist. At the end of the second year, the company had done about $600,000 in business. In the coming year, it would make only about $100,000 more as Potvin failed to go to trade shows and generally neglected the business. Instead he followed Ludwig around, confronted him, even told the story to the trickster's weeping wife, who eventually left him. When Potvin lied and said that his brother Claude, would be coming to town to make trouble, Ludwig retorted: "Tell your brother if he doesn't want to find his little brother with a bullet in his head in a ditch, don't come to my part of my world." Suddenly Potvin wasn't so sure about this bluffing game.

Yet, after a year and a half of badgering Ludwig by phone and in person, Potvin got most of his money back—about $30,000 in cash and the rest in machinery. And two years later Ludwig died of cancer. The lesson the relentless Potvin learned from all this is not that it pays to pursue a con man. He puts it more simply, without elaboration, in a single sentence that might be inscribed on every entrepreneur's wall.

If it sounds too good to be true, it probably isn't true

"You know it's too good to be true, but you learn to fool yourself," Yves Potvin says now. "You learn not to look at all the signs because you don't want to believe them. It was too good of a deal, and it was what I needed." Today, even in dealing with reputable equipment dealers, he sends someone to personally inspect—to *touch*—any machine he is thinking of buying.

Ashamed, Potvin had to admit the Sting to his brother and sister, which he did in a long tape-recorded confession. He sent it to them in 1989 as a prelude to a personal meeting where he announced his intention to buy them out and return the company to sole proprietorship. He had been feeling like an employee, especially of his sister, who had criticized Potvin for giving himself a $10,000 bonus the year before when the business had turned a $56,000 profit and he had taken only $25,000 in salary. What if he wanted to go to a trade show in Paris and have a couple of days off there—would he have to check with Francine? Speaking with Bolton, he had said, "I think we will destroy our family with this pressure." The accountant had approved his partnering with family members two years before, theorizing that if an entrepreneur must have investors, those with close blood ties might be the best ones. In this case he was only half right: Potvin could have remained partners with his brother. Now Bolton urged him to pay off both siblings—counsel that at first sounded like sacrilege to his client.

At the meeting in Montreal, Francine Potvin—who saw her investment as her retirement package—said it had all been a misunderstanding; she didn't want to sell. Claude agreed that his brother had a shotgun clause in their partnership and all he had to do was pull the trigger. Potvin offered each of them double their $50,000 investment. Claude replied that the company would be so successful that in ten years his brother would be happy he paid them $150,000 each. Which he did, although Bolton says, "At the time, it didn't warrant the premium paid." For all the pain Potvin went through, the experience was instructive.

Be very clear, from the beginning, what you and your partners expect of one another

Early on Yves Potvin had endured one painful experience with his first restaurant partners whom he had felt contributed so much less to the venture. His family partners presented a different problem, "If you want a partner, you have to have one that complements you," Potvin says now. He had brought his siblings into the company as silent financial associates, but his sister in particular believed she had the right to second-guess his decisions. "The only partnership I have seen that works is where one is an operational guy and one is in production or in sales—you know, where they each have their function and they say, 'I know I can't do marketing or production.'" Because his own weakness is finances, he considers his accountant a kind of partner, although Ken Bolton owns no shares.* Bolton says minority shareholdings often don't work, especially if the partners are merely investing money, rather than their skills. "A partner can provide financing, but a successful business is so much more—it's a culture, it's a market that's developed. Banks can do that [offer financing] and will not have any influence on the corporate culture. ... The entrepreneur will deliberately set aside seeds to sow for next year. But the financing partner will say, 'We don't need any more plants.'"

---

*Years later, when he was letting his controller go, Yves Potvin would ask his accountant to become an active partner in the company and offered him shares—"for peanuts," recalls Ken Bolton, who demurred. Potvin now is relieved that Bolton passed: "I think that it is good that we are not partners because I am not sure if we would have the same friendship." Their personal relationship is close enough for the client to name his accountant godfather to his daughter and for the two men to schedule an ongoing series of Scotch nights, where they get together over the amber liquid and brainstorm. "By the end of the evening," Bolton says, "we've pretty well got our lives planned—and are not looking forward to the morning."

In its fourth year of business, Yves Fine Foods had planted two new products in the marketplace—Veggie Wieners and Veggie Chili Dogs. The way that they and the original tofu wieners and deli slices were now being marketed proved to be the essential growth hormone for success. The clever strategy would take the company to the $1-million level of sales in 1989 (two years later than the initial business plan projected) and twice that the following year. While the products had first been featured in the all-vegetarian environment of health-food stores, they were generally sold during the early years in the meat sections of supermarkets (and, according to U.S. industry research, 96 percent of vegetarians shop in supermarkets). It was bad positioning, Potvin knew, because his health-conscious consumers often didn't make it to the meat or deli counters. Better that his products should be placed in produce sections, where some stores were putting these vegetarian-based packaged foods. Many supermarket managers weren't convinced. So he began gleaning hard data from other stores where the move from meat to produce departments had increased sales by as much as 500 percent. *Produce Business*, an American trade journal, points out that "this merchandising strategy also attracts women, who are traditionally strong purchasers of produce and often are looking for something healthier to offer their families." Impressed by Potvin's figures, the major supermarket chains began making the switch and within a year some saw sales double. If they hadn't believed his research, he says, his revenues today would be one-fifth of what they are.

In 1990, needing a methodical left-brainer to complement his less-disciplined, right-brain creativity, Potvin hired his first food technologist. Hien Trinh, a Vietnamese woman who is still on staff, was initially charged with finding a replacement for the albumen used to bind the meat analogues. At the time, the Japanese began buying egg whites in huge quantities to make their suddenly popular mock-crab products. All at once the price of albumen doubled and while it represented only five percent of Potvin's ingredients, it became 40 percent of his cost. Working on a tip from an insurance-salesman friend with a Ph.D. in food technology, he had Trinh experiment with the salt and acidity levels in the products, which could ultimately affect the binding properties. Replacing the egg whites dramatically improved the company's profit picture. Meanwhile the technologist helped develop new products, including the forerunner of a hamburger analogue, Veggie Garden Vegetable Patties. She worked with Sam Okomoto, the company's first in-house chef and a graduate of good Vancouver restaurants.*

It was a natural progression from making meatless hot dogs to creating a burgerlike product. But the doing of it during 1991-92 was another dark passage for Potvin. He had renamed the company Yves Veggie Cuisine and commissioned an eye-appealing new design and logo from Vancouver's Ken Koo Creative Group. The East Georgia plant expanded next door to produce patties and the burgers then under development. A pilot program had proven the feasibility of soy-based hamburger patties made in small quantities, but full-scale production required new technology from Israel.

The burger was the first of the products to be cooked with a new proprietary technique, which Potvin would rather not see in print. Testing in Holland and then back home with European and North American equipment went well. When actual manufacturing began, however, the burgers bloated, fell apart, and lacked the necessary bite, or mouth-feel. The first suspect was the acid in a new mustard being used. Go back to the old stuff; no difference. Try other ingredients; still a problem. Weeks went by. The technologists were flummoxed. Working until all hours, Potvin was strung out, mentally and physically as well as financially: he had hired ten new employees, leased 464 square metres of additional space, and announced the date of a major launch of the burger product.

"It was his darkest hour, no doubt," says Bolton. "We had successfully licensed use of technology from the Israelis, which required about $350,000 U.S. in capital investment in the form of equipment—an oven, moulding and packaging machinery—representing 100 percent growth in the assets of the company. [In total the investment to develop the burgers was roughly $600,000.] It's the only time I ever saw Yves depressed. He was putting it all on the table."

---

*Today Yves Veggie Cuisine has eight people working in food technology and quality assurance, along with a professional chef—one of the largest research and development departments of any Canadian food company of similar sales volume. Some of the products are in their 30th generation of development. In 1998 all the products were certified kosher, meeting the strict dietary guidelines of the Orthodox Union, which led to a problem during the Montreal ice storm when the kosher tofu supply from that city was cut off.

Finally Potvin called in a specialist from Israel who took a red-eye flight to Vancouver and spent the next week dissecting the problem, working with the technologists to repackage the ingredients so the burgers would neither bloat nor crumble in their bags. "We came up with a new product and somehow this one was binding," Potvin says. "We never figured it out. Same ingredients, just a different way of putting them together.★ And it was scary because we thought it may happen again." It didn't, and Veggie Burger Burgers were launched in 1992 to reasonable success in what has since become a crowded market.

His competitors now include such industry giants as Pillsbury, with its Green Harvest vegetable burger, and Worthington Foods' Morningstar Farms, the market leader in the $252-million frozen meat-substitute category. Among the many others are Gardenburger of Portland, Oregon, a small company but number two in this category, which made a marketing and media splash in 1998 when it spent $14 million on a TV campaign that centred on a $1.5-million commercial aired on the final *Seinfeld* episode.★★

Such expenditures are beyond the ken of Yves Potvin, who contents himself with being the continental leader in the fresh meat-substitute category—without any consumer advertising at all. He spends only about $100,000 a year on ads mostly aimed at the food industry, in effect coaxing grocers to stock his products in their produce sections. "To do a proper advertising campaign," he says. "You probably have to

---

★Veggie Burger Burger, along with several other products, has since been reformulated as virtually fat-free. Its ingredients, in order of quantity, are water, soy-protein product, onion, wheat gluten, natural flavours, vegetable gum, pea fibre, malt extract, tomato paste, evaporated cane juice, yeast extract, carrageenan, salt, unidentified spices, vinegar, rice starch, beet-root powder, and citric acid. It contains .2 grams of fat and 11 grams of protein. Potvin is disarmingly honest about the product, which competes with about 50 others in the North American market: "Ours is not the best. We're the best wiener and the best [deli] slices and best ground round, but we're not the best burger. And that's because it's a fresh product and not frozen. You can flash-freeze and capture the moisture in a product that you can't with the fresh."

★★Gardenburger began life the same year—1985— as Yves Potvin's company, but with a meatless patty that founder Paul Wenner made of leftovers from his vegetarian restaurant in Gresham, Oregon. When the restaurant failed, he continued to sell the patties from his van under the name Wholesome & Hearty Foods. It went public in 1992, its stock soaring to $30 from $3 amid speculation that major burger chains were thinking of using its patties. When the rumours proved untrue, shares subsequently plummeted.

spend $400,000 to $500,000 in print and millions on TV. We're grow-ing 40 percent a year and usually you start advertising to the consumer when the growth starts to slow down. We are also the type of company to do guerrilla marketing"—one-on-one approaches such as product demonstrations and information packages directed to potential buyers. One principle Potvin has learned applies to many other products or ser-vices in other industries.

Realize that you may have to educate your consumer

"Yves has been very, very deliberate in educating the consumer about the end use and the end benefits of his product," says his accountant, Ken Bolton. Potvin believes you can't take it for granted that the consumer knows your particular brand or even the existence of a leading-edge kind of product like his. "This is a new category and people don't know about it and we don't have millions to spend on advertising," he says. Instead he will-ingly disburses $400,000 a year in supermarket product demonstrations throughout North America. "We feel they're products that you have to put in your mouth. And you say, 'Wow, this tastes good—and it's good for me, too.'" The com-pany recently published a brochure of recipes that discusses the healthy benefits of soy protein ("a good source of naturally occurring isoflavones, [which] act like a form of natural estro-gen"), and this year is releasing a cookbook based on its prod-ucts. All the packaging continues the educational process by offering product updates and nutrition data—"soy foods can sustain energy longer than many other foods"—and even pre-senting the corporate vision on the reverse of each label. Potvin: "You have to educate the consumer not to be afraid of this new category."

After the Embarrassing Burger incident, as Potvin introduced other products and won several product and business-excellence awards, sales continued to soar—from $2.3 million in 1992 to $12.5 million in 1996. That was the year Yves Veggie Cuisine moved into a new plant and offices on Annacis Island, an industrial park in the Lower

Mainland municipality of Delta. Getting there was no cakewalk. A couple of years earlier Ken Bolton had arranged for Potvin to acquire the land from another of his clients for $730,000. Even though the company had a solid track record with the Royal, the bank had no confidence in the company's growth forecasts of 30 to 40 percent a year. At the 11th hour before the land deal was to close, Bolton moved Potvin to the Bank of Nova Scotia, which lent him the money. He now needed to borrow a further $5 million for the building itself. The Bank of Nova Scotia referred the company to Bank Italia, whose Canadian president visited the site and assured it of a loan. "And on that verbal authorization," Bolton recalls, "we went ahead. We've entered into a building contract and there are D-8 Caterpillars on the land—and there is no financing." The bank had suddenly, inexplicably, backed out. Bolton began scrambling, doing dog-and-pony shows for the Hongkong Bank of Canada and the Bank of Montreal. "Within the next 21 days—my darkest days with the company—I put RoyNat and the TD Bank together to finance it."

Afterward, Potvin says, his accountant confessed to him: "I was trying to stay calm, but inside I was panicking. I didn't know where to go, we knocked on every bank door, and nobody wanted to finance it." Meanwhile his client had been telling him: "Ken, we will get the financing. Don't worry. We'll find a way." The way Bolton found was to split the total needed into different loan packages, so one bank would cover the construction and the other the equipment. "It was much scarier for me than it was for Yves. He's not rattled easily."

The new facility has 5,109 square metres for manufacturing, packaging, warehousing, shipping, sales, and administration, including 139 square metres for research and development. The lobby sets the tenor of the place: tasteful light wood, expensive variegated tile, and a cone of gorgeous fresh flowers in the reception area. A Vision Statement hangs in the lobby opposite a wall of awards. A winding staircase leads to the executive offices; on the first floor, the smell of tofu wieners permeates the air, which is also filled with the sound of the 22 languages the 225 employees speak.

Moving in three years ago, the nonunion staff actively entertained the idea of becoming members of a Canadian Auto Workers local. The union drive followed the firing of a longtime electrician who never did

110

upgrade the qualifications he had been paid to do. Potvin, rattled this time, met with a group of employees to remind them how he had helped over the years with loans and profit-sharing schemes, such as the current one that gave them about $1,500 a year. He also pointed out nice little touches in the new building that included a patio and a basketball court. His countercampaign was enough to head off the union. Since then, he has resurrected an employees' council and acted on its recommendations for emergency-loan and company-backed RRSP funds and such additional benefits as three more vacation days.

Potvin also tries to lead by example. The first week in the new building, he cleaned up the company kitchen twice a day with two employees, setting the standard and taking his turn like everyone else on staff. Later, when a disgruntled employee kept stealing china from the cafeteria, the president announced that he wasn't going to ask employees to bring their own plates or introduce plastic ones: the company would simply keep replacing the china until the culprit stopped—which he did.

Be a cheerleader for your employees

"My job as president is I sign cheques, I have to create a vision, but I'm a cheerleader," Yves Potvin says. "I have to cheer my staff. I'm the queen of the beehive. We all need a queen and employees need somebody they respect, who represents them, who they feel proud about. ... They have to feel good about themselves, and therefore when we have our picnics and barbecues every month and a half on the patio upstairs, we celebrate the birthdays and one-year anniversaries for working here, we celebrate when somebody's pregnant, getting married. So I'm the cheerleader. I pump them up, I reward them, I congratulate them, I joke. Cheerleader might not be the right term, but I'm the guy who has to make them feel good." He tells new staff about the corporate values statement, which includes "open communication, listening to each other, commitment to team goals, a spirit of cooperation, sharing successes and responsibility, having fun." He also lets them know that the company respects its employees' varied cultures: "We love that you're from Salvador because we think it's an asset for the company." A regular newsletter reports employee awards, sales and production achievements, birthdays and anniversaries—and personalizes the president by letting them in on his life, such as announcing his marriage and even reporting on how he proposed to his wife.

Fourteen years after starting Yves Veggie Cuisine, Potvin is reaping the harvest of a crazy idea and a mess of soybean curd. He drives a Land Rover, has taken his extended family on an Alaskan cruise, and is moving into a 557-square-metre Tudor-style home. His company has become so successful that competitors are coming after him with cash in hand. As natural-foods consultant Michael Weiner points out, "None of them still know how to do some of the things he does with meat analogues. They used to accuse him of putting stuff in his product that he didn't declare on his label." Among those that have approached Potvin is market leader Worthington Foods.

So is he selling? "That's a good question. My wife asked me that not too long ago: 'What would you do if you sell the company?' I said, 'First of all, I don't want to sell it at this stage. I'll never say I won't sell the company in the future, but I sense that it's so exciting right now because we're developing the market, it's very creative, very challenging, and now we're putting in a line of fast-food restaurants attached to the brand." With that move, as with so many others he has made since he started, he seems to be running ahead of the pack.

TrendWatch

The Futurist, the journal of the nonprofit World Future Society, pointed out last year that in the United States, "diners are walking out of restaurants in droves, taking their meals with them. The number of restaurant-prepared meals eaten off premises now [exceeds] those eaten on the scene. ... The to-go business is booming and complete dinners—sides and all—are becoming the most popular take-out items." In a recent issue, Canada's *Profit* magazine predicted the top-ten business opportunities for 1999, and leading the list was "gourmet home-meal replacements." That's exactly what the new Yves restaurant chain is offering: upscale "ready meals" made from all of the parent company's products, which can be eaten on the premises or taken to office or home. Of course, the concept goes well beyond that. "It's our lifestyle," Potvin says. "You grab a sandwich, it tastes good, and you say, 'I'm going to buy it in the supermarket and make it at home.' And by the way, this is the recipe. How many companies give recipes of what they do? ... I think the restaurant has potential to be bigger than the manufacturing."

Chapter Four

The Passionate Vintner

Harry McWatters, Sumac Ridge Estate Winery, and Hawthorne Mountain Vineyards

November 1968. On that blustery first day he spent within the Casabello winery in Penticton, British Columbia, Harry McWatters knew he was addicted. Escaping the snow of one of the coldest winters in the Okanagan Valley, he had opened the heavy, dark doors and stepped into the warmth of the brick-and-beam, Mediterranean-like interior. It was the first winery the amateur winemaker had ever visited: California redwood storage vats, Portuguese brandy barrels, gleaming stainless-steel fermentation tanks bubbling with the essence of grapes, and the young reds and whites ripening in row upon row of bottles. By day's end, the 23-year-old—at the time perhaps the highest-earning moving-company salesman in western Canada—agreed to become the very first vendor of the winery's offerings. Drunk on the aromas, colours, and flavours of the wines, he discovered only afterward that his salary was little more than half of what he had been earning, slightly sweetened with an opportunity to buy shares in the company. By then he was too far gone: Casabello had spoken to him with the seductiveness of its adapted Italian name, "beautiful house." As McWatters would later describe the winery for which he worked for 13 years, "I felt like I had come home."

September 1998. The brief detour off busy Highway 97 north of Summerland, British Columbia, wends up a hill past a golf clubhouse to a pine-bordered parking lot. And suddenly it is all there. On a bench of land above Lake Okanagan, clusters of tiny green Johannisberg Riesling grapes undulate in long rows to a horizon of arid, conifer-studded hills. Under a hot sun softened by a cool autumn breeze, the wands of irrigators slowly circle, wetting vines grown from cuttings laboriously hand-clipped and planted in 1981. Spread over the 6.8-hectare site bordering a nine-hole golf course are fermentation chambers, barrel cellars, champagne caves, a bottling line, and a warehouse to hold the 50,000 cases of vintage wines crafted here each year. Tall new buildings with steep, alpine-style blue roofs house a well-patronized retail wineshop, a well-regarded restaurant, and the offices of the profitable Sumac Ridge Estate Winery—Harry McWatters, cofounder and president. "We're very proud," he says of his own corporate home, which he, his family, and his partners have built in less than two decades. He whispers the words, as if to avoid disturbing the capricious gods of winemaking.

Harry McWatters is the most high-profile vintner—winemaker and wine merchant—in the fastest-growing wine region in North America. Here in British Columbia, in the Fraser and Okanagan Valleys and on Vancouver Island and even the little Gulf Islands, more than 50 wineries are creating award-winning vintage reds and whites, sparkling, fortified, and ice wines, on fewer than 1,215 vineyard hectares (compared to Ontario's 40 operations drawing on 4,455 hectares). McWatters and a partner have a respectable share of the B.C. industry. Immediately across Lake Okanagan another compact vineyard grows the grapes that make Sumac Ridge's ice wines, which have attracted regular customers as far away as Taiwan. Just north of the American border, in the near-desert around the town of Osoyoos, the winery has the 46.5 hectares of the Black Sage vineyard, planted in premium grapes that make red wines capturing honours at international competitions. And a half hour's drive south of Summerland, at Okanagan Falls, the partners have 69.2 hectares along Green Lake at their other winery, Hawthorne Mountain Vineyards. Within a few years, they expect it to be producing even finer wines than Sumac Ridge at twice the volume.

At 54 McWatters may be in the peak years of his personal vintage. He is a walking, talking billboard of the zest and *bonhomie* that wine can generate. Only his hair, which went grey over two terrible years in the early 1990s, belies the youthful energy he exudes. In his effusiveness about the health-promoting effects of his products, he likes to mention the so-called French Paradox, the theory suggested by some medical researchers that the people of France, while indulging in rich foods, are relatively less prone to some major physical problems because of the wine they drink.* "One study shows that moderate daily consumption of wine reduces your risk of heart disease and stroke by 45 percent," he says. (Actually, a major report puts the risk reduction at 40 percent by drinking two glasses of wine a day). "That's a pretty good reason to drink wine alone. The fact that it tastes good makes it a pretty easy medicine to be taking."

McWatters is something of a paradox himself. A relentlessly independent businessman, he has long manipulated the government rules that sometimes constrain his enterprise. His was officially the province's first estate winery—defined as a medium-size operation creating wines mostly of grapes from their own vineyards—and remains the oldest winery of any kind in the Okanagan Valley to be operated by its founder. As John Schreiner, a *Financial Post* writer and the author of *The Wineries of British Columbia*, says, "In an industry that is overregulated and affiliated with some of the legacy of Prohibition, Harry has never minded pushing the envelope to expand the rules and make them more flexible—and other people have benefitted." Despite McWatters's self-interested stance, he has brought the industry together as the founding head of the Okanagan Wine Festival and the B.C. Wine Institute, and most recently as chairman of VQA (Vintners Quality Alliance) Canada, the quality-control organization that has enriched the image of Canadian wines.

With his merry, bearded face and round, squat body, notable for its expansive girth, he looks like a Friar Tuck, although the monk's robe is replaced by his summer uniform of sandals and khaki shorts. The exuberant McWatters seems ever eager to belly up to the banquet table of life and sample whatever adventure is set before him. Yet the paradox is that, aside from indulging in food and drink and his passion for running a winery, he is a workaholic with no moderating avocations, except for his too-few escapes in snowmobiling and houseboating (last summer he didn't spend a single night aboard his 11-metre, 24-year-

---

*In the words of Dr. Serge Renaud, director of France's National Institute of Health and Medical Research, "The French Paradox could be defined as a high level of risk from high levels of cholesterol, fat, and hypertension, yet a much lower death rate, one of the lowest in the world, from heart disease. This is due ... to wine drinking in France."

old boat on the lake). He went through two partners before settling on his current one, a keeper named Bob Wareham, and he has always involved his family in the active running of Sumac Ridge. While his wife, Kathy, has recently stepped back, the children—still in their twenties—are well poised to take over the business someday: daughter Christa-Lee is a sales representative ("In 1998 she probably took more money home out of the company than anybody, including me," her father says), and son Darren is warehouse and distribution manager for both wineries. Wareham says: "Christa-Lee is her father's clone." But Darren has told his dad: "This isn't my passion. I mean, I love it and there's no other business I want to work in. But you have to understand I have my hobbies"—such as coaching minor hockey and competing in Ironman triathlons.

Hobbyless Harry McWatters, on the other hand, might still be at work deep into the night, only to have his wife call wondering when he is coming home for dinner. "I get so enthralled in what I'm doing that time has no meaning at that point," he says. His enthusiasm has infected his peers in an industry that is only starting to mature a decade after the effects of free trade—removing all price protection—shocked it into a survival mode. "We've got a lot of youth in the industry—a lot of wineries that have a lot of maturing to do within the business community, within the wine industry, from a world perspective, and some of them at this point may be a little bit naïve. I think experience is going to change that. The reality is, we are also developing a number of wineries that have been around for more than ten years. Take the ones that were here pre-free trade. They lived through some major challenges, they did a lot of business maturing, they had to really take a hard look at whether they were going to survive and if so, how? And the ones that went through that grew up real fast. Today we have a common bond in the fact in that enough of us who said we were too old and too stubborn to retrain—we weren't exiting this business, we had a passion for it—we had no choice but to band together and make things happen together."

That is how he defines his own role at his two wineries: "Having a partner like Bob has enabled me to go out and do what I do best—and that's make things happen in the marketplace. And not have to worry about whether or not somebody is taking care of the problems that might arise—the corks haven't arrived for tomorrow's bottling or whatever the crisis of the day may be—while you're 3,000 miles away trying real hard to convince the LCBO [Liquor Control Board of Ontario] that they should be listing some more Sumac Ridge products."

Only a quarter of those products are sold outside British Columbia. Within Canada they can be found in liquor stores as near at hand as the Prairies and as far away as Newfoundland, where Bob Wareham grew up, worked for John Labatt Limited, and now makes an effort to keep them stocked. The rest of the Atlantic provinces don't carry them. "Every province is like dealing with another country," says Gwen Coleman, a marketing consultant for the two wineries. In Ontario a persistent wine buyer can find their Chardonnay, Cabernet Sauvignon, Merlot, and Meritage—a red blend of Cabernet Sauvignon, Cabernet Franc, and Merlot. In Quebec, where French wine rules, an Eastern Townships restaurant called Auberge Georgesville serves a Sumac Ridge Gewürztraminer, and in 1998 the provincial liquor board imported 56 cases of the Cabernet Sauvignon after the 1995 vintage won an international competition in Montreal.

It was the first Canadian red ever to take a gold medal at Selections Mondiales, one of the world's more important wine and spirits competitions. In 1998, the tenth anniversary of the event, there were 1,718 entries from 35 countries; another Sumac Ridge red, the 1995 Meritage, came home with a silver. Those awards followed the 1995 Merlot's being named Canadian wine of the year, taking a trophy for best red wine, and a gold medal at the 18th annual All-Canada Wine Championships in Windsor, Ontario, the largest and most prestigious domestic competition. One judge, Michigan wine wholesaler Rick Lopus, commented: "The Sumac Ridge was spectacular. I think red wines are going to be the future of Canadian wine."* Not to slight the whites: a 1996 Sauvignon Blanc, also from the Black Sage vineyard, took a gold, too. McWatters, noting that 1995 was the first year fruit had come off these vines, asks

---

*But how does it taste? In naming Sumac Ridge B.C. Winery of the Month in late 1998, *Vancouver* magazine wine critic Memory Walsh described its 1996 Merlot ($17.95 in the province's liquor stores) as full-bodied: "Even in a difficult vintage, generous black cherry and current flavours cushion firm tannins, and an acid backbone extends the finish in a long close. Skilful use of oak barriques, predominantly French, reinforces both concentration and charisma—a credit to the concept of B.C. reds."

rhetorically, "If that's what we can do in year one, where are we going to be in ten years when we've got mature vines?"

What he would like to do is sell much more product in the well-wined United States and Europe. The way to do it, he believes, is to keep stressing the industry's VQA standards, which are government-regulated in British Columbia and industry-run in Ontario. Under the rules of VQA Canada, any wines submitted for this quality designation face panels of experienced, respected tasters. In Canada the rejected wines simply don't get the VQA stamp of approval; in South Africa, however, the also-rans can't even be sold. "I don't think were strict enough on that," McWatters says. Australia, New Zealand, and the state of Oregon, among others, don't allow any wines to be exported unless a panel has tested and confirmed them as representative of the area.

All of Canada's best attempts have not impressed Europe—yet. "We can't get access because they haven't accepted our standards overall as a national wine standard. So we're fighting to get that. The only way to get it is the kind of credibility we have with VQA. We'll probably sell more wine in the United States long-term than we will in Europe. But the reality is, until we can go to France and Germany and Italy and sell some wine, there's going to be people at home who just don't believe we're as good. It's international credibility." Credibility like the gold and silver medals presented to Sumac Ridge at Selections Mondiales and the gold for its 1996 Pinot Blanc Ice Wine at the 1998 World Wine Championships in Chicago, where its mark of 94 was the highest ever given to any Canadian winery in the competition.

The wines that won well over 100 awards in 1998 for Sumac Ridge Estate Winery (for the second year in a row) are all gold compared to the dross that Harry McWatters made and drank as a teenager in Vancouver. Born in Toronto, in between older and younger sisters, he was ten when the family moved west in 1995 and his father became district manager for the Toledo Scale Company. Five generations of McWatterses had worked for the business, and both the boy's grandfather and father died on the job. When a heart attack felled his dad, the 13-year-old Harry was devastated. As well as a successful executive, the senior McWatters had been a part-time entrepreneur, selling used scales that he refurbished in his basement. About the time of his father's death—"I'm not sure that it didn't make me just that little bit more independent," his son says now—Harry began selling light bulbs door-to-door and newspapers down on the Vancouver docks, while setting pins at night in a bowling alley. "I always had money in my pocket as a kid," he insists. On the side, he took up boxing and early on, in a foreshadowing of his future, developed a taste for wine. In Toronto his father had bought high-alcohol reds from Italian wine-makers and routinely kept a jug in the refrigerator and let the kids have a little with meals. When Harry's mother remarried in Vancouver, her new husband served them wine, too. Her son didn't start making his own plonk until the rest of the family moved to Winnipeg for his stepfather's new work and Harry stayed behind—ostensibly for a summer job but really because of his girlfriend. It was at her place that he experimented with "potato champagne," a stew of spuds, raisins, yeast, and water. "I started making wine when I was 16," he recalls. "By the time I was 18, I was actually making wines I could drink, and by about 20, I could actually convince others to do the same."

Harry was also learning to be a cook of sorts by frying burgers at a Dairy Queen, which led to a stint as a kitchen helper at a hotel in North Vancouver. He had other jobs to support himself in an attic apartment as he went back to school: delivering and occasionally selling for an appliance store and helping his stepfather, now back from Winnipeg, in his paint-contracting business. Some of his earnings went to buy the first of a string of cars he acquired over the years, classics such as a spiffy 1956 Buick convertible and a zippy 1965 Pontiac Beaumont he bought from the dealership of an up-and-comer named Jimmy Pattison.

"School interfered with my enterprises," McWatters says now. Although he took correspondence courses and attended night classes, he never finished high school, lacking a credit in English literature. He did get involved in a youth organization called Demolay, a kind of Catholic Junior Achievement, where he began to learn public speaking. A Safeway produce manager saw him at one event and offered him his first full-time work; he spent three years in a dozen locations selling garden supplies as well as handling produce (the leftover fruit of which he used to make his wine). The selling energized him: "If I didn't feel that I made a sale or made things happen today, tomorrow would be really tough." He learned more about the psychology of salesmanship in a two-year course in merchandising and marketing that the Vancouver Board of Trade sponsored on Saturday mornings at the University of British Columbia. What he learned in particular has proven useful throughout his career.

Entrepreneur = Salesperson—and you sell a lot more by listening than by talking

It is a fact that most self-employed people don't recognize: they are really in the selling game. In an Angus Reid survey for the Canadian Professional Sales Association Group—of 862 people who already had or thought of having their own business— 38 percent believed business relationships were the key element in entrepreneurial success. Yet only four percent considered good salesmanship the major factor. As association president Terry Ruffel points out, "entrepreneurs clearly understand that moving their product or service is critical. But when you call these skills 'sales,' entrepreneurs simply don't identify with them." Harry McWatters certainly does, but he says there are salespeople and *salespeople*. "I guess the one thing I learned continually throughout life is a good salesperson sells a whole lot more by good listening than they ever do by talking—and I don't believe that all salespeople are good listeners. The more they listen to what their customers' needs are, the more they can fulfill those needs. And there is nothing really difficult about that. Sometimes you can create the need. In the wine business, there is a bit of an emotional attachment to buying a bottle of wine. There's a lot of things that can influence it. We ask customers: 'What style of wines do you like? What was the last bottle of wine you bought? Are you buying something that goes with the food you're buying?' If you do lots of hand-selling as we do, then you start to build a trust." From such intelligent listening in his own wine stores and at public events, McWatters says, his wineries have tried to create products and packaging that reflect the generalized opinions expressed during one-on-one selling.

When McWatters was about 18, his father's successor at Toledo Scale took him to lunch and asked, "What are you going to do career-wise?" When the young man said he hadn't decided, his would-be mentor replied, "Well, you know your family has been in the scales business for a long time and I've already made some arrangements if you want to pursue that."

"Whatever gave you the idea I wanted to be in the scales business?" a surprised McWatters wondered, sounding a little like a Horatio Alger hero. "If I'm successful in life, it will be because I earned it and not because my name is McWatters." (Today, when asked why he didn't pursue that business, he notes dryly, "At my size, I'm sensitive about scales.")

On his final day at Safeway, a former schoolmate invited him to work in his paint-contracting firm. That job evolved into an informal partnership of the two friends in a body shop, where McWatters painted cars in return for some equity and good pay. But half a year later, wanting to pursue a career in sales, he answered an ad placed by a local affiliate of United Van Lines. It was a family moving business, and his job as salesman eventually led to a position as sales manager. In three years, he learned the tricks of the trade, such as comforting housewives by promising to have their china packed extra carefully—knowing that the additional weight of all the china barrels would mean more money for the movers. McWatters was called a booking agent and believes that at the time—the late 1960s—he was the highest-earning one in the western Canadian moving industry. Not only that, he had a company car.

Part of his job was to solicit corporate business. As a promotional gimmick, every month he sent likely prospects watchbands with clip-on calendars. One target was Hiram Walker Distillers; when McWatters gave a local rep a year's supply, the grateful recipient showed up with a bottle of Imperial whiskey and became an instant friend. One day he told McWatters that Casabello Wines in the Okanagan Valley was hiring Hiram Walker in Vancouver as its sales agency, but the distillers had no wine specialist. Would he be interested in joining the recently built winery as its first salesman and working out of the Walker office? He knew of McWatters's interest in wine and his sterling sales record with the moving company. Casabello had opened on Penticton's Main

Street in 1966, with about $400,000 from local businessman Evans Lougheed and a group of 40 investors and a $100,000 grant from the federal government. Selling the winery's products would be a challenge: at the time, advertising of wine was forbidden and Casabello had an image problem after the first vintage it put on the market, in the previous year, was recalled because of bacterial problems. But the vintner who made that wine had been replaced and Casabello was now truly committed to quality.

Sure, McWatters was interested enough to phone Lougheed, the winery's managing director, and then meet in Vancouver with its well-connected corporate secretary, Chester Johnson, a Vancouver forestry honcho. "Well, I am very interested," he told Johnson, "and I am interested in wine and it certainly is an opportunity to put my hobby and my profession together. So what type of money are we talking about?"

The answer was $6,000 a year—or about $10,000 less than he had been earning with the movers. And he had to have his own car.

McWatters had bought a cheap house from a friend, moved into it, and was making mortgage payments. His heart wanted him to take the Casabello job, but his head knew he lived well beyond the $500 a month being offered. "I would love to do this, but I can't," he told Johnson.

A week later Evans Lougheed, who was also a real-estate developer and Avis car-rental franchisee, phoned to convince McWatters to at least fly up to Penticton to see the winery. Casabello's new winemaker, a gruff old German, met him and his girlfriend of the moment at the airport in the swirling snow and then drove him in a pickup to the welcoming Italianate facility. And, from the moment he met Lougheed, McWatters was hooked.

"Evans is sitting there telling me about what his plans are and what their potential is," McWatters recalls, "but there was never any doubt in my mind from the time I sat down to talk with him. There was never any doubt that this was an easy project—that they wouldn't be able to produce enough wine to fill the demand in the short term." There, on the spot, the 23-year-old hotshot salesman decided to follow his heart, after all. "By the end of the weekend, we shook hands and I was taking the job"—and he left without knowing exactly how much they would pay him. The answer came later: $550 a month—only ten percent above the original offer—but with a chance to buy some equity in the winery. What the hell; he accepted.

Pursue your passion and you'll find your career

"I have said thousands of times that the next day that I have to go to work, I am not going. I do what I love," Harry McWatters says 30 years later. "I just can't imagine getting up in the morning and having to go to something where I hate working—and that happens even in the wine industry." He tells the story of a talented Sumac Ridge winemaker who couldn't wait to leave work at the end of the day. Harold Bates was taking courses to fulfill his secret passion to be an Anglican priest, which he confessed when McWatters asked him about his long-term plans. "I just made a mistake telling you," he said. To which his boss replied: "We're pursuing our dream and I encourage you to do that—you'll be much happier. And you'll be a lot more valuable to us while you're here if you are doing that." It is wisdom he now passes on to his own daughter and son. "A lot of people have said I must be really pleased that my kids have come to work with me and I say it's irrelevant. But what I am pleased about is this was not their first career path. They decided that they were going to do other things. They might have pursued their education elsewhere with that in mind and then realized how much the wine business is part of their life. This is my dream, I'm living it, I don't want anyone else living it for me. They developed their own dream and it is different from mine, but it is in the same industry." This kind of intensity, enthusiasm, is important whether you are creating a company or running one. American economist David Birch, speaking of entrepreneurship, told *U.S. News & World Report*, "The first rule has to be that you do something you really love—you can't make it otherwise." And Deborah A. Coleman, vice president and CFO of Apple Computer Corporation, was quoted in Tom Peters's *Thriving on Chaos* "I don't think you should ever manage anything that you don't care passionately about."

"When I started in the wine business," McWatters says, "there were two kinds of wine consumers in the province—those that took it out of the brown paper bags and those that didn't. We were appealing to those that didn't fall into either category." Casabello was making slightly upscale generics with names such as Vino Rosso, Vino Bianco, and Angelica, a sweet dessert wine, all of them packaged with innocuous brown-paper labels that Lougheed's wife had helped design. The bestseller was the plainly titled Dinner Wine, Medium Dry Red. Many of these wines were the best that British Columbia was producing at the time, made from classic European vinifera varieties of grapes rather than the more disease-resistant but inferior-quality hybrids. Their major competition in this so-called premium category was the Castle Wine Company, the province's first winery, while Calona Wines was in the bottom-end jug-wine business. For the first six months, McWatters focused on government liquor stores throughout the province to reassure them that the winery's products were now bacteria-free, as well as to convince them to stock the wines so local restaurants and hotels could find a ready supply on the shelves. That done, he could concentrate on expanding the line and marketing the new products imaginatively in hope of raising the ridiculously low prices Canadians were then paying for domestic wines—as little as 95 cents for a 750-millilitre bottle.

Eventually he pushed up the price of Casabello's better products—those made from varietals (grapes of a single variety) such as Canadian Burgundy and Riesling—to an unprecedented $2.35. Soon after, he had a phone call from the sales supervisor for Andrés Wines, the much larger Ontario-based winery, the aggressive marketer of the infamous Baby Duck sparkling wine. "You know, Harry," the man said, "You have a lot of guts. I just saw the new prices. We knew that somebody had to break the $2 price barrier because nobody is making money at less than that. But, boy, $2.35—I just want to wish you luck."

Part of the products' ensuing success was their packaging, which included a stylish label with a description of the wine and a list of other wines printed on the reverse so the consumer could read this commercial after emptying the bottle. McWatters pushed for corks instead of screw caps and the development of a line called Estate Selection (although Casabello's "estate" was a mere 4.4 hectares, occupied by a house and an orchard as well as a miniature vineyard). He also recommended selling a down-market Gala line of generics that cost $1.05, a dime more than the competition.

Perhaps Casabello's biggest coup during his 13 years there was the Canadian launch of wine bottled in take-home glass carafes vacuum-sealed with metal lids, an idea pioneered by California winemaker Paul Masson. In 1974 McWatters had been actively scheduling public wine-tastings in restaurants for fund-raising service clubs and church groups, a marketing strategy that began when Vancouver restaurateur Jon Levine agreed to have the events three nights a week in an unused banquet room at Jon's Pizzarama. To make it classy, McWatters bought Mexican carafes from an import house; seeing how successful a gimmick they were, Casabello spent $20,000 on moulds to make carafes to hold the wine it sold in liquor stores. And it sold so well that McWatters earned a $1,000 bonus and got a $500-a-month raise.

The increase in sales from the carafe wines came at a crucial time: in 1972 Casabello's board of directors had agreed to give Labatt a five-year option to buy the winery for $1.5 million and a bonus based on profits in the fifth year. The big brewer immediately began investing capital in the company, introducing the province's first bag-in-a-box wines and insisting on watering some other wines to increase profits. The year Labatt took over the winery, Bob Wareham was parachuted in as vice president and general manager. He had been controller of Labatt's Chateau Gai and Chateau Cartier wine group in Toronto. Now he offered McWatters the marketing-manager position, which required the Vancouver-based sales manager to move to the Okanagan Valley with Kathy, his wife of 29 years, and their two young children. "Conceptually Harry was such a great marketer," Wareham says. "We were very complementary. He certainly is an A-type personality who likes being in front of people. I'm more of a backroom guy who gets finances in place, construction done, and deals with people issues."

In spite of Labatt's opposition, the two managers wanted to use more varietal grapes to produce premium Chenin Blanc, Chardonnay, Riesling, and Gewürztraminer wines. McWatters became close with Lloyd Schmidt, one year older and quiet of personality, a second-generation grape grower who had become Casabello's vineyard manager. Both were distraught at the down-market direction the new owners were taking the winery, so distraught they started to discuss going out on their own. In 1977 the Social Credit government of Bill Bennett had developed regulations allowing for so-called cottage wineries, those with vineyards of 8.1 hectares and producing no more than 90,920 litres a year.* The idea was to encourage higher-quality products by mandating that a cottage winery could not add water and sugar to wine nor extract more than 682 litres of juice from each tonne of grapes.

McWatters and Schmidt did a business plan that showed they would need an annual production of about 113,650 litres to operate a viable business. They approached the head of the provincial Liquor Control and Licensing Branch, who hinted he would be flexible. They also asked for a broad interpretation of the rule requiring that the wineries under this legislation have 8.1 hectares of their own vine-yards. That request was prompted by the fact that the property they wanted for their new winery had only a few hectares suitable for vini-culture; the rest was a golf course. McWatters's chief criterion for a site had been proximity to a chief road, based on the high amount of drop-in traffic he witnessed at Casabello's retail wine shop on the main street of Penticton. One possibility south of Penticton didn't have enough land adjoining a highway. But Schmidt remembered the owners of a golf course at Summerland offering to sell out to Casabello some years before. He and McWatters paid a pricey $12,500 per .4 hectare for 15.3 hectares, with the course, a club-house, a restaurant, and a house thrown in as part of the deal (they sold the house later for about $85,000). And it was all spread along the evocatively named Sumac Ridge, north of Summerland, just off the well-beaten Highway 97. The only problem was that little more than 3.6 hectares could be planted in vines. Undeterred, the partners made a deal with a grower to exchange a five-percent interest in his 5.2-hectare vineyard across Lake Okanagan near Naramata for shares in the winery-to-be; no money changed hands. At the same time, they convinced the licensing branch to let them buy grapes from other growers for their first vintage. All of this manoeuvring reflects one of McWatters's personal rules.

---

* It was Harry McWatters who in 1979 convinced the provincial government to change the name of cottage wineries to the classier "estate," Of the seven original estate wineries, only Sumac Ridge, Gray Monk, and Gehringer Brothers are still flourishing.

Some rules are made to be broken, but break them intelligently

"It's easier to beg for forgiveness than to ask for permission," Harry McWatters says.★ In his world, this means that if a bureaucratic regulation is patently stupid, figure out a way around it and then approach the powers that be with cap in hand but the solution about to be (or already) in place. "You know, you can't just have a hard-and-fast rule because not everybody fits the mould. We are government-regulated, but I just don't believe that most people who are policy and law makers—particularly when it comes to the wine business—are dealing in logic. They haven't lived on a vineyard. They don't have the experience. There are lots of people who take exception to the fact that we have pushed the envelope in a lot of cases and we have got away with it. ... But the restrictions that were put on us were unrealistic in the first place, particularly when it came to the limit of how much wine we could produce. If we were producing product that is 100 percent Okanagan Valley-grown, it was a quality product, and there was a demand for it, why would the government ever want to put a restriction on how much we made? You would think that they want us to be producing a whole lot more to create more jobs and pay more taxes." The relaxing of the 8.1-hectare rule stuck in some competitors' craws. McWatters quotes them as asking the licensing branch: "If I just go and buy 20 acres [8.1 hectares] of dirt, will you grant me a licence?" His response is that he and Schmidt were serious players with a long history in the wine industry and "I think all along there was no doubt in [the licensing branch's] mind that our intent was certainly genuine and that we were for real." And by gambling on being proactive, rather than passive, they helped change the rules for an industry.

★In a paraphrase of the remarks made by U.S. Navy Rear Admiral (Retired) Grace Murray Hopper, who said in a 1987 Washington speech: "If it's a good idea ... go ahead and do it. It is much easier to apologize than it is to get permission."

The upshot: by the time the two hopeful vintners were ready to launch, the branch had increased the allowable annual production to 136,380 litres and let them open with 8.1 hectares composed of their own raw land and the producing vineyard they had acquired across the lake in a simple swap of shares.

Thanks to a sympathetic Bob Wareham, they already had their first vintage secretly fermenting in the cellars of Casabello: about 1,500 cases apiece of Chancellor (a Claret-style red), Verdelet (a white French hybrid), and Okanagan Riesling (another hybrid white, of indeterminate ancestry). Now they had to create a winery. From the first, it was a family operation. To buy the land and buildings for $475,000, the partners mortgaged their houses and took out loans from relatives and the Federal Business Development Bank. In McWatters's case, he'd had clear title on his house, after receiving about $40,000 from selling his Casabello shares to Labatt, and he borrowed money from his mother, mother-in-law, and brother-in-law. On Valentine's Day 1981, the two families descended on the golf course, cleaning out ponds and getting the pro shop and restaurant ready for the season while planning to convert the clubhouse into a winery. Kathy McWatters, meanwhile, took an accounting course and began doing the winery's books.

The previous December, McWatters and his partner had gone on a week's holiday from Casabello to take cuttings of vines at a vineyard in Sunnyside, Washington. It was cold and foggy and the fog condensed on the thick vines, so cutting them was like shattering glass. They insisted on doing it themselves: "We wanted them all to be straight, 20 inches in length, and at least pencil thickness, and we wanted even internodes—the space between the buds. We were pruning the guy's vineyard at the same time, so we would get select wood. We were out there before daylight, and at the end of the first day, when it got too dark to work, we headed into the hotel restaurant and had a couple of hot rums and dinner, went back to our room, and I can remember taking off my jacket and starting to get undressed, then laid back and I just instantly fell asleep. Talk about exhaustion." They left the cuttings in a Washington nursery to propagate, returning in February to knock off all of the growth up to the top two buds. In mid-May, the two fathers and their five children—the McWatterses' just seven and nine years old—began planting the cuttings on what had been the first, second, and half of the ninth fairways of the redesigned Sumac Ridge golf course.

Using ropes marked with fluorescent paint, they measured precise rows 2.1 metres apart and spaced the plants 1.5 metres apart (today grape growers use lasers to do the same work). "We lifted up the ropes and went along the rows with a tractor and an auger, dug a hole 20 inches deep, and by hand put in a layer of moist mixture with a little bit of top soil and peat, put the plant in, and then another handful of peat on top of it with a bit of blood and bone, so the plant would stick out and catch the moisture."

Within eight months, they were making wine on-site in tanks built by a local stainless-steel contractor. Grapes of the 1981 vintage were challenging, high in acid. "It was lots of hard work," McWatters remembers. "We didn't have the right equipment, we had built it on a shoestring, and we ended up going through a lot of labour-intensive procedures that you wouldn't otherwise do. About four o'clock we would go downstairs and start to bottle, Kathy would stay and make dinner for both families and look after any customers, and our kids were stamping the numbers on the ends of boxes." Meanwhile, McWatters and Schmidt and the latter's wife and son might be operating a mechanical bottling and corking line. "Lloyd, Noreen, and I, and often Alan, would be here till one o'clock in the morning to finish up the bottling. The motivating factors were that our product sold for $4.95 plus tax when it first went to market—so it was $5.30—and every time we put a bottle down we would say $5, $10, and after a case, here's another $60. At midnight you need that kind of motivation."

Much of their energy went into the golf course, which the previous owners—wanting to develop a neighbouring subdivision—had demanded that McWatters and Schmidt run for five years as long as it proved economically viable. While both the course and the restaurant generated necessary cash flow, they were as labour-intensive as pruning vines. And the retail store on the first floor of the old clubhouse was so successful from the start that within a few months of opening it had run out of wine and could serve only coffee to visitors. Over the next couple of years, the partners increased production and added new varieties: Chardonnay, a Muscat-type Perle of Csaba, a rosé, a crisp, dry, delicate Okanagan Riesling, and even an unusual Sauternes-type Chenin Blanc made from grapes affected by a fungus that focuses sugar and flavour. They were among the first in British Columbia to use barrels, particularly French oak, to ferment their products. Schmidt's son, Alan, became a vital part of Sumac Ridge's winemaking.

Yet, although their wines were selling, McWatters and Schmidt were struggling. They were repaying the FBDB loan and had an operating line with the Canadian Imperial Bank of Commerce. Within a year, in those inflationary early 1980s, the interest on their loan had leaped from 14.25 percent to 25.5 percent. The tensions of continuing losses caused cracks in the partnership. "We got to the point where it was challenging to communicate," McWatters says. "I'm sure he would have a different side to this. But there were things that Lloyd bought or committed to that, in my opinion, it didn't matter how bad we needed them, we didn't have the money. And that just added to the stress. We didn't dislike each other. We just couldn't work together." Because they didn't have a formal shotgun buy-sell clause in their agreement, it took them about 18 months to negotiate a possible split. In 1985, McWatters told his partner to buy him out and—while Schmidt weighed the offer—even briefly considered acquiring a troubled winery called Claremont in nearby Peachland.

Schmidt found an investor willing to buy his partner's share, but the company's bank, worried about the winery's loss of marketing expertise, said it wouldn't relieve McWatters of his personal guarantee of $715,000 if he sold out. He told Schmidt to satisfy the bank before Sumac Ridge's rapidly approaching annual general meeting. But by the Sunday the shareholders met, Schmidt had done nothing to take his partner off the hook with the bank. McWatters went into the meeting with enough votes to carry the day. "That was probably the toughest day of my life, knowing I had proxies and was going to elect a slate of officers excluding Lloyd, and resume management of the company on my own." If Schmidt made the arrangement with the bank within the next three weeks, McWatters assured him the buyout would go through as planned—"but I just can't turn anything over without having my guarantees taken care of." After his partner walked out and the new slate of officers was elected, McWatters left the meeting to learn that his son and daughter had rolled a golf cart and got badly burned, with

Darren breaking his arm, and both ending up in the hospital. "It *was* the worst day of my life," their father recalls.

Two days later, Schmidt decided to sell his half of the company instead. While his son stayed on to make wine, he moved to Ontario's Niagara Peninsula region to become a grape-growing consultant. He sold to an investor McWatters had found. Bud Richmond, who had run a plywood-retailing firm and had a two-hectare vineyard nearby, was willing to be involved for five years. "Bud ruffled a few feathers. He was a little bit of a rough gem, but he was a good partner." While he oversaw vineyard production and grower relationships, McWatters assumed more of the business operation and his wife operated the wine shop.

The new partners became aggressive about marketing the retail store to tour groups, including those run by seniors' organizations and Overseas China Voice, which brought in busloads of Hong Kong tourists. During the tourist season, they advertised locally on radio and in newspapers to attract other holidayers. They continued with a provincially operated program that offered $25,000 in matching dollars to do on-site programs to train the staff of the B.C. restaurants that bought nearly 70 percent of their wines. It was good business: when selling to restaurants, Sumac Ridge kept the entire markup. And McWatters redesigned the label with an artist's painting of the winery for the 1985 vintage.

In 1987 Harold Bates joined as vintner, bringing his eastern reputation as a creator of Brights President Canadian Champagne. The partners began producing sparkling wines from a selection of 30 different grape varieties. They were the first to be made in British Columbia by the classic second-fermentation method, but McWatters had the wit not to offend the French and call them champagne. Sumac Ridge's first bubbly was Steller's Jay Cuvée, made from Pinot Blanc, Pinot Noir, and Chardonnay grapes and named for the cheeky blue jay that had just been voted the province's official bird. Before leaving to join the Anglican priesthood, Bates also produced some good Gewürztraminers that helped polish the winery's image.

Then, in 1988, all the ground rules changed. For the past decade, the B.C. Liquor Distribution Branch had protected domestic wineries by guaranteeing them 66 liquor store listings and marking up their wines by only 66 percent compared to imports' 115 percent.

Overnight, the Canada-United States Free Trade Agreement destroyed all such defences against American interlopers. Suddenly the Canadian wine industry was in crisis, no longer able to use trade barriers and price protection to pass off lesser products.

Certainly, the B.C. wine business had been maturing from plonk to palatable products. McWatters himself had been a key ingredient in the fermentation of that process. He was the winemaker that local tourism officials first called upon to be the founding head of the Okanagan Wine Festival, an annual celebration of the grape harvest that began in 1981, the year he was launching Sumac Ridge. He had suggested they import actor and gourmet Vincent Price as a celebrity patron, but instead they wound up with Glenn Ford, who grew some grapes on his property. The war-movie and western hero was not only afraid to go up in a helicopter to view the wineries, he also fled most autograph seekers and refused to judge a chili contest. In its second year, the festival eschewed any celebrities and held its first wine competition. ("They were technically well-made wines, but for the most part from hybrids," McWatters remembers. "Some of the judges had difficulty with it. I think we were a little ahead of our time.") Over the next few years he oversaw it, the event would lose more than $100,000 and consume much of McWatters's time. But it was another example of his overt leadership, a putting into practice of a strongly held conviction.

Get involved in your industry—if you want to help shape its future impact on your own operations

In the early 1980s, Harry McWatters had suggested that four other companies join him in starting the B.C. Estate Winery Association and open the Okanagan Estate Wine Cellars in a new Victoria development—the first such retail wine store in the province. Forming the association was his way around the liquor regulations that prevented a lone winery from launching an off-site store. "Our philosophy, when we started this winery, was no different than it is today: if you're not going to take an active role in industry issues, industry events, then you have to suffer the consequences when it doesn't go the way you think it should," McWatters maintains. "Not by any stretch of the imagination, because of our involvement, does it always go the way I think it should. But you get a lot of consensus and input from other people, and we've had a number of things that have been very successful," including the Okanagan Wine Festival, which now schedules two events a year, has extended the valley's tourist season to Thanksgiving, and gives the provincial wine industry a high-profile presence. Over the past decade, his partner, Bob Wareham, has seen one of McWatters's principal roles as dealing with larger issues in their trade. "You needed to be out there controlling the future of the industry. It was going through an evolution—the VQA program was in its infancy but had to be sold to the public. And it's made the industry."

The program that ultimately made the industry was born of desperation. When the Free Trade Agreement and the more global General Agreement on Trades and Tariffs eliminated industry protections beginning in the late 1980s, Canadian wines faced their first serious price competition. "We had met with government trade negotiators provincially for about two years," McWatters says, "and we were pretty much assured by them that the wine industry was going to remain unscathed [after free trade]. At the 11th hour, the federal government sold out the wine industry. I can't put it in any more gentle terms than that. But that shouldn't be surprising, because Ronald Reagan was the president of the day, came from California, and I'll bet he had more than one friend in the wine industry. ... It was just a bad deal all the way around. Having said that, I also believe that from the consumers' perspective, it was the best thing that could ever happen. And I think as we get another 20 years behind us, the wine industry is going to say it was the best thing that ever happened, too." In response to the FTA and GATT provisions, the federal and B.C. governments handed out $28 million in funds, primarily to let provincial grape growers yank second-fiddle vines and replace them with better European styles—or to get out of the business altogether. While so many took the latter route, lowering the value of the 1989 harvest by $10 million to a mere $3 million, the optimists replanted. Among them was McWatters, who the following year was instrumental in creating the British Columbia Wine Institute. Grape growers and wineries each contributed a levy

amounting to $50 a tonne of their crushed grapes to establish this lob-
bying and marketing weapon.

The Institute's major contribution to the future of the industry was
the adoption of Vintners Quality Alliance standards, which were first
formulated by Ontario wine makers in 1989. British Columbia followed the next year, using slightly different wording (some of which
their eastern counterparts later accepted). The intent was the same: "to
help guarantee superior-quality Canadian wines, affecting all areas of
quality control in winemaking, from what grapes can be used and
where they are cultivated to the taste of the finished wine and the
labelling on the bottle." McWatters, who became the wine institute's
chairman, says that "people who were buying British Columbia wine
before the VQA program often felt they were playing wine roulette—
they'd get a good bottle and then they'd get something else." In 1998
sales of VQA wine across Canada totalled almost one million cases, and
most insiders concede that the program saved the industry.

But in the furor that followed the Free Trade Agreement, British
Columbia's wineries had clutched at several straws to stay afloat. One
of them was to capitalize on the provision that permitted the importing
of bulk wines and selling it at domestic prices. The large commercial
wineries jumped on this exemption, which was designed to replace the
volume of grapes lost when growers pulled out their inferior vines. The
enterprising McWatters decided to exploit this market, too, by selling
both Okanagan and imported wines in very basic bulk form. The idea
nearly proved to be his undoing. The vehicle he and his then-partner,
Bud Richmond, chose in 1989 was Valley Wine Merchants. Their new
company opened a Vancouver outlet called Wine on Broadway, beside
a Liquor Distribution Branch location, to offer a variety of wines drawn
from large stainless-steel beer kegs fitted with taps. Similar to long-
established shops in Europe, it allowed restaurateurs, pub owners, and
individual buyers—who brought their own bottles— to buy bulk wine
at a reasonable price. Exactly how reasonable became the issue: just
before opening day, the Liquor Control and Licensing Branch placed a
floor price on bulk wine of $6.20 a litre. Valley Wine Merchants had
planned to sell some of its wines for as little as $4 and $5 a litre. Now
anyone could go to the liquor store and get similar wine, packaged, for
the same $6.20 price tag they could at Winery on Broadway.

There were other setbacks. While the partners had been promised $125,000 in a provincial make-work program, they received only $64,000. They had expected a $150,000 operating line of credit at the Bank of British Columbia, but at the last minute got only $100,000. These developments, along with the unexpected pricing rule, left them reeling. They quickly reduced their staff numbers, and twice a week McWatters routinely made the four-hour drive from Summerland to Vancouver to keg the wine into the early-morning hours and to generally manage the operation. His state of exhaustion wasn't eased by the squeeze the bank was inexplicably putting on the company. Near the end of 1990, when the business began failing, the bank placed an injunction on Valley Wine Merchants' receivables from the LDB and actually seized McWatters's house for a time. Over the two frantic years he ran the company, McWatters's hair literally turned grey. In his enthusiasm for the idea of a bulk-wine store, he had ignored a reality that any entrepreneur must consider.

Realistically size up your competitors—especially their influence in the industry—before launching a major project that might threaten them

"What I learned," Harry McWatters says of his Valley Wine Merchants experience, "is that you really need to know the environment you're in, the other forces that are at work. What I didn't know was the kind of pressure being put by the commercial industry of the day on the LDB [Liquor Distribution Branch]. Lots of people from the LDB have since retired and shared some of the kinds of pressures that were applied. But I also was told very clearly that somebody with a commercial wine interest had a very strong tie to the Bank of B.C. and implied that there was no way we were going to make it. We would have made it if the bank had given us the breathing room. We were at a break-even. We had accrued a fair amount of debt that needed to be serviced, but our operating costs were being covered by our sales, and our sales were growing dramatically." Another way of wording the lesson: "Make sure that you're familiar with the things that are working behind the

137

scenes, the things you can't see—how strong is your competition? I didn't view them as competition. I didn't think they viewed me as competition—we weren't selling packaged products. There's no question we were going to erode some of their market, so I guess there was a little naivete to it. And this pressure that was brought to bear, combined with the influence they brought to bear on the bank, tied our hands."

The company never declared bankruptcy. The partners, between them, personally lost an estimated $300,000; others took a bath, as well, with Sumac Ridge being the largest creditor. In 1990 the winery sold the golf course, and a discouraged Bud Richmond, his five-year deadline looming, pulled out of the business. In May 1991, Bob Wareham—who had advised against the Valley Wine Merchants venture—bought into the winery for $250,000. As he describes the operation then, "it was barely in the black." Sometimes there wasn't enough power available to plug in two large pieces of equipment. However, his on-site managerial talents and financial expertise helped sort out the money problems.

And, over the next few years as their VQA wines began attracting attention, the partners saw compound growth of more than 21 percent annually. They felt confident enough to expand. For $431,250, they bought the 46.5-hectare Black Sage vineyard near Osoyoos to grow grapes for red wine, and for about $3.2 million, they acquired the former LeComte Estate Winery to transform it into Hawthorne Mountain Vineyards. As well as tapping various banks for loans to build a better infrastructure, they used an innovative investment vehicle to finance expansion: a tax-sheltered venture capital corporation offering, with a minimum subscription of $10,000. The VCC could be placed in a registered retirement plan and after five years allow an investor B.C. tax credits. They first used it in the mid-1990s to raise $2 million for Sumac Ridge; the investment group got a third of the business, which then had an appraised value of $4 million. Later, another VCC generated $1 million in return for 20 percent of Hawthorne Mountain while a group of private investors got 30 percent for putting in $1.5 million.

Speaking in late 1998 of the VCC that revitalized Sumac Ridge, Wareham told me: "There was no other alternative. It's a very good tax vehicle for a small business to raise money. A lot of it's coming in through RRSP contributions so you can get your income tax reduced, and the provincial government was giving a 30-percent tax credit so you as an investor would have only $3,000 of the $10,000 in there but get dividends on the original investment. And it's patient money—they have to stay in there for a minimum of five years. By that time, we'll have done some kind of public offering. That's a work-in-progress. ... "

Within a few years, Hawthorne Mountain could be producing 100,000 cases a year, twice Sumac Ridge's volume. The partners have kept the LeComte label as more of a market-entry line. "Some of the wines were pretty good, some were pretty charm-free," McWatters admits. LeComte products can use wines that don't meet the standard for Hawthorne Mountain, which is 100-percent vinifera varietal wine. The winery itself is entrancing. Visitors turn off Highway 97 near Okanagan Falls onto the country charm of Green Lake Road and drive up to the century-old stone house, encircled by acacia trees, that serves as the office and an airy wine shop. In the lee of the mountain named for the brothers who settled here, the winery has an old-world feel. Wine tasters can sit under a grape arbour as they look out over the valley to Skaha Lake or stroll the vineyard-ringed grounds where a pet cemetery honours the collies of the British major who lived here until 1974. The most pleasing aspect of the place, however, is the quality of the wines it produces.*

---

*Under its own label, Hawthorne Mountain makes the white Gewürztraminer, Riesling, Chardonnay, Chardonnay/Semillon; the red Merlot, Meritage, Pinot Noir, Cabernet Franc, Gamay Noir, Pinot Meunier, and Lemberger (a superb variety popularized in Washington State); the sparkling HMV Brut and Empress Brut; and the specialty Select Late Harvest Optima, Oraniensteiner and Ehrenfelser Ice Wines. The LeComte label includes Proprietors White, Gewürztraminer, Gewürztraminer Dry, Riesling, Chardonnay, Vineyard Select, and Auxerrois (all whites), and Proprietors Red, Pinot Noir, Chelois, Marechal Foch, and Reserve Red (all reds). Sumac Ridge makes the white Chardonnay, Dry Gewürztraminer, Okanagan Blanc, Okanagan Blush, Pinot Blanc, Riesling, Sauvignon Blanc, White Meritage (half Blanc, half Semillon); the red Okanagan Reserve, Private Reserve Chancellor, Merlot, Cabernet Sauvignon, Cabernet Franc, Meritage Red, Private Reserve Pinot Noir; the sparkling Blanc de Noirs, Steller's Jay Brut, and Prestige 2000 (a champagnelike bubbly for the millennium); and the specialty Elegance (a sweet Muscat), Pinot Blanc Ice Wine (including a 50-litre sampler size), and Pipe—a port-style fortified wine that McWatters christened, using an old name for a barrel, only to learn later that in French slang it means "blow job." The *Globe and Mail*'s David Lawrason visited B.C. wineries in late 1998 and either Sumac Ridge or Hawthorne Mountain made his list of "the most interesting and best wines" in each category.

Nice as Hawthorne Mountain is, as good as its wines already are, McWatters and Wareham are in a continuing acquisition mode. At this writing, they had a verbal agreement to buy a 40-hectare vineyard in the Okanagan that would, in McWatters's words, "give us another 500 tonnes of grapes and a lot of room to expand our product line." They are also looking south in hope of acquiring a U.S. operation, which would allow them to expand in the American market well beyond the current three-percent of their total sales. What will help propel their growth is Harry McWatters's careful reading of the shifting fashions in his industry and the logical progression of tastes to an appreciation for better wines.

TrendWatch

"Today I see no end in sight for the growth in more intense-flavoured wines, both red and white," Harry McWatters says. "The order of the day is flavour, flavour, flavour. And if it's Gewürztraminer, it better be the most powerful Gewürztraminer and most intense fruits you can get. Don't compromise that. When it comes to Cabernet Sauvignon, they want big, bold reds they can chew. The challenge is they don't want to take them home and cellar them, as much as we encourage them to do that. We wait a minimum of two years before we release them, and big, bold reds still aren't ready to drink after two years. So we have to make them bold enough to get their attention, soft enough to make them tell their friends about them. If they're going to take them home and drink them when they're 25 months old, they've got to be very approachable." The other trend is parents' introducing wine to their children over family dinners. Perhaps not with the ease with which McWatters himself did—"but I think they're going to become more that way. And as they do, we may not have a group of youth that come up drinking solely soda pop. They may get some exposure to wine. My

gut feeling is that it's happening a lot more frequently. I watched it through my kids—their friends
all drink wine." But he warns that the industry can't
intimidate newcomers into the wine world. "Let's let
them embrace whatever the wine is. If they want to
start drinking sweet and muscaty white Zinfandel, so
be it. If they like our Blush, we can get them to love
our Gewürztraminer, and it's not going to be a big
step before we've got them drinking Merlot." Rather
than the plonk he himself used to make and drink
when he was in his teens.

The Tourism Impresarios

T he article on the Forum page of the *Vancouver Sun* in August 1998 was a strange challenge to the Canadian government. "It's time to take back one of the world's great railway journeys," the headline urged. The author was an American, a Florida transportation attorney, who noted that a private rail operator was running tourist passenger trains between Calgary, Kamloops, and Vancouver along the stunning southern route once plied by the historic Canadian Pacific Railway. The CPR's successor, VIA Rail Canada, had launched this service itself in 1988—operating only in daylight to allow tourists to view the Rocky and Coast Mountains in all their magnificence—and ran it at a loss for two seasons. Pressured by the Brian Mulroney government to privatize this Rocky Mountaineer route, VIA awarded the rights to Vancouver's Great Canadian Railtour Company, whose posh service soon began turning a profit. In his article, the lawyer and train buff, Donald Pevsner, noted that the no-compete clause VIA had signed with Great Canadian would expire in late 1998—when it would behoove the government to let VIA once again run The Canadian passenger train on the preferred route between Calgary and Kamloops. He said the private railway's president, Peter Armstrong, "had no right to dictate national policy on transcontinental passenger rail operations beyond 1998."

It could be argued that an American had no right to dictate such policy, either—a policy, incidentally, that Ottawa has announced it is not about to change in favour of VIA. But the point is that the privatized Rocky Mountaineer was running along a legacy of Our Nation's Past and through the natural wonders of western Canada, whose presence places an extra burden on any tourism operator. From the disappearing grasslands of the Prairies to the overcommercialized centres in our western mountain parks, the West's physical features and the natural and human-shaped resources they contain are flashpoints in Canadians' fight to preserve our environment. Because this half of Canada is more wild, less developed and populated, and has a younger, more vulnerable history than the East, we tend to react more violently to any trespasses on its soul.

Peter Armstrong, one of the featured Tourism Impresarios, has been made well aware of his responsibility in maintaining the integrity of the heritage he is exploiting with his rail service. A 16-page tabloid newspaper given to all his passengers celebrates the history of the rail line and the people it has served, and Armstrong commissioned historian David J. Mitchell to write a 144-page hardcover book, *All Aboard!*, a well-researched and -illustrated chronicle of the building of the route through the Rockies.

Armstrong is fortunate in that his rail operation has little potential to blight the landscape or deplete natural resources. Those are common risks for most western-based tourism operators who deal even more directly with the environment. One such entrepreneur I originally considered for this chapter is Bob Wright, the Prairie-bred founder and CEO of the Oak Bay Marine Group of Victoria. The continent's major sports-fishing empire had been selling more than $50 million worth of expeditions to 40,000 fishermen a year while operating marinas, trailer parks, residential developments, and tourist attractions in British Columbia, the western United States, and the Bahamas. It all began to sour in 1996 when some species of the B.C. salmon that Wright was promising customers were declared so endangered that the federal government severely limited catches. Recreational anglers, mostly American, began cancelling their trips that year when a zero-retention policy affected chinook off the west coast of Vancouver Island and the Queen Charlotte Islands. In 1998 Ottawa banned fishing for coho salmon. This all left Oak Bay reeling. Wright had already earned the nickname "Mad Bob" for the unsubtle negotiating style he wielded to fight the commercial fishing industry and to take politicians to court. More recently he has been less vocal, appearing to let others speak for an industry that routinely earns the wrath of professional fishers and environmentalists alike.

Of course, the concerns for the havoc that tourists can wreak are not confined to western Canada, as Tourism Impresario Dennis Hurd of Atlantis Submarines knows well. Although based in Vancouver, he operates his undersea passenger vessels in several tropical countries— none along Canada's West Coast. When he moved into Hawaii in 1987, the Sierra Club and similar groups mounted a campaign protesting what they considered the company's Disneyfication of the sea bottom with artificial reefs. Atlantis quickly dropped its original idea to place concrete sharks and sea monsters underwater amid the scientifically designed metal structures and remnants of real ships and planes. And after much public protest it also backed away from its plan to lease a chunk of the ocean for its exclusive use. As it turned out, the artificial reefs built with the help of University of Hawaii researchers proved to be a benefit to sea life, and the Atlantis submarines have a much more benign impact on sensitive corals than scuba divers who can brush up against them and destroy centuries of growth in this vital fish habitat.

Both Hurd and Armstrong are typical of western enterpreneurs who are riding the wave of what's termed "soft-adventure" tourism—some of them, such as kayaking and whitewater-rafting operators, riding it quite literally. In his book *Voltaire's Bastards,* Canadian visionary John Ralston Saul points out with irony the "widespread and desperate need of people to experience unstructured excitement at almost any cost, providing it is organized and the responsibility is taken by the organizer. ... It is the logical child of the Club Meds, spas and package tours." It is also, as both Impresarios have realized, the growth area of a growing industry in this country that has become particularly pivotal in the economic health of the westernmost provinces.

Tourism is creating more jobs than anything else in Canada (the 6.5-percent expansion recorded in 1997 was the highest in a decade).

That is especially true in British Columbia, where the $8.5-billion-a-year sector is the province's leading job producer and is second only to forestry in overall economic contribution (across Canada, tourism ranks as the 12th-largest industry). The province has been outperforming the rest of the country in drawing American and overseas tourists, whose collective numbers climbed by 3.2 percent in the first six months of 1998. While Japanese visitors declined by 6.8 percent, our southern neighbours have increasingly been lured to British Columbia and the other western provinces by the low value of the Canadian dollar and the escalating number of trans-border flights resulting from the United States-Canada open-sky agreement. In British Columbia the Whistler sun-and-ski resort had a 50-percent increase in American visitors last summer, Victoria was predicting its first billion-dollar tourism year, and Vancouver was named the best international destination by the North American Travel Journalists Association.

Yet even Saskatchewan, which is not always perceived as a strong magnet for visitors, is more and more dependent on tourism. The province's fastest-growing sector is already the fourth-largest industry, generating well over $1 billion a year and employing 42,000-plus people. American sportsmen are lured there by the fact that Saskatchewan is the only place in Canada to allow the well-stocked hunting and fishing grounds of game farms. But ecotourism has a rising share of total spending, in particular the tours—by canoe, fish-boat, balloon-tired vehicle—to view the tens of millions of waterfowl that congregate every autumn on Saskatchewan's lakes, rivers, and sloughs on their way to winter nests. I would happily go back to the province and reexperience the thousands of sandhill cranes I watched in 1998 restaging on an island in the North Saskatchewan River, just minutes after I had enjoyed a good country-restaurant meal that ended with a tall saskatoon-berry pie.

The ruggedly handsome West is well positioned to profit from the coming flood of retiring American baby boomers who will wash through the world in the next dozen years, seeking enviromental beauty and soft adventure on their vacations. "Baby boomers value things that are natural, as opposed to synthetic or man-made," the Canadian Tourism Commission noted in a 1998 report. "If tourism is to capitalize on the boomer market, operators will need to pay attention to nature and the natural. ... Sophisticated baby boomers will have to be sold a unique experience as opposed to a product."

Which means whalewatching in northern Manitoba, walleye-fishing on Saskatchewan lakes, and whitewater rafting on Alberta rivers—not to mention luxury train journeys through British Columbia's wild mountains and safe submarine dives in warm waters around the world.

Chapter Five

Mr. Submarine

Dennis Hurd, Atlantis Submarines

The small white submarine gleams under the glaring Hawaiian sun as it perches less than a kilometre out on the calm sea. Waves of ultramarine dissolve into hues of jade as they approach the palm-rimmed Kona coast of the Big Island. The crew of three on the deck are in blue shorts and open-necked, short-sleeved white shirts with gold epaulets that suggest they are sailors in some tropical nation's laid-back navy. Thirty-two of us passengers, mostly young and middle-aged couples, clamber down the ladders in two hatches to find ourselves in a long cigar of a cabin. But this is no *Das Boot.* Soothing Muzak with a reedy, Asian-sounding score floats in the air-conditioned, pressure-controlled atmosphere. Forty-eight moulded bench seats, back to back, position us in front of big circular viewports for maximum viewing. The bow is a domed acrylic window, which offers the moustached pilot his own 360-degree panorama of the Pacific's crystalline waters, clear as far as 36 metres. "Permission to proceed with this dive," he says dramatically over the loudspeaker.

"Now dive! Now dive!" a disembodied voice commands from the surface.

As ballast tanks fill with seawater, vertical thrusters powered by batteries slowly submerge the sub. Instantly we are swarmed by fat black surgeonfish and a school of curious, frying pan-sized bluestripe snapper. Peering in at us, lured by the promise of puppy chow trickling from external tubes, the fish follow the vessel as it proceeds at a stately one knot or less. We are soon amid stony coral reefs formed on beds of lava that flowed into the sea 18,000 years ago. Here, at about 21 metres, a cleaning wrasse is tidying up a sleek unicornfish.

"Something's got the fish on the portside spooked," notes one of two narrators, a copilot stationed at the stern (the other attendant is quietly translating for the lone Japanese couple aboard). "You might see a bluefin trevally lurking about."

We do, and over the next 45 minutes the young man disgorges a fountain of other facts, such as an adult parrotfish's annual production of half a tonne of the white sand that made Hawaii famous. In a 22-page personal dive log, we record sightings of sea urchins, black durgon, and the longnose butterflyfish that Hawaiians call *lau-wiliwili-nukunuku-oioi*. We don't see the rare whale shark, like the one that a sister sub found filling its deck as it surfaced off Waikiki and had to resubmerge to free. Eventually our vessel descends to 47 metres, where shy garden eels poke their heads out of the sand. Now the pilot releases compressed air to mark the sub's location for the passenger tender always patrolling above. As we surface, surrounded by fish, sunlight shears through silvery bouquets of bubbles. "That was fantastic!" a man from Alabama drawls.

For $69 U.S., we have gone where scuba divers go, seen the underwater wonders they see, and had a dry-skin, no-sweat experience that at least simulates theirs. Throughout we have been comforted by the knowledge that, if power failed, the buoyancy of the sub would propel it automatically to the surface and, if it somehow got snared below (as one of these Hawaiian subs has, with no passengers aboard), the emergency air supplies would last at least 24 hours. This is what travel officials call soft adventure, mixed in with a little ecotourism, and a privately held Vancouver company has made an industry out of it: manufacturing the vessels and operating them on its own and with partners and franchisees in ten international warm-weather resort locations.

Tourist subs are one of those terrific ideas that seem so obvious in hindsight, and if Atlantis Submarines didn't create the concept, it has built the largest fleet of them—14 subs and two deep-diving submersibles—along with the only successful business of its kind in the world.* Since 1985 it has sent more than six million passengers on

---

* Other companies in other countries have tried and mostly failed in building and operating tourist submarines. The Finns got into the business in 1986, but ceased operations three years later. Mitsubishi, which wanted to joint-venture with Atlantis, ended up building two subs based on the Finnish model and continues to run them in Japan, reportedly with little success. France's Comex and Switzerland's Sulzer began building passenger subs in the early 1990s and have since sold them off. Even a Russian military design group, Rubin Central, built one, which attempted unsuccessfully to operate in Antigua. At last report, other small individual sub businesses are running in the Bahamas, Canary Islands, Egypt, Spain, Taiwan, Italy, Israel, South Korea, Taiwan, and the islands of Bali and Saipan. Only the operations in Korea and Mallorca, Spain, are said to be more than marginal. In Vancouver, Atlantis often gets mistaken for the local operations of Phil Nuytten, who over

220,000-plus dives, generating annual revenues of about $30 million in the past three years and modest 1997 net earnings of $2.26 million. Along the way, it has become the largest single tourist-attractions operator throughout the Caribbean, where net profits rose by 82 percent in 1997, and in the Hawaiian islands, where it is imaginatively weathering the tourist downturn by managing and marketing other major attractions.

The unassuming admiral of Atlantis Submarines (International Holdings) Inc. is Dennis Hurd, a technocrat-turned-entrepreneur, a professional engineer who engineered the financing, design, manufacturing, and operation of these passenger subs without having to go public. He is the founder, president, and largest shareholder. With his unkempt lava-black hair, salt-and-pepper moustache, dark eyes slitted from sun-struck seas, and a penchant for wearing rough wool sweaters around the office, the compactly built, 56-year-old Hurd looks more like the sailor and submarine operator he was than the executive he has become. Yet he has the business credentials to carry off the role. A thesis short of his M.B.A. from the University of British Columbia, he went to work for the Federal Industrial Development Bank in Vancouver for four years as an assessor of cash-shy companies seeking loans from the Crown corporation. The wannabe entrepreneur and a partner later launched their own company to inspect oil pipelines and platforms in the Gulf of Mexico. They used innovative deep-sea mini-submersibles developed by International Hydrodynamics, where they had worked before that Vancouver pioneer of the sub-sea industry folded.

It was there, in the gulf waters off Texas—seeing the excitement of executives he would take down for a ride—that Hurd had the idea of building and operating passenger submarines. He began planning the prototype in 1983, and within two years *Atlantis I* was entertaining

---

30 years has been designing underwater devices, including his recent Newtsub Deep-Worker 2000 personal sub for scientific, military, and commercial uses, and the Newtsuit, a deep-sea diving suit with its own atmosphere being used by the Canadian and U.S. navies, among others. In 1997 Nuytten lost his public company, Hard Suits, in a $16.5-million hostile takeover by American Oilfield Divers Inc. of Louisiana; he has since started another company, Nuytco Research Ltd. He is involved in a joint venture with a Seattle adventure-travel company, which sometime in 1999 hopes to take passengers down in two- and three-person submersibles to view the perfectly preserved wreck of HMS *Breadalbane*, which sank in the Canadian Arctic in 1853 while seeking survivors of the Northwest Passage expedition of Sir John Franklin. The passengers will actually learn to pilot the subs and take the controls during the $10,000 expedition beneath the ice.

151

tourists off the Cayman Islands, British West Indies. By the end of the 1980s he boasted more subs in his fleet than the Canadian navy had in theirs—well, that totalled only five—including the first in American waters, off Kona. He earned a Canadian Award for Business Excellence, and in 1992 *Profit* magazine named him one of the top-ten Canadian entrepreneurs of the past decade.

Which is not to say that Hurd's helmsmanship has always been dead on course and his voyage as smooth as the lagoons along the Kona coast. In 1996 Atlantis closed its mismanaged joint venture in the Bahamas, where it was a 50-percent partner, after only three years. Its four-year-old operation in Cancun continues to lose so much money that the company and its 60-percent Mexican partners have considered shutting it down. And the manufacturing of its 15th sub, destined for Malaysia in 1998, halted in midstream when the local partners pulled out of the deal because of the Asian economic flu.

Even Hawaii, where five subs operate off Kona, the island of Maui, and Honolulu's Waikiki Beach, has become a troubled paradise for Atlantis. "Hawaii is our most important operation because it provides the most revenue," Hurd points out, furrowing his well-lined brow. "We're 25-percent owner, but there's also a licence fee, so our cash position is substantially higher than 50 percent." As Asians, especially the Japanese, retrench financially and reduce their travel spending, the state has become a relative basket case. Tourism generates a quarter of Hawaii's tax revenues and gross product and a third of its employment—and in 1997 alone Japanese tourists spent $800 million less on the islands. For Atlantis Hawaii, that translated into $523,000, a 22-percent drop in net earnings.

Staining the financial picture further in the past four years has been the emergence of the company's only competitor anywhere, an established Japanese-Hawaiian ground-transportation operator that seems determined to keep losing money by selling rides in two subs off Waikiki at half the Atlantis price. But the most emotionally—as opposed to economically—upsetting problem arose from the scuba-diving operations that once supplemented Atlantis Hawaii's submarine tours. Several of its own divers, entertaining passengers with fish-feeding shows, have been injured and some have sued the company. And a business that it bought to take Honolulu tourists out to scuba-dive has faced the most humiliating and horrifying setback any underwater operator could encounter: causing the death of a customer at sea.*

Hawaii has always been a different kind of deal for Dennis Hurd, his staff, and his corporate directors. Certainly it is an obvious place to do business. As well as a popular holiday destination for Japanese and other Asians, it is the third-most-visited state for Americans, after Florida and California. Atlantis began operating there in a joint venture in 1988, following an unexpected two years of battling with environmentalists and confronting a U.S. federal law that forced it to find American partners. Even after the submarine began diving off Kona, there were other problems, if somewhat more minor and amusing. One day during the first two months, after the sub had submerged, a male passenger unzipped his fly, and in an amazingly athletic manoeuvre, began performing an act of autoeroticism. The attendants had to forcibly remove the man from the vessel. Later on the odd female passenger would flash Atlantis divers feeding the fish around the sub, briefly pulling down her top and exposing her breasts.

Atlantis Hawaii had these dive shows for eight years. When I visited the Honolulu office in the spring of 1998, I met a young blond employee with one foot bandaged in preparation for an operation the next day. A company diver, she had suffered the bends and her crippled foot was a legacy of her accident. Diving had proved to be more dangerous than operating a sub because there were too many individuals making too many individual, unsupervised decisions and taking too many chances underwater. Feeding moray eels with fish guts on long broomsticks led to one diver's being bitten in the armpit. When feedings near the ocean bottom caused the eels to become aggressive, the divers moved the show nearer the surface—and still the fish attacked.

---

*To be fair, Atlantis's submarine crews have often rescued swimmers and others who find themselves in trouble in the sea, and in 1995 the Barbadian staff saved the lives of a pilot and 11 passengers on an Air Mustique flight that crashed at night in the open ocean 32 kilometres off the coast of Barbados. When others couldn't locate the victims, Atlantis employees—relying on their knowledge of the area and calculating ocean drift to estimate the probable position of the survivors three hours after the accident—raced their passenger boat to the scene, cut the engines, and listened in the silence until they heard the pilot's calls. All but one passenger survived.

Other big fish called ulua would circle divers and charge and bite if attracted by waving arms. A 1.8-metre barracuda seriously injured one diver's hand. Meanwhile other divers got bad cases of the bends, caused by too-rapid compression of air as they surfaced.

Not only did the company have its own divers to worry about, it was running a business called Atlantis Reef Divers, which took neophyte and often unfit as well as experienced and healthy scuba-diving tourists off Waikiki Beach. In the summer of 1996, one customer died of a heart attack while diving. Then about a month later, a 24-year-old woman visiting from Japan was left behind in 10.6 metres of water during an introductory scuba tour when the Atlantis dive boat returned hurriedly to shore. Her sister tried frantically to communicate her disappearance to the boat crew, none of whom could speak Japanese. Only when they landed did a Japanese-speaking employee translate the sister's horrific message. By the time another boat found the diver, she was dead.* The irony is that Reef Divers had lost half a million dollars in six months, and Atlantis Hawaii CEO Darrell Metzger was about to pull the plug on the business the day after Labour Day. "We left somebody behind out there—what are you going to say?" he asks rhetorically now. The resulting lawsuit was resolved in less-litigious Japan; Metzger says the company got off lightly.

Don't cling to what looks like a bad idea just because you were once in love with it

No customer of the Atlantis submarine operation has ever died or been seriously injured because of the company's negligence. However, a Japanese diver's death was front-page news in Hawaii for weeks, tarnishing the good corporate name that

---

* Reporting on the death, the *Honolulu Advertiser* wrote: "Several customers on the dive said they couldn't understand [the instructor's] attempts at Japanese. One said it was 'incoherent.' The boat's captain ... told the Coast Guard his schedule was 'fast and furious,' with a short turnaround time between dive groups. The *Hilton Rainbow I* was running ten minutes behind schedule. During the boat's return it was learned that [the woman] was missing, but nobody knows what happened to her just before she died. Follow-up tests showed her equipment was in working order. The Medical Examiner's office determined only that she drowned."

Darrell Metzger had been effectively burnishing since he had joined the company in 1995. He had already stopped the dive shows accompanying the submarine tours because of the danger to the professional divers, not to mention the lawsuits they were launching against the company. So why hadn't Atlantis Hawaii got out of the dive business long before when signals of a potentially dangerous operation kept arising? One reason might be that scuba-diving is the second-most-popular tourist activity in Hawaii, after attending luaus. Dennis Hurd admits that problems started to surface early on, but "in the Caymans or Barbados we haven't had any diving accidents from the shows. [Before the troubled Atlantis Bahamas location shut down, it featured—perhaps a little desperately—divers in chain-mail suits hand-feeding reef sharks.] In Hawaii I don't know why we have all those kinds of accidents." He continues to speak wistfully of the idea of the dramatic feeding displays, especially Kona's: "It's such a shame because that was such a great show." Yet sometimes abandoning one long-loved idea yields a better one. An irony of the show's demise is that the dive tours are now probably more educational than sheer showbiz. In the words of Kona operations manager Doug MacIlroy, who is passionate about his love of the underwater world: "It's meant that in order to maintain the same level of entertainment, copilots have to be more focused and articulate and attuned to their audience."

Like most extraordinary entrepreneurs, Dennis Hurd has always been able to fall in love with a concept and pursue it with a quiet passion—in spite of perceived problems and outright skepticism. Born in land-locked Timmins, Ontario, he spent his teenage years living along the Indian Ocean. He moved to Port Elizabeth, South Africa, with his parents and four siblings when his civil-engineer father, Roy, became assistant to the managing director of Ford of South Africa. That was where Dennis first became enamoured of the sea. "The standard procedure on a Saturday would be to get their bicycles and their spearfishers and go down the coast," Roy Hurd remembers of his son and his many friends. Dennis says: "We would go after school, every weekend, every chance we got. We were probably much more heavily involved in things

like open-ocean skindiving and spearfishing than most people."
Returning on his own to Ontario at 18, he echoed his father by taking
civil and structural engineering at Queen's University in Kingston. He
had planned on studying ocean engineering at graduate school. Taking
a breather, he settled in the sailing nirvana of Vancouver and worked
for Public Works Canada designing docks and breakwaters. With his
business genes now clicking in, he completed most of his first year of
an M.B.A. at the University of British Columbia, majoring in finance
and operations research. His studies got interrupted again as he and a
couple of Queen's buddies bought a rundown 20-tonne, 18.2-metre
working schooner to sail from Nova Scotia to the Caribbean. "I was the
only sailor and I wasn't very good," Hurd confesses. "We pretty near
sunk it a couple of times." They spent 18 indulgent months sailing and
working in the Bahamas, where he wound up surveying and supervising a subdivision project. At the time, though, he never considered taking any tourists out on the boat as a business.

Back in Vancouver, he made a couple of halfhearted attempts to finish his M.B.A. thesis. "I never felt any driving need to have the degree.
Long-term, I never wanted to join a big corporation where that would be
essential. I wanted to start my own company." He and a friend spent a
few months pursuing the possibility of starting a systems data-processing
service, but the concept was too new for most local businesses. Instead,
he went to work for the Industrial Development Bank, becoming a specialist in assessing the health and prospects of small industrial concerns,
large hotels, real-estate developments, and marine businesses looking for
federal loans. He interviewed presidents, marketing people, accountants,
even customers. Over four years, working for what was often a bank of
last resort resulted in a remarkable paid education for a budding entrepreneur. Hurd came to realize the truth, among many others, that not
everyone who starts a company is necessarily the right person to manage
it long-term. "Maybe they'd done all the marketing themselves, for
example, and obviously couldn't continue to do that but didn't recognize
it," he says now. "Or in their accounting systems, their CFO—who used
to be a bookkeeper—just wouldn't be able to make it happen. Could they
really grow with the business?"

There was another, seemingly straightforward truth for embryonic
entrepreneurs that he came to understand—one that within a few years
would resonate in his own business.

Don't underestimate the start-up capital your business needs—and, once launched, always keep careful track of your cash position

Larry Ginsberg, the Canadian co-author of *Small Business, Big Money*, urges new businesses to have at least a basic financial plan that outlines the following year month by month. "Once you create this road map, you should be able to anticipate any potential financial problems early enough to find a solution. Many businesses fail because they simply run out of cash." Dennis Hurd agrees, based on his experience with the Industrial Development Bank and, later, Atlantis: "It's all to do with being awfully careful about not running out of cash. Some of the outfits we visited [for the federal bank] were start-ups. Underestimating your start-up capital required is probably a classic. I think everybody does it. We did it. ... When you're going in, you're reluctant to put in too big a contingency— 'why raise a whole bunch more money than I need?' We managed to get interest-free repayable loans from the [federal] government. But our timing assumed they'd distribute that money to us at certain times and they didn't. So that was actually a big problem. In the nick of time, the government distributed it. But it was a scary thing—suddenly, you're completely out of control. ... It's a crucial lesson. You must be damn aware of what your cash position is. And for people who turn over a lot of cash, like some manufacturers, if they lose control of their financial affairs they can one day wake up and realize that suddenly their receivables aren't coming in. If guys who owe you money find out that you have problems, they hold back. And if the guys you owe money to find out you've got problems, they're all over you, right in your face, trying to get what they can out of you. So it snowballs."

One of IDB's clients, for whom Hurd did some consulting, was International Hydrodynamics of Vancouver. It was the world leader in deep-sea manned submersibles, which could tend North Sea oil rigs to depths of 2,000 metres. I first encountered Hyco, as it was popularly known, after its mini-sub *Pisces III* was trapped on the floor of the Atlantic Ocean off Ireland in 1973. Writing the dramatic story for *The Canadian* magazine of the three-day rescue operation to save her pair of pilots, I interviewed two of the trio of divers who had founded the company a decade earlier. Hyco, technically strong, managerially deficient—and cash-short—had recently taken on new majority partners: Peninsular and Oriental Steam Navigation Company, Britain's fabled P&O. And not long after the rescue, it hired Hurd away from IDB to run its *Taurus* submersible program, designed to send a mini-sub in place of a tethered bell to position workers underwater around deepsea oil rigs. When the petroleum industry rejected that concept, he went to Texas to run Hyco's submarine servicing of oil rigs in the Gulf of Mexico. As the company began to come apart, despite P&O's backing and many millions in federal loans, Hurd returned to Vancouver.

Teaming up with Allan Trice—the Hyco cofounder who had emerged as the hero of the deep-sea sub rescue—he made a bid for a lucrative drill-ship-servicing contract Hyco had been fulfilling before it went belly up. Roy Hurd, now back in Ontario and co-owner of a successful foundry, worked with his son on the offer to the receivers, but an American company got the contract. So Dennis Hurd and another partner formed Offshore Engineering Corporation and resurfaced in the Gulf of Mexico to revive the oil-industry submersible business. When that profitable venture began flattening out in the third year, they regrouped in Vancouver.

It was 1983 and Hurd felt the time was now or never to get serious about the idea that had long been simmering on the entrepreneurial side of his brain. He kept recalling the fact that, during his first stint diving in the gulf, the oil-industry honchos he had chauffeured under the sea were dazzled by the experience. In the quiet winter of 1977, he had even started exploring the prospect of turning small subs into tour boats in the temperate seas of the Bahamas. But soon realizing that he needed a vessel that would seat more than the three that Hyco submersibles held, he put the concept into dry dock.

It wasn't a new idea. The first tourist submarine was built for the 1964 Swiss National Exhibition, taking 32,000 passengers, 40 at a time, to the bottom of Geneva's Lake Leman. When a plan to use the sub for passengers in the United States ran aground on American marine regulations, it was converted to a commercial vessel. Meanwhile, in 1983, Vancouver marine archaeologist Robyn Woodward (daughter of the local department-store and ranching Woodwards) and her husband, Phillip Janca, began taking scientists and visitors down to explore the Cayman Wall off Grand Cayman at up to $300 U.S. a trip. They had bought a couple of the same three-person Hyco research submersibles that Hurd had already rejected as uneconomic.

While still involved in Ocean Engineering, Hurd and his partners— now including Al Trice—went to see the organizers of Vancouver's Expo 86 about doing submersible tours in False Creek during the world's fair on transportation. "It was really a bit of a lark," Hurd told me, especially since he had to admit that "you're not going to see bugger all underwater." Expo officials were interested, but again the figures didn't add up using small subs. Ocean Engineering's principals amicably went their separate ways, taking their shares of the respectable profits, with Dennis Hurd determined to chase his vision of larger, cost-effective tourist submarines.

Cleverly he commissioned an artist to paint a colour illustration of a stubby submarine with four large viewports and a fishlike fluke on each side—far from the sleek final version he would eventually build. But it gave substance to his dream, and he began walking it around to travel agents and tourism officials, including cruise-ship people in Miami, government and travel agents in the Caymans, and the Bahamian tourist office in Toronto. Most were as excited about the proposal as the oilmen had been. "So I thought there were worse things to take a bit of a risk on," he says in his laconic style.

But would anybody else agree? He had $80,000 in savings from his previous business. By now he was married (to Susan, a physiotherapist from England) and had two of the four children they would raise; there was no thought of mortgaging his house in Vancouver—"I don't think I ever would."* He could try the banks, but based on his own experience with the IDB, he felt they would take one look at his cockamamie idea

---

*After a brief article I wrote about Atlantis appeared in *BC Business*, Susan Hurd called to say that I hadn't caught some of her husband's strongest characteristics: "He's an incredible family man—so devoted to the kids. ... [Within the company] he seems to generate a huge amount of loyalty—everybody's incredibly devoted to him. ... His integrity is incredible. When he went into Mexico, where you have to buy people off, he refused to buy into that. ... But he's the worst procrastinator that I know—the main lights in our kitchen don't work. He says, 'We'll work something out.' Dennis is absolutely brilliant—especially at home—at delegating things. For instance, he gave Darrell [Metzger] in Hawaii total freedom to do what he thought best."

and laugh him out of their offices. He was less than thrilled about the thought of going on the volatile Vancouver Stock Exchange. That left one other avenue, which translates into a piece of advice from the Hurd entrepreneurial canon.

Don't be too proud to approach friends and family for early financing

"You hate losing their money," Dennis Hurd acknowledges in discussing how he approached his family for start-up investments. But he believes that if you candidly warn those close to you— "Look, this is a superhigh risk"—then they should be offered the chance to invest. Because if they are not and the idea works, he says they could come back on you: "Why the hell wasn't I offered some of this?" They should, however, be investing money they can afford to lose: "I want to invite you into this opportunity, but you could lose all of it in a nanosecond." His father recalls his son's initial hesitance to approach the family and his admonition that "what you're getting into is a gamble. It isn't a sure thing." However, "the family wanted to get involved and I guess we didn't listen to him. It was exciting and we had confidence in him." In fact, as well as Roy Hurd, Dennis's sister and two of his three brothers became early, substantial investors. The youngest, who owned a metal-stamping business, held back; his father quotes him as saying: "Dad, I don't think he'll succeed. But I've set aside 500,000 bucks if he ever needs it." As Roy Hurd says, "He never did go in. Dennis never did need it."

Roy Hurd had a partner in his foundry, Peter Kenny, another professional engineer who was a risk taker. Kenny would eventually invest even more than the $250,000 the senior Hurd did as they became the second- and third-largest shareholders after Dennis Hurd and continue as active corporate directors today.* Another early investor was an

---

*Lawyer and corporate secretary George Pellatt and Lucille Johnstone are also Atlantis directors. Johnstone began as a secretary/dispatcher with Vancouver's Rivtow Straits and built it over three decades into a tugboat-based conglomerate; after retiring, she served as vice chair in the privatizing and expansion of Vancouver International Airport. Other investors include three Canadian institutions: Crown Life, Metropolitan Life, and Lincluden Management.

Australian, Barry Bellchambers, who had once shared a house with Dennis and other bachelor friends in North Vancouver. Now he was living in Whitehorse, developing Yukon housing, hotels, and trailer parks, running a real-estate company, and getting involved in northern diamond-drilling ventures. Roy Hurd, who would come to know him well, describes Bellchambers as the quintessential entrepreneur: "He's been in and out of more bloody businesses. He makes some money and then he gets bored stiff."

Dennis Hurd christened his company Sub Aquatics Development Corporation and began gathering a part-time crew of consultants around him. Among them were engineers John Witney from Hyco and Tom Roberts from Ocean Engineering, along with a structural design specialist. (Today, among many long-term employees, Witney is general manager of engineering and production, while Roberts is manager of electrical engineering.) They planned a 28-passenger submarine, powered with lead acid storage batteries, with a fibreglass deck and superstructure around a steel pressure hull; 64.7-centimetre-round viewports of 8.2-centimetre-acrylic; and—most important—all the essential electrical, hydraulic, and pressure systems, closed-circuit life support, and motor and ballast controls duplicated for utmost safety. (It had a conning tower, but no periscope and not even a single toilet.) In the first year, Hurd raised $387,000, largely on the basis of his illustration, a plywood mock-up, and the sheer confidence he exuded to investors about his mastery of the technical details.*

Much of the funding during the first three years came in under the federal Scientific Tax Research Credit scheme, which gave investors a 50-percent tax break. (Sub Aquatics may have been one of the few genuine investments under that much-abused program.) By December 1984, Hurd had attracted another $825,000 in capital, largely to handle design costs. He went to the American Bureau of Shipping to seek

---

*James Miller, a physiology professor who was running Quadra Logics Technologies at the time (see page 319), was approached to be an investor in Dennis Hurd's new company and recalls an even less tangible mock-up. Hurd, he says, "had a cardboard replica of the submarine and would walk you into this thing—and that was his dog-and-pony show downtown to the investor group. You had to imagine you were sitting in one of these things looking out through little portholes. It's like right off in another planet. 'Dennis, this is not going to fly,' [I said]. First of all, he had no background or knowledge in marketing. But the guy just had the guts to go for it. Come hell or high water—that's Dennis's approach to doing it. People lined up to give him money."

assurances that this world authority on marine classification would approve the design plans, monitor construction, and ultimately certify the innovative prototype as seaworthy. That prospect in hand, he then approached Lloyd's of London for a comprehensive-insurance program that would cover passengers. Lloyd's underwriters agreed, placing the tourist sub in the same exotic and expensive classification as space shots.

Within six months, Hurd had another $1.25 million to cover construction. Roy Hurd and his partner had rounded up risk-oriented friends in the northern Ontario mining community, while Bellchambers was introducing Dennis to Yukon investors. One of them was a young lawyer named George Asquith, working for the past decade in former MP Erik Nielsen's firm. Meeting Hurd at lunch in Whitehorse, Asquith was mightily impressed: "Dennis didn't have any doubt whatsoever that he could build this vehicle and that it would operate and that it would be safe and client-friendly and environmentally sound—*that it would work*. That wasn't even an issue for him. He had also done the due diligence on all the regulatory things already, which was impressive to me as a lawyer because normally that's what entrepreneurs forget about." Asquith liked the idea that not only would the company be building the tourist subs but also operating them in high-volume, hot-weather tourist areas, where cruise-ship passengers congregate. He quickly bought $50,000 worth of stock and, after visiting Vancouver to see the sub under construction, invested as much again.

At first Hurd had felt less than confident about the specialized field of marketing. "I never doubted that it would be well received in the marketplace," Asquith says. "But Dennis's area of not feeling competent to make a judgement was in how many people can we get to ride on these things and what will they pay? And he had gone out and got a university professor to use his students to do all this research and obviously spent a lot of time coming to terms to understand it." Hurd's brainstorm was one that other entrepreneurs might well emulate. "We recognized that this thing was so unusual," he recollects, "and if we're going to raise some serious money for it, we better have a serious market study." How to get one done without spending a small fortune? He approached Ken Kendall, then a professor of marketing in graduate studies at Simon Fraser University, who—like a lot of academics—was looking for interesting real-life projects for his grad students. He assigned four of them ("Kenny's Angels," Hurd called them) to do 550 personal interviews, asking respondents whether they would ride a tourist submarine and what they would be willing to pay. The results were credible and encouraging: after eliminating all those disinterested or afraid of water, about 30 percent said they loved the idea and perhaps half of those would absolutely take the tour at a higher-end price. "That validated the operating projections," Hurd says. The SFU fee was negligible. "Normally we would have had a $30,000 bill. The deal was we give them a thousand bucks and they send their students in."

Construction proceeded throughout 1985 on *Atlantis I*—named by an employee's wife for the lost island of Greek legend, which then became a more melodious name for the whole company than Sub Aquatics. A large, dilapidated building along the False Creek waterfront was the assembly point for the sub. Hurd had farmed out the manufacturing to local businesses: a maker of pressure vessels and boilers did the steel hull; a fabricator of fibreglass car parts fashioned a 15-metre-long, $60,000 faring, the skin for a hull it had never seen. Technician Doug Fry remembers that when the faring didn't fit the hull, "we started with little strokes of a file and wound up with big swacks coming off with a power saw." Anyone who was interested could help out, night and day. Peter Kenny's son, David, worked on the sub, as did Dr. Bill Keen, a Vancouver radiologist and investor, and the visiting George Asquith.

"I can remember putting the bumper on one night," says Fry, reliving it years later in an open-air restaurant in Honolulu, where he now works as a maintenance and quality-assurance manager for Atlantis Hawaii.* "George and I were the only two there. It was like wrestling a giant anaconda—one length of it probably weighed a couple of hundred pounds—and we were on top of ladders 12 feet off the ground."

---

*Doug Fry is typical of many Atlantis employees in the interesting background he brings to his work: he competed in and taught ice-dancing in Canada for years and even coached the National Hockey League's Vancouver Canucks in power-skating one summer. What helped land him his job with the submarine company, along with his electrical-engineering training, was the fact that as a young man he had built kayaks and a six-person hovercraft in his backyard in Oliver, British Columbia. Another Hawaiian employee, Doug MacIlroy, served for six years on a U.S. Navy nuclear submarine and co-authored an unpublished novel that revolves around such a sub and the survivors of a global thermonuclear holocaust.

The factory, perhaps a century old, was a miserable place to work. Hurd reminisces: "It leaks and there's no heat and it was winter and everybody's down there—I mean, everybody—day in, day out, and health's starting to fade, colds and stuff, and this friend of mine was in a vitamin-wholesaling business. He came down with big boxes filled with all manner of vitamins. Then we collected everybody and he gave a lecture on what sorts to take. We laid all the boxes out. Funnily enough, I'm not sure that that didn't help."

Hurd had long since decided that the first Atlantis location would be the Cayman Islands, a British dependency of 33,000 people 720 kilometres south of Florida. A global tax shelter, the islands are also a tourist hot spot. One of the submarine pilots that Atlantis recruited— most of them commercial divers it then trained—was Mark Almaraz, now an operations manager in Hawaii. He worked in the Caymans for a year: "Besides the government, it had everything—the water was flat and clear, the visibility was 100 feet, and there were a large number of American visitors and three to five cruise ships in the harbour at any one time." But there *was* the government. Hurd's father and an enthusiastic Barry Bellchambers did the diplomatic work there, on and off for two frustrating years. "We were neophytes when it came to dealing with the Caribbean government," Roy Hurd says. "We spent interminable weeks waiting for permits." Bellchambers would hang out Saturday nights at a pub the port captain frequented in George Town, the Cayman's capital, and Hurd found himself going to church with his surprised wife Sunday mornings in hope of meeting the head of a crucial committee. Both of them called Dennis Hurd at different times to tell him he should find another location. Pressing the issue, he shipped the almost-completed sub to the Caymans before the government had granted approval to base the vessel there and allow foreigners to operate it. The sub went across North America in a massive truck trailer originally designed to carry MX cruise missiles, and then by ship to George Town—at a total cost of about $100,000. (Much later, when the company decided to exchange a 30-passenger submarine in Barbados with a 48-passenger one in St. Thomas, the swap would cost $519,000.)

Once the sub was in place—at a dock Atlantis built near the cruise-ship berths in George Town—the government relented and the tourist board started promoting this unusual new attraction. It probably didn't hurt that the company's lawyer was William Walker, O.B.E., an architect of the Caymans' offshore financial structure, and that one of the sub pilots—who has since become the Cayman location's manager—was the son of the minister of finance. For all that, business was slow to build. Location, location, location: the ticket office was in an old house a two-minute walk from the waterfront, too far from tourists. "So we rent this tent from Florida," Hurd says, "and put that on a parking lot, and storms come and blow the whole thing down—really Mickey Mouse. We put some cash registers in. We weren't set up for credit cards. We were just totally disorganized." And the problem remained: not enough people were buying tickets, especially the cruise passengers. What no one at Atlantis had realized soon enough was that the people on the luxury liners usually buy their shore excursions before they disembark, and the cruise companies can take six months to approve an excursion they will agree to sell onboard. Doug Fry says: "John Witney was our chief engineer and he took it upon himself to take a handful of flyers we printed up and went down to the cruise-ship dock and started handing them out. And he was nearly arrested. First of all, it was a customs area … " Bitter experiences can teach useful lessons.

Make the marketing of your product or service a priority in the planning stages of a start-up— not an afterthought

"We were all so excited and thought everybody else was so excited that once we put the sub in the water, people would just line up," Doug Fry says. And then there was the corporate belief that whatever marketing had to be done could be handled by the existing staff or nonspecialists. Dennis Hurd says: "I used to market [commercial] submarine services, Barry's sold everything under the sun. There was a girl up in Whitehorse who came to the Caymans as a marketing manager. She was also a very minor investor. But that was stupid of us because she never marketed a tourism product in her life— and none of us had, either. … I guess we should have brought in an expert tourism person. We should have had a better—*a* marketing— budget. I don't mean to sound overly critical of us, but there were a bunch of things we didn't do right. We were really getting into a business we didn't understand and we didn't pay enough attention to say we're missing this expertise. I think if we tried hard enough we could have found somebody on some basis who'd had a good background in tourism marketing. It would have saved us a lot of hassle."

Atlantis did do some things right. It offered hotels and travel agencies free familiarization dives in the sub. Then it argued the agents down from a 45-percent commission to 15 percent by suggesting they take that amount as a down payment from each passenger, who would pay Atlantis the rest when they took the tour. Having the commission in hand, up front—rather than waiting for it to be reimbursed by the attraction operator—was a new idea for the local industry. Eventually the Cayman operation would begin to make money and in 1992 grow with the replacement of *Atlantis I* with a 46-passenger submarine and the addition of the two deep-diving submersibles that Robyn Woodward and her husband had operated there.*

Hurd and his managers were learning from their early entrepreneurial errors. Within a year of the Cayman launch, they would have first-rate marketing and public-relations people in place, both of them graduates of Expo 86. Deciding to have a presence at the fair, after all, the company raised another $2.1 million to hurriedly build *Atlantis II*, another 28-passenger sub, to market to the 22 million visitors from around the world. At Expo's end, the vessel began diving off the coast of Barbados. During the fair, Hurd had got to know Fred Lounsberry,

---

*What do you see at 300 metres that you don't at 30? As Robyn Woodward once reported in *The Financial Post*, the highly manoeuvrable small submersible takes you to "myriad deep-water species of black corals, madracis and madrepora fan corals resembling shrubs and flowers. … Delicate sea whips, dainty dandelion corals and vibrant orange sea fans stand out against the barren lunar landscapes of the deep." And there is a completely intact wreck of the 54.8-metre-long freighter *Kirk Pride* that an Atlantis pilot discovered in 1986. This was once called one of the three best tourist sub dives in the world. ("The price: $275 per person. It's worth every penny," said American consultant L. Bruce Jones of U.S. Submarines, Inc.) The others were in Martinique (since discontinued) and in Port Lucaya, Bahamas, where the world's only large acrylic tourist sub takes 44 passengers to rich marine settings they view through a transparent acrylic plastic hull.

a senior marketing executive selling the event in the United States Lounsberry (later the executive vice president of Universal Studios) took over marketing for Atlantis and quickly raised its profile in the travel industry. He hired another Expo grad as a consultant, Mike Leone, who still does the company's sophisticated PR and promotion out of Irvine, California. Major magazines, including *Time* and *National Geographic*, and TV shows such as *Good Morning America*, began featuring Atlantis.

Emboldened, the company built its first 46-passenger vessel, a third longer than the 15-metre prototype, and located her in 1988 at St. Thomas in the U.S. Virgin Islands, where more cruise ships called in at that time than anywhere else in the world. Meanwhile Atlantis was building another 46-seater, this one destined for somewhere in Hawaii. Exactly *where* became the problem of George Asquith, who had grown so fascinated with the company that he left his Yukon law partnership and joined Atlantis in 1986 to act as general counsel and handle corporate development. He was immediately immersed in getting regulatory approvals for the Hawaiian project. It proved to be even more of a bad trip than the Caymans had been and underlined the fact that, at this point, the company had still not fully learned its lesson about effective communications.

Settling in Honolulu, Asquith consulted with an enviromental expert and a state politician who was chairman of the Marine and Ocean Science Section of the House of Representatives. Asquith is a personable character, with pleasantly plump cheeks and small round glasses that give him a friendly appearance, and a quick intelligence that he expresses in a deep, confidence-building voice. But he got off on the wrong tack by agreeing with his advisers that Atlantis would be the first company to apply under an Ocean Leasing Act for exclusive use of 13 kilometres of the sea off Honolulu and the water corridor above it. He had already used sophisticated videos and informative speeches to woo state legislators, who passed resolutions supporting the request for the ocean lease. But the Sierra Club, among others, felt the legislation was designed to encourage ocean-mining and saw Atlantis as a precedent. Environmentalists had another concern: the company's decision to create a $1-million-plus artificial reef. Because the waters just off Waikiki Beach have virtually no natural coral reefs to attract fish, Atlantis began working with the University of Hawaii and the state government to build a fish habitat from sunken ships, airplanes, and concrete and metal structures. As laudable as the project was, supported by academics, the very word *artificial* raised flags, with protestors calling it a "garish, underwater Disneyland"—inspired by the original plan to place concrete sharks and sea monsters around the more legitimate structures. Almost 300 Maui residents lambasted the whole project at a three-hour meeting in June 1987.

"We filed the environmental-impact statements, did all the studies, and went out in the public forum asking for these ocean leases," Asquith says. "That raised all these big issues to the point where we got into a horrendous stink—protesters in the town hall with signs like "Get these people out of here" and TV and all. Although what people were really concerned about was the exclusive use of the ocean by any particular company or group, they came up with every other concern you could possibly think about. We got on everybody's radar screen."

By then the company had hired another consultant, the former state agriculture director, John Farais, who later became a director of Atlantis Hawaii. He and others advised the company to drop its application to lease a chunk of the ocean and address the other issues it had never really identified. Asquith met with tourist and environmental officials, boat captains and divers, to reassure them of the corporate good intentions. Meanwhile Atlantis focused on its first choice for a site: the Big Island's more welcoming Kona coast.* Even there it had to build a wooden tower and finance a study in which researchers were to monitor the movement of whale cows and calves—which never did appear.

All this kerfuffle had come as a large surprise to Atlantis, which believed it was environmentally pure. After all, its battery-powered subs are nonpolluting, releasing nothing more than compressed air into the sea, and potentially far less damaging to reefs than careless scuba divers breaking off pieces of coral. Not only that, the company had an educa-

---

*While the powers that be have been welcoming, Kona's environment has lately been less so. Since the volcano Kilauea began erupting with a vengeance on the Big Island in 1986, it has been belching about 1,000 tonnes of sulphur dioxide gas daily—what the locals call "vog." The pollution streams out to sea and gets swept back along the Kona coast where Atlantis operates. On bad days, it creates respiratory problems for some residents, burning eyes for tourists, and a haze that settles on the hills behind the resorts.

tional program, The Living Classroom, which it introduced in the Caribbean to take school classes on underwater field trips. Over the years, more than 60,000 students have participated (and Hawaii's program would one day earn it a gold medal for environmental education from the Pacific Asia Travel Association).

John Harrison, environmental coordinator of the University of Hawaii Enviromental Center, told *Hawaii Business* magazine later: "The Atlantis people bent over backward to accommodate state and federal officials. They were professional, confident, and nonconfrontational. They didn't try to hide anything." By August 1988, when *Atlantis IV* was launched off Kona, it had won over the Sierra Club and other environmental groups, which actually supported its application to operate in Hawaii. Along the way, the company discovered a wise axiom.

If your business has even the slightest chance of being controversial, communicate with the public from day one

"You have to consult a little bit more broadly and try to find out where people's sensitivities lie," George Asquith says. As Don Sa'agd, a University of Hawaii business-development specialist, would say of Atlantis later, "Because of their success in the Caribbean, they thought they understood the working of island governments, and that Hawaii would be a piece of cake. But they were wrong." The company had an environmental consultant from the start of its Hawaiian project. "He was voicing certain concerns," Asquith says, "but they weren't environmental concerns. This is an absolutely clean environmental project, so during the first part of the exercise we're saying, 'Don't worry about that.' I guess we were a bit too self-assured. We *believed* so much. I guess we didn't understand the communication exercise. Normally small companies and entrepreneurs who are really excited about their product, overwhelmed by it, don't understand—until they've been slapped down a few times—the need to budget time and resources to listen and put together a good communications program. 'My product is so wonderful,' [they say]. 'Why do I need a PR firm?' So you learn."

One battle was already won and another would soon be lost. The U.S. Coast Guard had to approve the first passenger submarine ever to operate in American waters and didn't really want to deal with the issue. As Dennis Hurd translates the unspoken fear of one official, "This could kill my career if these guys blow away a bunch of tourists." But another high-level Coast Guard official at the New York City headquarters was more amenable. "He sat in the room with John [Witney] and me one day," Hurd recalls, "and said to his staff, 'This is a really unusual situation, something that's going to take a ton of work, but I want you guys to make this happen.'" The other battle ended less positively. Despite earlier indications to the contrary from high levels in Washington, D.C., Atlantis proved not to be exempt from the Jones Act, which requires that vessels carrying cargo or passengers between U.S. ports must be owned principally by Americans, built in American shipyards, and manned by American crews. So Atlantis arranged to have the sub manufactured just across the border in Washington State and set about finding American majority partners. Merrill Lynch was helping the company raise another $5.5 million at the time, and the lead Toronto investor introduced Atlantis to three American investors, all from Indiana, who assembled 29 others to back the Hawaiian venture. The Vancouver holding company owns the maximum 25 percent of Atlantis Hawaii allowed under the U.S. marine legislation.

The same year Kona came aboard, Atlantis Submarines had its first franchise agreement— with a high-profile Japanese tourism operator in Guam. The Micronesian Pacific island is a U.S. military base and a tourist magnet, mostly for the Japanese. The operator acquired *Atlantis V* and continues to pay the company five percent of his revenues (declining since the drop in Asian tourism) under a comprehensive licensing agreement in which Atlantis controls all the operating standards. In its 1990 move into Aruba, in the Caribbean off the Venezuelan coast, the company developed the licensing agreement further to include a two-percent fee for a fund that covers overall branding and marketing of the Atlantis name and logo. Originally a minority partner in Aruba with Japan's Kawasaki and an English shipping company, Atlantis now owns 94 percent of the shares in an operation with increasing cash flow and a year-to-year reputation as the island's most outstanding tourist attraction.

The Bahamas were another obvious target for a tourist sub; in 1993 Atlantis entered into a joint venture there with Bahamian partners. It had done a market survey, which was encouraging, and a weather-and-wave monitoring study, which steered it away from the area of Nassau where all the tourists gather. Instead it decided to bus customers to a corner of New Providence Island where the oceanscape was more inviting. The idea was to turn what should have been a 45-minute ride into a highly entertaining narrated island tour, stopping at a pirate cave and ending at a submarine site where James Bond movies were filmed. The reality was somewhat less, as Dennis Hurd so directly puts it: "I'm going to sit your ass on a hot bus with a lousy driver who's going to ask for a tip and he'll stop to chat with his buddies for 20 minutes."

Another problem was the quality of tourists, who were less free-spending than expected. After the first 18 months, when revenues failed to meet projections, the Bahamian partners kept trying to convince Atlantis that things were changing: the government had switched to one that was more protourism, a $300-million casino coincidentally named Atlantis had opened up, the cruise ships were coming in greater numbers. But by October 1996, the company bailed out, with a loss of about $800,000. It had all come down to that bus ride and the fact that Atlantis couldn't be in the driver's seat and couldn't maintain the quality of the tour.

Whenever possible, don't depend on suppliers you can't control

"It never did work out because that tour really took about an hour," Dennis Hurd explains. "We knew people didn't like being on a bus, no more than you or I would. But had we been able to really control it the way we wanted and create a good piece of product ... " Bahamian regulations precluded that: "Not being able to own the buses and hire the bus drivers, it turned out we just couldn't control it—which was obviously a crucial part of the problem. The thing we should have understood is that we *wouldn't* be able to control it." And in tourism, isn't it vital that the attraction operator must dictate quality? "Yeah. If we'd been smart, that's what we would have figured out. Pretty expensive mistake. We should have got out a lot earlier."

Cancun, in 1994, was another joint venture, this time with one of the wealthiest men in Mexico and the son of a prominent politican. George Asquith spearheaded the negotiations with the government and the partners (both of whom request anonymity for fear of kidnapping). Again, location has been a factor in discouraging revenues: the dive site is too shallow, the currents and surface winds too strong, and El Niño weather hasn't helped. Combine that with the devaluation of the peso and the resulting disappearance of indigenous Mexican tourists and it is understandable why Hurd says frankly: "We think we might be able to break even this year. If we can, we'll be okay. If we lose a bunch more money, we're gonna bail. How would we have done that differently? I don't know, because God, it's still a good market, you know—over two million tourists a year in Cancun."

The Hawaiian islands attract seven million tourists a year, which is why Atlantis has located five vessels there in the past decade, one of them the world's largest passenger sub, a 30-metre vessel holding 64 passengers. With the slump in tourist spending, and a predatory competitor in Honolulu, the considerable cash flow the company once counted on is in decline. But Atlantis Hawaii has cut costs back to 1994 levels and taken on management and marketing contracts for two major tourist parks on the island of Oahu—Sea Life and Waimea Valley—and a marketing and sales contract for the largest attraction to come to Honolulu in decades: USS *Missouri,* the Second World War battleship where the Japanese surrendered, which resurfaced in the Gulf War.

This aggressive broadening of markets is the intelligent handiwork of Darrell Metzger, who in three years has transformed the joint venture from a submarine-tour company to a true attractions-and-entertainment business. M.B.A. in hand, the southern Californian joined the Disney Corporation and ended up as head of human resources when Disney acted as consultants to the Japanese operators of Tokyo Disneyland. He came back to North America as a consultant for the 1984 Summer Olympics in Los Angeles and Expo 86, where he developed promotions for the fair in key western U.S. markets. By 1990 he was running Hong Kong's failing Ocean Park, a cultural, entertainment, and marine-life attraction. In the turnaround, he nearly doubled attendance and had to lower prices because the nonprofit park was making too much money. He was ripe for a return to the United States when Atlantis Hawaii came calling in 1995.

After George Asquith's role as diplomat in setting up the Hawaiian company, Metzger and Dennis Hurd have usually restricted their involvement to the directorial level. But they have leaped into the day-to-day fray at key moments. Once was just pre-Metzger, when the upstart local competitor tried to squeeze state officials into letting him use the Atlantis dive site off Waikiki for one of his subs, arguing that the area was designated for three vessels. Atlantis had created the 2.4-hectare artificial reef by sinking a U.S. naval ship, a Korean fishing vessel, and remnants of two airplanes and placing concrete pyramids there in collaboration with the University of Hawaii. Asquith successfully lobbied against the intrusion (while the company repositioned its Kona sub and crew on the site for several months to preempt a third competitive vessel).

The Vancouver holding company also looked over Atlantis Hawaii's shoulder when the joint venture was seeking a new CEO. "Certain areas we get more involved in," Hurd says. "For example, we outsourced the headhunters who hired Darrell and made a point to the board that this was the way to do it. ... Darrell is a smart guy and he certainly understands attractions." Coming in, Metzger added a director to the board, Jack Lindquist, a former president of Disneyland, and began reorganizing priorities to emphasize the bottom line as much as operating standards. He hired a new CFO, who had worked for NBC television for many years, and general managers to set up profit centres on the three islands. To battle his competitor, transportation tycoon Robert Iwamoto, Metzger introduced a time-limited $10 ticket promotion in 1998 during Atlantis's tenth anniversary—which goosed business from locals tenfold.* Most important, he is trading on the

---

*Atlantis also marked the anniversary by making history with the world's first live underwater remote-radio broadcast. From Atlantis subs in the Atlantic and Pacific Oceans, Virgin Islands and Honolulu dignitaries carried on a beneath-the-waves long-distance phone conversation which, in a clever piece of marketing, was broadcast live by local radio stations.

management contract with Sea Life Park and Waimea Valley and Adventure Park to offer Japanese travel wholesalers a $99 package that includes the sub, both parks, and a choice of rides ranging from all-terrain vehicles to river kayaks. He has also beefed up a retail store that sells Atlantis products and leased a Waikiki trolley that takes passengers on tours while acting as a highly visible mobile billboard for Atlantis. Another package combines the narrated trolley ride with the sub dive and a tour of a jewellery factory for the price of the sub alone. Recently Metzger increased the Atlantis marketing budget by ten percent to more than $2 million a year. And he has opened a reservations centre and a telemarketing office in Reno, where labour costs are cheap, that is cross-selling other companies' attractions as well as all the Atlantis Submarines offerings around the world.*

There is talk of buying the two Hawaiian parks from their New York City owner. (Noting that they were for sale earlier, Hurd says, "We were a little disappointed that as a group we weren't aggressive enough.") To attract repeat local business, Metzger has already added a butterfly exhibit at Waimea and a children's pirate lagoon and a swim-with-the-dolphins attraction at Sea Life. Combined, the parks and the three Hawaiian sub operations are drawing 1.3 million tourists a year (the state's next-largest tourist operator is the Polynesian Cultural Center, which attracts 800,000). The marketing of the USS *Missouri,* which opened in Pearl Harbor in 1999, has added another 620,000. And Metzger is looking at other possibilities, both inside and beyond Hawaii. While careful not to step on Vancouver's toes, he also thinks he may have access to more funds than the holding company does. His three-page personal list—"not for Dennis or the board"—ranges from a $2-million offshore platform at Waikiki with underwater viewing to a submarine operation in Singapore.

The Singapore submarine is also on Hurd's wish list. But at the moment he has a sub, *Atlantis 15,* in various pieces around Vancouver. The vessel is waiting for partners in a Malaysian public company to

---

*Among the pitches Atlantis makes to potential corporate clients in a lavish brochure is: "Each dive can be customized especially for your company. We can post underwater signs, proudly displaying your company logo. Or we'll create a special R.I.P. plaque for your competitor and attach it to Davy Jones' locker. How about a champagne toast on the ocean floor or your company CEO waving at you ... dressed in scuba gear, of course!"

revive their interest after the economically battered Southeast Asian federation had its currency devalued by half. The joint venture had ambitious plans for a $40-million operation that would serve up to 140,000 students a year at a marine-science camp centred on two 48-passengers subs. Hurd is now casting about for other projects as his core engineering crew takes on the odd temporary commission, such as building from scratch the exotic cooling systems for Ballard Power Systems' fuel cell.

Meanwhile, in the Caribbean, Hurd has bought Shorey International, the largest operator of semisubmersible tourist boats in the region, for between $5 and $6 million.* New submarine sites that have been considered include Miami (rough seas would have meant building a hugely expensive bargelike breakwater); Alaska (too seasonal, as are Vancouver and Europe); and Cuba ("too early," Hurd says). The real growth area will be Asia, and the president of Atlantis Submarines believes his basic product line is beautifully positioned to meet a couple of ongoing vogues.

TrendWatch

"I don't think you'll see any lessening in terms of the volumes of people going on holidays," Dennis Hurd says. "There's a bunch of baby boomers who are moving up into their wealthier years. If anything, that's going to grow in volume. Ecotourism when we started was just a new word. People want to do more than just lie on a beach. They want to interact, do things. And the submarines solve this—'I'm doing something, I'm interacting, it's fun, it's educational.' And another component is soft adventure. So [Atlantis has] got some nice components to it, as good tourism products have. Education's good, but that should just come through the fun of it. It's really

---

* Semisubmersibles, like those Atlantis already operates off Barbados, are the poor man's submarines. For a much lower price, the tourist gets to sit in an air-conditioned cabin a couple of metres below water while the vessel skims the surface. If the submariner has a scuba diver's view, the semisub passenger has a snorkeler's.

entertainment. If you learn some stuff, that's so much the better. If anything, those elements are becoming more pronounced. And one amazing thing going on is this cruise-ship business. It's staggering. They're half our business in the Caribbean. We sell our product to all the cruise ships, and it better be a good product and you better treat the passengers well. And they've got a ton more ships coming on." All, he hopes, bursting with passengers who might want to have an adventure under the sea as well as cruise sedately along its surface.

Chapter Six

The Railroader

Peter Armstrong, Great Canadian Railtour Company

Not far out of Calgary this morning in July 1998, the sun is creeping above the fat shredded-wheat rolls in the fields and the beige-and-blond cattle ruminating along the cliffs of the Bow River. "A deer! Wildlife!" somebody shouts. A little doe munches in the crease of a slope. Later, a pair of large-antlered elk lope across a track paralleling ours. We are rollicking along the foothills in an air-conditioned observation car of The Rocky Mountaineer—the tourist-train service that slices through the portentous peaks of southern Alberta and British Columbia. We are about to step down the spiral staircase to the rose-dotted dining car to breakfast on eggs Benedict, smoked salmon, and Alberta steak. There are about 70 of us in one of two dome cars, mostly middle-aged and older couples. In plush lounge chairs, we sip on champagne and orange juice, gaze out the wall-and-ceiling windows, and listen to the occasional commentary from the much younger attendants in snazzy green vests and white shirts who patrol the aisles, pampering us.

All at once, the Rockies rear up in the morning haze. The train is soon amid the ramparts and sculpted turrets that lent it their name. After a brief stop in the resort town of Banff to pick up the bulk of the 376 passengers, some of us stroll to the back of the car to stand outdoors in the vestibule, open on three sides to the sweet air. "You can't do this on any other train in Canada," Roger, a former VIA Rail employee on a sentimental journey, assures us. It is here, where we could reach out and almost touch the evergreen giants and mountain flanks, that the feeling of a rail adventure looms largest. But outside or in, this is an intimate encounter with nature. We watch for grizzlies and mountain goats and spot osprey families in their grand nests atop old telegraph poles—and the raven that, hearing the train whistle, routinely flies alongside the cars to the locomotive where one engineer will hold out a large cookie for the bird to snaffle up. The tight curves, bridges spanning turbulent rivers, tracks descending a kilometre of grade, twisting tunnels (one 20 minutes long), all remind us just how remarkable an exploit was the running of the original rail lines through this malevolent, enthralling land.

This is the only all-daylight rail journey through the western mountains. We stop over at the halfway point in Kamloops, British Columbia, for a bountiful buffet dinner, a remotely historical music revue, and an overnight in a medium-quality hotel. Next morning, linking with rail coaches from Jasper, we return to our dome car with trepidation: its air-conditioning had failed for a few hours yesterday in the 40-degree Celsius heat of this arid country, which a couple of weeks later would be ablaze with forest fires. But it is cool enough now as we roll through the surrealistic sagebrush- and pine-studded hills. A civilized lunch on white linen—wine, beer, and good lamb, beef strip loin, salmon filet, or cold Pacific seafood plate. Then we are in the Coast Mountains above roiling Hell's Gate Canyon and, before long, dropping down into the Fraser River Valley to Vancouver, where we pull in on schedule at 5:00 p.m. A middle-aged woman from Minneapolis, well travelled, tells me, "It was more than I thought it would be. There's nothing between you and nature. It's expensive but not overpriced. I got every dime's worth."*

For $868 U.S. (then about $1,085 Cdn.), she had got the deluxe two-day train tour, hotel room, and all meals—what the North American Travel Journalists Association judged in 1997 to be the Best International Attraction (yes, the very best of any tourist draw in the world outside the United States). The Rocky Mountaineer route is run by Great Canadian Railtour Company of Vancouver, the largest private rail operator in North America. While leasing four locomotives from General Motors, it owns 37 standard coaches, and four bilevel dome

---

*Another pleased passenger, this one unconcerned about price, was Microsoft's Bill Gates, who along with his wife, Melinda, took the trip in 1997 with a minimum of fuss and later wrote the company: "We can't imagine a better way to take in the majesty of your country than aboard a train. We thoroughly enjoyed our time with you and wish to thank you for making our travel most enjoyable." He also sent a letter to chef Oli Nichum: "The meals were superb and we enjoyed the care you took in preparing them." Gates enclosed copies of his book, *The Road Ahead*.

cars, a parlour car, a club car, a smoking car, and six baggage cars; its rolling stock includes the first new Canadian passenger rail coach to be introduced in four decades.

Great Canadian has been refining the experience since its first trip through the mountains in 1990, which was ripe with auguries. It, too, suffered air-conditioning failure yet managed to impress most of the 400 major travel representatives aboard and the secretary of state for external affairs of the time, Joe Clark, who kept repeating a phrase the company would steal as its slogan: "The most spectacular train trip in the world." That year The Rocky Mountaineer had 11,700 guests on 40 departures and lost about $900,000; in 1998 it had more than 50,000 on 126 departures and recorded its sixth straight year of profit. The exact figure remains the private affair of its president and CEO—and 86-percent shareholder since last year—Peter Armstrong, a strapping, well-born ex-doorman at the Hotel Vancouver who from the start has railroaded the company to success without government subsidy.*

Great Canadian has managed such a feat, unlike VIA Rail Canada, the heavily indebted Crown corporation. Responsible for intercity passenger rail transportation, VIA had launched The Rocky Mountaineer as an untypically entrepreneurial venture in 1988. Two years later, compelled by federal government cost-cutting, it sold off the tourist rail service to a private consortium engineered by Armstrong. Ever since, he has been fighting the shades of the original operator. Once, to avoid a court battle when his company was floundering, he was forced into paying off a former VIA executive who had bid against him for the business in 1990 and was now suing him. Then, through the

---

*Its potential competitors on the western-mountain route are VIA Rail and American Orient Express, both of which run day and night on their transcontinental routes, missing some of the most glorious scenery in the dark. However, The Rocky Mountaineer acts as a selling agent for both rail services and offers daylight mountain trips aboard its own trains as part of VIA's 11-day Toronto-Vancouver package, which in 1998 cost $3,305 Cdn. ($2,644 U.S.). The privately owned American Orient Express, featuring deluxe mahogany-and-brass vintage rail cars but no observation coaches, was charging $6,930 Cdn. ($4,990 U.S.) for an eight-day Vancouver-Montreal trip with side tours in several cities. Passengers on both trains sleep aboard, rather than overnighting in hotels. The Mountaineer has two levels of service: the deluxe GoldLeaf, offering seating in an observation car with a dining room, and Signature, with regular passenger cars and meals at your seat, which in 1998, high season cost $585 Cdn. (then $468 U.S.).

court alternative of mediation, Armstrong won a $5-million settlement from VIA for having misrepresented what it was handing over in the sale of the service. And in 1997 he effectively used the court of public opinion to foil VIA's attempt to double the frequency of its own tourist-season trips through the Rockies. Federal transport minister David Anderson of Vancouver declared: "It would be inappropriate for VIA to significantly increase its capacity in competition with a private-sector operator." In 1998 Ottawa's all-party Standing Committee on Transport, in a report on the restructuring of the Crown-owned service, recommended "that the government ensure that, with regard to competition in the passenger rail sector, no undue hardship be placed on the private passenger rail operator by a passenger rail subsidy, thus ensuring a level playing field."

Not only that, committee members discussed the real possibility of either full or partial privatization or public-private railroad-franchising partnerships to operate various rail systems now run by VIA. Expecting public bids to be announced sometime in 1999, Armstrong has been working on a paper to present to Transport Canada—"to tell them what to avoid in the process of commercializing, franchising, or privatizing. And I only came up with 15 pages of things," he says mischievously. "We particularly like tourism routes—through Montreal and the Maritimes to Halifax and the western transcontinental, which have great tourism potential." He has also talked to a group on Vancouver Island that wants to attract an operator to maintain and upgrade the local service of VIA's E&N Railroad there as well as scheduling tourist runs. "I think it's exciting for Canada," he says of all the possibilities. "If it's some kind of franchise deal for a couple of years, nobody is going to put their time and effort in to make it better, but if they have a real vision and the private sector takes it over … "*

If Great Canadian takes anything over, the visionary Armstrong—although his only remaining financial partner is his brother—will involve

---

*Peter Armstrong might have some high-profile competition from Britain: Richard Branson's Virgin Rail PLC, which operates the privatized western region rail service in Britain, and StageCoach holdings PLC, which runs the southwestern franchise, have expressed interest in a VIA Rail franchise. Ottawa has hired Britain's Hambros Bank, which oversaw the privatization of British Rail in 1992, to do business plans for country-wide franchising of the Canadian rail system.

many other people in the fulfillment of any venture. He will be capital-
izing on a principle he picked up the hard way since the day he stopped
being a doorman and started his own small transportation business.

Share your vision with your employees

"I was a pusher from behind and not a leader," Peter
Armstrong admits. "I did not explain myself very well and I
didn't invest the time to get people to share my vision.
Everybody comes to work for a paycheque. There's no question
about that. But they want to do something meaningful and they
want to know that at the end of the day they have been a part
of a success. ... People have to know what they are fighting for:
'Why do we want to do this?' We want to be proud that every
time a passenger has come off the train, they have had the experience of a lifetime. We're ambassadors for Canada, so this is
important. People like to be the best, but you can't ask them to
be the best without giving them the tools." At The Rocky
Mountaineer, one tool is a three-week training course created
by Vancouver service-excellence consultant and futurist Ann
Coombs, who shapes a clear-cut central vision for the onboard
attendants. She says: "I see Peter as genuine, caring, compas-
sionate, demanding but loyal." His staff obviously returns that
loyalty: of 96 seasonal attendants on the course last year, 90
were returnees.

Counting contract employees, Armstrong says, "about 350 people
depend on us for employment now. And, you know, you're thinking
about all those families and their dreams and their aspirations. They
wake up the same way I do, looking for a better day and trying to do
things better." Somehow he makes the platitudes sound plausible,
exuding a sincerity that has done well for him as he faced the continuing crises of his career. His commanding physical presence helps: just
under two metres tall, his full head of once-blond hair gone to silver,
although the broad, friendly face is still smooth-skinned in his mid-
forties. Stylishly suited, with a pinkie ring, gold cuff links and mono-
grammed cuffs on a white shirt even crisper than his staff's, he is a

strange combination of his private-school past and his hustling, one-of-the-guys background of hailing cabs for hotel guests.

We are in his office off Vancouver's Main Street in the 1919 Neoclassical Revival stone station that once housed the Canadian Northern Railway and that The Rocky Mountaineer now shares with its old antagonist, VIA Rail. His quarters are chockablock with rail memorabilia, model trains, and long-ago posters. The walls also hold a couple of telling reminders of how he got here. One is a framed reprint of a *Vancouver Sun* article from February 1997 with the headline: "Tiny B.C. firm beats out railroad giant for Banff run." The lead begins: "An upstart B.C. company has won its battle against the federal Crown corporate giant VIA Rail for the lucrative Banff-Jasper rail tour business." Across the room hangs an aphorism from Calvin Coolidge: "Nothing in the world can take the place of persistence. Talent will not; nothing is more common than unsuccessful men with talent. ... Persistence and determination alone are omnipotent."

If any story illuminates Armstrong's persistence, it is one that he tells on himself from his time at the establishment Hotel Vancouver. As a 20-year-old bellman in the early 1970s, he had to label and quietly deliver the *Globe and Mail* to every room overnight. His first try, he did it in two hours and 45 minutes, which the assistant manager said wasn't good enough—the norm was half an hour. Over the next few nights, the competitive Armstrong raced through the halls in running shoes, sweat-drenched, and by his final run had managed it in 29 minutes and 50 seconds. "Congratulations," his superior said, "you're the first guy to do it in under half an hour. Actually, you're the first guy to do it in under two hours."

Running papers and toting luggage seems like a strange job for the third child of a United Empire Loyalist descendant. His father was western Canadian and Asian vice president for the Nesbitt Thompson brokerage house in Vancouver. Peter went to the private St. George's School, where he didn't excel, having to repeat Grade 4 when he focused on baseball instead. By the next year, he was investing in stocks with his dad's advice and was once excused from class to attend the annual general meeting of Pacific Western Airlines, in which he had shares. In high school, he was a volunteer for the federal Conservatives on a winning election campaign and worked as a fishing guide in northern British Columbia. Along with majoring in girls at the camp, he got to know a holidaying entrepreneur who helped him put together a business plan for a company to repair four-wheel-drive vehicles in Prince George. It never happened, but Peter knew by then that he didn't ever want to work for a big company. And in Grade 12, deciding he didn't want to compete with his smart schoolmates in law or accounting, he went to see a friend of his father, the general manager of the Bayshore Hotel, who encouraged him to take the hotel-management course at the B.C. Institute of Technology.

When the dean at BCIT told him all the places were filled for the next semester, Armstrong wouldn't be brushed off and asked what it would take to be accepted. He met the several conditions (which two decades later he can't remember) and began the course. Trying to support himself, he asked second-year students what the best job in the local hotel industry was. Doorman of the Hotel Vancouver, they agreed. Off he went and met with the hotel's ancient head bellman, who said he could have a summer position to fill in for a vacationing doorman—if Armstrong could fit into the man's uniform. When it proved much too large for him, he fast-talked the seamstress at the uniform shop about how much he needed the job. She called the boss bellman, told him the uniform fitted Armstrong well, and then altered it to his size.

He began learning the trade from a doorman named Mike Miller, learning how important it was to cater to a guest's every wish and never to expect a tip—an education that would be useful in his later incarnations. (The first $50 bill he ever saw, however, was a tip from a grateful couple after he ran to a ticket office to get them on a train to Banff.) The big, brash young man was meeting visiting heads of state, entertainers such as Bob Hope, and local heavyweights such as *Sun* columnist Jack Wasserman. One day when the assistant general manager pressed him to have a tow truck haul away cars illegally parked at the hotel—one of which was Wasserman's—Armstrong went to the general manager's office and told him what he had been ordered to do. The cars weren't towed, but the assistant manager would get his revenge later by lying to Armstrong about how long it took to deliver the *Globe* door-to-door overnight.

The callow bellman had already discovered—by going through the garbage the cleaners brought from the administrative offices at night—

that he was making more money, with tips, than his immediate superior was. Perhaps hotel management wasn't the path to take. Armstrong began studying commerce at the University of British Columbia, moved into a fraternity house, dated a teacher-to-be named Wendy (who would become his wife), and kept working at the hotel.

It was there, in 1973, that he and his slightly older mentor, Mike Miller, noticed that on some summer days the local Gray Line tour-bus operation was turning away hundreds of potential sight-seeing customers. The company was operated by BC Hydro, the provincially owned utility, and suffered from bureaucratic mismanagement. Its only competition was a minor private double-decker business. The two doormen began researching the tour industry at the library down the block and at city hall, where Armstrong hired the licensing inspector's wife to type up their business plan—and convinced the inspector himself to invest $500 in their proposed company, Spotlight Tours.

The concept was high-quality daytime sight-seeing and especially nighttime entertainment tours during the summer season. Armstrong, matching Miller, invested about $5,000 from some stocks, bonds, and gold he had been buying. His brother, Bev, came in and so did Miller's father, Walter, along with some of his friends. In all, the two partners raised $27,000. In late 1974 that sum and a reasonable business plan convinced the Royal Bank to give them a $5,000 line of credit; the Federal Business Development Bank to advance $50,000 in a seven-year loan to buy two 23-seat tour buses; and a local Chevrolet dealer to finance a third vehicle. They bought them from an Alabama manufacturer who refused to give the young Canadians any financial break for buying more than one bus.

Like classic embryonic entrepreneurs, the partners did everything that first season—the summer of 1975—from driving to cleaning the brash blue-and-yellow vehicles, while overseeing a small crew of Armstrong's frat brothers and Miller's dad, who stickhandled the office phone. Gray Line's manager, now facing a second competitor, put more tour buses into action, vowing to run the upstarts out of business within two weeks. "And he came pretty close to doing it," Armstrong recalls. Among the factors that helped keep them alive was Miller's philosophy: "He taught me how to treat people, and one of the things that he taught me was brilliant—simple but brilliant: 'When we pay our

184

commissions to hotel desk clerks, pay in crisp brand-new bills.'" The rationale: at the end of the day, when the clerks were counting up their take, the pristine paper money would remind them exactly how much they had made for selling their guests on Spotlight Tours. The company survived by pursuing a tenet its cofounder still follows today.

Build meaningful personal relationships to make your business prosper

"When I wasn't selling tours on the street," Peter Armstrong says of his first tentative years in the tourist business, "I would be running around to the hotels, paying commissions, and talking it up with the people. ... I have always believed in building a relationship first. And what I started to do was build up a relationship with the people on the desk. I would know them and their kids and their interests and I would be talking about golf or tennis or whatever—I was selling myself and the commitment that I was making to them: 'You trust me with two or three of your guests a day and I will bring them back happy.'" He and his staff made them happy by relating to them as people, not just passengers. "When we had a stop, a lot of the other bus drivers would go and have a coffee. What we tried to do was stick with the group, not let them go off, and have a little chat with one and then talk to someone else. And by the end you had good quality time with each person—and it did great things for your gratuities." Hiring a couple of outgoing theatre students also helped. They would stress to their tour guests that this was a young company composed of college students who wanted to hear any complaints personally, but if the passengers had enjoyed the tour, would they please tell their bellman or desk clerk how good a job Spotlight was doing. The hotel staff would then pass it on to Armstrong: "I don't know what it is about your tours but everybody comes back and tells us what a great trip they had."

The nightclub tours, more fitful than predicted, lasted only the first season. What helped Spotlight's revenue stream was Gray Line's overreaction to its presence on the scene. Refocusing on the hotel trade, Gray Line now paid less attention to its contract for busing Princess Cruises passengers around town (Vancouver being the base for Alaskan cruises). Gray Line had started using lower-quality vehicles for these passengers; Armstrong told the cruise giant he would charge less and field a fleet of better buses. Princess used his offer to prod his big competitor, which suddenly realized it didn't want to risk losing the cruise business. "Well, the next time a cruise ship came in," Armstrong recalls, "all the Gray Line buses went down to the dock and the hotel service was lousy that day. And we went out and picked up all these people and looked great in front of these desk clerks who'd booked the business with Gray Line. It's the only way we got ahead."

But at season's end Spotlight Tours had spent $73,000 and earned $67,000, with Armstrong taking about $3,000 in salary. Miller—who had worked hard when off-duty from the hotel—and the other investors were dismayed that the fledgling company had lost money. "It turned ugly," Armstrong remembers, "and for many years I didn't have a good relationship with Mike, but there was nothing I could do." What he had done was offer to sell the company to his partner for $1; Miller declined and remained a doorman at the Hotel Vancouver, where he is a quarter century later. On the advice of the bankers, Armstrong then put Spotlight into soft receivership, paying off all the creditors, and bought the restructured company with a pair of new and older partners. Tom MacDonald and Don Baxter, who owned several businesses, including a tourist guide, invested a minor sum of money and used their administrative infrastructure to keep the business afloat. The next season, Spotlight made $5,000 profit on $105,000 in revenues, "which I was extremely ecstatic about," says Armstrong.

Spotlight was into its third season in 1977 when its principals heard that a Vancouver charter- and airport-bus company called Trailways of BC was about to buy a franchise from an industry major, American Sightseeing International, to operate tour buses locally. The threat of such competition terrified Armstrong and his partners. In a meeting with a Trailways partner, they suggested he might buy Spotlight and even offered, a little desperately, to come to work for him. He crudely

~ Marathon Man ~
Gary Charlwood
Century 21 Canada and
Uniglobe Travel

~ The Entertainer ~
Tim Gamble
Peace Arch Entertainment Group

~ Hot Dogger ~
Yves Potvin
Yves Veggie Cuisine

~ The Passionate Vintner ~
Harry McWatters
Sumac Ridge Estate Winery and
Hawthorne Mountain Vineyards

~ Mr. Submarine ~
Dennis Hurd
Atlantis Submarines

~ The Railroader ~
Peter Armstrong
Great Canadian
Railtour Company

~ Boondocks Warriors ~
Brad and Lori Field
Pacific Safety Products

~ The Hucksters ~
Jim Scharf
Jim Scharf Holdings

~ The Pathfinders ~
Ed and Shirley Fitzhenry
Pacific Navigation Systems

~ The Gamesman ~
Chuck Loewen
Online Business Systems

~ The Healer ~
Dr. Julia Levy
QLT PhotoTherapeutics

~The Samurai's Daughter ~
Kazuko Komatsu
Pacific Western
Brewing

told them he didn't need them or their company. *Oh, my God,* Armstrong thought, *our business is toast.*

In fact, a few months later the man called back and told them there might now be some opportunity to negotiate a deal. He introduced them to two managing partners of Trailways, who were quite frantically seeking help to unscramble what turned out to be the financial and legal messes they had inherited in taking over the company. Although doing upward of $9 million a year, it was hemorrhaging badly. The Spotlight principals, recognizing an opportunity, bought 56 percent of the business for what seemed like an astonishingly low $40,000.

On the December day of closing, Trailways had a working-capital deficiency of $400,000—or so the new partners thought. "That was before we counted up the drawers of payables that hadn't been marked," Armstrong points out. "The equipment was run down pretty bad. We were a quarter of million dollars late in our payment to the federal government on the airport contract. And the day we closed, All Fun Tours, which was our biggest customer [for gambling charters to Reno], went into receivership."

The next day, his commerce exams over, Armstrong went to work at Trailways; he never returned to UBC to finish his degree. His first job was an attempt to deal with a disgruntled driver at the airport who, after an argument with the dispatcher, was angrily stopping and starting his bus in a series of jackrabbit hops. "Every company has a rotten apple in the barrel," he says. "We thought we had everybody's rotten apple in our barrel. Part of it was that the previous management had beaten up on these guys so much. Some of the stories that we had heard were so atrocious that we can understand where it came from."

That same day Tom MacDonald asked Armstrong to cover for him at the Richmond office, where a bailiff arrived and told the young commerce student he was coming to seize #307, one of the All Fun buses.

"It's not here," he was told. "It went on a special trip to Reno till Friday night."

"You have that goddamn bus here when I get back because I'm seizing it," the bailiff demanded. When he left, Armstrong turned to look at the #307 bus looming behind the office's picture window.

His corporate education involved many such stratagems, so much so that within a few years his politically incorrect lawyer would describe him as "the Israeli of the bus industry—you take what you want and you attempt to legitimize it later." Facing a steep learning curve, Armstrong was responsible for sales and marketing—generating revenue—while MacDonald looked after legal issues and dealt with creditors. "And Tom was a masterful guy at building up relationships with people," Armstrong says, while admitting he wasn't. He pressed seasoned, much older managers to concentrate on the company's Spotlight sight-seeing division—with its short operating hours, high volume, and good margins—rather than Reno tours. He argued with drivers who were members of the Teamsters union and thought sightseeing was a mug's game until they saw the nonunion drivers empty their pockets of tips from tourists. To complicate matters, many of the union drivers were shareholders in the company. "The first two and a half years were very tough," Armstrong remembers, "and as the airport contract came up [for rebidding] in September of 1979, we first had to address the morale issue with our staff. There were things that I did and attitudes that I had that were just awful. I was a young kid who had a very little business that all of a sudden went very big and I had this grandiose idea that I was good. And I was arrogant, belligerent—and they were my best attributes."

One day a Teamsters president named Bill McLeod met with him over coffee. A gruff chain-smoker with a vivid vocabulary, McLeod said, "Peter, your methods aren't working. The problem I have with you is you do something stupid and you try to kick me and I end up kicking you back ten times." Armstrong was furious with the union boss: "I was steaming for weeks after, then I gradually realized that he was right. … I was dealing with guys that were 20, 30 years my senior and I was trying to tell them I knew everything about the bus service. And I didn't know anything—and the worst part of it was I didn't know that I didn't know anything." The know-it-all eventually came to accept a golden rule that works more often than not in business.

Don't be afraid to reveal your ignorance about important business issues

"I had this false bravado that I was some gift to the business world, and I wasn't," Peter Armstrong says of his young self. "If I was annoying a driver, he could do $5,000 damage to my coach and I would never know about it. So I started to change my attitude, I started to listen more, I started to recognize and to admit that I didn't know things—and that was one of the most challenging things I have ever learned in business. [As a boss] you have to make decisions, but there's no shame in asking questions. First I would ask a question and then I would listen. ... There's no monopoly on good ideas." As he so disarmingly describes the technique (which would later come into play at a critical moment in the bidding for The Rocky Mountaineer): "Never try to bullshit somebody when you don't know something. You can't lie to your employees and you can't lie to your suppliers and you can't lie to the government—and you can't lie. It doesn't pay."

"I think some of the old bus drivers would say that I was a son of a bitch to start with and they whipped me into shape," Armstrong says now. The sight-seeing division began contributing significantly to cash flow, which allowed Trailways to spruce up its equipment and start to pay the federal government the arrears it owed for the right to transport passengers to and from the airport. In 1978 that contract was coming up for renewal, and this time there were other bidders, including Perimeter Transportation, which had leased Armstrong's original Spotlight buses as its first vehicles. Trailways originally heard that it had won the contract, having argued that the competing companies didn't meet the criteria for volume of business and length of time in operation. Almost immediately, however, the government retendered the contract, and this time Perimeter won. Trailways launched a $60,000 court challenge, but—when the judge couldn't make a decision based on the facts at hand—lost in that arena, too.

It was a devastating setback. Suddenly about 40 percent of Trailways' business had vanished, a vital portion that had fed the company's other divisions. "We were in pretty tough shape," Armstrong says.

There was, however, another bidding war about to begin, one with roots dating to 1975 when Armstrong had worked on the successful political campaign of the formidable Grace McCarthy, a Social Credit member of the B.C. legislature. The Socreds became the government that year and McCarthy became deputy premier. She had agreed with Armstrong, then operating Spotlight Tours, that he shouldn't be competing with Gray Line, the money-losing, government-owned bus company—"this corrupt corporation," in his words. Once in power, she summoned him to Victoria to urge that he lobby government and Opposition members as well as the bureaucracy to sell it off. Which he did, quietly, and in 1979 the company came up for bid, the province's first Crown corporation to be privatized.

Trailways competed against some potent establishment names, among them financier and philanthropist Joe Segal, then chairman of Zellers. Yet in March 1979, half a year after losing the airport contract, it won Gray Line with an offer of $1.25 million.

Not so fast, at least one failed bidder decided. A bureaucrat friend of Armstrong in Victoria confirmed "there are some very powerful people trying to get your bid thrown out." Flying to the provincial capital, he learned that among them was Gordon Downing, a former speaker of the house who had bought the private double-decker sight-seeing bus line that had competed with Spotlight Tours. Downing had apparently written a letter to the chairman and directors of BC Hydro trying to overturn the Gray Line decision and allegedly impugning Armstrong's character. He had some ammunition: at Trailways Armstrong had, by his own admission, "played fast and loose" with the rules of the Motor Carriage Commission, which regulated bus transportation. "I didn't come with clean hands," he agrees. "My whole entrepreneurial spirit resented this trio of guys deciding on the future of the bus industry, and to me it was all a joke." As one instance, he found a way around commission rules that allowed him to run sight-seeing trips to Victoria and set up a shell company to funnel such business. Reflecting today on his finagling, he told me, "There is no accounting for the stupidity of youth. ... I didn't lie, I was so blatant in what I was doing. I just played with their loophole and drove a bus through it." Although he ultimately paid a fine of several thousand dollars, a week later the commission was forced to give him a sight-seeing license for Victoria because he had proved a public need for it.

Now, with the possibility of losing Gray Line, Armstrong sent a letter to BC Hydro chairman Robert Bonner. Dictated by his Victoria friend, a Hydro manager, it tried to refute Downing's charges against him. It succeeded: "I got in to see Bonner and a number of other people and we were able to turn the tide." What Trailways got in the government bus line was ten old buses and sight-seeing and charter bookings worth more than $1 million—about the same amount that Gray Line had lost the previous year.

Armstrong was the original president of the revitalized private company, in which he held 20 percent of the shares. Business flourished for a couple of years until a recession began biting into profits in 1981.* One of the provincial government's hopes for an economic shot in the arm during that decade was the Vancouver world's fair that became Expo 86. Grace McCarthy, as minister of travel industry, had been pushing the idea since 1978. Her protégé, Peter Armstrong, had immediately seen the opportunity the exposition presented and was the first person to purchase a ticket—in fact, in a well-publicized ploy in 1984, he had Gray Line buy a block of 5,000 tickets, worth $100,000 (and eventually more than 200,000 tickets). Those, along with the prebooking of 40,000 hotel-room nights, positioned the bus company admirably during Expo year. Expecting a profit of about $500,000, it would make five times that.

Less successful at the time was his ongoing relationship with the most active of his two partners, Tom MacDonald. The third principal, Don Baxter, stayed in the background ("Don is a brilliant guy, very quiet, unassuming but very insightful," Armstrong says). MacDonald, having sold his other businesses, decided to step into the role of Gray Line president, displacing his younger colleague, who then acted in various vice-presidential positions—often reluctantly. "I'm not all good news," Armstrong confessed to me. "A frog has a lot of warts. I would think that I would be a hard guy to be a partner with. Because I know I am a little effervescent, a little enthusiastic. I know I get off tangent a bit and I feel passionate about things."

---

*In 1981, Murray Atherton, now Peter Armstrong's vice president of marketing, first joined Gray Line to operate the newly acquired Snow Goose bus service between Vancouver airport and the Whistler ski resort. When the line ended up handling about 70 percent of all bus traffic to Whistler, Atherton had to sublease Gray Line buses and their more expensive drivers. He says: "I lost Peter about $100,000"—which is about what he lost him later when, in charge of sight-seeing sales, he negotiated exclusive agreements totalling that amount with several hotels, which led to a charge of monopoly and a restraining order against Gray Line. Atherton left to market hotels, became a consultant to The Rocky Mountaineer in 1990, and came aboard full-time four years later—this time to make Armstrong money.

The crunch came when, flush with cash, the two active principals began prepaying Baxter's shareholders' loans. Armstrong had been promised a third of the company, up from his 20 percent, but quotes MacDonald as saying, "We never signed that deal," and suggesting his junior partner could pack his bags and sue him. It would take Armstrong, consulting with a lawyer, three years to strike a deal to sell his shares to his partner—shares that two professional evaluators estimated being worth between $215,000 and $605,000. He got $100,000 cash up front and four payments of $50,000 apiece. Meanwhile he kept working for Gray Line, finally as executive vice president of corporate development. "It was the worst time of my life. ... I wasn't made to be an employee." In 1989, a bitter Armstrong left the company to figure out a better life.

The timing of his leave-taking was propitious. A year earlier VIA Rail, in a brief expansionary mode, began operating a train through the western mountains entirely by day. The original idea came from a retired Canadian National Railways engineer named Harry Holmes, who had restored a steam locomotive in Jasper. Before Expo 86 he had called the railways to suggest using it to bring tourists to the fair along a daytime route across the Rockies, through Kamloops. Instead VIA adapted the concept to use its own diesel engines on a once-a-week basis during the tourist season. At the time, Gray Line was doing about $1 million a year in tour and sight-seeing business with VIA passengers; Armstrong was a welcome guest aboard the inaugural Rocky Mountaineer trip. He recalls telling the railway's executives, including marketing vice president Murray Jackson, that they should get the private sector involved in running the train (among other problems, he thought the marketing was lacklustre). A year later Ottawa announced a major downsizing of Canada's passenger-rail company, including the elimination of The Canadian, its regular transcontinental service, and hinted at the possible privatizing of the money-losing Mountaineer.

Leaving Gray Line, Armstrong had only vague ideas about what he wanted to do—perhaps something in manufacturing. But the prospect of taking over VIA's tourist train became more intriguing. In June 1989, he hired a senior business consultant at Price Waterhouse in Vancouver to research the passenger-rail business and himself visited the only place in the world where privately run trains seemed to be making money: Alaska. The Holland America and Princess cruise lines put their passengers on their own trains in the state as add-on land packages to their sea voyages.

In July three VIA excutives came for a barbecue at Armstrong's home in Vancouver. The manager of VIA Tours, the railway's marketing director, and marketing VP Murray Jackson told him they knew of no insiders' management bid for the potential privatizing of the Mountaineer. A couple of days later Jackson phoned to say he was, in fact, putting together a proposal for the tourist train with other VIA executives and wondered if his recent host would be interested in investing.

Armstrong was soon at the railway's headquarters in Montreal, at the same time as Tom Rader, another possible investor. A former executive with Holland America's Westours subsidiary, which programs shore excursions for the cruise line, the American Rader had later built dome cars for the Alaska State Railway and established a rail-manufacturing business in Denver. Jackson and his colleagues wanted Rader to provide financing for new railcars for a privatized Mountaineer.* They wanted Armstrong to invest a large sum. He quickly learned that both the marketing and the business plans of the VIA managers' group were weak. "We were just dumbfounded by the lack of things they knew," he says. Brainstorming with them, he and Rader suggested changes to the business plan. Three months later the two potential investors were back in Montreal, only to find that the investment deal being offered made it, according to Armstrong, "better to put my money into a savings bond." Nor did the deal give him any assurance that he would be on the board of directors. "Yet I was going to come in with most of the money," Armstrong insists. "A big chunk of the money. They were going to come in with nothing."

Meanwhile, Armstrong says, this management group admitted to him that their masters at VIA had told them not to organize a business plan or take advantage of the inside information they had—or supposedly even meet about the idea of bidding for the Mountaineer—yet here they were planning a bid. "And I am thinking," Armstrong recalls, "here we are going into partnership with people who have made an undertaking to their employer, using their material, that they wouldn't

---

*The other colleagues were Christena Keon Sirsley, Bert Guiney, and Barry Dane.

do what they are doing—and we are supposed to put our money up for these people."

He and Rader, lunching with Murray Jackson the next day, announced they wouldn't be investing, after all. Jackson asked them to sign a letter of confidentiality about their discussions with the management group, which would have effectively prevented them from putting in their own bid for the train. When Armstrong refused, arguing that the VIA executive knew he had been interested in bidding all along, he says Jackson accused him of being a dishonourable man and angrily left the restaurant.

Not long after, in late 1989, Jess Ketchum remembers an excited Armstrong asking him to breakfast. Ketchum had been vice president of communications at Expo 86, where he came to know the man who had bought $100,000 worth of the fair's first tickets: "I liked how he didn't have a negative bone in that big body of his." Ketchum, who had become a friend, was now a corporate-communications consultant.

"I want to go into the railway business," Armstrong told him.

"Passenger rail?" his tablemate asked incredulously, knowing something about the rockiness of rail transport from his days with the B.C. government.

But Armstrong started making notes on a napkin, detailing how he would turn VIA's money-losing Mountaineer into a paying proposition and how he would like his friend's help.

As Ketchum points out today, "Peter was a pretty little guy in the scheme of things and there'd be major competition from some big companies. He never, ever, considered he wouldn't get it."

Armstrong began to put together a group of investors to finance a company called Mountain Vistas Railtour Services. Calling on both family and his by-now-broad network of business contacts, he got tentative commitments from three major backers. They had a combined net worth of more than $30 million, and the companies they controlled grossed $120 million-plus in 1989. His brother, Beverley, was president of Pacific Western Realty, a Vancouver real-estate development firm, and chairman of the 11-location chain of Red Robin Restaurants. Richard Browning was executive vice president of Pac West and president of a subsidiary. And James Houston was chairman and a principal of The Urban Projects Group, which had developed 8,000 housing units and 139,333 square metres of commercial properties along the West Coast.

Armstrong, working out of a Pac West office with about $60,000 of his own money, used his connections in the tourism, transportation, and hospitality industries to help pack his proposal with impressive names. People, that is, who would impress Charles Armstrong, the executive consultant handling the bidding for VIA. Peter Armstrong and Robert Hamilton, a chartered accountant then acting as a consultant on the project, had met with Charlie—a former senior vice president of Canadian National Railways—who told Peter he didn't want any fly-by-nighters muddying up the bidding process for the Mountaineer. Peter started organizing a rail-operations committee, including Richard O'Rourke, an ex-special-projects manager for CN Rail, and Arnold Sturgeon, a 44-year rail veteran who had revitalized the passenger services of BC Rail, the successful provincial Crown corporation. Looking for the most prominent railway name possible to chair that committee, Armstrong had his Price Waterhouse consultants go after one of their clients, Mac Norris. A graduate of CP Rail, Norris had spent the previous two decades at BC Rail, where he was retiring as president and CEO, having taken the company from a $58-million-a-year loss to a $65-million profit. After some hesitation, he agreed to chair the committee. As Jess Ketchum says, "He provided us with the credibility we probably didn't deserve." Norris also became a member of the board of directors headed by Rick Browning, who had now committed as an investor, along with Jim Houston, Rob Hamilton, and Armstrong's brother, Bev.

Mountain Vistas' lean management team had Peter Armstrong as president (and 10-percent partner), Sturgeon as vice president of operations, and Rob Hamilton, now vice president of finance and administration. Hamilton, an alumnus of The Arthur Andersen management-consulting firm, was an active principal in a hot-food-service business and a holding company for high-tech investments. Armstrong also assembled an advisory council led by high-profile local lawyer George Hungerford, a director of Eldorada Nuclear when Ottawa privatized that Crown uranium refiner, and a tourist and hospitality council under tourism consultant Ann Pollock, whose clients included Tourism Canada and the western provinces' tourist ministries. While neither group worked actively, their members' names looked good on paper.

Between November and March 1990, Mountain Vistas would spend $375,000 on its bid. After about 20 groups had shown interest in the

Mountaineer, only three made the short list: Armstrong's, Murray Jackson's, and Westours. The latter, an arm of Holland America, owned by gigantic Carnival Cruise Lines, had deep pockets and enormous experience in the travel industry (in the early 1980s it had negotiated with the two national railways about using their lines for a western tourist train service that never materialized). Westours was, however, American, while Mountain Vistas was resolutely Canadian—*western Canadian.*★ And the Jackson group was not only eastern in origin but had been stumbling badly in making its bid. For one thing, the rules said that a bidder had to supply its own locomotives, but when Jackson couldn't locate any, Charlie Armstrong announced a last-minute revision that allowed VIA to supply the locomotives for the winner.

Peter Armstrong needed some clout with both Canadian National and CP Rail (CN's privately owned competitor), whose existing track and services the Mountaineer had to use. An ex-railroader associate recommended he approach Howard Lyttle, a retired CP executive vice president. Because Lyttle was a doubting Thomas at first, Armstrong was forced to follow his rule of freely confessing ignorance: "Howard, we don't have the answers to your questions, I'll be honest with you. We don't even know how to ask these questions." Disarmed, Lyttle became a member of Mountain Vistas' rail-operations committee, and his presence helped the group to negotiate with CP, which initially gave the westerners a rough ride. Conferring in the bathroom at the end of the first meeting in Montreal—during which the railway's brass pontificated on how the Mountaineer would be run by CP rules—Mac Norris told Armstrong, "Holy shit, that was awful." Then Lyttle put his arm around the men and said, "God, that was great. They love us."

"The fact that we were a B.C.-based company was key," Jess Ketchum says now. "But in the final analysis, it was Peter Armstrong—

★ Two Americans, however, helped punch the first national railway through the western mountains: Major A. B. "Hell's Bells" Rogers discovered the crucial southern Rogers Pass route, and William Van Horne oversaw the major western construction. "This great Canadian enterprise was, in truth, an international effort," writes Vancouver historian David Mitchell in *All Aboard! The Canadian Rockies by Train,* a handsome, engaging book that Peter Armstrong commissioned in 1995. Along with listing the labourers from around the globe who worked on the line, Mitchell offers this surprising fact: "And, often overlooked, is the contribution of the native Indians of western Canada."

his strength of character and personality—who won the day." The winning bid, which Armstrong believes was by far the highest, totalled $7.2 million for the existing equipment, two additional baggage cars, and reimbursement for marketing commissions already paid. The sum even included $20,000 for senior VIA Rail managers to help with the transition to a private rail service.

The first sign that the transition would be anything but smooth came in VIA's list of tour operators it had dealt with to market the train. When the sheet of names arrived by fax, Mountain Vistas' marketing vice president, Rick Antonson, thought there had been a mistake: it was only half a page long. But, that was the entire list. And—surprise!—The Rocky Mountaineer's first trip of the 1990 season would start next month in Edmonton, where it had never before gone, and play host to Canadian small business and tourism minister Tom Hockin and 400 influential journalists and tour operators from the Pacific Asia Travel Association.

Armstrong quickly hired a crew of laid-off union rail workers and added his own onboard people (including his wife, Wendy, and her sister), then put them in tuxedos for the April inaugural run. To the amazement of rail veterans, CN gave the passenger train priority on its line to Jasper because of the commercial rates it was paying. But there were other snarls. The air-conditioning wasn't working in nine of ten coaches; a key union railwayman proved to be a womanizer and a drug addict who had to be kept in the baggage room for the trip; and when the train ran out of coffee cream, Ketchum had to jump off at Blue River, British Columbia, run to a grocery store, and ask the owner if she had 2,000 Creamos. Despite it all, the consensus of passengers was that the privatized Mountaineer would be an instant winner.

Aesthetically, perhaps, but not financially. VIA's lackadaisacal marketing campaign had lured only 7,000 passengers and, by season's end, the train had carried only 11,100. Great Canadian Railtours—as the company was now called—lost nearly $1 million. "I was pretty scared," Armstrong admits. "We knew we were in trouble." After some hard negotiations, the partners had to cede 38 percent of their shares to Vencap Equities Alberta when Canada's largest venture-capital company invested $2.5 million in the spring of 1991. That second year the Mountaineer increased its capacity to 600 seats from 500 and 30 departures from 20, but still lost about $2.9 million on 17,500 passengers. The next season the loss was a further $2.4 million on 20,500.*

The company was still dealing with VIA Rail, paying it for station services and train maintenance. Armstrong tried to win some concessions from the railway, but it was playing hardball with him, especially since he had gone to a mediator and accused it of having "negligently misrepresented" what it had sold him in The Rocky Mountaineer. He was asking for a settlement of $16 million. His case was largely based on the low number of passenger sales and bookings he had inherited in 1990 and VIA's failure to carry out its marketing plan for the tourist train in his first season. (Promising to market at the same level it had the year before—$2.7 million—VIA had spent only $175,000.) The mediator had recommended that it forgive Great Canadian nearly $2 million in indebtedness. Armstrong consulted with a lobbyist in Ottawa and then personally, and persuasively, presented his case to the politicians and bureaucrats for a final settlement that would give him another $3 million in credits with VIA. But the government railway was stalling on signing that agreement.

On November 12, 1992, Great Canadian had $4,000 in the bank, payables due of $1 million, including a payroll of up to $40,000—and no real revenue expected until May of the following year. Disaster, in the form of bankruptcy, loomed. Armstrong's partners were stretched thin, even willing to step away from their investments. He approached several other potential investors, to no avail, and finally his Albertan partners at Vencap Equities.** Asking them for a second cash infusion, of $1.1 million, he quotes CEO Sandy Slater as saying, "Peter, we'd bank on you for any other type of deal as long as VIA and the govern-

---

*One problem was the title of a TV show that kept getting rerun on the PBS network in the United States: *Last Train Across Canada* suggested that, with the end of The Canadian's run, Canada no longer had any passenger-train service. Speaking once to the head of the Association of Public Broadcasters, Peter Armstrong said: "If you ever wondered how effective your messages are to the viewing audience, I'm living proof of how good they are."

**Among the other potential investors was Holland America's Westours. "My partners and I approached them to see if they wanted to buy us out because we were in a pretty desperate financial situation," Armstrong says. "The discussion never got beyond [Westours'] Gordon Barr telling me he was going to fire me. That didn't bother me. But I could never get him to focus on any business terms."

ment weren't involved. So, unfortunately, we are not going to fund you anymore." At that point, Armstrong summoned up a strength he had learned in his youth—the real-life application of a seemingly simple piece of advice.

On crucial do-or-die issues, don't necessarily take no for a final answer

In 1972, wanting to take a hotel management course at the B.C. Institute of Technology, Peter Armstrong had refused to be dissuaded when the dean said all the places were full for the next semester. "A lot of people say I'm tenacious," he says. "I just don't always take no for an answer. I learned a long time ago that selling only starts when the customer says no. The key to that experience, and others along the way, is to find out what it does take [to get to yes]." When Vencap's Sandy Slater turned him down for more investment money, Armstrong said, "Sandy, I hear you. I appreciate the candour, but what will it take to get you to fund us?" Slater replied: "I'm sorry. You don't seem to understand. I am not going to fund you." Armstrong came back: "Sandy, you've got to give me something. You've got to tell me what it takes. I've got a week before disaster. I'm not going to sit back—what is it going to take?" Slater finally said: "Oh, gee, Peter, I don't know. Let me think about it." That was when Armstrong knew he had a chance. Slater, consulting with investment manager Michael Phillips and other associates, came back about an hour later to say Armstrong had to wrest concessions from CP and CN and get his settlement agreement finalized with VIA. Which he did: the two senior railways gave Great Canadian a grace period to pay its current debts—and they actually lent money to it—while in March 1993 VIA finally signed the agreement that gave the company more than $5 million in cash, equipment, credits, and debts waived.

In 1993 Great Canadian made a profit of more than $900,000. The company has been even more profitable every year since. And once it began making money, Murray Jackson resurfaced in Armstrong's life.

199

Harking back to 1989, and his demand for the confidentiality agreement that Armstrong refused to sign, the former VIA executive launched a lawsuit against him, alleging that he had agreed not to put in a competitive bid. Although Armstrong claims he wanted to fight, he says his board of directors didn't: "We paid him off. It pissed me off. ... It was an emotional thing for me because he was saying that I did something that I didn't do. I said, 'I respect the fact that I have got a board to make sure I don't do stupid things. I will do this, but I have to tell you I don't feel good about going about it this way—but it is the best thing for the company, providing certainty.' So we paid him $200,000 to go away."

In the first two years, Armstrong's ten-percent piece of the company had been diluted to four percent. With the company starting to turn a profit, his brother and Rick Browning began to ease out, leaving him to buy some of their shares and offer the rest in 1995 to the B.C. government's Working Opportunities Fund. Vencap's Mike Phillips had moved to the Vancouver-based investment fund as vice president of investment and helped arrange the $1.6-million infusion in Great Canadian Railtours.

It was during this time that Armstrong did something he had wanted to do for 20 years, something his fellow director and mentor Jim Houston had been urging on him.

As soon as you are eligible, join peer groups like the Young Presidents' Organization

It has been called everything from a secret international society of capitalists to the world's finest consulting service. The Young Presidents' Organization is designed to help its members become better executives through education and idea exchange.* To join (before a 40th birthday), a president or chairman and CEO must run a company with gross annual sales of at least $6 million U.S., or net revenues in annual commissions or fees of $4 million, and have at least 50 employees.

---

*An option to YPO is the Young Entrepreneurs' Organization for those 39 or under who are founder, cofounder, owner, or controlling shareholders of a business with annual sales above $1 million U.S. Like YPO, it stresses personal as well as professional development. In western Canada, there are chapters in Victoria, Vancouver, Calgary, Edmonton, Saskatoon, and Winnipeg (in the East, only Toronto and Montreal have chapters).

Years ago Peter Armstrong was intimidated by the people in YPO: "I thought, *They're going to ask all sorts of questions and on the financial side I am pretty good.* But I didn't want to get in some discussion where I didn't know the answer." When he finally did join, he met "some pretty impressive guys and they put their shoes on the same way I do—one at a time. You work together as a local chapter and you learn things. It could be about business, it could about dealing with family or with aging parents—a whole bunch of things. The education program is pretty exciting and dynamic." His wife has joined a spousal group, and even his children—16-year-old twin daughters and 13-year-old son—come along to some family events. He is in a forum group with one woman president and eight men. "And it's a chance to talk openly to colleagues with no ego, no game plan, no whatever, and they become your personal board of directors," he says. Yves Potvin of Yves Veggie Cuisine *(page 89)*, who is in Armstrong's forum group, remembers the railway man announcing last year that he was tired of dealing with partners. Potvin and others challenged him to buy them out.

The past few years have seen extraordinary growth for Great Canadian. In 1994 it bought the first of four dome coaches, built by old friend Tom Rader; the next year it increased the number of regular Daynighter coaches by four to 21; and the year after it ran the longest passenger train in Canadian history: 37 cars with 1,100-plus aboard. Then, by adding a second train in 1997, the company doubled its frequency of service to 126 departures a season. But as Mark Andrew, the newly appointed vice president and chief operating officer, points out, Great Canadian is much more than a railway company: "If we had to live on our two-day rail, we wouldn't be in business today. We are very much a marketing organization that also sells pre- and post-rail [tour] packages. Through just one of our packages you can see Niagara Falls, take the trans-continental to Jasper, then the Rocky Mountaineer to Vancouver—and we can fly you from your front doorstep to the train and back. Our future is predicated on our marketing."

There have been some bumps on the track, though. In 1995 Armstrong decided to buy out the 38 percent of shares owned by Vencap which, under the new ownership of Toronto lawyer/financier

Gerald Schwartz, had decided to divest itself of Great Canadian. But at the same time, Vencap was offering the stock to Alberta's Brewster Transportation. Armstrong tried for an injunction to delay the sale and, while he suffered a humiliating loss in court, the Royal Bank loyally provided the financing in time for him to leverage the buyout, which now had to match the higher Brewster offer.

That incident was a hiccup compared with the potential for disaster posed a year later when VIA Rail announced its intention to double the frequency of its own high-season trains through the Rockies. Mounting a full-frontal assault, Armstrong and consultant Jess Ketchum lobbied politicians of every party at every level of government, particularly in the city that acts as The Rocky Mountaineer's sleepover host. "Kamloops was the key to the campaign simply because the train has a monumental impact on the city," Ketchum says. "There have been 600 hotel rooms built there as a result"—and in 1998 the Mountaineer filled 33,000 rooms in all. When members of the Standing Committee on Transport were researching their report on "the renaissance of passenger rail in Canada," Great Canadian invited them on the trip through the Rockies. "Instead of 20 minutes," Ketchum says, "We had them for two days, and on the last day we took them into the boardroom and made our presentation." In June 1998, the committee called for "fair and reasonable" competition between the private and public rail sectors on "a level playing field."*

About then Armstrong felt flush enough to pick up the challenge of his fellow Young Presidents and buy out the last of his major partners, the Working Opportunity Fund, which estimated that it had made upward of a 65-percent return on its investment. That left only him and his brother, Bev, who retained 14 percent of the stock. (No wonder he was named the Canadian Venture Capital Associations's entrepreneur of the year in 1999.) Armstrong also felt confident enough to share some of the load with four new members of his management team. Among them was Mark Andrew, who had worked for the American-based Hyatt Hotel chain for 24 years, most recently as general manager of the Hyatt in Vancouver.

---

*By then Peter Armstrong's major antagonist at VIA Rail, president Terry Ivany, had stepped down at the end of his five-year mandate. Jess Ketchum says Ivany "was what got Peter up in the morning." Ivany's successor is Rod Morrison, who recently hit Armstrong with a huge increase for servicing Great Canadian's trains.

Sharing operational duties should prove whether Armstrong has made the transition from entrepreneur to seasoned executive. In the past, Ketchum says, his friend was "not beyond telling someone how to do his job in the minutest detail." Ann Coombs, the consultant who introduced her version of "service excellence" to Armstrong, says that when she met him five years ago, "Peter was not a delegator. He would not necessarily allow his people to take charge. But he's changing in terms of delegating. He's going to make this work."

Coombs is a spark plug behind at least one of Great Canadian's new business-building ventures—Meetings in Motion. In 1997 the company acquired two specialized, multipurpose coaches with lounge and boardroom space to offer firms rolling retreats on the Mountaineer. Coombs quickly booked $250,000 worth of business. Another innovation is winter train trips, prompted by four Japanese tour operators who sold their ski customers on a rail ride from Kamloops to Banff. "It was absolutely magical," says marketing VP Murray Atherton of the Christmas Express, which featured Santa Claus and a swing band for the 200 passengers. With $200,000 in marketing funds from the operators and the Canadian Tourism Association, Armstrong risked the $100,000 it costs to operate the train on a round trip. "We lost a ton of money," Atherton allows, although the response was encouraging enough to schedule four such tours in 1998 and 1999. Yet he says neither Asians nor the group tours are the future for the Mountaineer. Growth will build on individual travellers, 43 percent of them currently from the United States, 25 percent from the United Kingdom and Europe, and 20 percent from Canada.

To attract these markets to the Little Railway That Could—and possibly other rail operations in other countries—Armstrong hopes to ride on some intriguing developments that have transformed the tourism and hospitality industry in the quarter century since he was a hotel doorman.

TrendWatch

Peter Armstrong believes so strongly in his form of tourist-train travel that he is seriously talking to operators in Europe about potential franchises or ownership there and considering the possibility of Amtrak routes in the United States if and when they become available over the next few years. As for his Canadian line, he takes comfort in studies showing that, in future, sun vacations will be less popular than northern ones that offer wilderness experiences, even if a holiday trip through the Rockies happens to be aboard a cozy rail coach. And with his fellow boomers moving into their high-income years, he says, "People will have money to do things, so they'll be looking for quality experiences. Expectations are going to be higher. ... The consumer is less forgiving." He quotes disembarking passengers raving about how much they enjoyed being pampered for two days on his train. Futurist Ann Coombs understands: "People want to be nurtured now. On this train, you're nurtured for two solid days. You have extra services with wonderful commentary provided by people with grace and a passion for what they do." But she also sees the strength of Armstrong's business reflecting an increasingly important issue, especially for Americans: personal-security fears. "People are afraid. And the perspective is, that in spite of certain Amtrak crashes in the United States, trains are the safest way to travel." Especially a train with the history of The Rocky Mountaineer, where the most unnverving event can be the loss of air-conditioning in a glass-swathed luxury coach on a sweltering summer day.

The
Manufacturing
Magicians

In the spring of 1998, just as the wide skies over the Prairies were warming, I called Dan Haseloh in Kindersley, Saskatchewan. From a picture I had seen, where he looked rakishly handsome in a leather flying jacket and a Mickey Mouse tie, he appeared to be still in his thirties. That was young for the president of a manufacturing company doing about $2 million a year in business from a town of 4,800 people a long drive from Saskatoon. What fascinated me even more was the product in the background of the photo: a gyroplane. This cross between a helicopter and a plane had been briefly popular in the 1950s before too many poorly trained pilots began crashing the light rotary-blade aircraft. Yet here Haseloh was, four decades later, making enclosed two-seaters in kit form and selling them for $21,500 U.S. in 20 countries to buyers ranging from Yukon trappers to U.S. drug agents. On the phone, he mentioned that after high school he had had a direct-sales and marketing job and eventually ran a 15-person crew peddling cookware and silverware in Alberta. Now he had 22 employees working for him in his own company, Rotary Air Force. And in our conversation he made a point of stressing the safety of his gyroplanes and his insistence on selling them only to customers who had committed to take accredited flying courses.

As well as running his factory, Haseloh was also the company's test pilot and a demonstrator of gyroplanes at North American air shows and fly-ins. He would be in Florida in April; the closest he would get to me was Washington State at the beginning of July. Because I wanted to see him on his home turf, we agreed to meet in Kindersley at season's end. In late summer, I phoned his office number and a woman answered. Explaining my mission, I mentioned that Haseloh had asked me to call. I heard the phone drop. A few seconds later another female voice came on the line. When I repeated my introduction, the woman said, "I'm sorry, I guess you haven't heard. Dan was killed in a midair collision in June. That was his wife who answered."

I tell this story in homage to Dan Haseloh, who was not only venturesome in the air but also in business. He represented a breed of young Mavericks who have risked start-up manufacturing operations in small cities and towns, sometimes even villages, throughout the West. Kindersley itself, rich in the wheatland and oilfields of west-central Saskatchewan, has a strong manufacturing base, from Big Sky Steel Fabricators and Hill Acme Machine to Li'l S Woodworks and Beline Manufacturing, which fabricates agricultural implements and designs electronic controls, much of them for export. An industrial footing like this can transform a community in more ways than one: 80 percent of Kindersley's population is under 55, the opposite of most rural centres in the province.

Manufacturing Mavericks position themselves in nonurban settings for many reasons: cheaper land and buildings, government incentives, availability of local labour, lifestyle. They balance those benefits against drawbacks such as higher transportation costs and a shortage of highly skilled employees, many of whom prefer metropolitan attractions to rural charms. A case in point is the couple who moved to the little island in British Columbia where I live, less than 20 minutes from West Vancouver by frequent ferry, and started the evocatively named Bowen Island Brewing Company. They had come for the bucolic way of life, but the reality of having to bring all their raw materials on to the island and then ship all their product off proved much too expensive. They transplanted the microbrewery to Vancouver, where it operates successfully under its original name.

Many other western manufacturers do succeed away from the hurry-worry of the biggest cities. In British Columbia, for instance, 40 percent of the province's manufacturing establishments are located outside the Greater Vancouver Regional District. Werner Knittel, director of manufacturing for the B.C. division of the Alliance of Manufacturers and Exporters Canada, says, "I'm getting the sense that because of the high cost of doing business in the Lower Mainland, certain types of manufacturers are locating in smaller centres like Victoria and the Okanagan. The quality of life really does attract a lot of people to those two areas and they're very unlikely to leave." He mentions specialty entrepreneurial companies such as Dave Barron's AOG Air Support Inc. in Kelowna, which retrofits safety modifications to veteran utility aircraft such as the De Havilland Beaver and Twin Otter: "Their customers really don't care where their aircraft is serviced."

Of the two couples featured as Manufacturing Magicians on the following pages, one is also based in Kelowna—the Fields of Pacific Safety Products—while the Scharfs of Jim Scharf Holdings operate from Perdue, Saskatchewan.* They are *magicians* because it requires some legerdemain, some conjuring and juggling, to establish an industrial plant in most places in underpopulated western Canada, much less in a small centre away from a major city. By locating in remoter communities, however, these manufacturers are simply following the demographic drift of Canadians coast to coast. As economist David K. Foot says in his bestseller *Boom, Bust & Echo*, "Over the next two decades, as 9.8 million baby-boomers turn 50, we will witness a significant exo-

---

*The focus on these manufacturers in Saskatchewan and British Columbia is not to suggest that their counterparts in neighbouring western provinces are any less adventurous in locating outside major centres. Nor that the other two provinces themselves are any less interesting as manufacturing locales. In fact, Manitoba has a much more diverse industrial base than next-door Saskatchewan and—given the current economic decline on the West Coast—it is no surprise that Alberta recently bumped British Columbia to take third place in Canadian manufacturing, after Ontario and Quebec. Its industrial manufacturing shipments now nearly equal energy-sector shipments. Resource-rich Alberta has long witnessed the phenomenon of rural manufacturing. "It has been happening—very much so," says Bob Saari, provincial vice president of the Alliance of Manufacturers. He mentions the example of "this red-hot machinist" who moved to the village of Onoway, 60 kilometres west of Edmonton, took over a simple welding shop, and established a small custom-machining operation that has attracted complementary businesses. That would be Bernie Schulz, who left his work as a tool-and-die maker with Magna International in Toronto to resettle in a country environment with his wife and child. "I grew up in a small town in Germany," Schulz says, "and don't like the city rat race—life in the fast lane." Saari also notes "there are several companies who've moved out for the lifestyle to the Rocky Mountain House and Canmore areas." They make the move despite the fact that the provincial government, following Premier Ralph Klein's dictum that "the government is out of the business of being in business," offers few incentives to facilitate such nonurban industry.

dus from big-city Canada to small-town Canada." Among them will be prosperous new retirees: "It is already happening in the Okanagan and other parts of the B.C. Interior, where people from Vancouver and other major cities have settled after deciding to trade their city homes for some small-town tranquillity."

Brad and Lori Field were young marrieds living in the Okanagan Valley when they and some partners launched a business almost by happenstance. The Fields were there by choice (a national magazine not long ago declared their adopted home of Kelowna one of the ten best places to live in Canada) and saw no good reason to leave when they started making emergency medical kits and then body armour such as bulletproof vests. Their multimillion-dollar enterprise now supplies safety products around the globe, despite its location a four-hour drive north of Vancouver. "Two years ago we didn't rank," Brad Field told me in 1998. "We were nobody nowhere. Last year we really made our debut as far as the rest of the industry was concerned—'Where'd these guys come from, these upstarts from Canada? Where the heck is British Columbia, much less Kelowna?' Then this year we're one of the major players in North America. Biggest in Canada."

Being in a perceived backwater forces you to raise your profile, usually by in-person approaches to potential wholesalers and retailers in pivotal centres of high population. Which makes the success of Jim and Bruna Scharf's kitchen-gadget company more surprising, given his reluctance to leave their tiny Saskatchewan farming village for anyplace farther than Saskatoon. While he has attended his share of North American trade shows to promote their E-ZeeWrap 1000 plastic-wrap dispenser and other products, the innately bashful, home-loving Scharf refuses to appear at any more, asking his wife and an employee to go in his place. Meanwhile the couple has somehow managed to build their business by sending samples of their product line to suppliers and the media rather than selling it themselves with personal visits or employing a sales staff to represent them (although they have since hired a U.S. sales manager). "They said it couldn't work," Jim Scharf says of their unconventional long-distance marketing. "We made it work." And continue to make it prosper: Bruna is now using the Internet imaginatively to contact prospective retailers of their houewares—bridging the gulf between Prairie-bound Perdue and the rest of the wide world by that most modern of electronic means.

Chapter Seven

Boondocks Warriors

Brad and Lori Field, Pacific Safety Products

That August day in 1995 the two Mounties, members of a special-response team, had been clearing timber from a logging road block-aded by a group of Native protesters in Cariboo country near Gustafsen Lake, British Columbia. Constables Rocky Clelland and Gordon Molendyk of Prince George were among 400 police officers called out over that long, heated summer as a ranch owner tried to evict a group of Native people claiming a piece of his land as aboriginal ter-ritory. Suddenly, while the constables were removing the roadblock, a barrage of gunfire erupted around them. They leaped into their Suburban and desperately began backing it up as rounds from a semi-automatic AK-47 burst its tires, tore open the gas tank, and shattered windows. One bullet struck Clelland in the back, another got Molendyk near his right shoulder. "It was a 40-second ride through hell," they remember, and the only thing that saved them was the wrap-around body armour they were wearing. Clelland escaped with just a bruise the size of a grapefruit, his partner with only a burn where a slug had lodged between his belt and bare skin.* They both credited their survival to the Beast, the nickname for a bullet-resistant vest made of Spectra Shield high-threat ballistic material. So grateful were they that a year later the Mounties appeared as guests at the annual meeting of the vest's creator, a low-profile public company based in an unlikely location, the Okanagan resort-and-retirement centre of Kelowna.

---

*After one of Canada's longest criminal trials—ten months in a heavily secured Surrey, British Columbia courtroom—13 people involved in the armed standoff were sentenced to prison terms ranging from six months to four and a half years for offences that ran the gamut from mischief to the attempted murder of the two Mounties.

If the constables had been more seriously injured, the paramedics coming to their aid could well have been carrying emergency medical kits designed by the same innovative manufacturer, Pacific Safety Products. Medical professionals are using PSP's modular kits throughout Europe, Africa, Asia, Australia, and North America. Regular viewers of the hit television series *ER* and *The X-Files* might spot ambulance actors with the colourful kits, which were also highly visible in the 1994-95 TV space opera, *Earth 2* (a poster featuring a kit at the feet of the long-legged star, Deborah Farentino, hangs prominently in the corporate headquarters).

Pacific Emergency Products, the third-largest maker of these medical kits on the continent, is one division of this bipolar company. The other is Pacific Body Armour, which recently acquired a subsidiary, Canadian Body Armour of Brampton, Ontario. Together they now rank first in Canada and fifth in the United States among manufacturers of ballistic and knife-resistant vests and other highly specialized protective equipment for police, the military, and even paramedics and conservation officers. Scotland Yard uses CBA's armoured vests, and the Tokyo police force wears PSP's version, as Canadian peacekeepers did in Bosnia. The Kelowna company has also built elaborate land-mine-clearing suits—looking like space-movie costumes, they take 40 hours apiece to make—for Canadian military bomb-disposal specialists cleaning up that war-wracked remnant of Yugoslavia. And in a co-venture with an American leader in crash-safety products, PSP is making the Ballistic Advantage, an instant soft-armour system for vehicles, which can be fitted into a standard car in 15 minutes with no vehicle modifications or special tools.

If it seems a little improbable to find a world pacesetter in emergency medical kits and body and vehicle armour in Kelowna (area population: 120,000), consider its equally unlikely founding partners, a couple in their early forties.* Brad and Lori Field—husband and wife,

---

*In fact, Kelowna is well on its way to becoming British Columbia's third metropolitan area, after Greater Vancouver and Greater Victoria. Excepting some Lower Mainland municipalities, Kelowna expanded more quickly throughout the 1990s—at a rate of 46 percent—than any other western Canadian centre with more than 25,000 people. Reflecting this urban growth is the current $20-million expansion of the local airport, reportedly the swiftest-growing "national" one in Canada. Yet 45 percent of the city remains in British Columbia's Agricultural Land Reserve.

parents of two, president and corporate secretary, continuing coworkers—built the company on a good if simple idea, his overweening zeal and her reluctant faith, and three initial years of consuming work that yielded them not a cent of salary—oh, and on their charge card and a $1,000 loan from Brad's uncle. At three times over the first decade as a private business, they shared the stresses with different partners, some of them friends, none of whom have survived as co-owners. Since the Fields took PSP public on the Alberta Stock Exchange in 1995, they have managed to retain majority control and develop a sterling enough reputation in the global industry to attract as a company director the Canadian military hero Major General Lewis MacKenzie. But even now the tensions remain for the couple, at least quietly in the background, as they personally guarantee the corporate line of credit with the bank—which means they would lose their lovely new house high on a hill overlooking Kelowna, and numerous other personal possessions if the business were to fail.

That isn't likely. "I'm impressed with Brad Field," says Michael Hill, an industrial-technology specialist with Calgary's Acumen Capital Partners. "He's a fairly astute businessman. I have a pretty warm feeling about where he can take this company. He can do well over time. I think he's right—he has to build through acquisition to get some sort of critical mass that enables him to attract the world-scale customers and the public market's interest." In the 1998 fiscal year, through acquisition, a wider distribution network, and some significant special orders, the Fields came tantalizingly close to the $10-million sales mark needed to apply for a Toronto Stock Exchange listing; in the 1999 fiscal year, they expected to do $15 million.

Their success has come at some cost. The Fields, typical of most entrepreneurial couples, had to balance different talents, contrapuntal personalities, and his perceived need for an unrelenting presence at work with her desire for a normal life with a young family. For the first nine years, fighting for the very survival of the business, they didn't take a vacation until Lori announced one day that she was booking a lakeside holiday, and was he joining her? It would take Brad a few years longer to recognize that he didn't have to lead the company alone, that he could trust managers, that he could hire consultants for the expertise he lacked. He would shoot himself in the foot several times— metaphorically, with no recourse to any emotional medical kit to relieve the pain. Helping him survive through it all, however, was a human version of a bulletproof vest. Early on he realized that he could call on an unpaid confidant, an older and more experienced businessman who would offer hard-won wisdom that Brad Field would badly need.

Swallowing and digesting such advice, difficult as that often was, he has let it fuel his personal and corporate growth. "For the president of a small-cap company," Mike Hill says, "I'd consider him on the more sophisticated end of the spectrum—in terms of his business acumen on all fronts." Field has grown from a naïve up-country entrepreneur who, when told that Marubeni Corporation was seeking a company to supply body armour in Tokyo, asked, "Who are they?" He has become a much more worldly strategist who can juggle an AlliedSignal—a major American supplier of ballistic materials that introduced him to the giant Japanese trading company—and Du Pont, the U.S. company's heavyweight competitor in the synthetic-fibre industry. AlliedSignal was his original supplier when Field moved into body armour in 1990, but he pulled back from the Virginia-based manufacturer over, of all people, Oliver North of Iran-Contra infamy. The Marine-turned-conservative-talk-show-host has his own body-armour company, Guardian Technologies International.

Field began telling me the story of the falling-out with Allied as we were in the long tunnel that is his ballistics lab—the concrete-and-padding firing range at PSP's new, $2-million, 2,508-square-metre headquarters.* Showing me a rough-looking gun of 7.62 calibre, he said, "This is a deadly piece of work." It was a Tokarev, a standard Russian military sidearm. "There's millions of these things around. With the breakup of the Eastern Bloc, of course, they proliferated all over the place. And they're a nasty little round to stop. So we developed a ballistic package—ballistic composition specifically designed to defeat that high-performance round. We developed this package, and Ollie North ended up announcing that he'd developed it. And AlliedSignal supported him on it, which infuriated us because we had given them the data. We just said, 'Fine, if that's the way you want to do business, we'll do our business elsewhere.' We vote with our feet. There's other

---

*Which is tightly secured, unlike the former premises—a trio of buildings totalling 1,579 square metres—where in 1995 thieves broke in and stole several ballistic vests. Fortunately police caught them before they could use the body armour during a crime.

ways to stop those rounds, so we just went and figured out another way with another company's product, their raw material."

Yet he continues to maintain Allied as a sometime supplier. He had been on the phone with one of the company's salesmen that morning. "I see our old friend Ollie North is going down," Field said, remarking on the fact that the former Marine's business was bleeding badly. "A million bucks in sales—you're not going to survive on that for very long."

On the wall facing him as he spoke was a handsomely framed Group of Seven reproduction, with a plaque recording PSP's move into its new quarters. It was a gift from Du Pont Canada, AlliedSignal's rival.

On his desk, beside a pack of Twizzlers licorice, a Compaq laptop lets him check PSP's latest stock price and the production statistics on the factory floor below. In the bookcase behind him are the inevitable *Boom, Bust & Echo*, such inspirational titles as *Seven Summits* and *Going for Broke*, and military memoirs, including *Peacekeeper: The Road to Sarajevo* by Lewis MacKenzie, the former chief of staff of the U.N. peacekeeping force in Yugsolavia (the autograph inside reads: "Dear Brad, Many thanks—for all the support and protection!"). Atop the case is an amusing black dragon, which has become the company motif: "You can't pierce the scales of a dragon," Field explains. Here, on the city's outskirts, he looks out on a woodland hill where quail, pheasant, and the occasional deer drop by. Perched on the windowsill is an antique Singer sewing machine, a symbol of where the company came from.

Field is wearing a tie over a blue denim shirt with the monogram "TEAM PSP/Quality Through Teamwork." Bespectacled, his broad, high brow ascending as his hairline recedes, he stands no more than 1.6 metres, his face appearing almost too big for his body. Approaching his 40th birthday in 1997, he shaved his moustache, shedding several years. He looks too young, too small a package to be dealing at high levels in the world of big-boned SWAT teams and seasoned major generals leading military expeditions in battle-scarred nations.

Growing up the son of a road contractor in southeastern British Columbia around Christina Lake and then Cranbrook, Bradley Field was the shortest kid in high school. About 1.3 metres tall, he played on the basketball team only when the visiting Harlem Clowns needed some comic relief. An individualist, he preferred solo sports like skiing and rock-climbing. He loved poetry, disliked abstract mathematics, but excelled in more practical subjects such as geometry. From age six, he had wanted to study marine biology and attended the University of Victoria for a year before realizing there would likely be no job in that overcrowded field when he graduated. Instead he went to a deep-sea diving school in California and became a commercial diver off Vancouver Island, living on a boat and harvesting geoduck for the Japanese market.

After a year, he dropped that hard, dangerous work and moved to Kelowna in 1981 to pursue emergency medicine, another childhood passion. Settling in with an aunt and uncle, he tried to become a paramedic with the B.C. Ambulance Service. It wasn't hiring and, anyway, he couldn't get an ambulance-driver's licence because he was born blind in one eye, although that hadn't affected his driving stock cars in Cranbrook and, later, ice-racing vehicles around Kelowna. His first work in town was rolling fibreglass in a hot-tub factory ("by far my worst job"), but he graduated to the shipping department before moving on to become a full-time ski patroller on a local mountain. The job would at least allow him to keep his first-aid ticket current.

By then an old girlfriend had moved to Kelowna. Brad and Lori had begun dating in high school until he dropped her for two years and then resumed their relationship after graduation. The diminutive Lori, the youngest of five of a single mother who worked in retail, also went to the University of Victoria and left after a year's arts and science to take business courses at the Southern Alberta Institute of Technology in Calgary. Unlike her boyfriend, she never had any clear personal goals ("I still don't," she confesses). The summer of 1981, she joined Brad and began working in an insurance office while continuing to take professional courses. Together they volunteered with the Canadian Ski Patrol on weekends at Crystal Mountain. And it was there, two years later, that their business careers were born.

Along with one female and two male volunteers, they would brainstorm about designing a better fanny pack to organize and carry medical supplies, a pack that could be worn as easily on a ski lift as on the slopes. Their original design, incorporating Velcro pullout pouches with zippers for individual items, was the rough prototype for the current Pacific Safety Products medical kits. Field did the cutting of fabric, and the female patroller sewed the first packs at home. They soon had 30 orders, one from another patroller who worked at a local credit union.

214

Deciding to form a small company, Patrol Pack Systems, the quartet approached him for a loan. That was where Brad Field first heard words of warning he would wish he had heeded.

Think hard before going into business with friends

"You guys are going to start out as friends and end up as enemies," the credit-union loan officer told the four would-be entrepreneurs. "And you know what?" Brad Field says. "It's exactly what happened. We had no bankroll to speak of. We all had regular jobs to survive." The business-illiterate friends began bickering—"Well, I want *you* to put in more time." And soon, he says, "It got to the point where we were yelling and screaming at each other. I once heard that partnerships are great as long as you're not losing money or making money —somebody's saying I'm not getting my cut. We learned some tough lessons—that you don't go in ignorant. It's probably not worth the friendships to do that, because it really tore us all up. Fortunately most of us are now back talking. The thing just exploded in our faces, and we were doomed to failure right from the beginning. What you're doing when you go into business with friends or family, you're risking that relationship—is it worth the risk? For the most part, it's not. This one wasn't. Having said that, this company wouldn't be here today if we hadn't all done that."

In 1984, having made 100 fanny packs and 20 backpacks, the partners—now including a fifth man, who invested a small sum—went their separate ways. Neither Brad nor Lori had any talent for sewing, so they paid a woman with an industrial sewing machine to make the packs in her home. In the evenings, after work on the ski hills, Brad would spell her off, sometimes until 3:00 a.m. It was at this point that his Uncle Mark took pity and gave him $1,000 to buy his own heavy-duty machine (this first crucial investor has since had more than a 300-percent return).*

---

*Today one of the industrial sewing machines, a fully programmable model, costs the company $30,000; most of them run around $6,000. At the Pacific Safety Products factory, they are all operated by women; at Canadian Body Armour, some men work on the machines.

Field called a manufacturer who had already supplied backpack fabric to him: Dave Harley, a cofounder with his father of Far West Mountain Wear of Vernon, British Columbia. "Dave's another guy who started from zero, from the back of his dad's store, and developed it into a successful multimillion-dollar business," he says. At the time, Far West was the largest customer in North America for Gore-Tex water-resistant outerwear fabrics. When they first met, Harley was getting out of the backpack business and invited Field to visit him at his factory. When the young hopeful arrived, he asked for the well-established businessman. He was directed to a fellow about his age at a desk in the middle of the factory floor. "This company's probably doing $25 million a year at that point, and there he was, hair all over the place, ripped-up sweatshirt, and he's wearing gumboots. I said, 'No, *Dave* Harley.' 'That's him.' I thought, *Oh, this guy also has a hobby farm and just came in.* But that's Dave Harley. It indicated to me that you could be successful regardless of whether you were Bay Street. He was on the factory floor, he had a finger on the pulse all the time, knew exactly what was going on. I greatly admired that."

It was the beginning of a friendship that blossomed a year later when Harley brought an industrial sewing machine to the 74-square-metre house where the newly married Brad and Lori were now living and showed them how to use it. At the time, Field had an important potential customer for his packs. A couple of paramedics he had befriended on the ski hills, and even gone out on calls with, told him that the B.C. Ambulance Service could use a new emergency medical kit. He redesigned the original model—using tough ballistic nylon and reflective tape for a kit with a centre compartment and outer pockets—and put it on a table in front of the service's head trainer in Vancouver. The man, without even greeting him, said, "I'll take 40. How much? I want to put them on my training ambulances. If we like them, we'll buy 400."

The Fields soon outgrew their living-room factory, cleared out their windowless little garage to cut material, and hired a seamstress, their first full-time employee. They opened an account with Far West for fabric and another with Mountain Co-Op in Vancouver for buckles, webbing, and corduroy. They would make a couple of kits and sell them for cash flow to buy more supplies. They worked their Visa card, with its

$1,000 limit. "No bank would touch you with a ten-foot pole," Brad says. He was still employed on the ski hill and Lori at the insurance agency. When the first seamstress left, they hired a young Vietnamese refugee. "She was probably the hardest-working person I've ever come across," he says. "She'd have a yardstick and start pounding it on the table: 'Boss, boss, more work!' She'd eat her lunch at the machine. She really drove me to continue." After fulfilling the contract for 400 ambulance kits, they began making a couple of other styles, holsters to carry medical instruments, and a protective bag for paramedics' oxygen cylinders. Sales doubled to $40,000 in the second year and would double again in the third—still not enough to yield any salaries for the owners. Their new family company, Pacific Emergency Packs and Equipment, moved into the back of a silk screener's studio, bought two more sewing machines, and hired a couple of other Vietnamese women and one of Brad's rock-climbing friends to do the cutting.

And they now had a silent partner, Jack Peach of Vancouver, who had won $1 million in a provincial lottery, moved to Kelowna, and wound up working on the ski hill as his winnings ran out. He had invested $5,000 for 35 percent of the company. In 1986 the Fields replaced him with Merv Miller, a former government accountant in Whitehorse who bought out Peach for about $25,000 to get 45 percent of the company. "Pretty efficient guy, but nevertheless an accountant, only concerned about the dollar and margins, " Field says. "There's a reason you don't have accountants running companies. Our relationship soured real bad within a matter of months."

It would take two years for the partnership to end. Not only did Miller move them into a smaller space, but he also insisted on hiring his son as a cutter. When Field complained about the young man's work ethic, the father exploded and told his partner to buy him out right away or he would buy Field out. "And to add a little pressure, we had a bank line that we weren't using, but Merv went and paid everybody and put the bank line over the limit, so I had the banks all over me, too. And he said, 'Oh, by the way, I'm not working anymore. You can reach me at home.' Plus, my wife is nine months' pregnant. So I called on my old friend Dave Harley: 'I think I'm in deep shit here. I think Merv's going to get the company.' He said, 'Oh, no. Come up to my place this weekend. I'll have the beer cold and we'll go through it.'"

Field had recognized a fundamental that can prove vital for any embryonic entrepreneur.

Find and use a mentor

"Get a mentor—they've gone through it," Brad Field urges. "And it's suprising how many people are willing to be one." Toronto business consultant Chips Klein, a mentor in the Step Ahead One-on-One Mentoring Program, says, "A mentor is someone who's been there, done that, learned from the experience, and is willing to share that knowledge with the protégé. A good mentor should have been through the start-up phase, growth phase, recessionary times, changes in the economy, possibly even downsizing or bankruptcy, and has weathered all the ups and downs."* Field had such an adviser in Dave Harley, who had him come to his home in Vernon to discuss the partnership crisis in a calmer atmosphere. "It's a summer day and he's got a beautiful view overlooking a golf course," Field says. "'Here's the name of my lawyer,' he tells me, 'the name of my accountant. You go see them.' His lawyer said, 'No problem. We'll have you your company. Give me 30 days.' They put a deal together for Merv to be bought out for about $75,000 over three years. Between the accountant and the lawyer, they structured it so I could handle all of it. At the end of the day, we dodged the bullet thanks to David Harley, my mentor, and kept the company. Lori and I are the lone owners again. Full circle." It wouldn't be the last time they called on Harley, who early in their careers offered them this piece of advice: *The first million is the toughest. After that, it's just zeroes.*

---

*What is in it for the mentor? Chips Klein says, "Mentors get a rare opportunity to hone their interpersonal skills and reevaluate their own business practices." The Step Ahead One-on-One Mentoring Program he is involved with is a Toronto-based group aimed primarily at women entrepreneurs. The Peer Resources Network, a service of a nonprofit educational corporation in Victoria, has a Web site *(www.peer.ca/findamentor.html)* that gives tips on locating a mentor, a list of experts in mentoring, and even offers to help you match up with a potential mentor.

On their own now, their firstborn newly arrived, the Fields had to redouble their already herculean efforts. Lori took a two-day course in bookkeeping and came into the office with their daughter, who would sit in a car seat on a cutting table surrounded by about 15 employees. She brought Shaylee in for ten months until they could afford to hire an office worker. "I was literally nursing this baby while I was on the phone talking to customers," the mother recalls. "You do what you've got to do." Today she admits to having done it reluctantly at times. "I wasn't supportive of Brad. I thought he was crazy. He's a dreamer. Luckily he has the means to make his dreams come true. He doesn't hesitate—ever. He doesn't see roadblocks. I see everything as a roadblock."

Her husband says Lori routinely undersells herself: "She can do anything. She always was a top student. When she was in the insurance business, she had so many letters behind her name, taking courses, she ran out of space." But he agrees that she isn't a risk taker. "And that is a balance, which is a positive thing for both, because you feed off each other. People that conservative use you as an avenue—they really would love to take the risk, but their makeup won't allow them to. But they want to be part of it. That's good for me and good for her."

They needed all that balance to face a new crisis in January 1989. The fallout of the failed partnership had left the business reeling. "We were close to bankruptcy, but Brad didn't want to leave our suppliers unpaid," Lori remembers. Harley offered to buy the company from them, but the Fields agreed to give themselves another three months. "And in six months, everything was okay," she says.

By then they had a professional-looking catalogue promoting everything from paramedics' and firefighters' kits to cargo bags and dog harnesses for use in helicopter transport. Field had begun to tap the market to the south. He first attended an emergency-medical trade show in the United States, simply to get the lay of the land. After borrowing trade journals from his ambulance friends, he decided on placing an ad in *JEMS, Journal of Emergency Medical Services,* a key publication. The half-page display showed a dramatic photo of British Columbia's Bugaboo Mountains, which Field had shot while climbing, and gave the company's name and the simple message: "Built to withstand the most severe conditions. Dealer enquiries welcome." No product photos, no technical description, no hype.

The first American dealer was based in New York City. "And holy mackerel, I'm selling up a storm into the U.S. market!" Brad Field recollects, the surprise still in his voice. "But our first shipment was a nightmare, because I didn't know how to ship into the U.S., so I sent it in bond—and, in New York, to get something out of bond takes about three months. The dealer phoned up, and they were just beside themselves. We had to rebuild the whole shipment and ship it again, and by the time the second shipment got there they still hadn't got the first one. They kept them both, actually. But it was a big learning curve. Had to learn all about duties and brokerage fees and how to properly ship— pretty quick. But it became quickly apparent that the U.S. market was where the business was."

Most of his dealerships would result from his appearances at the tightly knit industry's trade shows. He had already got a small Federal Industrial Development Bank loan and now went after government grants to attend the American-based shows, which attract interested parties from around the globe. The fact that he had sold to the B.C. Ambulance Service, one of the larger such operations in the world, helped him do business with the Ontario Ministry of Health and then the New York Emergency Medical Services. Today 65 percent of his emergency products are sold in the United States.

Body armour is another matter. With major-league competitors down south—and even minor ones like high-profile Ollie North's company (whose products are "made in America from American-made raw materials")—very little of PSP's line is exported to the United States. So, the company sells anywhere else, including Asia, Europe, and South America. "The Americans are so bad at export, which is a good thing for us," Field says. "I just love it. And I hope they never learn."

But it was at an American trade show that he met an emergency-room nurse and product developer who led him into the armour business. Dan White, whom he describes as the epitome of the salesman, told Field he had a U.S. customer who liked the Canadian's utility vests but needed armour in them. Field was shocked and recalls himself asking: "Why would paramedics need armour? I don't get this."

"You're from Canada," he quotes White as saying. "Down here it's mandatory for paramedics to wear armour in 14 cities. They're getting called to violent crimes. They carry drugs. They're a target."

"Dan, I don't know bugger all about armour. I'm not interested in getting into armour. We can design the outer garment and we'll phone a U.S. armour manufacturer and see if we can't do a joint venture with them, get them to make the panels for the vests."

In 1990 the company started making the vests with armoured panels from a Florida supplier, which soon went into Chapter 11 bankruptcy after overextending itself during the brief Gulf War. Field then decided to get into armour, after all, to construct it in-house from layers of ballistic material made by AlliedSignal, the low-volume, high-end Virginia supplier he would rely on until the Ollie North hostilities. Two years later he and his staff of 35—which now included a plant manager and an accountant—moved into three buildings near downtown Kelowna. One housed a ballistic testing range where a riflelike weapon called a universal receiver could take barrels of various calibre sizes to fire at products up against a clay backdrop.* Field was assimilating the lingo of the industry, learning about "threat levels" (standards set by the U.S. National Institute of Justice for armour's effectiveness against various types of ammunition); "impact velocity" (a way of measuring the effects of anything from a .38 round-nose lead slug to a .30-06 armour-piercing bullet); and proprietary bullet- and knife-resistant woven materials with such names as Spectra Gold and Kevlar Protera.

He had begun learning how to learn as he was developing his emergency-product line.

Get as close to your customer base as you can

Brad Field believes strongly in working with the end users of his products. "If you're going to be in an industry, get involved in it to whatever level you can." He's not talking about head-

---

* My fantasy of donning one of the company's ballistic vests and being shot at—in a dramatic scene to prove how effective they are—was dashed when Brad Field explained that the sheer energy of the blunt trauma of a bullet, even if doesn't penetrate to the body, can be lethal. Which is why the the industry calls the vests "bullet-resistant," not "bulletproof." PSP does, however, guarantee the ballistic integrity of its vests for five years.

ing up business organizations, as Kelowna winemaker Harry McWatters does. He means getting to know your customers. "First off, I was involved in the industry as a ski patroller," he says. "So I knew intimately what I needed to do the job because I was my own customer. And I still am designing products and I will continue to, whether or not I use our design team as a conduit. The reason we have been successful is not because I'm such an incredible designer, but I had the foresight to be able to look at what the customers wanted and give them what they needed. Not build something and tell them that they should have it because I think it's what they need." On the body-armour side, he communicates with both small-town police departments and big-city tactical and SWAT teams. "Talking to them, going to their practice shoots—getting involved with the guys, sitting there over a beer or a coffee and saying, 'Here's what we got. Does that work for you? Oh, it doesn't—why? Oh, good point. That pocket's not going to work there because your protocol says you just don't do it that way.' I have a friend in the local police department who was a dog handler, and he was very instrumental in some of the things we've done. You have to be right there, involved, and as intimate as you possibly can be. If not, you're going to do a lot of guessing."

In later years, Field would follow up with customer-satisfaction surveys, done over the phone by an outside firm in Vernon, and quality-oriented questionnaires packaged with each item sold. The feedback became particularly imperative as the armour business began to eclipse the emergency products (which today represent less than 25 percent of sales). A recent phone survey, for example, confirmed what Field had been suspecting: the medical-equipment customers weren't being serviced properly. The questionnaires, which elicit about a one-percent return, have inspired some important innovations. One was prompted by paramedics who flew in a medevac helicopter with a floor of antiskid material that wore down the material used in portable medical kits. The idea, which the company has patented, was to make them with a detachable hard bottom. Another dissatisfied customer's complaint—

about the kits having "a chintzy little fabric handle that isn't indicative of the quality of the product"—led to the adoption of a standard heavy leather handle.*

The company's first decade was a little like slogging through a Vietnam jungle, always on the lookout for booby traps, never letting your guard down. It took its toll on Brad's wife and their children, now two in number and needing Lori's full-time attention. Meanwhile he was working from six until six, spending a couple of evening hours at home, and returning to work until midnight. "I was just fried. I was surviving on caffeine. ... I'm the type of guy who, when I'm married, I'm married for life. I don't take it lightly. If you take that attitude, then you will do whatever it takes to survive. It's going to get stressful. The transition point for us was taking the damn holiday. But that took nine years. Because I was so committed to the job that I wouldn't take a holiday. Maybe we'd go for a weekend, but that's it. So finally she just said, 'To hell with you. I'm booking a cabin at Christina Lake, on the water, no phone, no fax—you coming?' A week. And I didn't know if I could do it. Then I got there and I didn't know if I could come back. For the first couple of days, I'm pacing, I'm just antsy as hell. 'I'm just going to make a phone call at my brother's.' But by the end of the week, I'm mellow. Two weeks the next year and every year since. Now I'm entitled to four weeks off. Never happens—yet. But I'm getting a lot closer."

It had taken nine years for the company to earn a total of $1 million in sales, but just another 12 months to generate that amount in a single year. In 1994 the company restructured itself as Pacific Safety Products Inc. with the emergency-products and body-armour operations as separate divisions. One day Field was searching an Internet computer program called the Online Bidding System when he spotted a call for

---

*PSP has patented a system called adjustable elastic technology, which allows the user of an emergency kit to configure it to personal requirements with self-locking cards—rather than traditional elastic loops—to securely hold each item in place. And it has a patent pending for the Tribrid, a new combination of Kevlar and Spectra that is reportedly more flexible and comfortable than similar products. The manager of research and development is Brian Farnsworth, a Ph.D. in physics, who worked in R&D at the Department of National Defence and at Mustang Industries of Richmond, British Columbia, which recently subcontracted PSP to supply ballistic protection for its role in a $10-million National Defence R&D contract for the Solider System 2005 high-tech project to supply clothing and equipment for the Canadian military.

tenders for 5,000 load-bearing vests for Canadian peacekeeping troops, most of them destined for Bosnia. PSP had just completed a contract to make 100 less-complicated vests for RCMP officers heading to the same war zone. Now it bid for the peacekeeper body armour—or, as it turned out, underbid. "This was a stage where the company really broke out," its president reflects. "And that was the toughest time of my career."

The military vests were complex items with 120 components, including 17 different-size pockets for military gear and slots for bullet-resistant armour. Field and his staff figured that each would take about 180 minutes to assemble. The workforce doubled to 62 to handle the first 1,100 on a tight deadline. At the time, the factory was organized on the classic assembly-line, piecework model, where employees would cut up to 100 units in one batch and might have as many as six batches of different dye-lot colours floating around the floor. The system couldn't cope: at first the vests were taking 200 more minutes apiece to make and only hit the 180-minute target once briefly during the job. "To try and manage all these things was an absolute nightmare. The stress level was through the roof," Field told me. "I would literally have people breaking down in tears on the factory floor. At that time I had my cousin working for me to help manage the factory and we had her stressed to the limit. She was a basket case at the end of all this. My general manager quit, saying, 'I've had enough.' Then we had to lay off a bunch of people because we lost so much money on that contract—about $400,000. And that was the year we were going public."

Field wanted to bid for the remaining 3,900 military vests, but only after implementing some changes. Again he returned to his mentor, Dave Harley, who was running a successful but lower-profile company after new management had squeezed him out of the family business in 1989. David Harley Sportswear Ltd. used sophisticated computer-controlled equipment to make a line called Valhalla Pure Outfitters. Harley recommended that his protégé hire a consultant, a factory-floor engineer named Gene Barbee of Winnipeg's Gene Barbee & Associates.* Field had read an article about a system known as modular manufacturing, which stresses teamwork and peer support to increase productivity.

---

*Barbee, an international production engineer and efficiency expert, has acted as a consultant for such American companies as Wrangler Jeans and Sara Lee, which rank among the world's largest clothing and food conglomerates.

Coincidentally Barbee brought him a videotape on the same topic. Over three months, starting with an experimental group of eight employees, the consultant helped implement a process in which the production staff were split into teams of designers, cutters, seamstresses, and team leaders who liaised with one another. Now each team received a bin of components that would make a dozen full vests, to be assembled by the group working together—rather than disconnected pieces handed from one individual operator to another, with nobody taking responsibility for the finished product. In team-based manufacturing, Field says, "All of a sudden, they're all inspectors." They also had the satisfaction of completing one batch of ready-to-ship vests in the morning and starting a new batch after lunch. The first group had enjoyed the process so much that the other employees organized themselves into teams while Field was away on a road trip.

Coupled with this modular method was a locally designed computerized tracking system, Trax, which offers instant data on any product at any time in the process. It allowed rapid diagnosing of production bottlenecks and up-to-the-minute reporting to customers. Combined, the two systems revolutionized PSP's manufacturing. The company had won the bid for the remaining vests at a higher per-unit cost. This time each one took only 180 minutes at the start of the contract and a third of that time by the end. Not only that, but while the repair rate on the vests in the first contract was as high as 78 percent, it dropped to less than one percent in the second. And although the first time around, vest production had forced the company to abandon the making of emergency medical products—which incensed customers—this time they continued to flow through the factory. "There was no stress," Field says. "I didn't work overtime at all."

Modular manufacturing, which continues at Pacific Safety Products to this day, was a practical discovery Field made at this turning point.

Park your ego and call in consultants if you can't handle a crisis alone

"The lesson to be learned," Brad Field points out, "is to use the expertise out there. Call upon the factory-floor engineers, call upon the management consultants. Entrepreneurs are terribly bad for not using consultants because you think you know.

225

That's a fine line because you develop a culture within a business." Entrepreneurs want to be involved in more than the nuts and bolts of their business; they thrive on their own creative strategies and dislike having solutions imposed on them. As Field phrases that impulse, "Yes, I want to know how everybody else runs their business, but at the same time don't tell me. I'll do it myself and then I will put my own slant on it." In fact, he advises now: "Don't be afraid that just because you understand how other people do it that somehow by default you're going to lose the identity of what you're trying to create. You'll apply [the models] in a different way." And he warns against hesitating too long before calling in the experts: "It's like the Stop sign that gets put in after the car accident. You tend to wait until you're into the crisis and now it's hit and miss whether you survive. Well, fortunately, I still had some people to call upon."

All the while PSP was processing these military contracts, it was in the throes of going public. A local investment broker had suggested the idea to Field: "I started to look into it and talked to Dave Harley about it. He didn't say no"—even though Harley had kept his own new company resolutely private. At this point, with the children in school, Lori came back into the business part-time to help handle the paperwork required to list on the Alberta Stock Exchange. She would become corporate secretary. "We had a rough year," she says. "It was a very stressful time. This was like putting a puzzle together and not knowing whether you have all the pieces." Her husband, who had hoped he could just buy a book called *How to Go Public 101*, says, "We floundered our way through it. I thought the underwriters were there to really get the ball rolling. I was waiting for them and they were waiting for me. So we wasted about three months." The process, which he expected to take six months, took a year.* But the initial public offering sold out in half an hour on the ASE, raising $1.6 million to reorganize the factory and launch the company more solidly in the body-armour industry.

---

* He had a lot of company. A 1998 Ernst & Young study of executives in 500 Canadian enterprises revealed that nearly half thought, looking back on their going-public process, that they had been badly prepared. Those companies that later proved successful, by market standards, had lavished more attention before the initial public offering on revising

The Fields pushed to make sure they ended up with corporate control—65 percent then, 54 now. They became directors along with Dave Harley; André Lorent, president of Western Tradeco Inc., who has developed armour-piercing weaponry and military vehicles; and a friend of his, the retired but still high-profile Major General Lewis MacKenzie, who warned them, "If you're wanting me on the board for the prestige of it, you'd better do it quick." In fact, the company played down MacKenzie's presence so much that one day when Roger Soar, vice president of product development, was in Ottawa, a key military contact came up, slugged him on the arm, and said, "You didn't tell me Lew was on your board."

Being a publicly traded company brought unpredicted new pressures. A corporate submission for a recent National Quality Institute entrepreneurship award (which PSP didn't win) spelled out how dealing with brokers, shareholders, lawyers, and securities commissioners has affected Field's role: "He went from being a hands-on manager, fixing sewing machines, testing bullet-proof materials, troubleshooting production problems, dealing with banks, handling employee relations, etc. to being in a top-end management position. He had to learn to let go of the little problems that surfaced during the day, and allow the staff he had hired to do their jobs. He spent a lot less time on the production floor and most of his time in his office on the phone."

Letting go was painful. "This is your baby and to have somebody else start raising your kid is not a comfortable feeling," Field admits. But there was the reward of realizing that employees knew what they were doing and that if he empowered them, as he did by organizing them into teams, they would perform and take the load off him and middle management. Since modular manufacturing began, PSP still has only one production manager, although it is doing ten times the volume.

These days one of the full-time employees is Lori Field, who spends three months a year preparing for the annual general meeting and fills in for others, as she was doing in the customer-service department when I visited. While conceding that her coworkers probably see her as

---

areas such as strategic planning, investor relations, accounting, and executive compensation. A big surprise was that the key element in a good IPO was setting up a well-organized employee-incentive program—in his case, Brad Field did a preliminary seed-stock offering and made it available to employees, many of whom chose to buy in.

the boss's spouse, she says, "I've never looked at myself as the Wife. I see myself as just another employee." The Fields seldom work together. "When I decided to come back, the business was so much bigger," she maintains. "I can literally not even talk to Brad all day long."

The year after going public Field was talking constantly to shareholders upset about the price of the stocks. Most of the investors were Kelowna-based, in for the long haul with a local company they could get to know. But some were less-patient speculators who had bought PSP stock on margin and called him first thing every morning demanding to know what he would be doing to hype their shares. Field insisted the company had gone public for the long term and he didn't intend to spend copious amounts of time and money doing market plays. Mike Hill of Acumen Capital Partners agrees with his approach: "He went through a phase where he was worried about the stock price, but that's become less of an issue as he matures. Overall, the company has to perform and that's what the market will reward."

Focus on your business, not your share price

"Forget the stock price, focus on the bottom line, focus on doing good business," Brad Field recommends. "If you get all caught up in what your share price is every day, you're distracted from what you should be focused on. If you do what you say you're going to do, you will get support on your stock and it will reflect the value of the company." What he came to understand was that speculators who called to urge him to boost the value of their holdings "want you to spend a ton of money promoting the stock as high as you can get it so they can sell it. ... Suddenly you realize that there's nothing you can do, so you might as well just save your money. And a lot of people will argue the point with me, and rightly so, that you owe it to the shareholders to keep the stock in the forefront. But at the same time, there's got to be a balance. The minute you take your eye off the target, you're potentially going to get in trouble. ... And understand that you are going to have to deal with the irate investors, with the flippers, and accept them as being part of the game. They're not doing bad things. Welcome to the world."

The stock has since fluctuated as high as $1.20 but has generally hovered around 70 cents. When I spoke to him, Field figured this was a fair number, considering recent earnings per share of two cents and a generous multiple of 30. "So you want higher stock value?" he asks rhetorically. "Make more earnings. It's fairly fundamental." He allows that being in the boondocks might affect the price of PSP shares, as a *Financial Post* article once suggested, but says the larger factor is that the company has been trading on the Alberta Stock Exchange. "A penny stock on a small-cap exchange—that's two strokes against you right there." In the 1997 fiscal year, PSP spent $80,000 on investor relations; the next year the board agreed to put that money toward the bottom line instead.

As the company gears up to go on the TSE, it has an intriguing story to tell new investors. One of several fresh chapters is the involvement with Marubeni Corporation. In late 1995, AlliedSignal introduced PSP to representatives of one of the world's largest trading houses, who at the last minute were seeking to replace another body-armour supplier to furnish the Tokyo police department with ballistic vests. Field met with them in Vancouver and didn't think anything would come of the deal until his chief financial officer phoned one night a month later and asked him if he was sitting down. "There's an order for a million dollars sitting on the fax from Marubeni in Japan," the CEO said. Field quickly had a friend give him some basic Japanese etiquette lessons and listened to language tapes before flying off to Tokyo, where his delivery of some key phrases so impressed his hosts that they told him later they had decided to stop talking in Japanese in front of him. After working two shifts to complete a $1.2-million order for 1,100 vests on time, PSP received a $920,000 order for another 800, and Field went back to Japan for a two-week tour. Further orders may be forthcoming.*

Another major plot twist in the corporate tale is the 1997 acquisition of its major competitor, Canadian Body Armour. Although the Ontario

---

*For all his boning up on Japanese ways, Brad Field admits to two embarrassing gaffes in his dealings with the trading giant. One was when he let his vice president of sales fly to Japan with an expired passport and it took a Marubeni representative to spring the man from an airport security room and give a personal guarantee to get him to the Canadian consulate before leaving Tokyo. The other was when Field was playing an early-morning game of golf in Phoenix with a Marubeni rep who asked him: "Is that a new fashion statement?" In the darkness, he had put his shirt on inside out.

company was profitable selling lower-end general products, its two principals approached Field at a trade show about buying them out. The older partner was thinking of retirement and the younger didn't want to run the company on his own. PSP paid $800,000 and 1.6 million of its common shares for its rival, with the cash coming from stock warrants purchased by a Vancouver investor in a nail-biting transaction at last-minute bargain prices. The co-owners agreed to stay on as managers, but Field confesses to moving in on the company with a heavy hand. "The first mistake we made was to assume that people would embrace our culture. So here we are, on our high horse: 'We're going to tell you guys how to do it right.' What in essence you're telling these poor people is: 'You've been doing it wrong, you boneheads.'" Retreating, he had to let go a plant manager PSP had parachuted in to run the new subsidiary, replacing him with existing employees.

Since 1997, Pacific Safety Products has gone through turbulent times. "There was a serious rift in the direction of the company," Field said in mid-1999, "and it became apparent that we were disconnected with our board." Between the previous October and February, the entire board of directors had changed except for the founding couple. Major General MacKenzie decided to retire gracefully, to be replaced by a friend of his, Major General (Retired) Barry Ashton of Calgary, who has a degree in business as well as service in Bosnia. However, the Fields asked for the resignation of André Lorent while Brad's mentor, Dave Harley, left in frustration. "It was very hard to see him leave," Brad Field says. "He felt he wasn't seeing what he wanted to see. ... We're nowhere as close as we used to be." What Harley was seeing was an abysmal bottom line in fiscal 1998—a loss of $514,000—despite growth of 65 percent. The other new directors are Mel Kotler of Kelowna, president of the western Canadian division of Fabricland, and Joe Little, president of Sumalta Investments of Calgary, who has been an interested minor investor for several years. With the new board taking an active role and the company finally beginning to reap the benefits of its acquisition, prospects have since improved dramatically. "This year we're forecasting growth of 15 percent and we are now having the most profitable year we've ever had," Field says. "We're going to make more profit in 1999 than all the other years combined—about three-quarters of a million dollars."

Orders at both Brampton and Kelowna have been building: 10,000 high-performance ballistic vests worth $2.5 million for a South American country that prefers to remain unidentified; 3,255 soft body-armour vests in a $555,000 contract with the RCMP; another body-armour order valued at nearly $1 million for Scotland Yard. With $250,000 in funding from the Canadian defence department, PSP is doing a three-year research program on American-made nanocrystalline tiles that might prove to be terrific bullet stoppers.*

The Fields had to cancel a trip to Disneyland with the kids because of the workload and a determination to get back in the black. Brad did find more time for the family, taking them to Phoenix and going skiing in Kelowna, as well as pursuing his golf game in summer and ice-car racing in winter. At the office, he is on the lookout for further acquisitions, perhaps in the burgeoning body-armour industry. Yet he isn't neglecting emergency medical products—the business that got them started. It is part of a larger market that is on a continuing growth curve.

TrendWatch

"Businesses are almost always created through opportunity," Brad Field says. "And we happened to walk into an ideal opportunity. So it wasn't that I went and researched anything to get started. Having said that, demographics do and will continue to play an important role in how we look at markets." He points to the baby-boomer population—9.8 million Canadians, who began entering their fifth decade in 1997—and what their presence might mean to medical products. "Well, we see an aging population. We see a greater demand for medical services. We see increased sales, an increasing demand for those products." *Boom, Bust*

---

*When the company's product developer, research scientist Roger Soar, first called about using the ceramic tiles for this purpose, the American manufacturer—Nanophase Technologies Corporation of Chicago—laughed and said, "Don't be ridiculous. They'll break." To which Soar replied, "Of course, they'll break. What actually stops the bullets is the degradation of the ceramic, which is slower than the degradation of the bullet."

& Echo, which he keeps handy on his bookshelf, agrees that the Canadian health-services sector will offer opportunities for sharp investors. And he quotes Toronto economist/futurist Nuala Beck, who says that high-knowledge industries like health care (where 40 percent or more of workers are professionals, technicians, or other "knowledge" workers) represent the future: five of the top-20 job-creating industries are related to health care. Field speaks for himself, those in related fields, and other opportunistic entrepreneurs when he says, "You have to be there."

Chapter Eight

The Hucksters

Jim and Bruna Scharf, Jim Scharf Holdings Ltd.

Perdue, Saskatchewan (population: 420), rears up gently 60 kilometres southwest of Saskatoon on a straight road through flatland punctuated this October 1998 day with oases of autumn-gold poplars and plump hay rolls in the harvested fields. On the outskirts along Highway 14, where the inevitable Esso and Shell stations contend, two thriving implement dealerships, Moody's and Can-Don, keep the place alive as a trading centre. Perched along the prairie-wide road into the village is the Perdue Legion, across from the Masonic Hall and not far from the United Church and the Hotel Perdue—Bar-B-Qed Steaks/Hot Dogs. The modern school houses 140 students from kindergarten to Grade 12; a curling rink and community hall complex has a two-lane bowling alley and a branch of the Wheatland Regional Library.

Much of the village's commercial action happens off the main drag on Ninth Street. Its broad expanse terminates in one of the two Saskatchewan Wheat Pool grain elevators, languishing after the summer's poor crops. On one side sit Perdue Valumaster Hardware (Fall Bulbs Now in Stock), the little redbrick post office, and the village and rural municipality offices that share space with the local credit union. On the other is an insurance agency/notary public/motor licence issuer and the Lucky Dollar Foods store, with a poster in the window advertising "Ladies Nite Out—Come and Relive a Night on the *Titanic* ($25 with cocktails, dinner, and a live band)." And then there is the one-story, metal-sheathed building that is the head office and assembly plant of Jim Scharf Holdings Ltd., the developer and distributor of the Lettuce Knife, the Bagel Buddy, the Bakeware Buddy, the Grocery Grip, the Heavenly Fresh Odor Absorber, and its flagship kitchen product, the Enviroll System E-ZeeWrap 1000—the patented, award-winning dispenser of 1,000-foot rolls of plastic wrap—"As seen on TV."

The company is like a rustic contemporary clone of Winnipeg-born K-tel International, whose carnival-like commercials have been littering our television screens since the 1960s, pitching nonstick pans, lint brushes, and blue-collar record albums.* Jim Scharf Holdings has also spent many millions of dollars on TV throughout North America and in several other countries, including shopping channels in Israel and Mexico. And in the spirit of K-tel's founder, who had earlier hawked vegetable cutters along Atlantic City's boardwalk, the husband-and-wife entrepreneurs behind the E-ZeeWrap commercials have even been known to throw in a free slicer and dicer with every dispenser. For the past season, they have paid $50,000 for the on-screen services of Sandra Schmirler, the western Canadian curler who was a Nagano Olympics gold medalist. She demonstrates their products in a national saturation campaign on CBC Television, sweeping all the competing plastic-wrap containers off a kitchen table while declaiming, "To be a winner, you've got to give your best every time." The Scharfs negotiated a deep discount with the network, which was a sweet follow-up to the deal they had done years ago with stations across Canada to run their commercials with no up-front payments, just a share of their national sales.

For a couple who might sound like market-savvy, city-slicker hucksters, Jim and Bruna Scharf have surprisingly rural roots. A couple of blocks from Ninth Street, on the edge of the village, is the farmstead where they and their two teenage sons live and work their 3,240 cultivated hectares, which stretch south and west from here for 24 kilometres. Their home is still the packaged model from Beaver Lumber that Jim built with friends and family, with a basement paid for by Bruna's savings. Their one big luxury is a later addition, an indoor swimming pool, which is Jim's stress reliever. Most of their funds have gone back into the business and the farm, where they grow wheat, canola, three different types of mustard, some malt barley, and the one crop that saved them the summer of 1998: lentils.

"Farming is in the toilet now," Jim Scharf tells me in the familiar countryman's complaint, "and in our area here we had no crops. We'll be

---

*K-tel has since moved to Minneapolis, where it now specializes in packaged CDs of golden oldies, country, polka, and love-song collections, promoted heavily on TV and the Internet throughout the world.

collecting crop insurance because the yields were so low. It forgot to rain." (He wasn't crying wolf: Prairie farmers faced financial devastation as wheat prices fell by 41 percent and hog prices by 65 percent.) Not that he'll be hurting a whole lot. Along with the estimated $3.5 million in sales from his kitchen-gadget company in 1998, and two good grain-growing and revenue years back-to-back as recently as 1995-96, the family has just had a bumper harvest of the sun-loving legumes called lentils.* The timing was superb: the Scharfs have been exporting trial shipments south of the border of yet another innovation, Instant Lentejas, their bilingually named, imaginatively packaged, quick-cooking product that bids to be the Minute Rice of the lentil world—at least in the Spanish-speaking southern United States and Mexico. "It's bigger than E-ZeeWrap," Jim says of the product's potential. So excited is he about the legume that in 1999 he planted a 48-hectare test plot of organic lentils as well as the conventionally grown variety.

The husband and wife, still in their early forties, have been running this international enterprise together since 1986. She not only does the accounting and payroll, but also quarterbacks packaging design, an Internet site, and all trade-show promotions. One survey labelled their company the fastest-growing on the Prairies. They have determinedly maintained its base in a village that even Saskatchewan folk might find hard to place (Perdue in French means, appropriately, "lost"). As a third-generation farmer, Jim has a deep allegiance to the land around here, but Bruna is more of a big-city person and would gladly spend much of the year in Saskatoon. Neither is currently loyal to the village itself, however, which explains the homemade sign on their headquarters, written in dripping red paint: "Building for Sale." There is that, and the fact that they are now also having some of their E-ZeeWrap dispensers manufactured in and distributed from a factory in Toronto as a possible backup if they do pack up. Their lack of fealty to Perdue arises from the unsuccessful battle they waged against a $12-million Saskatchewan Wheat Pool hog farm that will begin operating this year eight kilometres west of town. They fear the pollution of area water and,

---

*Lentils are among the so-called pulse crops—those leguminous plants with edible seeds such as peas and beans—that Prairie farmers are increasingly growing and selling for good prices. Canada is not only the world's second-largest producer of these crops, after India, but it is also the largest exporter.

more pointedly, the odours that might seep into their products' packaging and shipping containers. Jim Scharf effectively used the province's media to make his stand ("If the barn comes, I'm gone"), alleging that three of the seven rural-municipality councillors deciding on the project were also investors and the reeve was actually selling shares in it.

Scharf has a penchant for conflict, as becomes clear when he shows me around the family farm and later tells me the story of his entrepreneurial company. He is in his usual jeans and a floppy, short-sleeved mustard polo shirt that drapes over his vast belly. With his voluminous double chin, deeply creased brow, and monk's balding pate, he reminds me a bit of the old Hollywood character actor S. Z. "Cuddles" Sakall (the headwaiter, Carl, in *Casablanca*). At first the tour is pleasantly historical, revealing Scharf's heritage. "That's my grandfather's tractor," he says. "We still use it, a 1952 WD9. It's probably worth about $500, compared to that one—$200,000, $225,000. We have three of those."

There is the new shop, 464 square metres, which today houses a water truck, five snowmobiles, a motorcycle, and two sets of golf clubs, which the Scharf sons will use on the driving range they are building on the farm. And there is the old Quonset hut where their dad put together an E-ZeeWrap prototype and some of the quirky and practical products that preceded it. The place is still decorated with his father Clarence's ephemera, a baroque backdrop for the beery conversations the elder Scharf would have with his pals. One wall is hung with frying pans that Clarence collected from old homesteads, now bearing the names of their owners. Another is papered in pictures and quotations from his heroes, including John Kennedy and John Diefenbaker (he was a Tory backroom boy), and assorted maxims that would inspire any entrepreneur. "To make money," he quoted a Perdue printer as saying, "you have to do something that will make you money while you're sleeping." Jim Scharf nods. "That's so true. That's what my lawyer tells me."

He recalls one of his dad's own lines: "Any damn fool can buy something. It takes someone to make something." It is clear where the son's talent for tinkering came from. Clarence Scharf built a conveyer system to load railcars with his grain; an electric mixing mill to blend straw and minerals to feed his cattle; and in his early seventies, a paddle-wheel houseboat atop 18 barrels, which he floated on a shallow coulee. He died in 1995, aged 81. Being father to his only son, who had three older sisters, he was an exacting taskmaster. "I had a very hard teacher," Scharf says. In personality they weren't two peas in a pod. "The Hotel Perdue is the local bar," he tells me. "I've never been in there. My father was in there every day. He loved to party. When I was 21, I was so shy I wouldn't even pick up the phone."

Today he has Bruna to force him into facing the world. His Italian-Canadian wife has a round face with a big dark puffball of hair and the full-blown body of a Renaissance model, which she dresses up in tasteful fashion. "He hates flying, putting on suits," she says. "He likes to wear jeans and be himself." One morning, in 1997, she was trying to get him to the important International Housewares Show in Chicago, just after a shipment of their wrap dispensers destined for the United States had been held for ransom in a dispute between a customs brokerage and a trucking firm. It was the day of their flight, she had packed all the suitcases, and was at the office working, but her husband was still in bed. "He was depressed big-time. I had to do a selling job. Within a half an hour, I had to get him up and showered. My throat was sore from screaming and yelling at him. I don't think I've ever done that before." On the flight, she remembers, "I didn't hardly talk to him, but by the time we got to the hotel room that night, we had a good talk. The next day he said, 'Thanks for convincing me.'" But they agreed that this would be the last trade show he would ever attend; she would represent the company from now on. She knew that when Jim was a young man, his shyness had kept him home on winter days and nights, developing products rather than socializing, and it was only his resulting success that pressed him to put his reticence on hold and meet people to market his handiwork.

The operative phrase about what he did back then is "*developing* products." For the truth is that, although he is invariably credited with their invention, Scharf didn't originate the plastic-wrap dispenser or most of the items he has sold over the years. And in some cases, he told me, he simply walked away from their creators when disputes arose and then proceeded to refine their innovations and peddle his improved designs. That has left him in bad odour with at least a couple of the originators, one of them the man who brought him an early version of the Odor Absorber that Scharf now sells. Yet the Saskatchewan farmer who invented the plastic Lettuce Knife ("cuts like a regular knife without browning lettuce") and its sister slicers, the Bagel and Bakeware Buddies, is profiting from his relationship with the combative entrepreneur.

As we continue our tour of the farm, I realize Scharf is far from shy about picking a fight, no matter how public it becomes. He tells me about his canola crop this year, which yielded only about a third of what it could have because of what he claims were the ill effects of the chemical he used on the grain. "I'm in a battle with the chemical company," he says casually of a prospective lawsuit. Later he points out a metal box on his property that contains phone switches and other wiring belonging to the provincial telephone company, of which he is not a customer. When one of his sons accidentally ran over the box while farming, SaskTel charged his father $450 in repairs. That resulted in a Scharf-inspired story in Saskatoon's *StarPhoenix* that began: "A Perdue farmer says if he must pay for damage to SaskTel property, SaskTel should pay him to put their equipment on his land." Scharf was quoted as saying: "They get all these easements for nothing and this is how they treat us for being nice guys." The same newspaper had backed him in an editorial over his fight against the hog-production facilities that Sask Pool is building near Perdue. Noting that the venture had divided the community, the editorialist wrote, "Saskatchewan needs to diversify its economy, but not at any price."

However, those fights are just small potatoes compared to the one Jim Scharf Holdings has been involved in with a competitor over patent infrigement of the E-ZeeWrap 1000. The series of suits and countersuits that erupted between them has already cost the Scharfs at least $70,000 in legal fees, and they estimate that their rival's tactics have meant a $2-million drop in their market share. At the very least, they say, it is likely responsible in large part for the approximately $1-million decrease in their 1998 earnings from the $4.5 million recorded the year before.

Don't depend on a patent to protect your innovation—unless you're determined to back it up both legally and financially

"A patent is a nice piece of paper," the plainspoken Jim Scharf says. "It tends to keep the honest people in the world—the bigger businesses—straight. You have to be prepared to defend it, otherwise the patent is nothing." The man who brought him the Lettuce Knife has applied for patents on the gadget. "Is it worth it?" Scharf asks rheotrically. "Marketing is everything. I would apply for the patent-pending stage—then you're protected. It keeps the legitimate guys out. It's only about 500 bucks. Then I would flog the shit out of it—is this thing really good? Then you got to patent it in about a year. And then you know whether it's worth doing or not." For E-ZeeWrap, patents have cost him anywhere from $3,000 to $5,000 per country, depending on complications. "These guys tell you they got worldwide patents—it's a bunch of garbage. I've got Mexican patents, U.S., Canadian patents. I could've had European, but this lawsuit was going on and I said, 'How am I ever gonna defend this?' Forget it. I spent about $15,000 on Europe and then quit. So there is only one way to defend it in Europe or any other country—and that's low price."

How Jim and Bruna Scharf of Perdue, Saskatchewan, reached the point where they are dealing in the millions of dollars in a global marketplace, developing dispensable kitchen gadgets, overseeing their manufacture, assembly, and package design, shipping them worldwide, advertising them on television, attending trade shows, and fighting off competitors is a classic tale of Canadian grassroots entrepreneurialism.

In this case, the roots go back to the early 20th century. Jim Scharf's paternal grandfather moved to the area from Manitoba, built a three-story brick house with turrets—the Castle, the locals called it—and began farming on the rich Saskatchewan soil. His maternal granddad, meanwhile, was more of a conventional businessman, opening an ice-cream parlour in Perdue in 1910. Jim's father grew up without a mother when she left with the youngest of her three sons and the hired hand. Clarence Scharf stayed on the farm and married a quiet girl with the intriguing first name of Queade. She was both similar and dissimilar to the unusually named young woman Jim would wed; Bruna is thrifty, like her mother-in-law was, but she is hardly a homebody.

As the only son among four children, young Jim went straight from high school on to the family farm. He had already been earning money as a student, renting 28 hectares from his father, raising hogs, and building them a barn.* His extreme shyness kept him at home, rather than going out to curl or drink with the guys, and his handiness with tools kept him occupied. One of his first avocations after becoming a full-time farmer with his father was assembling 15 swathing machines for resale. For fun he built a dune buggy out of a Volkswagen, learning how to do the wiring and engine work, and winning third prize in a Saskatoon custom-car show.

His timidity was most apparent in the fact that Bruna was his first girlfriend, a blind date in 1974. She was one of three kids in an Italian-Canadian family that moved to Kelowna, British Columbia, from Coleman, Alberta, when her coal-miner father died when she was five. After high school, she came to Saskatoon and was an 18-year-old doing office work at a trucking company when mutual friends set her up with the strapping Jim Scharf. At 20 he was such a naiif that she had to introduce him to pizza, a food he found much too spicy. But he was an ambitious young guy, and they were married two years later.

As a city girl, Bruna never did quite take to rural life. Even today she insists, "People say I live in a glass bubble. I don't get involved in the community." Yet as well as performing the farm-wife chores, such as cooking three squares for a hungry family and hired hands, she did crafts, including needlework that she showed at local shows, and for a time had a cake-decorating service in Perdue. In his winter off-season, the newly married Jim capitalized on current crazes. When waterbeds were popular, he remembers thinking, *Hey! That's the answer!* So, for a year, he constructed 15 fancy wooden beds with mirrored headboards and built-in drawers. "But, of course, I didn't know how to sell them," he admits. In 1980, as satellite television surfaced on the Prairies, he began peddling the receiving dishes and making their mounts. "It was a nightmare," he says. "You'd get it set up and then it wouldn't work." He has no idea whether he ever made any profit on the project. During his three years selling the dishes in the local area, Bruna says dryly, "He learned a lot about customer service."

A more successful venture was one of his few inventions, a farm tool he machined in his shop and marketed with a friend. The Safety-Hoe

---

*Another Maverick, Chuck Loewen of Winnipeg's Online Business Services, also put himself through high school on the proceeds from buying and selling hogs *(see page 285)*.

is a long-handled steel implement with an offset curved blade specially designed to fit through the tailgate of a truck box to clean the last ten bushels of grain from the corners. He had a partner, another local grain farmed named Mel Elliot. Similar devices had been sold, but their new design made the hoes patentable. It was the first test of Scharf's theory that marketing is more important than any patent protection. For a year and a half, beginning in 1985, the partners sold hard through trade shows and even 4-H clubs, but in the end managed to unload only 6,000, earning perhaps $20,000 between them. Today they still have 1,500 in storage. From that experience, Scharf learned something fundamental that he was able to apply to future projects.

Don't assume that it makes economic sense to handle all—or even most—of the elements of the manufacturing process yourself

The Scharfs are very modern manufacturers: they don't actually make their products on their own site but may handle some steps in the system and have the know-how to choreograph the entire procedure. While Jim Scharf made the prototype Safety-Hoe, and he and Mel Elliot assembled the first production models in his farm shop, they soon realized it was smarter to have a specialty shop in Perdue manufacture the basic parts in bulk. Not only did it make economic sense, but the partners could also expend their limited time and energy on selling the tools. That experience would convince Scharf to pursue the same pattern in the E-ZeeWrap business. Again he made early models in his Quonset hut, while knowing that it would pay to use experts whose factories were set up for major runs. "There are so many other people out there to do it for you—and do it better—unless you want to spend millions of dollars setting up a plant," he contends. Until recently the Scharfs continued to hire local people on a part-time basis to assemble and package all the plastic-wrap dispensers in their village warehouse. Even that has changed recently with the contracting out to a Toronto factory of the whole process—from manufacture through delivery—for about ten percent of the product at up to 20-percent

241

less cost. "Why duplicate what somebody else can do for you?" Scharf says. "It frees our money for marketing and everything else. And you don't have your assets tied into a whole bunch of things that could change tomorrow [such as a possible move from Perdue]. So we remain very flexible that way."

A spin-off from the Safety-Hoe caper was noted in the very first media mention of Scharf when *The Western Producer* reported: "His wife Bruna says she and other family members have watched him change from a shy farmer to an enthusiastic salesman." Bitten by the entrepreneurial bug, quelling his trepidation about public appearances, Scharf was ripe for the E-ZeeWrap adventure that began to happen in 1985.

The story that has never been told is how the Scharfs came to realize the enormous, if less than obvious, potential of a product designed solely to dispense polyethylene-based food wrap. They were among the people of Perdue who first heard about the concept from a former local who had gone to the West Coast and become a promoter on the Vancouver Stock Exchange. Coming home, he apparently convinced several villagers that plastic wrap could be their fortune. Scharf says the man had brought along an Edmonton-made dispenser moulded of plastic that was similar to a metal version that the veteran American food company Borden, Inc. had been selling for years. The money to be spun from this promotion was not in the initial sale of the dispenser itself—however profitable that might be—but in the ongoing sale of large rolls of wrap to supply such a device. That's 1,000-foot rolls, rather than the usual 100-footers you buy in Saran Wrap or Glad Wrap cardboard containers. Several Perdue residents had liked the promoter's spiel and, when he upped and departed for other pastures, were allegedly left confused and disgruntled—and at least four locals lost a total of many thousands of dollars.

Scharf was one of them. Still believing in the basic idea, he decided to do something about it. The Edmonton dispenser was designed to sit on a kitchen counter, and in his judgement it didn't work very well. What if, Scharf wondered, it could also be mounted under a cabinet both to save space and make it easier to use? His handmade prototype was crafted of spruce with the spindle from a paint roller holding the roll of plastic wrap. The second version was steel with oak end pieces and piano hinges of metal spot-welded in his farm shop. The first run was about 1,000 dispensers fabricated by a Saskatoon machine shop. Some of them were sold door-to-door, Scharf's father bought a lot and gave them away; people generally liked them. An improved model had integral hinges that were punched out and shaped from the metal of the box. It worked well but was expensive to make and demanded a $49.95 price tag to be viable.

The name was equally a problem. Scharf says the promoter had already been using the word *easy* as part of the name. "Everything in the book is tradenamed *easy*," he says. The Scharfs tried many variations on the word until they came up with the special spelling of E-ZeeWrap 1000 (the number reflecting the length of the roll). Jim's advice: "Spend your money on a trademark rather than a patent. That's all Coca-Cola has is a name. It's hard to come up with a name that's trademarkable and something that's identifiable with the product." Between the first and second production models, the Scharfs hired a Saskatoon designer to clean up the crude original rendering of the logo. Bruna has since continued to stage-manage the bold graphic design of all their products.

The expensive metal version, even with 1,000 feet of wrap, proved to be a tough sell. Over the next five years, the couple would dispose of only 5,000 dispensers. Their first major marketing program was a six-week campaign on a Saskatoon television station to generate direct-mail response. "Totally bombed," Scharf remembers. "It's pre-Christmas. Perfect timing, but it didn't pull. *But* the employees [of the station] bought over 20 units. So that's what keeps you going." The one-minute commercial, which cost at least $6,000, failed to sell the sizzle, focusing instead on such dry details as its heavy-metal construction and oak ends. Eventually the Scharfs would learn to pitch the product's benefits—its ease of use and waste reduction—covering off its quality quickly with two brief phrases: "lifetime warranty" and "money-back guarantee."

At the time, Scharf says, he panicked: "I was forced to get on the road and go sell, go cold-call on a store, something I hated to do with a passion." He and a friend covered Saskatchewan in less than a week, driving to almost every key small town, ten a day, trying to set up a dealer network and convince retailers to buy the dispensers outright. In one town, nobody would accept them unless on consignment, returnable if they didn't sell. ("Never do consignment unless it's your last choice," Scharf now says.) While placing as many as 500 units with dealers who to this day remain loyal to the product, he still had a large inventory left. By now Bruna was well involved, taking orders on the toll-free lines in their home, invoicing, and shipping dispensers and the refill rolls of plastic wrap sourced from a Toronto supplier. The Scharfs began taking space at trade shows and exhibitions, including a gruelling one in Edmonton where they spent two weeks working out of a 1.7-metre-wide booth.

By 1987 E-ZeeWrap's sluggish sales were all the more frustrating given the sudden success of another offbeat product that the Scharfs were making and promoting. The new Canadian dollar coins had just been issued with an illustration of a loon on one side. Inevitably they became known as loonies, which ignited some entrepreneurs' imaginations. One of them was a friend of the Scharfs, who approached them with the idea of a coin bank called the Loony Bin. They modified his idea to do a product named the Loony Nest, had a graphic designer sketch the idea, took it to a trade show, and came back with 600 orders. When the friend balked at their adaptation and protested at the cost of having a professional design done, they proceeded to do the project on their own. Renting space in the building on Ninth Street that they would one day own, they assembled a boxlike bank from two sizes of precut wood. "I counted over 20 different versions that hit the marketplace," Jim Scharf says. "We were one of the first. We sold over 30,000. They wholesaled for about nine bucks a pop, retailed from 15 to 20 bucks. Half a million dollars of retail sales, about three years. Never made any money, but I learned a lot about marketing."

For a time, it looked as if they would make a profit on their Loony Nests, especially when they sold about 600 units at an Edmonton wholesale gift show compared to only about 40 E-ZeeWraps. That contrast drove them to renewed efforts in selling the dispensers—and, as it turned out, to a minor disaster. A man Scharf met in a Saskatoon print shop, who claimed to be in advertising, said he could mount a direct-reponse mail campaign, combined with a radio promotion, that would saturate Saskatchewan. He saw the Scharfs coming. They paid him $45,000, and Scharf says they received nothing in return. "The stuff got printed, but the post office supposedly lost all the bags of mail. So we had to bring in the post office fraud squad, and they got involved and tried to track this down. [The promotional pieces] never got mailed. But about a year later I met with someone who does mail drops and all these things are sitting at a drop in Regina, so they ended up shipping them back here. Meantime we're doing radio and the radio stations got stung. And I found out afterward that this was all a scam. I went back and questioned the guy and said, 'What the hell's going on here? All this stuff didn't go out!' So then he threatened to sue me. It's kinda like a weasel up against the wall. So my lawyer went to work and then all of a sudden the guy went away. He just left the country. Never did find out where he went." The Scharfs had to swallow an embarrassing lesson.

Always double-check the credentials of your suppliers

It seems so obvious, yet in practice so many embryonic entrepreneurs—overeager to get things done, out of their depth in fresh fields of endeavour, and much too trusting—often overlook this piece of advice: When dealing with companies delivering services to you, as Jim Scharf says, "Always ask for references. Nobody should ever have a problem giving you references. If they don't want to show you their credentials, dump them. Man, I've got scammed on different things."

While E-ZeeWrap generated sales of only $163,000 in 1989, another product the Scharfs produced briefly was immediately profitable. That year they began marketing small wooden crates for the gift industry. Purdy's Chocolates and a Red Deer brewery were among those who purchased these Create A Gift boxes to package their wares. "It's the only product we ever did that made money right off the bat," Scharf recalls. "We did maybe $75,000 worth of crates." Those were welcome sales, since the rest of the business was stagnant and finances were running low. In 1986 the Scharfs and Jim's dad, Clarence, had been forced to refinance their farming operations. The Royal Bank had called in the senior Scharf's notes and, after searching fruitlessly for a friendly bank, father and son managed a loan with the federal Farm Credit Corporation Canada. The transaction involved the younger Scharf buying a section of land from Clarence on a borrowed $208,000 over three decades (the son still owes

$154,000 on the loan). It was enough cash to wipe off all of the father's and some of his own debts incurred by his E-ZeeWrap investments.

The Scharfs stopped selling their money-spinning gift crates when they became involved in a wholesale redesign of the dispenser. In 1990 they approached the Saskatchewan Research Council, a Crown corporation that receives about 70 percent of its financing from private-contract work. Council researchers had already designed a better spindle for the rolls of wrap. Now, Jim Scharf told project scientist Orville Olm, "I've gotta cheapen this thing. I gotta bring the cost down, but it's gotta look high-end. I don't want it to look like a piece of plastic hung under the cabinet. It's gotta be good or I don't want it." Olm spent 18 months developing a handsome new product, one that would not only be made of plastic but also work more efficiently. In reinventing it through computer design, he picked up on the Scharfs' suggestion that the bottom of the dispenser, where the plastic wrap emerges, should be textured in some way so the wrap wouldn't stick to it. Olm's major innovation was to create a series of a dozen parallel ribs that prevent such cling. He also designed a two-piece product with an extremely sharp cutter bar of plastic, rather than metal, and one that dispenses the wrap evenly and opens easily for refilling with pressure on two side buttons. In the end, the Scharfs had a mould that they could then take to Hara Products, an injection-moulding operation in the manufacturing hotbed of Swift Current, Saskatchewan, to mass-produce the dispenser at a cost that is probably well below $2 per unit. All in all, after an investment of about $65,000, the device was now eminently workable and they began gathering new patents for the redesigned version.*

Tap into provincial-government experts for specialized industrial research and development as well as the usual business R&D

The operator of the injection-moulding company in Swift Current had told the Scharfs the Saskatchewan Research Council was their best local bet for computer-aided product

---

*Jim Scharf didn't bother telling his dad how much money he had spent in redeveloping the dispenser: "If I had told my father I could've bought a quarter of land with it, he would've had a fit. 'You nuts, Jim Scharf—or what!'"

design. It was a sensible suggestion: provincial research establishments like the SRC or the Alberta Research Council often have a wide range of expertise to offer businesspeople. And because they are funded partially through government grants, their fees can be lower than those for equivalent research in the private sector. Jim Scharf was wary: "It was the biggest investment I ever made. I didn't know if the thing was going to work." But the dedication of the project scientist was impressive. Years later it also helped convince the Scharfs to pursue such knowledge in developing their instant-lentil product, when they went to Saskatchewan Wheat Pool researchers who were already experimenting with the bulk production of the quick-cooking legumes. Summarizing his decision to use the SRC, Jim Scharf says: "It was the biggest risk I ever took in my life. And it's what made us today."

"So finally they got the thing to work and then we did a run of 2,000 units," Scharf says. "We're putting them all together in our farm shop ... and now we really got some money invested in those things." All Jim and Bruna had to do was sell the things for anywhere from $30 to $40 retail with a fine-tuned name and package design. To call attention to the fact that the 1,000-foot rolls of wrap were environmentally friendly—replacing ten 100-footers with all their packaging—they invented the word *Enviroll*. Bruna was working on the redesign of the package with a graphic artist who suggested adding the word *system* to make it sound even more significant. Today the dispenser's bright and busy cardboard container bears the trademarked name "The Original Enviroll System E-ZeeWrap 1000," along with copyright artwork—a cartoon strip and photographs showing its use—and descriptions in six languages, symbols of the awards it has won, and a smiling Sandra Schmirler (while a catalogue inside describes the company's other kitchen products and the instruction sheet has a laudatory article about Scharf from the magazine *Saskatchewan Business*).

Given Jim's reluctance to travel, the Scharfs attempted some pretty basic marketing. Noting that *Canadian Living* had a direct-marketing section, they sent the Toronto-based magazine a sample dispenser. A representative phoned to say the product wasn't suitable for the publication and asked where to return it. Take it home, they replied, and use it in your own kitchen. A month later the rep called back to say the magazine was now delighted with E-ZeeWrap and would feature it in the mail-order section four times running. The Scharfs were particularly pleased that a competitive plastic-wrap manufacturer had paid to run a large ad in *Canadian Living* at the same time. They did the same long-distance marketing with major retailers, sending off samples and hoping the dispenser's quality would sell itself. Their first big order came in late 1991 when Eaton's acquired $50,000 worth of E-ZeeWraps. Early in the new year the Scharfs attended their first major trade fair, the Canadian Houseware and Home Improvement Show, where they won awards for best retail packaging and best new houseware product—"against Black & Decker, Braun, all the big guys," Jim says.

With such a promising start, he and Bruna bought the building they are now in for about $26,000 from a bank and spent another $10,000 refurbishing it. But they were soon facing another financial crunch. Western Economic Diversification Canada, the federal agency, had given them $60,000 to market the product. A $10,000 public-relations campaign, using an American PR firm to pitch E-ZeeWrap during Chicago's International Housewares Show, generated not a single article.* The Scharfs had better luck on television. The first year they were advertising the dispenser with a 1,000-foot roll for a mail-order price of $39.95 and offering the TV stations 50 percent of the revenue. The usual industry percentage for these so-called PIs—per inquiries—was half that. Meanwhile they tried to interest retailers in handling the dispenser, without much success. The second year of commercials priced it at only $24.95 with a 500-foot roll. "Plus we give away this rolling slicer-dicer that was all over U.S. TV for 20 bucks," Scharf says. "You could buy this thing so cheap [less than $2], so we give it away with our product." On these direct sales, the company was merely breaking even.

But by now—1993—the more profitable retail sales were starting to climb, and while the couple wanted to continue with a supportive TV

---

*However, a more recent PR campaign—run by Cheryl Hirsch Communications of Encino, California—was a major success. For instance, a columnist for the large chain of Gannett Suburban Newspapers extolled the virtues of E-ZeeWrap, while the Lettuce Knife was well promoted on food pages of such major newspapers as the *San Diego Union-Tribune* and the *Plain Dealer* in Cleveland.

campaign, they had run out of cash. As Scharf puts it, "The banks told me, 'You'd better get a new hobby.'" Again the Scharfs followed their instincts and a philosophy that might have some resonance with other entrepreneurs.

If you are shy of funds—or even if you aren't— don't be constrained by the conventional marketing rules

Jim and Bruna Scharf were landing retail accounts, including Woolco and Canadian Tire, simply by sending their products to potential retailers instead of spending the usual large sums on a marketing campaign combined with supposedly essential in-person visits. Now they phoned up TV stations across Canada with an intriguing offer. Jim told them, "Look, I've got all these distributors who want to carry this product. I got no money for you. I've spent it already. But I'll give you a piece of the pie." What he offered them was anywhere from a quarter percent to three percent of the total national sales of E-ZeeWrap— depending on the size of each TV market—in return for their running a certain number of commercials. Thirty station managers, from the Maritimes to British Columbia, bit on this extraordinary gimmick, which was negotiated entirely by phone from an office in Perdue, Saskatchewan (where Jim's office has a colour photo entitled *Our Farm 1997* next to a poster that reads: "Whether you think you can, or think you can't, you're right.") "And nobody knew what the national sales were but me and Bruna," he notes. "They just went on our credibility." When you are short of money, Scharf says, "you figure out a way to do something that's impossible. No deal like that would've been made if I had money."

The company attracted some strong retailers domestically. Cotter Canada, with about 450 True Value hardware stores and V&S department stores in rural areas nationwide, was among the first large accounts to list E-ZeeWrap. Head housewares buyer Dorothy Keizer says the Scharfs are one of her favourite suppliers. At one point early in their relationship, she reported the rapid pace of sales: "They are buying like drunken idiots. Unbelievable!" Other majors now handling the product in this country include Wal-Mart, Zellers, Home Hardware, and London Drugs. In other countries, sales have been mixed. A home-shopping channel in Mexico sold $200,000 worth before the peso fell, while a similar channel in Israel ordered three pallet loads. There have been exports to Britain, Spain, Poland, South Africa, and even Iceland. Having been stung by foreign distributors, the Scharfs insist on immediate payment by credit card before shipping product offshore.

Until recently the toughest market to crack has been the closest, the United States, where only about 30,000 units had sold until 1999. They have a warehouse in Mobrige, South Dakota, and a sales manager in Detroit. In anticipation of an expanding American market, the couple got a $1-million line of bank credit in case they had to carry inventory and they have done what Scharf calls "mega-advertising, a little over three and a half million dollars."* Some of the money went for game shows, including *Jeopardy*, where a ten-second, $6,000 tag line at show's end mentions that all contestants receive E-ZeeWrap. One unusual deal was a barter arrangement with Turner Broadcasting, which runs CNN, among other channels. They bought three substantial ad campaigns with Turner, paying half in cash and half in products valued at their full retail value. Then, when the broadcaster couldn't figure out how to sell most of them, the Scharfs bought the products back at a lower price. All of this advertising had been calculated to convince American retailers to begin stocking the plastic-wrap dispenser on their shelves, but to little avail, even with Turner's national sales manager calling up such chains as Wal-Mart to suggest they carry the product. As Scharf told CBC-TV's *Venture* in 1998 about his forays into the United States, "I'm almost at a loss. I don't know what to do." At that time, their U.S. accounts included kitchen-gadget and gift-store chains and the impressive-sounding Ace Hardware, a chain of about 5,000 stores. However, each Ace location orders its own merchandise and relatively few have taken E-ZeeWrap. Then, in mid-1999, the Scharfs' American fortunes changed overnight

---

*In late 1998, the Scharf's began testing a direct-response TV commercial throughout the United States that offers E-ZeeWrap at $19.95 with a 500-foot roll of wrap instead of the 1,000-footer.

when they closed a significant deal with the U.S. K-mart chain to handle both E-ZeeWrap and their line of Buddy knives. "We are going to get very, very, very busy," Scharf predicts.

Their earlier lack of success south of the boarder was partly due to a patent-infringement fight that they claimed was interfering with their sales of E-ZeeWrap. As they tell it, the dispute began when a salesman got a purchase order from an eastern Canadian discount chain for 20,000 units of a cheaper dispenser that was based on their patented design, complete with nonstick ribs on the bottom. Their competitor agreed to settle the resulting case out of court, paying them $25,000 and promising to change the design. Which he did, removing the ribs, but still keeping the bottom textured. After the Scharfs' lawyer sent his lawyer a letter of complaint, the competitor launched a lawsuit based on the belief that Scharf would tell retailers, particularly a large U.S. chain, that the man was still infringing on their product. Meanwhile he had changed his dispenser again to a completely smooth bottom. He and the Scharfs now have claims and counterclaims outstanding in court.

Scharf says the result of all this legal volleying had been to discourage retailers, especially those they had targeted in the United States, from handling E-ZeeWrap. To counter the losses they have suffered in 1998, they have focused more than ever on the large American trade shows to attract new retailers. While Bruna is attending them now with an employee from Perdue, in the past they both appeared and soon came to realize that they had to distinguish themselves from the pack.

Make your presence known at trade shows with as many promotional devices as you can

"When we do the houseware show in Chicago, very seldom do we just go with the booth," Jim Scharf points out. Some promotions are cheap, some expensive; some work, some don't. "One time," he says. "We sent out $5 lottery tickets with a Canadian Mountie on them, trying to get the top 100 buyers to our booth—'The last draw is the last day of the show, so come by and check out your ticket.' We had two guys show up, but they were big guys." The Scharfs also use the in-house TV channel in the major hotel frequented by attendees, paying about $4,000 U.S. for a one-minute commercial on programs that show trade-show news. "That stuff works very well," Scharf says. They have also run commercials on CNN news programs that play on kiosk TV sets at the Chicago show. Most recently that promotion, combined with E-ZeeWrap ads on buses travelling to the event, cost them a half-price $20,000. "The [International Housewares Show] is huge," Scharf says. "I've been seven times and never seen it all. So you have to make yourself stand out somehow."

The Scharfs' company has been a standout at several trade fairs, including California's Gourmet Products Show, where E-ZeeWrap was named best product in 1996. These shows are ideal venues for introducing merchandise, such as the Grocery Grip the couple are peddling on behalf of its Saskatchewan inventor. It is simply a nylon handle with an extended, upturned hook centred under the grip to hold several plastic grocery bags efficiently and carry them comfortably. Their Heavenly Fresh Odor Absorber, which uses activated coconut-shell charcoal—supposedly the best of all such air purifiers—can hang in refrigerators and lockers if you don't mind its chubby-cheeked angel design. To the Scharfs' credit, the odoureater is assembled in Saskatoon by Cosmopolitan Industries, which employs more than 350 adults with mental or other disabilities.

Among the couple's recent innovations—which include the packaging of aluminum foil in 1,000-foot rolls for the same dispenser that parcels out plastic wrap—the most radical departure is their Instant Lentejas. This precooked-lentil product was inspired by the one man Jim Scharf names as a real mentor: the late Raj Manek, who was Saskatchewan's regional director of economic development in Saskatoon. He first consulted Manek when considering a serious entry into the waterbed market, which the director discouraged. It was about a decade later when he met his mentor again, using him as a sounding board for various projects. Although never in business himself, this Canadian of East Indian origin had two successful entrepreneurial brothers and kept well informed on industrial trends. When Scharf approached him about doing something value-added with the lentils he was growing, Manek took him to see a team of Sask Pool researchers precooking the legumes in bulk. At first the scientists refused to share their knowledge with a possible competitor, but when the angered regional director was persistent, they showed Scharf their operation. Still, it wasn't until his mentor said, "Think of it as Minute Rice," that the farmer saw the entrepreneurial possibilities, particularly in the lentil-eating, Spanish-speaking United States and Mexico. And it was only Bruna's involvement that encouraged her husband to pursue the product with any passion: "Without her I wouldn't be doing instant lentils," Scharf insists. "I just grow them. I need her input."

It was his wife who worked with a food consultant and graphic designer and even came up with the name—Nona's Instant Lentejas. *Nona* is an Italian name for grandmother (and sounds just Spanish enough); Bruna suggested that a photo of her own *Nona* adorn the package. Their product takes only 14 minutes to cook, at least twice as fast as regular lentils. Early reports indicate acceptance by the target ethnic market, with some stores in California already reordering. The Scharfs are hoping that consumers will be attracted by the ease of preparing what is a low-fat, cholesterol vegetable high in protein, complex carbohydrates, and dietary fibre. They even provide appetizing lentil recipes in a slick brochure and on their Web site (*www.ezeewrap.com*).

Bruna is entirely responsible for their Internet presence. "I don't know how to turn the computer on," her husband admits. Their site is attractive and works well, offering visitors a rounded portrait of all the products and the laurels they have earned, media coverage, frequently asked questions ("Why does my dispenser make a chattering noise?") and, perhaps most important, incentives to interest potential distributors. On her own, Bruna has been making creative use of the Internet in her off hours to actively seek out potential wholesalers. Working from Perdue, Saskatchewan, the Scharfs are becoming part of a phenomenon that promises to be the Net's most significant payback.

TrendWatch

As the American magazine *Inc. Tech* reported late last year, "Business-to-business commerce dominates activity on the Internet. This year companies buying from other companies will account for $17 billion of the total $21.8 billion in Net transactions (excluding financial services), and on-line business-to-business sales will surpass $300 billion by 2002, according to Forrester Research." The Scharfs' contribution to this total, small as it is, is simple and clever.

Using search engines, Bruna located retailers throughout North America and sent them an e-mail letter urging them to view the couple's Web site. The homey-sounding letter points out that theirs is a husband-and-wife business and they are farmers, as well. It also offers free delivery on all wholesale orders, free samples, guaranteed refunds at any time, and full customer satisfaction or money back. The first round of letters drew a surprising 25-percent response. "We tried to do direct mail before," Jim Scharf notes, "and if you're lucky, you get a five-percent return." For someone who admits to being computer illiterate, Scharf is almost as excited about the potential of e-commerce as he once was about the future of plastic wrap. "The Internet's going to be big," he announces. And in case anyone missed the message, he adds, "Big, big, big, big."

The
High-Tech
Entrepreneurs

P ositioning themselves in the world is what entrepreneurs do by creating their enterprises. With typical Maverick innovation, some high-technology entrepreneurs in Calgary have taken that concept quite literally in the kind of companies they have started. They rank high among the pioneers around the planet who are applying a fascinating technology based on signals from an aggregation of 24 American defence department satellites orbiting in space. It is called the Global Positioning System, or GPS. The satellites broadcast ranging codes to GPS receivers on Earth, which measure the time delay between the signals the satellites send and the ones they pick up. A receiver can then determine the distance between a satellite and the user of a GPS device and pinpoint a geographical location anywhere on the globe to within at least 30 metres. In a further, more expensive refinement, the error between an apparent code range and the true range can be computed as a differential correction, which can then be applied to other receivers in the local area to improve the accuracy of the user's position to within millimetres. The practical uses include the expected—doing geographic surveys with incredible precision—and the less obvious, such as showing car and truck drivers the fastest routes to their destinations and mapping farmers' crop yields to let them program their machines to do the most cost-effective fertilizing.

255

Calgary has become a scientific and creative hub in this field, which has flourished since the American military released GPS for civilian use in 1993. That same year Ed Fitzhenry, one-half of the High-Tech Entrepreneur couple portrayed in the next chapter, outfitted a plane with GPS equipment to stage the first-ever precision approach using the technology. "We had an association with some people at the University of Calgary who really are world leaders in GPS application," the chairman of Pelorus Navigation Systems says, explaining how he managed the feat. "They've written papers, been acknowledged by their peers—and just coincidentally, here *we* are."

The transfer of such technology is becoming an important role for Canadian universities, which in the past decade have spun off more than 300 companies from their academic research. The University of Calgary, for instance, has benefitted the private sector both indirectly and quite directly. Take the example of Michel Fattouche, an associate professor in the electrical and computer engineering department at the university, and Hatim Zaghloul, who earned his Ph.D. in physics there. In 1995 they cofounded Cell-Loc Inc., a publicly traded company that makes and markets cellular-location and tracking systems using GPS in a different way. Its patented Cellocate receivers can track the exact location of a cell phone in emergency situations, even when it isn't in use (and by 2001, cellular companies in the United States will be bound to offer such a service). A Cell-Loc receiver incorporates a GPS receiver—not as a locating device but as the most precise of time-pieces—and the timing from the satellite signals has the accuracy of atomic clocks, to a millionth of a millionth of a second. Last year the company's first major customer, a large North American wireless carrier, placed a $500,000 order.

Another intriguing local GPS-based company is Ellipse Spatial Services, which Rob Pryor started six years ago from a spare bedroom in his Calgary home. He has no direct connections with the university; in fact, although he studied engineering technology and mathematics at Fraser Valley College in Abbotsford, British Columbia, Pryor says, "I'm not really certified in anything. It's more the vision and following through on it. I've just taken existing products off the shelf and put new uses to them"—such as a recently completed $750,000 project for a gas-transmission pipeline installation in Alberta. Ellipse employs differential GPS receivers to quickly capture accurate data when high-pressure petroleum pipelines are laid underground. The data can help pinpoint potential problems such as weakened pipes. The pipeline operators use bar codes—like those on grocery products—to identify individual pipes. "To reduce human error during data collection," Pryor says, " we scan the bar code of each individual pipe joint. This bar code links the pipe's chemical and mechanical properties, joint-weld data, and other features to a geographical point."

Differential GPS is the basis of Ed and Shirley Fitzhenry's navigation systems which their company, Pelorus, is manufacturing for worldwide marketing by the multinational Honeywell Inc. That strategic alliance exemplifies how local initiatives can attract deeper-pocket partners from outside who take existing technology to more rarified altitudes. Ed Fitzhenry says: "There has been a transformation in the province fostered by the forward thinking of the Peter Lougheed government." He points to the support that Premier Lougheed's administration gave to the 1992 dismantling of NovAtel, the provincially owned cellular manufacturer and marketer. "They took flak for this," he says, "but in my view that was the genesis of the development of Calgary and Alberta generally as a technology centre." Among other things, hiving off the company into private holdings attracted world-calibre players in the industry to the province, including Northern Telecom, which acquired the cellular-systems business, and Canadian Marconi, which in 1998 took a majority stake in the NovAtel division that was reborn as a GPS specialist. As a result of this sort of activity, Fitzhenry says, "Even though oil prices are in the sewer, we're seeing this vibrant economy."

The concept of high technology as a saviour of western Canada is a new one. Talk about high tech in this country and the places that pop into mind are usually bound by Ontario's borders, towns such as Kanata near Ottawa and the Toronto outpost of Markham. Yet the West has some dazzling entrepreneurial stars in the universe of computing, electronics, telecommunications, precision-engineering, robotics, biochemistry, and health-care products.

In British Columbia, this collective industry ranks third-largest and the province has at least two global leaders revolutionizing their important fields. Ballard Power Systems is by far the most advanced developer of fuel-cell systems destined for tomorrow's battery-powered cars (attracting Ford Motor Company and Daimler-Benz as major partners, with Ford alone investing $600 million), and Creo Products has transformed the worldwide printing industry with its trailblazing computer-to-plate technology, which eliminates the traditional film process in converting computer data to printing plates.

Alberta—which spends more per capita on research and development than any other province—shines beyond its preeminence in GPS and cellular technology. Not surprisingly, Calgary has twice the per-capita national average of scientists, mathematicians, and engineers. That's largely due to the the petroleum industry based there and the rich R&D in energy technology it generates. You expect the presence of companies like Secure Oil Tools of Edmonton, whose low-cost metallic-filter technology to increase the productivity of oil wells has given it broad international markets and offices in Barbados and Venezuela. Less predictable is a biopharmaceutical front-runner like Biomira Inc. of Edmonton, which is in the final phase of testing its long-awaited vaccine Theratope to treat women with advanced breast cancer. Biomira was born in 1985 after two University of Alberta researchers, an immunologist and a pharmacist, compared notes over a beer at the faculty club and decided to capitalize on their combined interest in diagnostic cancer research. If Theratope's final clinical results prove positive, the long-simmering public company is about to come to the boil with exceptional earnings—and could help position Alberta as an emerging biotechnology centre.*

Saskatchewan, meanwhile, has staked its turf in agricultural biotechnology. Important international corporations have been lured to work with local experts in Saskatoon, now among the top ten cities in

---

*In typical scenarios for high-tech companies, which are the target of stock players hungry for undervalued properties to invest in, Biomira, Ballard Power, and Calgary's Cell-Loc all created short-lived stirs in late 1998 when American media discovered them. *Business Week* mentioned Biomira's vaccine along with a favourable comment from a large Minneapolis investor, sending the shares soaring to $17.13 on the Nasdaq Stock Market before they sank to $4.81. A positive *New York Times* story about Ballard's fuel-cell technology—"they may have the Holy Grail," a transportation expert with the Union of Concerned Scientists said—boosted the company's stock by $5.80, a ten-percent gain. And Cell-Loc gained 51 percent in three days after trumpeting that it would be featured on a TV show hosted by *Forbes* magazine's chairman.

the world for this specialty. The hometown companies tend to bear unwieldly names like MicroBio Rhizogen Corporation, whose bacterial products enhance pea and lentil production around the world; Philom Bios Inc., which uses fermentation technology to create safe, cheap bio-herbicides and biofungicides for western agriculture; and Bioriginal Food & Science Corporation, which makes the trendy nutritional plant-based products called nutraceuticals.* Bioriginal's president, Rick Kulow, earned a special citation for innovative product develop-ment in the 1998 Canadian Entrepreneur of the Year awards.

While Manitoba has never been known as a hotbed of high tech, in at least one area—information-technology consulting—the province has a star that is creating its own galaxy in North America. Online Business Systems of Winnipeg is the creation of Chuck Loewen, a High-Tech Entrepreneur whose career and counsel are explored at length in his own chapter. Loewen grew up in a Mennonite farm fam-ily and in 1986 founded one of Canada's most consistently fastest-growing companies, now operating across the continent. Online is an IT consultant, computer-system trainer, and custom software-package developer. Given his conservative background and the industry he is in, it would be fair to surmise that Chuck Loewen should be among the most serious-minded of the Mavericks. Not at all: he thinks of his entrepreneurial business, profitable from the start, as a wonderful game and himself as a gamesman. With the self-assuredness and poise that spring from his success and allow him this sense of play, he would be the last one to need a GPS receiver to position himself in the world.

---

*There is a multibillion-dollar global market for neutraceuticals and "functional foods" that result when health-promoting ingredients of one food are extracted and added to another common food—oat bran in white bread, for example—or turned into a neutraceutical pill or powder. The Canadian Neutraceuticals Innovation Centre in Portage la Prairie, Manitoba, is developing the industry in that province and across the West. In 1998 the University of Alberta opened a Functional Foods Centre of Excellence, which is research-ing connections between diet and chronic disease as well as developing neutraceuticals.

Chapter Nine

The Pathfinders

Ed and Shirley Fitzhenry, Pelorus Navigation Systems

The MD-80 jet making its approach to New Jersey's Newark International Airport on September 21, 1998, was laden with American politicians, government officials, journalists, aviation representatives, and a Canadian couple with more than a casual interest in being aboard. As the blue-and-white Continental Airlines plane touched down, its passengers became participants in an historic event. They were on the world's first commercial flight to land while using a Differential Global Positioning System—DGPS—that relies on a constellation of 24 satellites in space. If it wasn't quite as momentous as the Wright Brothers' inaugural manned liftoff at Kitty Hawk in 1903, it did rank right up there with the first instrument-landing systems tested in Britain during the Second World War.

All of these systems are designed to guide an aircraft when poor weather conditions make a safe visual approach impossible. What distinguishes the DGPS is that it refines the raw broadcasting signals that pilots receive from satellites in space and positions their planes even more precisely to ensure an uneventful landing no matter how rotten the visibility. Even without the so-called differential capability to correct the satellites' unrefined data, GPS itself had been a landmark in more ways than one. The American Department of Defense called upon the network of satellites during the Gulf War and then unveiled the system for civilian use in 1993. That year the head of the U.S. Federal Aviation Administration said, "GPS is the single most important advance in air navigation since we started flying airplanes." And DGPS was the next giant step: the superior commercial application of the satellite-tapping technology, making precision approaches smoother and many times safer at as little as a 12th of the cost of traditional landing systems for a typical medium-size airport.

Ed and Shirley Fitzhenry were on the flight from Washington, D.C., to Newark that first day of fall. Husband and wife, they are the cofounders of Pelorus Navigation Systems Inc. of Calgary, which helped develop and now manufactures and installs all the ground-based hardware for DGPS. In 1995 the modestly financed Pelorus, with its 30 employees, entered into a strategic alliance with Honeywell Inc., the $8-billion U.S. multinational with a workforce of 50,000.* Honeywell is marketing the systems around the world and supplying airlines with the GPS equipment their planes need to link with the world's most sophisticated aircraft-navigation technology.

For the Fitzhenrys, the trip to Newark was the touchdown of a long entrepreneurial flight that began 15 years earlier when they ran an airplane-engine repair business and an air-charter company—both of which went belly-up, leaving them with only a small navigation-systems distributorship. Ed Fitzhenry, witnessing the successful satellite-assisted landing of a commercial jet that September, could reflect on his days as an executive with a half-dozen oil companies in the early 1980s. His work took him by plane to Arctic outposts where the lack of any approach aids would often force planes to turn back without landing. "When you got there," he says, "I could see the pilots were really faced with quite a dilemma—whether or not to push the envelope of safety."

Since the birth of Pelorus (named for an early navigational instrument like a mariner's compass), the pathfinding Fitzhenrys have been helping reduce such risks. Their public company has designed, built, and set up navigational and meteorological systems of varying degrees of sophistication at more than 200 airports, helicopter pads, and marine platforms on six continents. Flying into almost any airport of any consequence in Canada, the pilot of your plane will be depending on their Distance Measuring Equipment ground station. Yet the couple who have made this high-tech equipment and marketed it around the world are well aware that even in North America, fewer than half of all active runways used by commercial carriers have precision-approach

---

*Honeywell supplies control systems for homes and buildings, industry, and space and aviation, where it is the world's leading supplier of avionics systems for commercial, military, and space markets. Its technology has been aboard every American manned space flight since the first Mercury program and is on almost every commercial aircraft today.

and landing aids (only five percent worldwide). "And as specialists in air-navigation systems," Ed Fitzhenry notes, "it concerns us considerably that 53 percent of all serious commercial aircraft accidents take place during the approach and landing phases of flight."

The U.S. Federal Aviation Authority estimates 48,000 airports around the globe have runways long enough to land jet aircraft, which makes them potential customers of precision-landing systems. Most of them don't have such electronic aids because conventional technology is costly, hard to put in and maintain, and won't even work in many hilly locations. Approved by the FAA, the new Pelorus-Honeywell product answers all these complaints, the Fitzhenrys say, and they are counting on it to become the landing system of tomorrow. They are, in fact, betting their own future on it as they await the widespread introduction of the high-tech equipment required on planes to make their system operable. While Pelorus provides the technology on the ground, Honeywell furnishes the technology in the air—the avionics—which the airline industry is only now starting to adopt. Continental and nine other airlines are involved in consortiums that the FAA has charged with designing and implementing GPS-based navigation systems. Honeywell, meanwhile, is targeting 1,400 major international airports that might upgrade to this standard.

Mike Hill, the market analyst with a professional-engineering background who watches Pelorus for Acumen Capital Partners of Calgary, says, "We don't expect large-scale adoption to occur until the 2001 time frame. ... For investors who currently hold Pelorus stock, patience will be required." For newcomers who want to take a flyer on the technology, Hill is cautiously optimistic: "Pelorus should be considered a long-term speculative play with upside potential at current price levels." He was one of the observers on the memorable Washington-Newark flight, which he has described as the start of a new era in aircraft navigation. More pragmatically, he adds, "From a marketing perspective, this event signalled that this technology is at the point where it can be used for revenue-generating flights." From a public-relations perspective, it doesn't hurt that the U.S. National Aeronautics and Space Administration is already using two of the Pelorus-Honeywell systems for its shuttle-training aircraft to support astronaut instruction, flight-testing, and data collection.

While they are waiting for the upside, the Fitzhenrys have taken steps to lighten the financial load on their company. In 1998, at a youthful-looking 61, Ed bumped himself upstairs to become an unpaid chairman and appointed Mike Beamish, for six years engineering vice president with Pelorus, as president and CEO. The previous year Shirley had essentially retired from Pelorus, although she still comes in occasionally to help out with the accounting. That was only one of several responsibilities she had assumed since starting to act as a corporate navigator to her husband's piloting of the company and its predecessors a decade and a half before. He says simply, "Shirley has been responsible for just about everything." She was corporate secretary, oversaw the vital insurance and treasury duties, spearheaded ISO quality-assurance certification by the International Organization for Standardization and, when the company went public in 1987, handled investor relations. "Shirley has been as integral as one can be," Mike Beamish told me. "She was not an ornament—she was a trusted confidante."

With her soft voice and a fair-skinned face that is round and warm-looking, she was certainly an anomaly in the industry, especially when accompanying her husband on sales trips to the Far East. At first, she says herself, "I was thought of as Ed's wife. Like the oil industry, aviation has always been male-dominated and it's hard." But she changed the skeptics' attitudes in becoming the point person with Transport Canada and attending trade shows and conventions as a working partner, off on her own dealing with suppliers and clients. "I'm pretty black-and-white; I was going to say I follow the rules. Ed could get carried away with his creativity and his risk-taking and his adventuresome spirit. I enjoy all of this, but I'm very conservative. In a company context, I tend to play the devil's advocate, and that's why I think we did so well together."

His creative and risk-tolerant nature had certainly surfaced in 1993 when he had a "clootched-together" GPS device installed on a borrowed airplane to make what he billed as the world's first such precision approach, even though this prototype really didn't comply with the official industry specifications for the system. Then Fitzhenry got himself on a Canadian-government sales junket to Vietnam with the express purpose of spending some quality lobbying time with transport minister Doug Young. He so impressed Young with the potential of Global Positioning Systems that the minister invited the deputy minister of Vietnam to visit Canada at the government's expense, with a highlight being a demonstration of the Pelorus version of GPS. With the media and government officials on hand, the company was demonstrating satellite navigation, all right, but this time performing only a charade of a precision approach—an approach that, given the state of the technology available at the time and all the witnesses present, would have been too dangerous to chance. "What it was," he admits now, "was a media event." And he smiles his Irishy grin which—along with his thick thatch of pewter hair, large nose, and rosy face—make him look like George Segal playing an engaging movie con man.

For someone who spent the first half of his career employed by others—working for the Man, as he puts it—Edward G. Fitzhenry showed some enterpreneurial tendencies very early on. One of two children of British working-class immigrants, he was born in 1936 in London, Ontario, where he was a lackadaisical student: sports and a blond girl named Shirley were among the few highlights of his brief fling at high school. He quit in Grade 9, aged 15, to work as a beaker-scrubbing junior lab technician in the plant physiology department at the University of Western Ontario. For the first time, he became intrigued by learning and eagerly read the books the professors lent him, on topics ranging from science to classical music. "Working with Ph.D.s," says Shirley, who was then dating the dark-haired, pleasant-looking Ed, "he realized how little he knew." Now wanting to become a pure mathematician, Fitzhenry stayed in the laboratory for five years while taking the requisite Grade 13 night courses to enter university. During this time, he had what he still considers his first entrepreneurial experience, if "entrepreneur" means a risk-taking self-starter in effective control of an enterprise. He came up with a scheme to educate himself that offers a lesson that has guided him through life.

Communicate your passion to your suppliers and clients so they can buy into your objectives

Trying to get his final year of high school without passing through the four earlier grades, Ed Fitzhenry was rebuffed as a part-time student by the educational establishment. "I was really quite upset about it," he says, "so I found out who the best teachers were in the city of London and I interviewed them and offered them a proposition. I said, 'You teach me to get through Grade 13—I'm not going to take all the rest of it, but I want to do this—and I'll pay you, of course, but I'll give you a bonus if I get 80 or 90.' And some of them were pretty good and I was pretty generous because teachers don't make a whole lot of money—and they were intrigued with the concept." In fact, the occasional teacher refused both the bonus and any payment from this keen student. What he was doing, Fitzhenry now realizes, was having them buy into his objectives by convincing them how serious he was about his education. "I wanted to get good marks because that was the only way to get into university, and so I had to have somebody who identified with that objective, who could share it with me." In later years, he saw the power of displaying his zeal to people outside as well as inside his companies. In Pelorus the mission is "safe, reliable landings," and he says, "I try as much as possible to share my passion for this with everybody. I just feel that I want to make sure that people understand what we're trying to do. ... It's also a way of validating your own dreams—whether they're worthy of having other people participate or not."

He did get into Western as a 20-year-old, and in his first summer off became a more active entrepreneur. Leasing a car from a local driving-school owner, he barnstormed six small towns around London to give driving lessons. He set up in each place for two weeks at a time and then moved on, making better money than his buddies. But in the second summer he was seduced by the prospect of a reliable paycheque from steady employment, working for the first of what would become a long line of petroleum companies. Although he was a clerk in the Shell Oil bulk plant in London, Fitzhenry used to accompany the truck drivers and salesmen on their rounds. "Just to see what the hell they did," he says now. "It was a whole goddamn new world for me because I'd been in university and my father and mother never had any business experience." His cuss words belie a literate mind. Fitzhenry's routine duties at the time veered him in another educational direction when he saw the often indecipherable correspondence that crossed his desk. He realized he could benefit by focusing on English literature and other arts subjects instead of business courses or even the math he took in his first year. (Today, as a management adviser to the University of Calgary, he urges healthy funding for arts programs. "That's the heart of the university," he insists. "That's where the knowledge is, and the M.B.A. guys ought to be exposed to more of it.")

Graduating, intrigued by business, he accepted a job that Shell offered him to take over a badly run bulk plant at Owen Sound on Georgian Bay northwest of Toronto. As a trainee manager with a staff of four, he sold petroleum to new clients as well as servicing existing accounts such as bulk-carrier ships and retail service stations. By now Fitzhenry was married to his high-school sweetheart, Shirley, who soon gave birth to the first of their two daughters. In his mid-twenties, he was mature enough to seek out two middle-aged mentors at corporate headquarters in Toronto. Their counsel helped teach him to keep looking for associates of integrity who inspire trust—qualities he still values more highly than straight financial experience when choosing his corporate directors. Owen Sound also showed him the importance of community involvement, in the form of a highly successful Shell Toy Town promotion he introduced there to collect gifts for needy children. (In his sixties, he continues to stay involved with the Alberta Research Council, the Calgary Airport Authority, and the university, among other institutions.)

In little more than a year, Fitzhenry showed such promise that Shell brought him to Toronto to oversee a territory of about 40 service-station dealers. Most of them were clever mechanics-turned-entrepreneurs who made him realize that "it didn't take university to be a good businessman." His progress with the company was swift, as he worked on the acquisition of the White Rose gas-station chain based in Atlantic Canada and then moved into Shell's finance department to manage and invest incoming funds. Soon after arriving in Toronto, he started an evening M.B.A. program at the University of Toronto to match his frontline learning with some further formal education. In the early 1960s York University was gaining its independence from the University of Toronto and its business program offered Fitzhenry a scholarship to complete his Master's there on a full-time basis. It was a compelling proposal: he became president of York's first M.B.A. graduating class as well as leading it in final marks.

Shell offered him a job in finance again, but Fitzhenry was feeling entrepreneurial, even though he and Shirley were feeling the pinch. The day he graduated, his wife remembers, they had no money for milk so she had to spend a silver dollar one of her husband's corporate mentors had given them as a memento of the birth of their first daughter. The ambitious Fitzhenry soon had five jobs, four of them teaching. In Toronto he lectured part-time on business correspondence at Ryerson Polytechnical and on English to Indo-Canadians at George Brown College, and full-time on business mathematics at Seneca College. A long drive away in St. Catharines, he gave an undergraduate course in marketing at Brock University and began to understand a truth he respects to this day.

If you want to keep learning throughout your career, teach

As the Japanese proverb has it, "to teach is to learn." Not every entrepreneur can afford the time and energy—nor has the background or self-confidence—to teach what he or she knows. But in my experience of the breed in Canada, a surprising number do welcome the opportunity to lecture at least informally in colleges and business schools, drawing from their own careers for seminars and colloquia. And they come away amazed at how much information and informed opinion they possess to communicate and often at how their encounters with students can kick-start their own thinking. While the usual advice is to keep learning throughout your life, teaching—in whatever form— adds an entirely deeper dimension to education. As Ed Fitzhenry points out, "I've never learned so much about anything as I did when I taught. If you don't know anything about a subject, go and teach it—and then you've got to learn." Preparing for even a simple question-and-answer session with a classful of bright students usually demands some self-examination, analysis of personal business style, and questioning of the conventional wisdom in your field. Teaching formally as

Fitzhenry was, he didn't have to bone up for the business-math course but did for marketing, where he was dealing with case studies and sophisticated concepts about consumer products and market research. "I had to be at least one chapter ahead of the students," he says, "and while I wasn't pushing back the frontiers of knowledge, I got a real joy out of it." Even later, as a busy senior executive in the oil industry, he made space in his career to teach part-time at York University.

Fitzhenry's connection with York landed him a fifth job as a management consultant. A marketing professor there asked him to write brochures and make presentations for the university. That led to links with Ford of Canada, for whom he did dealer training, as he later wound up doing for Imperial Oil's Esso dealerships in tandem with an independent clinical psychologist named Dave Jackson. After a year on his own, Fitzhenry quit his teaching jobs to become part of a lucrative consulting practice with Jackson and his associates. In the two years they worked together—billing nearly $1 million annually—one of their marketing-research clients was the Canadian division of Sun Oil. Fitzhenry's consultation to the company on unbranded and self-serve gas stations prompted Sun to offer him a position as marketing and research manager in Toronto.

"The kids were young," he explains, "and the practice was going sideways and the economy was a bit tight—and I went conservative." Still, he enjoyed Sun Oil for most of the five years he worked there: "It was a great job and I wanted to be president." He got as far as manager of corporate planning. The American oil company was involved in Canadian retailing and refining as well as developing the Alberta tar sands and drilling on the East Coast and in the North. His final role there was as member of a negotiating team trying to acquire the Canadian operations of California-based Union Oil, which wanted to pull out of this country. When Sun's head honchos in the United States rejected the deal his team had shaped, Fitzhenry exploded: "I threw my papers all over the office."

By coincidence he then got a phone call from Maurice Strong, the head of Ottawa's fresh-from-the-crate Crown corporation, Petro-Canada, established in 1975 to expedite oil and gas exploration, research, and development. Strong was a persuasive figure with his management background in energy and financial corporations and his recent prominent postings with the United Nations. Fitzhenry was philosophically opposed to the strongly nationalistic sentiments that the Liberal government of Pierre Trudeau had mustered to justify Petro-Canada. Yet the visionary Strong persuaded him to move with his family to Calgary to become chief financial officer of the new state-owned agency. "Maurice convinced me I could make a difference, together with some other people who also came from the industry." In fact, he says, he never did manage to. Banging heads with president-to-be Bill Hopper and knowing how unpopular Petro-Canada was with the private oil industry, Fitzhenry lasted only one year while the federal corporation acquired Atlantic Richfield's Canadian assets. "We agreed to part company," he says. "It wasn't my best hour and I felt I'd let the family down."

Once again he flirted with the idea of becoming an entrepreneur, this time in British Columbia's Okanagan Valley—either to buy a wood-working company there or restore an old paddlewheeler and take a chance on turning it into a gambling casino. ("Don't bet on it," an unimpressed Shirley told him.) Instead he went back to working for the Man in a roundelay of oil-industry positions. He was corporate planner for Ashland Oil Canada briefly, then helped sell it to Kaiser Resources, where he worked for little more than a year. Edgar Kaiser Jr. spun Ashland off to Jack Gallagher's Dome Petroleum, Canada's preeminent energy conglomerate, and Fitzhenry became special-projects manager there in 1980. He prospered from these transactions, making hundreds of thousands of dollars from his investment in Ashland, and Dome gave him stock that would earn him even more.

One of the projects he undertook at Dome was rationalizing the corporate air force of 20 planes and helicopters. And it was while playing this part that he really came to understand the vital nature of instrument-landing systems in Canadian aviation. He would fly to remote northern reaches like Tuktoyuktuk in a high-performance, 15-passenger G2 jet with sophisticated avionics aboard. Sometimes the aircraft had to detour hundreds of kilometres in foul weather because the gravel airfield below had virtually no other navigation aids except for a simple nondirectional beacon, which was absolutely useless in fog or heavy cloud. "It was always on my mind—why would that be?" he recalls. "And so I took a look at nav aids."

But not immediately. He and Shirley were finally about to find their path in the long and convoluted journey they had taken since their days in Owen Sound. First Fitzhenry had to abandon the comforts of his current cocoon. With a nice nest egg from his oil-company investments, he wanted to hatch his very own business. Calgary, at the dawn of the 1980s, was still riding the oil boom of the previous decade. Out of many opportunities, Fitzhenry chose to buy Munro Aero Engine, paying about $200,000 in cash and a few hundred thousand in future earnings, and an air charter business called Meridian Aviation, which sold for roughly $1 million—all to be paid out in future earnings, in return for his assuming several million dollars' worth of debt. Munro repaired and overhauled airplane piston engines; Meridian had a fleet of five planes—from Cessnas to Citations acquired on lease-to-purchase plans—and good charter contracts to take oil-drilling crews to the north country. And within Meridian, Fitzhenry started a small navigation-systems business.

"Suddenly we had 60 employees," Shirley Fitzhenry says. "That's when the hard work really started. " With high-school courses in basic bookkeeping, she had worked for Great-West Life Insurance as a secretary in London and a trainer of office employees in Toronto, and even oversaw young women in residence at a Toronto nursing school. "Ed asked me to come in and help three days a week," she says. "Mostly in the office areas, helping to get the accounting organized and making sure their company files were up-to-date. I can't say I didn't have sleepless nights with Munro and Meridian, but we never missed a payroll. There were a lot of times when Ed and I didn't take salaries."

Then, in 1983, her husband says: "Everything went to hell in a handbasket. The economy—interest rates went to 26 percent. And we had leases, loans to the banks. Munro was a pretty good business, but Meridian had all these airplanes leased and they were highly leveraged. One of the ways you made money was the aircraft actually appreciated in value, so it seemed like a good idea [to own them] at the time. Except the economy turned and the interest rates went up and the oil companies didn't honour their contracts and said, 'Well, sue us.' The banks called the notes and that was the end of the company. And it brought Munro down with it. ... I lost virtually everything I had."

"That was tough," Shirley says. "We had some great employees—and that was emotionally the hardest part for us. So you start all over again. That's what you do."

As Fitzhenry told her at the time, "Shirley, the jig is up. I'm going to have to work real hard and I don't have a job and the oil industry has gone to hell around here. I think we're going to have to live on our wits like we used to."

"Is there anything I can do to help?"

Well, yes, there was, he told her: come in and work for the little company he was considering.

They mortgaged their house, and out of the minor navigation-aids distributorship they had conducted within Meridian—the only legally unencumbered part of the business—formed Pelorus Navigation Systems. It was a private company, and Shirley, who handled the incorporation, was the founding shareholder. Two pilots became their equal partners, one of them working on marketing; the Fitzhenrys bought them out by the second year. The staff consisted of Ed, Shirley doing the office work, and two technicians who did installations and repairs to the systems in airplane cockpits. Working out of a couple of rooms in the Executive Flight Centre at the Calgary airport, they were in close contact with pilots and the all-important local Transport Canada officials.

Pelorus had two basic product lines. One was a California-built avionics device that worked with a Global Navigation System (GNS, as opposed to GPS)—specifically the Omega system of radio beacons operated by the U.S. Navy, which some aircraft relied on for en route navigation rather than for landing assistance. The other was Distance Measuring Equipment, a ground-based system manufactured by a company in Kansas City. Pelorus leased the airborne equipment to petroleum companies and the DME to airports. In 1985, Fitzhenry persuaded the DME manufacturer to let him make an improved version of the equipment in Calgary using its original printed circuit boards.

"DME started to take off," Shirley says, "and that's when Transport Canada began to take an interest in Pelorus. At that time Ed and I started going to Ottawa to meet industry people at Aerospace Industry Association of Canada meetings, and dedicated a lot of time to making those contacts. There wasn't a company that didn't know Pelorus by the end of that first year. I was part of the decision-making team and really knew what was going on. I was the contact with Transport Canada for a lot of things."

Another product was looming on the horizon, touted as the future of the industry: Microwave Landing Systems. MLS was superior to existing systems, especially for those petroleum clients whose planes had to land on ice runways in the High Arctic. In 1986 Pelorus acquired an exclusive distribution deal from the New York manufacturer and supplied and installed the first MLS in a Canadian airport (the Jasper/Hinton field in Alberta). This line proved popular, too; one of the customers was the airport in Nanaimo, British Columbia, which had a Pelorus DME but was still facing too many aborted landings when the wicked coastal weather closed in. When the mayor said the airport couldn't afford the hefty price tag for a new MLS, Fitzhenry advised him to initiate landing fees to finance the system—and meanwhile he would see if he could find a bargain for Nanaimo. About a month later an airport developer in Houston, Texas, called to say he was going into receivership and had an MLS to sell. Fitzhenry flew down to meet the vice president of the Texas Commerce Bank and offered $200,000 for the $1.5 million piece of equipment.

"It's got to be worth more than that," the bank receiver said.

"If it is, then you sell it to somebody. We don't have much time. I have a customer for it back in Canada."

"It's a deal."

And, as Fitzhenry tells me, "One of my engineers went down to Texas with me and we took this landing system off its moorings, put it on an American Van Lines Air Ride van, and got out of Dodge City."

This was the same sort of chutzpah that led him to his next big adventure. Pelorus was doing splendidly by now, earning $1 million after tax on $5 million in sales. It went public in 1987, raising $2 million when the Alberta government introduced a stocks-and-savings plan that allowed provincial residents to write off their investments in Albertan companies against their provincial taxes. So the Fitzhenrys were primed for expansion when the U.S. manufacturer of MLS mentioned the need for specialty Distance Measuring Equipment that would work with his sophisticated microwave system to provide ten times more precise readings. He gave them the name of a Norwegian aerospace company, Delcom Electro, that was working in the area of precision DME. Fitzhenry flew to Oslo to meet a crew of bright engineers from the University of Trondheim now working for an owner who was a real-estate developer. Fellow enterpreneurs, the two company presidents got to know each other well, visiting back and forth, although they never could make a deal on transferring the new technology to Canada. Then Fitzhenry got a call from Johan Wessamann, the managing director and chief engineer of Delcom, who said "a lot of guys in blue suits"—receivers from a Norwegian bank—were on the premises to take over the company.

Off Fitzhenry flew to Oslo and accompanied Wessamann to the bank to negotiate the purchase of the distressed Delcom. He warned the engineer that he would be telling the receivers that the equipment and the technology involved were inferior—"the stuff is lousy."

In earlier negotiations, the owner had been asking the equivalent of $2 million Cdn. for only part of the company. The offer Fitzhenry made the bank was $60,000. When Wessamman heard the number, his figurative jaw dropped. It obviously fell even farther when the bank accepted. What the wheeler-dealer from Canada was counting on was a basic law of negotiation.

In deal-making, always look for your leverage — and if you don't have any, create it

"Leverage is a fundamental principle in business," Ed Fitzhenry points out. "Whenever we're in a situation today with Honeywell or anybody, I always look for leverage. If you want something from somebody—you know, not in a love relationship but a business relationship—then you need leverage, you need to have a very shiny star. And it has to be real shiny relative to others, or larger, or something creative. There has got to be something that gives you some edge." And in the case of the Norwegian aerospace company, once valued at $2 million, for which he paid $60,000? "The perception was that it had no value and that it was just going to dissipate. Our leverage was that we were there and we had the money to pay them—albeit a pittance. No one else was prepared to step up." And if you don't have any true leverage? "Make it," he says, as he did in part by suggesting that the company wasn't worth much while knowing that the bank was more interested in the owner's real-estate holdings. Fitzhenry would effectively use leverage again when it came to negotiating a strategic alliance with Honeywell on GPS technology: "We had a working prototype, but it was more than that. The other thing we had was customers: we had three sales here in Canada and one in Australia and that really turned Honeywell around. There has always got to be something."

In acquiring Delcom Electro, the Fitzhenrys were buying the brains of Johan Wessamann and four other crack engineers who remained in Oslo for a year before three of them moved to Calgary. Wessamann was among that trio, and while the others stayed in Canada for only two years, he was here for five, leading what Fitzhenry believes was "the smartest engineering team for DME in the world." The wattage of Distance Measuring Equipment determines the distance that it can transmit a signal. Wessamann invented the state-of-the-art kilowatt (1,000-watt) DME, which is used for navigation while an aircraft is en route from airport to airport, while the 100-watt DME is useful only for landings.

Pelorus also pioneered the adoption of DMEs to guide helicopter landings on the icebreakers of the Canadian Coast Guard and the marine platforms of oil companies' deep-sea drilling rigs. One of those rig installations was worth about $250,000, with a 50-percent gross margin, and Pelorus did 15 of them. By 1992, thanks to such profitable deals, the company was able to retire its $1.1 million in long-term debt.

Not every deal worked. In 1986 Pelorus had installed Canada's first fully Automated Weather Observation and Reporting Systems for airports. A device developed in California, it seemed pertinent for Canada, especially to serve smaller, remoter airports where it was uneconomical to have observers on-site to record the often fearsome weather. "We thought it was a big product," Fitzhenry says. "We were trying to sell stock and we thought it was important to establish that this was an innovative company." Getting the licensing and technology rights to AWOS, Fitzhenry approached the federal Atmospheric Environment Service. "I went a little too far with it and said, 'Look, why doesn't Canada use this as the aviation weather network? It's cheaper, better, and look at all the money you can save.'" The savings would have come primarily from replacing the many round-the-clock weather observers in place at airports across the country. But he says their superiors didn't want to reduce their empire by cutting the payroll. "So they found a way to screw me," he insists. Officially they rejected his AWOS on the theory that its anemometer, a wind-measuring device, couldn't pass a severe icing test. "Well, there's no anemometer in the world that would endure this icing test, and their anemometers don't," he argues. At the time, the government weather people retorted that it was no problem if one of theirs didn't survive because their observers on-site would see it was gone and could warn pilots. "Obviously," Fitzhenry says now, "we'd thought of that. We had a device in there that would fail-safe, always worked, and said the system's not operating. They wouldn't buy it." In the end, only a few airports purchased the system.

Pelorus had better luck selling Johan Wessamann's precision DMEs throughout Canada and around the world. In 1992 he further improved the product by adding a telemetry-monitoring function. A centrally located computer could now dial up a navigation system at a remote airfield and determine if a component was malfunctioning. In seeking foreign distributors, the Fitzhenrys would first learn who distributed for companies like Canadian Marconi or CAE Electronics and then pitch them. Occasionally they would encounter cultural barriers, as they did in South Korea. Shirley always travelled with Ed on these overseas trips and, he recollects, "In the Korean adventure, in particular, I think we came close to not getting the agent we wanted because we had a woman in our entourage. She was front-row centre because she was an executive and owner."

The Korean agent was an elderly man, whose son took Fitzhenry aside to say his father didn't like women in the workplace and asked that Shirley not attend a meeting scheduled with airport and government authorities. That situation gave rise to a Fitzhenry precept.

When pursuing global business relations, respect other cultures, but don't compromise your own principles

In dealing with a Korean business culture where women weren't necessarily welcome, Ed Fitzhenry had to walk a tightrope. "I took a hard stand as nicely as I could and said, 'Well, I respect your culture and your values and I wish I had understood that aspect of your company before. That's a shortfall. I didn't learn enough about you and where you are and that's not characteristic of me or my company. We made a mistake and we will improve. Now I want you to learn something about my culture and where I'm coming from.' And I went through the fact that we're all born equal and even said, 'If you're going to do business with our company, then you're going to do business with Shirley and me, sometimes with Shirley alone, sometimes with me alone, and that's the way that it is. We've got the best product and we'll be sensitive to your culture, but you have got to figure out how to do business with women.' And he did so." After a lunch with both Fitzhenrys, where they spoke as both marriage and business partners, and Shirley asked him questions about his wife and daughters, the son melted and has done business with her ever since. "The lesson," Fitzhenry says, "is do your homework first, learn the culture, but the correlate of that is don't betray your principles and values in doing business internationally."

For all the success Pelorus was experiencing internationally, however, the Fitzhenrys could see some disturbing blips on the radar screen, like enemy fighter planes poised for attack. MLS was no longer being touted as the system of the future, and precision DME sales were starting to fall off. The popularization of the superior Global Positioning Systems during the Gulf War and the release of GPS for civilian use afterward meant that potential landing-system buyers were deferring their purchases until the satellite system was well in place. Pelorus began working with the GPS experts who had gathered at the University of Calgary and then with ARINC, a large not-for-profit engineering company in Minneapolis owned by and serving 40 airlines. Its brilliant engineers also had contracts with outside agencies, such as the FAA and the American military, for whom they had done the original work on GPS satellite guidance systems. Ed Fitzhenry approached ARINC's president about utilizing its technology for precision landings using differential GPS. Fitzhenry says the meeting went well: "I play a little golf—I'm not very good at it, fortunately—and he whipped my ass and we made a friendly relationship."

Mike Beamish was representing Pelorus in a world organization called the Radio Technical Communications for Aeronautics Committee in Washington, D.C. In 1992, 20 years after getting involved in the Alberta high-tech industry, Beamish had joined the company as engineering vice president and as a director with a six-percent shareholding (currently 16 percent). Now Fitzhenry sent him to sit on the RTCA subcommittee, along with ARINC, Honeywell, and other heavyweights. The group's task was to develop specifications for using differential GPS to land aircraft. When Beamish reported back, his boss said, "God, we've got to get this first. We've got to have some leverage. I don't care if it meets the spec— let's just clootch together a prototype and we'll make a big foofaraw." Both the engineers of ARINC and the local academic experts contributed their expertise to help Pelorus beat the world in making the first precision approach using a primitive form of differential GPS. It happened, however, on a clear November day in 1993, and the plane had a visual fix on the airport at all times. "We had a half-assed radio technology that applied to this sort of thing," Fitzhenry says, "and we put it all together in a clumsy machine and put a GPS on light twin-piston turboprop we borrowed from a guy—and we actually did a precision approach. And it was quite good. We knew that our system didn't comply with the [RTCA] specifications. All we wanted to do was get in the game." The media were on hand for the event, along with representatives from the FAA and ARINC, and Pelorus was suddenly a prominent player.

The follow-up was another media event the next year when Doug Young, the Canadian transport minister, imported Vietnam's deputy prime minister for a demonstration of differential GPS. "We actually used the GPS for navigation, but we wouldn't have done a precision approach because it was too risky," Fitzhenry recalls. Among those on hand was Keith Aakre, who had been a helicopter pilot in Vietnam, a country he loved, and was now marketing vice president for Honeywell.

Pelorus was swapping information with ARINC, which under its president had decided it would get involved for the very first time in developing its own product to sell: differential GPS. The idea was that the small Canadian company could then market the product internationally. But a complication arose in the form of an American company called E-Systems (since acquired by Raytheon, a major U.S. defence contractor), which was part of the military establishment, specializing in spy products. Moving in on ARINC when its friendly president unexpectedly died, E-Systems looked as if it would displace Pelorus as the DGPS marketer. Ed and Shirley Fitzhenry were about to step into a meeting in San Diego when ARINC's engineering vice president warned them that the pair of E-Systems people in attendance had accused them of cheating and other malfeasance. As the meeting began, Fitzhenry directed a question to his accusers: "You said that we don't have integrity and we've done some bad things and I'd like to know what you're talking about. Let's get it on the table. If there's a problem, we should deal with it."

The room fell quiet. Then the E-Systems people replied, "No, we have no problem. We think that you're a fine company."

Fitzhenry had called their bluff, but Pelorus's relationship with ARINC didn't survive: "I had one more meeting where E-Systems, the FAA, American Airlines, and ourselves were there to talk about the installation of our system at Dallas-Fort Worth airport. So here I was talking about putting a system in and E-Systems puts on the table a brochure of our system with no mention of us and it just said 'E-Systems Satellite Landing System.' Amazing.* Shirley knew that things were going badly and I got a call from her stating that our old friend [vice president] Jay Mesiti from Honeywell had called, asking about our landing system and whether there might be some opportunity for us to work together. So I flew to Phoenix, Arizona, to meet Mesiti and walked into the room where about ten Honeywell executives are saying, 'Tell us about your landing system.' And I said, 'Well, look, first of all I'm going to tell you about this relationship that I've had and I don't want to say anything out of school, but here is the situation—I am not happy with it. They've got our technology and it needs some work and we're looking around for somebody to help market this thing.' And poof! From there on in, Honeywell said, 'Well, we are the ones.' They really wanted to move it along and finally flew their executives up here and said they were going to stay until they had a deal. And they did."

---

*Recently, Ed Fitzhenry says E-Systems' deal with ARINC eventually "came unglued" and the company wasn't prospering as part of Raytheon. "They haven't got a certified system yet and they haven't made any sales and they haven't demonstrated any systems. They have had a lot of problems."

279

The leverage Pelorus wielded was the agreement it had reached to install the world's first DGPS precision-approach and landing systems at Melbourne Airport for use by Airservices Australia as well as the pact with the Saskatchewan government for systems at the Regina and Saskatoon airports. The deal with the province was to open a factory in Saskatoon to manufacture the products, where ten employees currently put them together, with subassembly work in Calgary.

In the exclusive teaming deal signed in January 1995, Pelorus would participate in the research and development of the DGPS product officially called the Honeywell/Pelorus Satellite Landing System SLS 2000; get it certified in Canada; and do all manufacturing, installations, and customer training. Honeywell would handle certification in the United States and most marketing and product support around the globe. It was a joint venture, with each partner investing only in its areas of responsibility (Honeywell has spent an estimated $30 million-plus on the project to date). In developing the strategic alliance, Fitzhenry decided to define the principles that should underly such a relationship. He and his wife flew to Cancun, Mexico, for a week's holiday, during which he did some heavy reading. Then, after discussions with Shirley, he established some guidelines for the business affiliation. While they may not apply to every entrepreneurial company getting into bed with a bigger partner, the collective point they make is all-embracing.

Establish guiding principles before entering into a strategic alliance

"While we're in the vanguard, the reality is that we were a small company with a staff of 30 people," Ed Fitzhenry says. "To compete successfully in global markets for large multiyear, multi-unit contracts, we needed more credibility and we needed help. The kind of help that's found in strategic alliances with large corporations who have well-established management systems, financial muscle, technical bench strength and, most important, marketing capacity." But not just any old big company: "We were looking for an ally who was prepared to embrace five principles that are critical to the survival of a technology-based alliance. The first thing we look for is a partner who wants a long-term relationship. Secondly, we ask that our partner share our value for the continuous growth and development of our people. We want to be a brain centre, too. Next, we not only look for alliances that want our technology, but also for a commitment to share technology both ways. And both partners must be committed to participation in marketing. Our experience has taught us that all elements of the system—technology, manufacturing, and marketing—must be integrated to continually deliver value to customers. Finally, we look for a strategic partner who shares our commitment to total quality management, a company that strives for excellence in every dimension: in customer service and satisfaction, profitability, productivity, human resources, marketing, innovation, social and environmental responsibility, and so on across the entire spectrum of business functions. Quality is not part of excellence—it's all of it."

To finance its part in the new alliance, Pelorus completed a successful public issue in 1995 of 1.2 million common shares worth $780,000 and private placements a year later of $2.4 million and $3.6 million. "We knew we were going to need more time," Fitzhenry says. "It turned out to be a bigger project and Honeywell turned out to be a more demanding partner than we anticipated." Among other things, the senior partner has been pushing for the eventual manufacture of 200 systems a year, compared to the ten Pelorus was making by the end of 1998, when Fitzhenry told me, "We've got teams of people installing systems right now in the U.S., Brazil, Australia." But the reality is that, although the FAA approved the Honeywell/Pelorus ground station in the summer of 1997, the aviation industry is awaiting cheaper avionics: receiving units aboard the aircraft that will cost only about $50,000 apiece compared to the current $125,000 and are expected to be available from an American supplier by the turn of the century. As the latest Pelorus annual report notes, "While revenue for 1998 was up significantly over 1997 at $2,136,372 versus $817,087, sales of SLS systems did not meet expectations, primarily due to the lack of suitably priced, suitable avionics."

The Fitzhenrys are holding their breath, too, waiting for the expansive growth that should follow the introduction of the lower-cost receivers. Shirley's retirement in 1997 cut costs, and the following year Fitzhenry relinquished the CEO role and stopped drawing a salary. Mike Beamish, with his electrical-engineering and management-consulting background, is essentially in charge of the day-to-day business. He is well recovered from a heart attack he suffered as a new VP five years earlier. "It substantially changed my life," he says. "We'd just launched our prototype GPS system and the world was rosy. Ed and Shirley were incredibly supportive to the point where I was looking under rocks wondering why they were so nice. Ed and I had several chats regarding succession. I was his retirement project, and when I had the heart attack, now it had to be Plan B. For several years, we agreed I would not succeed Ed because of the concern for my health. This was a very caring Ed. There was a turning point in Pelorus's evolution in 1996-97, where because of our association with Honeywell, our market capitalization had gone from a few million to $80 million. When I joined, we had about three million shares outstanding trading in the 50- to 60-cent range. And now eight million shares in the $8 range. Ed was dreaming the big dream and we needed more people. We brought on three senior people and I was happy—now it was not all on my shoulders. Then the stock fell out of bed." The downturn happened in early 1998, about the time Pelorus was going after another company, Atlantis Aerospace of Toronto, which makes simulators for pilot training. When the shares declined, the takeover attempt ended. "The market turned against us and we went from $8 to a couple of dollars a share," Beamish says.

Since then, Fitzhenry has been on the hunt for other possible acquisitions to backstop the landing-system business. "We're betting that Honeywell can make this happen and that the technology will take hold," he says. "And it's a good bet. But I would like to hedge it a bit and see what we can do with an acquisition and enlarge our possibilities."

Meanwhile he and Shirley divide their time between homes in Calgary and San Diego's Rancho Bernardo, playing some winter golf and tennis and pursuing some new personal paths—in his words, "exploring a new dimension to our relationship." Part of his ongoing role as chairman, along with mentoring Mike Beamish, is to identify new opportunities and complementary products that might provide short-term cash flow. This requires him to keep current with industry patterns.

TrendWatch

The use of simulation in the field of aviation is one of the possibilities that excites Ed Fitzhenry. "That's why I was keen about Atlantis Aerospace. It's something that will save lives and money and time—the technologies are here for us to learn through simulations as opposed to the school of hard knocks. And you can simulate just about anything. Maintenance training with complicated equipment in the field, for example—tying together all of our remote operating and maintenance capability with the simulation experience." Another slowly emerging trend, which involves partner Honeywell, is the integration of all systems in an airport, including security and retailing, even cleaning, as well as aircraft landings. "Anyone who has figured out how to run a total airport environment efficiently will then be able to franchise that. I see airports becoming franchises. ... The early stages of the trend are toward common administration, and when that takes hold, then we can look for systems that they can manage efficiently." He isn't aware of anyone doing this quite yet, but says, "Honeywell is making moves to position themselves in that game, and we're positioning ourselves to be in Honeywell's game. Whenever we look at new product and new business opportunities, we try to see them in the context of where they'll fit in the big scheme of things in a couple of decades from now. And whether we've got it right or not remains to be seen."

Chapter Ten

The Gamesman

Charles (Chuck) Loewen, Online Business Systems

As a boy growing up in a fatherless home, on a hard-scrabble mixed farm in Manitoba, Chuck Loewen worked with pigs, feeding them and mucking out their manured barn, morning after early morning. Then the bottom fell out of the market and his Mennonite mother backed away from the hog business. A few years later, when he was in high school, Loewen got a loan, rented the barn from his mom, and began raising hogs again to finance his education. "I trust you will be careful with the analogy," he tells me nearly two decades later while allowing that there are comparisons to be made between his teenage agricultural venture and the private company he now runs as a 36-year-old. Online Business Systems is one of western Canada's most successful information-technology consultants, computer-system trainers, and custom-software-package developers. Marketing to blue-chip clients throughout North America from offices in its home base of Winnipeg and in Calgary, Vancouver, and Minneapolis, it has made a profit every year since its almost-accidental founding in 1986. For the past four years, this otherwise low-profile enterprise has appeared on *Profit* magazine's list of the fastest-growing companies in Canada—most recently it ranked 17th, with five-year revenue growth of 2,655 percent to 1997. A year later it was generating nearly $12 million. And perhaps more important, management consultants Arthur Andersen & Co. and *The Financial Post* keep naming Online one of the country's 50 best-managed private companies.

If any analogy is to be drawn between pigs and PCs, says Chuck Loewen, it is the stick-to-itiveness demanded by both businesses.*

---

*No direct relation to Ray Loewen, the former president of The Loewen Group, the funeral-services giant now based in Richmond, British Columbia, which began as a Mennonite family business in Steinbach, Manitoba (see Introduction, page 9).

"Growing up, we had no options," he says. "We had to keep doing what we were doing. That was our livelihood, that was how we put bread on the table, and every day the farm work had to be done. Pigs are a lot of work. Today you have automated feed systems and barn cleaners and so on, but in those days it was carrying pails of feed to pigs and cleaning the manure off the barn floor. There are lots of unglamorous things that need to be done daily after the excitement is gone." At Online the demand is the day-to-day maintenance of staff and customers; he says the comparison is often made that "we are farmers and we are farming our customers and we plant seeds and we maintain them and ultimately we harvest. ... And it doesn't end necessarily when it is time to go home. On the farm, if we needed to work through the night, we would." Now, with Online 13 years old, he says, "Most days I will go home at six and bring work home with me, but in the early days, the first six, seven years of business, it was 18-hour days, day in, day out. I started without any money."

If Charles "Chuck" Loewen is beginning to sound dishearteningly sober-sided, a little too intense, and as dour in character as the stereotype of the Mennonite-farm background from which he sprang, it is time to add some colour to his portrait. For this is an owner-manager who believes in viewing business as a game—with all the team participation and even fun that this implies. He once defined his management style as TLC, which stood for Teachers, Leaders, Cheerleaders (and he would act as all three). But it could equally have meant Tender, Loving Care, which is the nutrient he has used in sowing and growing his business. He and his two partners have treated their employees as highly involved, empowered members of a troupe of bright young talents who have to park their egos and work together. In the competitive IT world of North America, where Winnipeg—and perhaps even Calgary and Minneapolis—aren't naturally among the first places a computer whiz might think to settle, Online has attracted 150 first-rate employees. "Many people who have used Online say Loewen and his staff are some of the smartest people in the business," notes *Winnipeg Free Press* business reporter Martin Cash. They come and stay because of the coddling and encouragement their bosses lavish on them. The ongoing award for being a best-managed company largely reflects this corporate attitude. It is epitomized by the fact that two women who joined the Winnipeg office as receptionists, with no technical background whatsoever—one of them had to ask Loewen how to operate a fax machine—were given training courses and quickly graduated to become competent computer specialists.

"You can write your own ticket here," says Shelley Malo, who had been an immigration consultant in Calgary before returning home to Winnipeg and trying Online for a transitional job. She started as a 28-year-old receptionist—"a shock to my system"—but soon became Loewen's executive assistant. After deciding that a technical-writing course the company paid for was too dry, she went to lunch with her boss to discuss her murky future. Within a couple of months, she had done "a lot of feet-first learning" and was part of a team dispatched to Prince George, British Columbia, to implement software programs for a lumber and plywood client. "I was the expert," Malo recalls of that six-month experience. "I would phone Chuck on his cell at home and he would always make me laugh and be supportive. I was never walking on eggshells. And I never felt as proud of any other experience I've had." She is now an integral part of Online's forestry division, which has sold its software to other forest-products companies, some of them in Oregon and Georgia. Another package the company has developed, in partnership with a software firm, targets health-care systems, from the scheduling of physicians' services to the operation of an entire regional health authority.

These are a mere sideline to Online's two core businesses. One is its training programs, which account for only ten percent of its revenue. They include upgrade courses in several Microsoft applications; Powersoft's PowerBuilder client-server environment; Java programming language; and Vision Jade programs that generate Java applications specifically for business (five-day-course fees average about $2,000). In technical training for, and the dissemination of, both PowerBuilder and Jade programs, the company has been a North American pioneer. Its most visible training success has been the package it put together for Human Resources Development Canada. Unemployed, often computer-illiterate people—with postgraduate degrees in anything from political science to commerce—get classroom instruction and workplace experience with companies that inevitably end up hiring them as Microsoft-certified systems engineers (the courses, from 12 to 15 months, cost $14,000, half of it paid by the employers). All of the graduates have found work, two of them with Online. This strategic alliance earned the company the first-ever Microsoft Business Innovation Award for Skills 2000 programs in Canada—educational programs addressing the critical shortage of IT professionals. As training manager Susan Goldie points out, placing grads in jobs with the corporate partners helps build future relationships with these companies. Online has also used the program to introduce itself to potential clients who might be interested in offering their workplaces to the apprentices being trained.

But the main source of Online's revenues is consulting—helping companies choose, implement, upgrade, and maintain their computer systems. Not surprisingly, its clients include several majors in its home province, among them the Manitoba Telephone System, the City of Winnipeg, and United Grain Growers. UGG, Canada's oldest grain-handling cooperative—once farmer-owned, now publicly held with sales of $1.9 billion—is a key account, and applications manager Terry Light says, "Online knows how to implement client/server systems.* We are impressed with the speed with which we manage to get things addressed." Over the years, the consultancy has worked for high-profile companies based elsewhere: IBM Canada, Air Canada, and The USA Group of Indianapolis, a financial-services company with about 30,000 employees.

Operating in these sophisticated circles, Chuck Loewen has the big, bucket-slinging arms and wide-open face that bespeak his rural roots. His hair is blondish and his chin prominent, while small silver oval glasses sit on a broad ski-lift nose that saves him from being capital-*H* Handsome. He leans to stylishly casual clothes, such as intensely hued tops over black pants. Although his demeanour is quiet and comforting, there is high energy in the air at Online's Winnipeg headquarters. The offices themselves mirror Loewen's pervading philosophy: "Maintaining a positive attitude will magnetize others around you with

---

* Online was among those riding the early wave of client/server, which is—as defined by *The Computer Desktop Encyclopedia*—"an architecture in which the client (personal computer or workstation) is the requesting machine and the server is the supplying machine, both of which are connected via a local area network (LAN) or wide area network (WAN). Since the early 1990s, client/server has been the buzzword for building applications on LANs in contrast to centralized minis and mainframes with dedicated terminals."

a positive attitude, and you will not only bring the best out in people, the best people will be drawn to you." The physical surroundings certainly help: the century-old Brokerage (or Donald H. Bain Building) is a yellow brick and cut-stone beauty in Winnipeg's historic downtown Exchange district, a national historic site that movie makers use as a backdrop for period films. The split-level, five- and three-story building, which once housed the West's oldest grocery brokerage, is half a block from the well-treed greenbelt, picnic tables, and benches of Stephen Juba Park and its public dock along the Red River. Inside, Online has exposed the lofty ceilings, warehouse beams, and open piping and then decorated in earth tones. The reception area, with its wicker furniture and two bold paintings in primary colours, establishes the relaxed yet vibrant mood of the place. A river of enthusiasm runs through it, expressed by Shelley Malo when she says, "I've never had so many male and *female* mentors—so many women managers I can model after."

Loewen seems comfortable sharing his authority with his on-the-job partner, Tim Siemens, director of technology. (There are 13 outside investors.) "Chuck is a natural relationship builder," Siemens says. "It's innate. And it's not manipulative." Loewen's inspiriting mindset, his sense of play in business, springs in part from a seminal encounter he had early on in his career. Acting as a consultant for a Winnipeg distribution company, he heard the owner loudly chewing out one of his 40 employees one day while the rest of the staff kept their heads down, pretending to ignore the situation. Afterward his client stopped by Loewen's desk, slapped his back, and said, "Chucky, it's just a game. It's just a game." The man meant it: he played his business like a real-world game. "He would be on the phone with Zellers, which was famous for never paying before 90 days, and would do this Academy Award-winning performance: 'Yours is a big company. I'm just a small businessman trying to make ends meet. Who is your boss? Let me talk to your boss.' So he would talk to that person and then say, 'Who is *your* boss?' Then an hour later he would be on the phone and just laugh and laugh: 'I got them—we're getting a cheque next week!' And it wasn't the fact that he needed the money, but it was the game—he had gotten his way." That was a negative demonstration of a more positive belief Loewen himself had.

Take your business seriously—yet treat it as much as possible like a great, fun-generating game*

"Business is obviously a very serious game," Chuck Loewen acknowledges. "There's potentially lots of hard work and things that need to be done that are undesirable, but if the underlying principle isn't fun, then why are you doing it?" Online regularly gets its employees together for dinners, nights at the racetrack, paint-ball and go-cart outings, gives them football and hockey tickets, and sponsors a corporate team in dragon-boat races. More tangibly, they also get three extra personal days off each year, receive performance bonuses, and participate in a profit-sharing plan. Loewen sounds less like the businessman once named Manitoba's Entrepreneur of the Year and more like the father of two young children when he chooses the example of fictional nanny Mary Poppins, who encourages her charges to clean up the nursery with a spoonful of sugar to help the medicine go down. "As soon as you think of any task as a game," he says with not even a teaspoon of irony, "it becomes fun and it's easy to do." He recalls a weekend with fellow members of the Young Entrepreneurs' Organization where he and another man won all the card, dice, and word games being played. Why, the others wondered, did he and Kevin always win? "The answer is that we enjoyed the thrill of it," Loewen says. "I enjoy the *game*."

Chuck Loewen grew up in a Mennonite farming community, which frowned on the worldly pleasures of smoking, drinking, and even

---

*I had to tell Chuck Loewen of a book called *The Great Game of Business* by John P. Stack, the president and CEO of Springfield Remanufacturing Corporation, a Missouri engine rebuilder that Stack and 12 other managers resurrected from a failing division of International Harvester—boosting SRC's stock price by 18,200 percent. He and his employee shareholders "turn business into a game that everybody in the company can play. It's fun, but it's more: it's a way of tapping into the universal desire to win, of making that desire a powerful competitive force. Winning the Great Game of Business has the greatest reward: constant improvement of your life and your livelihood. You only get that reward, however, by playing together as a team, and by building a dynamic company." Loewen says, "That's it exactly."

dancing. Instead he, his older brother and sister, and younger brother played board games. Some of them, contests of strategy such as Monopoly and Risk, were well suited to a future entrepreneur. Games were for Sunday afternoons when they weren't attending school and working in the grain fields and hog barn of the 162-hectare farm their mother ran after her husband died of leukemia when he was 35 and Chuck was seven. Eleanor Loewen, forced to run the farm and the family on about $13,000 a year, had the help of church people and the many relatives who lived around Rosenort, a hamlet of a couple of hundred people in southern Manitoba. Loewen, who had 88 first cousins, remembers three uncles who would bring their combines around at harvest time.

One of his own chores was taking care of the hogs, but his ambitions went well beyond the farmstead. To earn money in high school, he pumped gas, and in his first bout of entrepreneuralism, he sold milk to fellow students from an old Coke cooler. In Grade 9, he says, "I was the smallest kid and the youngest age and there'd always be people who were bigger and stronger stealing. It didn't really make sense. The amount of money to be made from selling milk might have been $10 a month because of shrinkage and [the fact that] only a third of your student body enjoys drinking milk." So why bother? "You know what it was? It was the *game* of it." A more enterprising venture was a scheme the 15-year-old concocted with his physical-education teacher, Bob Fisher, to sell volleyball shoes and other athletic equipment to student athletes throughout the south of the province. The pair diligently researched suppliers and markets, estimating they could earn $30,000 a year—but with all their planning they missed the volleyball season and never did revive the idea the following year.

Failing this attempt to create a Roots-like empire, Chuck returned to the hogs his mother had abandoned when prices were depressed. He approached the local Mennonite credit union for $8,000 to buy the pigs and feed and rent the barn at favourable terms from his mom, who also guaranteed the loan. The 350 animals generated an annual profit of about $2,000 during his last two years of high school (where he became student-council president while his marks remained average) and in his first year at the University of Manitoba.

Loewen, knowing that farming wasn't a moneymaking option for him, had thought vaguely of becoming a chartered accountant.* University introduced him to the concept of computers as a possible career choice. It was an exciting era: as the 1980s began, IBM was just marketing its first PCs, running on Microsoft's MS-DOS system. By his second year, Loewen was enrolled in a computer science co-op program that sent students out in the field to work with industry. His first internship was in Toronto with Geac Computer Corporation, then a supplier of hardware to libraries and financial institutions (now Canada's largest software company, with more than 3,000 employees). His semester there as a software engineer—testing and documenting programs, even writing a manual on intercomputer communication— was successful enough to attract the attention of professors in his own department. They hired him part-time next term to advise other students on the Geac systems they were using. His third work placement was with IBM Canada, which had him implementing a security system for the City of Winnipeg's mainframe computer and designing and teaching a mandatory course on the system to the city's IT department. Oh, and making contacts that would prove profitable in years to come.

The day after Loewen wrote his final exam in 1985 he got married. In his first year of university he had met a vivacious 1.5-metre-tall nursing student named Carolyn. Although her background was Scottish Canadian, not Mennonite, that was a nonissue for Loewen. "Christianity as taught by the local Mennonite church—I have not totally bought into it," he says. "All of the details of the future life are irrelevant. We don't know what they are. So there's no sense getting into a pissing contest." The bluntness of the final phrase sounded vaguely shocking coming from his lips.

Loewen graduated with a B-plus average and terrific field experience. As Carolyn joined the Victorian Order of Nurses, he decided to work for five years and then get an M.B.A. at the University of Western Ontario—all as a prelude to launching his own business. Rejecting an offer from IBM because it would entail travel away from his new bride,

*At a time when farms had to increase in size to stay solvent, Chuck Loewen's mother's 162 hectares became increasingly less viable. She waited until all the children had left home before selling out and moving into Rosenort and later remarrying. Today Loewen's younger brother is a contract hog farmer, a less risky way of farming, while his older brother is a cement-truck driver and his sister is a school principal in Los Angeles.

he took a job with a five-person computer-consulting firm in Winnipeg. The promise was that he would soon become an executive and within a few years a corporate director. The reality was bleaker: "The president of the company was an unethical criminal." An example of the man's lack of ethics, Loewen says, was refusing to admit to a large institutional client that the computer company couldn't create a certain program yet charging for all the useless work on it, anyway. Within a couple of months, the recent grad, just 22 years old, was savvy enough to escape from the benighted company, which eventually went bankrupt, taking other businesses down with it.

It was December and the City of Winnipeg had a position for a computer specialist opening up in May. Perhaps, he thought, while waiting, he could do a little freelance consulting for a few months. Early in the new year Loewen negotiated a deal with a tour company to rent space in its offices in return for overseeing its computer system. He had hoped to get a $4,000 grant that the Manitoba NDP government was offering young entrepreneurs who took workshops on marketing and creating a business plan. But his proposal to start an information-technology consulting firm was turned down on the theory that the market was saturated. "That was a huge blow because I had no money," Loewen recalls. "So we tapped out our Visa card to get this going." *We* meant his wife and him and *this* was a firm with no business other than the barter arrangement with his landlord. He named it Online Enterprises, choosing by chance an image that would gain greater currency in the Internet world to come (within a couple of years he also registered its current name, Online Business Systems).

Loewen began cold-calling potential clients, offering to develop software and build them computer systems. His first work came from a tour-bus company run by a family of Mennonites—which helped get the young man from Rosenort in the door. While computerizing their bookings, he locked horns with one sister in the business who thought computers were a waste of money. That challenging first account began to teach him about the common Luddite mentality of the time; the system he devised was convincing enough to sway the sister and stay viable for the next decade. He soon landed other clients, including a job-placement agency and a bridge-building company. "So by the time May came around," he says, "I already had too much work that I had sold." He told the city's IT departrment he was too busy and having too much fun to take the promised job. And he never did get his M.B.A.

Among his early clients was the distributor who considered business a great game. Working as a consultant for him taught Loewen another lesson, one he passes on as practical counsel to any wannabe entrepreneur.

In a small start-up company, cash flow is paramount—keep on top of it in the most tangible way you can

The distributorship the young Chuck Loewen acted as a consultant for had 40 employees, but the owner—rather than relying on his bookkeeper—was insistent on making the bank deposits himself each day. When his consultant asked him why he bothered, the man replied, "Because I can feel the money going in. And I write the cheques, so I can feel it going out, and I always know exactly how I'm doing. Because I can feel it." Allowing someone else to physically handle the money, he believed, made it too much of an abstraction. "And until about three years ago," Loewen says, "I always made the bank deposits for that very reason—I couldn't have agreed with him more. ... Because you have got to realize, especially as a small business, cash is king. We have always said here that the long term will take care of itself. We have to make sure the short term works." To this day, he still gets daily e-mails detailing all the bank deposits. But, to his regret, he doesn't have enough time to keep up with all the accounts in the hands-on way he once did. "I don't know anymore," he muses. "I used to know every balance of every account. ... I would know what they all owed us and what time period. ... It's the idea of actually feeling that cash."

In 1987, with his clientele beginning to burgeon, he asked a friend from university to help him out evenings and weekends. Dave Neufeld, a fellow Mennonite, was working for Cargill Ltd., the Canadian subsidiary of the American agribusiness empire. When Neufeld's moonlighting work proved much more interesting, he joined Online, which moved out of the tour-business office to larger quarters in a downtown office building that was designed as an incubator for IT companies. One prominent client now was the Winnipeg branch of Core-Mark, the national food-distribution company based on the West Coast—a $50,000 account. Meanwhile Loewen had developed pharmacy software for a husband-and-wife company to market and a general-purpose accounting program in an effective Canadian-created language called ZIM. He was using the accounting package as a wedge to introduce Online's services to small businesses.

Within two years his company had moved well beyond its beginnings as a lone-wolf start-up. Loewen was an employer now, with a receptionist, colleague Dave Neufeld, a software developer named Bruce Penner he knew from university, and his first partner, Malcolm Crooks. The branch manager for a Montreal-based company specializing in manufacturing software, Crooks had been working in the same building, where he and Loewen often chatted. He was an industrial-engineering grad with a sales and marketing flair. Over a cafeteria lunch, he agreed to join Online on the understanding that he could acquire equity in the company after three years. His immediate role was to sell its consulting services and a more advanced (and cumbersome) accounting-software package Loewen had developed with an accountant, using the American language called Clipper. Crooks went on to handle recruitment and the development of new offices as executive vice president under Loewen as president and CEO.

As Malcolm Crooks came onboard, Neufeld decided to take a position with the Manitoba government at a much higher salary —"which is a huge blow to the spirit because he has been a big part of getting things going," Loewen says now. "And then the phone rings and it's a company out of Ottawa [working for Revenue Canada] that has seen our Yellow Pages ad. We have always had a Yellow Pages ad, and my advice for any entrepreneur is to use them. They are going to get together a consortium to implement the GST across the county and they need people in every jurisdiction." Online agreed to handle the software implementation of the new Goods and Services Tax in Winnipeg and Brandon, Manitoba, and Thunder Bay and North Bay, Ontario, in a contract that Loewen remembers aproaching $200,000. "And back then that was a big contract," he says. "This was great except it was a distraction from selling the software, but it was such a good distraction that it was worth it. Then, about two months later, we get another call from the Yellow Pages, and it's Air Canada and they're looking for UNIX experts. *Now* it's clear-cut—Microsoft sort of rules the world. But in those days it wasn't clear and so we had lots of UNIX expertise and had built some of our systems on a UNIX derivative, which is a different, non-DOS operating system.* So we knew this stuff inside and out. ... It was a $12,000 contract and it was a distraction, but we take it. Well, that $12,000 contract turned into a $1-million piece of work over the next three years." The initial job was to create a system to shuttle files back and forth in the coordination of all Air Canada suppliers, such as Hertz and Hilton, that were plugged into the Aeroplan frequent-flier program. That led to Online's overall managing of the airline's UNIX operating systems.

"It's still a grind," Loewen remembers, "but we are having fun with the grind and always the promise is there of bigger and better." All of this expansion demanded financing. In the early years, Loewen was drawing no more than $20,000 a year as a struggling entrepreneur while fellow students who had graduated in computer science were earning far more as employees for established companies. "It was a little bit of a tough sell at home because all my friends now were making $40,000 a year," he admits. "And here I am still working twice as hard and taking all that risk and having to borrow money." He and Carolyn had bought a house, and as he decided to expand, the lenders wanted the real estate as collateral. While his wife viewed him as an absentee husband, she was generally supportive of his goals, although having the house at risk was upsetting.

In 1988, he approached a Winnipeg credit union, which was Mennonite-controlled and demanded that clients taking out loans be of that faith. When the loans officer mentioned this provision, Loewen balked at first, arguing that the credit union couldn't enforce it. When she insisted it could, he said he didn't attend a Mennonite church but

---

* *The Computer Desktop Encyclopedia* defines UNIX as "a multiuser, multitasking operating system that is widely used as the master control program in workstations and servers. There are many versions of UNIX on the market, and, except for the PC world, where Windows dominates, almost every hardware vendor offers it either as its primary or secondary operating system."

had grown up in one. That was good enough; he got a small operating line of credit. "A business needs cash to grow," he says, underlining the obvious, and during those first few years he had to refinance at least every nine months. It was about three years into Online's life when the credit union insisted on having his house as security for the operating line. During these years, he began to formulate some theories about dealing with lenders.

Understand the real role of a financial institution— which is to lease safe capital to low-risk borrowers

Chuck Loewen mentions the old one-liner about a bank or credit union being an institution that gives you an umbrella when the skies are clear and then wants it back as soon as it starts raining. "Entrepreneurs, full of vim and vigour," he says, "mistake the bank's role as the entity that will share the risks with them to see the entrepreneurs' dream come true. Not so. That said, banks and credit unions can and do play a vital role in any company." Among his words to the wise: If you think you are someday going to be an entrepreneur, borrow some money well before you need it—as he did in raising hogs in high school—to establish a good track record. "Put the money in an interest-bearing account and over time pay off your loan," he advises. "This will establish a very positive lending history and will give you a great start if you ever do go into business." Once in business, try to learn what motivates your potential lender and make a well-researched presentation in a way the banker will comprehend and relate to. Always let the bank know in advance about any potential bad news on the horizon. And, Loewen stresses, "Always understand—you are the entrepreneur, he or she is the banker."

In 1991, just two years after leaving, Dave Neufeld returned to Online. That was the same year Tim Siemens joined to oversee technology development and on-site delivery to clients. He and Loewen had much in common: Siemens was raised as a Mennonite on a Manitoba farm and graduated in computer science from the University of Manitoba at the same time. He had since worked for the City of Winnipeg and a major oilseed crushing company before moving to Vancouver to become the chief architect of new systems development for Elders Grain, part of a large multinational. When that job disappeared, he came home to handle information services for the Manitoba Cancer Treatment and Research Foundation. "My strengths," Siemens says, "lie in taking a look at all the technologies out there, what their capabilities are, what sort of business problems they address, and the likelihood of market acceptance."

Once at Online, he proved to be the consummate techie, well equipped to surf the client/server wave washing over the computer world while "Malcolm was pushing growth and Chuck was relationship-building—he's a natural entrepreneur." Siemens had an agreement with the two partners that he would have a piece of the company someday.* Meanwhile he leaped in to carry out a Manitoba Telephone Systems contract Crooks had won to develop specialty software for the MTS Telecom group. At the same time, often from 5:00 p.m. to midnight, Siemens choreographed a United Grain Growers contract Loewen had landed to set up the hot new technology of the PowerBuilder client/server environment.

The UGG deal was a turning point worth many millions in the years that followed. The grain-handling cooperative has been a dream client: not long after the relationship began, Loewen received a call from its IT director, who wanted to see him immediately. Warily Loewen went to his office, only to hear the client say, "It's important for UGG to have Online succeed because UGG needs to succeed. So we will do everything we can to make sure you're successful. When you send us an invoice, we will pay it the same day we receive it." Suddenly cash flow was no longer a problem, Loewen says: "Here is a cheque, guaranteed 25 grand every month—you can count on the day that it's going to be there." This arrangement ended about three years ago when UGG became publicly held instead of farmer-owned. But the company recently underscored its commitment with another dramatic gesture.

---

* As of 1997, Siemens owned 10.1 percent of Online, Crooks 33.3 percent, and Loewen 56.6 percent, but in 1999 Crooks left the company. "Some original people no longer add as much value as they once did," Loewen remarks. Crooks's shares were bought out through internal funds and a $1.6-million convertible debenture held by 13 outside investors.

After reporting that an Online competitor had offered not to charge a fee to do a project for which Online would have charged $40,000—and hearing Loewen's assurance that "whatever it takes, we will do it"—UGG replied: "Nobody else is going to do this system for us. Just go ahead and do it and send us the bill."

In dealing with large organizations like UGG, one secret of Online's success has been to hew to a simple slogan.

Undersell—and overdeliver

In his contribution to *Anatomy of an Entrepreneur*, published by the Young Leaders Committee of Winnipeg, Chuck Loewen writes: "The best that you can be known for is doing what you say you will do. A sure way to build that reputation is to make sure you set your expectations well in advance and then always meet or exceed those expectations. What this often requires is underselling an idea or promise and then overdelivering. How you do this will vary with your type of business, but a simple example is as follows. When I think I will be two or three minutes late for an appointment, I phone ahead [on a cell phone] to say I will be ten minutes late. Then, when I arrive only five minutes later, I appear early." A more complicated example comes from Online technology director Tim Siemens. The developers of the new Vision Jade progams to generate Java-language applications specifically for business claim that it works ten times faster than competitive products. "We're cynics here," Siemens says, having found that in one project he oversaw, Jade was just 3.1 percent faster. That's all he is claiming for it with clients. If it performs better, they will be pleasantly surprised. He echoes his partner: "Set expectations correctly—undersell and overdeliver. It's a hard thing to do. But it's a key thing for a project's success."

By 1992 Online Business Systems was on a rapidly ascending growth curve that would see the company expand by 40 percent annually and its staff more than double to 45 over the next three years. (The Loewen family had grown, too, with a preschool daughter and son.) In 1994 the three principals agreed that it would be shrewd to go after American business, which could be done competitively in Winnipeg for the lower Canadian dollar and earn a 35-percent premium on the work. Their first target market was Minneapolis, just an hour's plane ride south, an established IT centre with the largest number of head offices per capita in North America.

"It never quite worked out for a number of reasons," Loewen admits. "Minneapolis is also an old boys' town and we're a bunch of foreigners coming into the city and saying, 'We're here. Send us work.' Now we have done millions of dollars of work there, but it hasn't come as easily as here and Calgary. Here we are so well-known and so connected in the community that there is no project in Winnipeg that occurs without our involvement. Whereas there we are a small player." Malcolm Crooks opened the Minneapolis office, which at one point had 15 employees— Americans in sales, Canadians in production—trying to attract the breakthrough client that hasn't come yet. Under a new local manager, the branch made its first reasonable return in the third quarter of 1998 after a couple of years' losses. Independent of the Minneapolis office, Online has found other work in the United States, particularly in the forest industry, through word-of-mouth recommendations from American consultants encountered at international conferences.

Calgary has been a more welcoming venue for the company's services. Since its opening in 1996, the branch there has mushroomed to 30 employees, led by a local manager. To get it up and running, Online hired Calgarians and sent a couple of Winnipeg staff to work on a project for a B.C. client based in Prince George. That gave the office enough momentum to propel further sales—in a variety of industries other than oil and gas. Surprisingly the only clients linked to petroleum are pipeline utilities; the others are in fields such as financial services and forestry. The Vancouver branch, launched last year, is also a forest-based practice, run by a salesman versed in the industry who markets Online's suite of forestry-software packages to large Pacific Northwest mills: LOGS is a comprehensive woodlands operation system to manage all elements of harvest operations and contractor relationships; MILLS is an integrated wood system that manages each stage of the sawmill process, tracking the production and sales of lumber.

Reflecting the Loewen flexibility, another employee with forestry expertise works out of Eugene, Oregon, simply because that's where his girlfriend is. For a brief three months, Online also had a Los Angeles office. A man who dressed like a senior executive and had seemingly exceptional credentials, including an Oxford education, approached the company to join him in marketing accounting software to sizable companies across the continent and overseas. "When really what should have happened," Loewen says, "he should have joined Online"—which would have meant his spending six months in Winnipeg showing his stuff and learning the corporate culture. In hindsight the company failed to follow up on the man's alleged track record, soon realized he was in way over his head, and pulled out of the joint venture.

Generally, Siemens argues, "we hire the best and brightest—not just brightest technically, but they have to be able to talk to people, do project management, and understand the entire life cycle of a customer relationship. And risk-taking—that's part of the game, too." The Winnipeg head office has lured many computer professionals from other Canadian centres despite the city's reputation for miserable weather and a stagnant economy. They come from the other western provinces as well as Toronto, swayed by low house prices and short commutes. "I am a huge Winnipeg proponent," Loewen says. "It has three weeks in the winter when it's obnoxiously cold. ... It has got a very nice summer climate. It has the lakes and cottage life available to the middle class." And to ensure that the city's admittedly vibrant cultural life stays that way, he and his colleagues make healthy donations to institutions such as the Royal Winnipeg Ballet. Loewen himself is on the University of Manitoba President's Council and the advisory board of the *Winnipeg Sun* and chaired a technology committee for the Pan Am Games. "We take out of the community and we have to give back," he says.

In 1995, with staff numbers swelling, Online moved into its current home. The company had cased 20 buildings before settling on the post-and-beam warehouse downtown by the river and having the interior revamped with funk and flair over four months. That was the expansive year the company realized it had to move beyond its limited credit-union lender and select a big bank to finance its growth.

Shop around for a bank with the same care you would for any big-ticket purchase—don't necessarily buy the first sales pitch you hear

Knowing that its business south of the border would increasingly require the international reach of a bank, Chuck Loewen and his colleagues started looking for an appropriate lender early on. "I realized that the day was coming—maybe a couple of years away—where we would need a bank and we should start building that relationship before we needed them," he says. "We talked to a number of different banks and we received offers. The rates were similar and we would obviously grind rates down to a level we thought was appropriate." In the end, the deciding factors focused on the personal approach each bank took in seeking the company's account, how complementary its people were with Online, and how enthusiastic they were about its progress and promise. "Find a banker who has a personality you click with and who is excited about your business," Loewen advises. The Royal Bank proved to be the most professional in the marketing of its services, actually approaching Online through a referral before the company had contacted the bank. Shortly after meeting with an account manager and the head of the Royal Bank's department specializing in knowledge-based industries, Loewen had a slickly coordinated phone call from the Manitoba region's vice president, pointing out his availability to Online at any time. "I could see that it was cleverly orchestrated," Loewen says, but he was so impressed that his own company now incorporates similar follow-up calls from the partners to potential clients. "I really felt that the Royal Bank wanted our business."

Despite his good relations with the Royal Bank, Loewen exercises his right to be aggressively proactive with the financial institution. Two years ago, during its annual refinancing round, Online requested ten changes in its financial arrangement, all but one of which the Royal Bank approved. The tenth was for a more comfortable debt-to-equity ratio. "We likely don't need it," Loewen told his banker, "but I don't want to be in a position where we have to make bad business decisions because we're worried about cash." The bank insisted on reviewing the corporate financial statements and then repeated its demand that, based on current debt, Online must agree to maintain a minimum equity at a specified amount. The company wanted a debt-equity ratio of no more than 2.5:1. When the bank representative demurred, asking Loewen to sign the agreement without that change, he told her, "This is bothering me, and if you think back to the first visit when you called on me, and you said knowledge of a company and management strength were more important than the assets the company had—you remember that discussion?"

Yes, she recalled it. Now the bank's general manager, she had then been the account manager who had made the first contact with Loewen.

"Okay," he said, "I want you to say to me in a clear and unwavering voice that that was all bullshit and it was just marketing hype, and if you can say that to me, then I will sign this and we will go ahead."

"Chuck, I'll phone you right back."

About ten minutes later she called to say that the bank would agree to Online's debt-equity demand.

"If they want to play that game," the great gamesman says now, "then they have to practise what they preach."

Loewen will likely be going back to the bank in the near future to fuel the growth that he hints at in our talks. When I ask him if there were any significant expansion plans, he replies, "In my head." In Canada or the United States? I ask. "We are looking at options both in Canada and the U.S. ... We have chosen to build a world-class information-technology company out of Winnipeg. ... And so one day, potentially, we will go public. We are financing our own growth, profitable growth. The money all goes back in the company, so if we need or desire to grow faster than we can afford to, then we have to go raise some money. And if you want liquidity of your shares in the company, [going public] would be a way."

Given the success of Online Business Enterprises as one of the fastest-growing and best-managed private companies in the country, continuing expansion seems inevitable. To support that growth, the three partners will have to keep recruiting well-trained, intelligent IT professionals—get them into, and keep them in, the great game of business. Looking ahead, Loewen realizes that won't necessarily be easy.

TrendWatch

Early in this decade the cost of hiring labour in Canada became double the cost of adding smart machines to do equivalent work. There are some Canadians who will obviously profit from this trend: those who are not only adroit with computers but also have the communication skills and teamwork that working on information-technology projects demands. A Northern Telecom report in 1998 predicted that the shortage of high-tech professionals (computer scientists and electrical engineers) in Canada could total 50,000 by 2000. "The next ten years will see an increasingly larger need for IT people," Chuck Loewen says. "And the worldwide ability to produce these people will not keep pace with the national need. This is a great time to be in technology. There are tools like Vision Jade [the program that creates Java applications for business] and there's more coming that reduce the amount of work. So instead of taking 1,000 hours to do something, now it might only take 400 hours. And there are so many things that have to be done, can be done, and if the price is cheap enough *will* be done. ... It's a boom industry in a time when the economy is doing well, because companies are looking forward to how they can use technology to grow. And when the economy is stalled or going down, companies are looking to save money. How do we save money? We do it by automating things with computers." Information technology, Loewen predicts, will inevitably continue to be a growth profession for the next decade. "After ten years, my crystal ball is broken."

The Gender Pioneers

Julia Levy and Kazuko Komatsu, meet Audra Hollingshead.

Dr. Julia Levy is a cofounder and the current president of QLT Photo-Therapeutics Inc. of Vancouver, which is on the verge of launching the world's only cure for a common eye condition that leads inevitably to blindness in the elderly. Kazuko Komatsu has formed several entrepreneurial companies and in 1990 took over Pacific Western Brewing Company of Prince George, British Columbia, the largest domestically owned independent brewery in western Canada. The truth is, I might just as well have profiled microbiologist Levy as a High-Tech Entrepreneuer and beer maker Komatsu as a Palate Pleaser. They are trailblazers in their respective fields. But they also epitomize the Gender Pioneers, those Maverick women who trek intrepidly into uncharted territories where their very presence is unusual, if not unwelcome.

I have labelled Levy the Healer, not merely for her preoccupation with treating cancer and eye conditions, but also for the salutary manner in which she handles her 160 employees while competing in the worldwide marketplace. With three honorary degrees to accompany her Ph.D., she is the 1998 winner of the Canadian Women Entrepreneurs' award for International Competitiveness. It was partly a tribute to the strategic alliances she has crafted with foreign pharmaceutical power-houses. She is believed to be the only female CEO among the continent's 350 public biotechnology companies with a scientific, rather than a strictly business background. And likely the only one whose husband works for her in a senior position, as vice president of corporate development. While sympathizing with the battles other women have waged, Levy says that in her 63 years she has never let herself be put down because of her own womanhood.

When I did ask about the gender thing, she replied, "Never thought about it. Whenever I was confronted by it, I was really astounded that there would be men who had made assumptions that I would want to stop working. It was so *never* in my consciousness that when it happened, I'd say, 'Of course, I'm going to go on. It doesn't matter whether I have children or not, I'll find a way.' And I did. It was in other people's heads, never in mine. And I never anticipated any kind of gender bias. I was very confident, I think, that I could do well. I was confident and probably naïve. I think it made me oblivious. I'm one of the most unparanoid people I've ever met. If someone's really trying to do dirty on me, they've really got to hit me on the head. I'm always very optimistic, I assume the world's a nice place, and I want to live my life feeling that—so I choose not to pick up the rock and see what's crawling around underneath. Unless I really have to, I don't."

Komatsu, a Japanese immigrant to Canada, also keeps winning honours, among them the Federal Business Development Bank's B.C. Entrepreneur of the Year award and a Canadian Commemorative Medal for her philanthropic and business contributions. Interestingly she, too, employs her life partner: Harry Mayor is the brewery's operations manager, and he is fiercely proud of her working feminism and the womanly warmth she has brought to her macho-image businesses—from exporting logs to running a fish-processing plant. A recent comprehensive case study of her brewery by the University of Western Ontario's Richard Ivey School of Business quotes Mayor as saying: "Kazuko is passionate about taking care of her employees and I firmly believe that she has established a unique situation for B.C.—one where there is genuine mutual respect between management and the employees. Ever since she took over, not one issue has ever gone to arbitration. All issues are resolved efficiently and amicably. If you don't believe me, ask the union steward. He even sends her flowers when she is sick." Kazuko Komatsu may be a Samurai's Daughter, as I call her, but she is a peace-loving heir to that bellicose tradition.

The stories and sagacity of Komatsu and Levy are explored in the final two chapters. Although both are based in Vancouver, they have never met, and neither knows Audra Hollingshead of Edmonton. I would love to be in the same room if all three ever did trade tales and confidences. Distinctive as they are, collectively they present a rounded portrait of the experienced western Canadian woman entrepreneur—Levy and Hollingshead both in their early sixties, Komatsu about 50 (although the latter two are surprisingly coy about their ages). Audra Hollingshead was among the many other women I considered portraying in full, and if she weren't virtually retired, except for occasional teaching of her globally gained wisdom, she would merit a chapter of her own.* As it is, I did interview her in depth, and some snapshots of her life and career serve as a fitting prelude to the other Pioneers, both still actively engaged in their businesses.

Hollingshead has been an independent information and deal broker through most of her career. Among many other transactions, A. Hollingshead & Associates has facilitated the sale of tens of millions of dollars' worth of British turnkey hospitals to mainland China, done a three-way deal financed by Japanese interests to ship Canadian coal to

---

*I had a lot of choice, ranging from Christine Magee, the 39-year-old cofounder of Sleep Country Canada of Richmond, British Columbia, with its 50-plus mattress stores from Ontario west, to 43-year-old Brenda Andre of Winnipeg, who started by driving a lunch truck, bought the mobile catering business, and then with silent partners acquired nine outlets (more than any other Canadian franchisee) of the Tennessee-based Perkins Family Restaurant chain. Both women have high profiles as spokeswomen in TV commercials. Western female entrepreneurs are well represented in organizations like the Women Entrepreneurs of Canada ("We CAN")—at (416) 361-7036 and www.wec.ca—for those with businesses at least four years old or having annual sales/revenue of $250,000. The recently formed Women Business Owners of Canada is a nonprofit "virtual organization" with a database, Web site (www.wboc.ca), and toll-free number (1-888-822-WBOC). An Angus Reid poll done to mark the Business Owners' birth shows that 78 percent of Canadian men and 80 percent of women agree that owning or operating their own businesses has enhanced their lives. But, starting out, women are 15 percent more likely to have mentors and 40 percent more likely to take a course beforehand—although 25 percent less likely to have written a formal business plan.

East German steel mills, and put an Iranian buyer together with an Albertan-based seller of offshore oil rigs. In the hospital deal during the late 1970s, she says her cut—typically taken only after a win-win conclusion—totalled hundreds of thousands of dollars.

Not bad for the daughter of a postmaster in Morse, Saskatchewan, whose dyslexia kept her from high marks in school ("I can't even add milk money," she says) and discouraged her from a university degree (although not, decades later, from serving for six years on the Senate of the University of Alberta). The tall redhead went to work in the big city of Edmonton for Retail Credit, where she reviewed the reports of credit checkers—one of them prominent-author-to-be W. P. Kinsella—and did credit investigations that taught her how to ferret out information for her later deal-making. Her marriage to a local photographer produced two daughters, but when it began to fail in 1969, she suggested the family have an adventure in Australia. That was where she started musing about possibly acting as an intermediary to move products between one country and another. It would later be the scene of one of her happiest ongoing successes: she negotiated a pact with a Hong Kong knitwear factory to provide products to an unemployed Australian divorcée with two children, who today distributes to agents all over her country and continues to give Hollingshead two percent of her take.

Hollingshead's marriage ended after her return to Edmonton. With a $5,000 divorce settlement, she invested in a couple of rundown houses as an equal partner with a friendly local realtor. That simple transaction, she says, snowballed throughout the 1970s into a mini-empire that comprised 40 houses in Edmonton, a motel and a lodge in Alberta, another lodge in British Columbia, property in Mexico and Arizona—both locales where she lived briefly with her children—and even a string of racehorses. She helped find the real estate, managed it, and invested her substantial earnings. When both the property and stock markets took a dive around the turn of the decade, she turned to her more global pursuits.

During the 1978 Commonwealth Games in Edmonton, she got involved in protocol (and a decade later would become director of protocol for the Winter Olympics in Calgary). Through an Asian man visiting Alberta with a delegation, she met an elderly Hong Kong wheeler-dealer improbably named Charlie Chan, "older than God and absolutely charming" as she puts it. Hollingshead says he put her together with contacts in the British colony and on the mainland who could use her go-between services to source western materials such as airport and ship-docking facilities. One of her more bizarre adventures was a journey to Bolivia in 1983, ostensibly to investigate the activities of an American land developer operating there. She says she called the Bolivian ambassador to Canada and persuaded him to let her determine on behalf of his government whether the development was a scam—in return for an eventful trip through his country. In finding the operation was legitimate, she once had to leap off a slow-moving train into the black of a tropical rainforest night to view the land site. And in the courtyard of a hotel in the central Bolivian capital of Santa Cruz, she hid behind a pillar as gangsters raced up the stairs to the landing above her, burst into the room beside hers, and machine-gunned its occupant to death over gambling debts.

. Through it all, Hollingshead insists, she maintained her femininity. "If someone asked me what I attributed my success to, I'd probably be smart-assed and say, 'Because I never wore trousers.' A lot of cultures do not feel comfortable with women in pants and therefore I never wore pants. ... And a great part of my success is writing thank-you notes. They never forget you because it's so unusual." That's one of the ladylike tips she offers in her seminars for economics and commerce students on international business and social etiquette and in college courses titled Street Fighting 101.

"I'm just a generalist, a putter-togetherer," she says. Audra Hollingshead has been much more than that, as have the other women I have gathered here under the label of Gender Pioneers. She, Julia Levy, and Kazuko Komatsu have been role models in the way they do business and conduct their careers—in their we-all-win philosophy, their overt caring for associates, their professional and personal integrity. They are well met.

Chapter Eleven

The Healer

Dr. Julia Levy, QLT PhotoTherapeutics

Call it happenstance, serendipity—or simply luck, as Julia Levy calls it. Whatever the label, the combination of circumstances that would eventually land QLT PhotoTherapeutics Inc. of Vancouver among the 25 leading biotechnology companies in North America began germinating two decades ago during Levy family outings on an island in British Columbia's Inside Passage. It was born of a mother's observation of her children, followed up by a scientist's pursuit of illumination—a word that in this case also has the literal meaning of a physical light. As a mother, Levy had noticed that when her son and daughter played outdoors at their Sonora Island vacation home, they would sometimes suffer what looked liked burns on their skins, which could then blister. Suspecting that contact with a plant caused the condition, yet confused because there was no predictability to the flare-ups, the scientist in Dr. Levy (a Ph.D., not an M.D.) approached a colleague at the University of British Columbia. The plant biochemist asked her if the island had cow parsley, a wild chervil with large white flowers. It did, and, as he explained, the juice of the plant was harmful to the skin, but only when the skin was exposed to sunlight. Cow parsley molecules are photosensitive, he said, and researchers were examining other such molecules in various substances. Their findings promised a possible way of treating cancer: a photosensitizer drug might be delivered to cancerous cells and then a laser targeted at these toxins to turn the drug on and kill them.

Not long after, when a graduate student said she would like to do her Ph.D. on these fascinating new drugs, Levy encouraged her and eventually began to focus on them herself, helping to develop a revolutionary product called Verteporfin, which has since been trademarked as Visudyne. Within a decade of first accidentally learning about photosensitizers, she convinced her partners in the biotechnology company she had since cofounded that they should acquire the rights to Photofrin, one of the drugs already in clinical trials. At her urging, they abandoned much of their other research. In 1992 QLT PhotoTherapeutics became the first company anywhere to gain regulatory approval to market a light-activated pharmaceutical product like Photofrin in the hugely promising field of photodynamic therapy, or PDT.*

Biotechnology is a crazy business. How many industries have to go through so many regulatory hoops to get a product approved? And in how many other industries could a company attract tens of millions of dollars of investments without delivering a major product to the market for more than a decade?

Those questions are now largely academic for QLT. The technology it harnessed—PDT—is successfully employing Photofrin and Visudyne to treat various cancers, autoimmune diseases such as a skin malady called psoriasis, and one form of an otherwise incurable condition, known as age-related macular degeneration—AMD—that is the leading cause of blindness in the elderly. Levy's company is in the concluding phase of its clinical trials for this last disease. Her pioneering work in its treatment results from another personal involvement: her helplessness at watching her remarkable mother go almost blind with AMD. By the year 2000, Visudyne should be the first on the market to efficiently treat the 500,000 new cases of so-called "wet" AMD that surface worldwide annually, half of them in North America. (The wet version—about ten to 20 percent of all AMD cases—is caused by new blood vessels that leak fluid and eventually scar the retina. The cause of the incurable "dry" version—which Canadian publisher Jack McClelland has—is unknown.)

---

* Here is how the technology works, in QLT's own words: "Treatment with photodynamic therapy consists of a two-step process beginning with administration of the drug, or 'photosensitizer,' by intravenous injection. While circulating in the bloodstream, the drug attaches to molecules called lipoproteins. Because cells undergoing rapid proliferation require a greater amount of lipoproteins than non-dividing cells, the drug is delivered more quickly and in higher concentrations to these types of cells. Once the concentration of drug reaches appropriate levels in target cells, it is activated with a pre-calculated dose of light at a particular wavelength. The activated drug subsequently causes the conversion of normal oxygen found in tissue to a highly energized form called 'singlet oxygen.' The singlet oxygen, in turn, causes cell death by disrupting normal cellular functions. Neither the drug nor the light exert any effect until combined."

Visudyne's potential is enormous, as analyst Christine Charette of Nesbitt Burns in Toronto has pointed out in recommending QLT as a "most attractive" stock buy: "With such a large patient population, the lack of available treatment for the majority of patients, and the absence of significant competitive products on the horizon, [Visudyne] is well-positioned to reach peak sales of over C$500 million." Less formally, Charette says, "I haven't seen this kind of opportunity in biotech since I started covering it." In early 1999, as the company's stock climbed by 24 percent, analyst Ezra Lwowski of Toronto's Yorkton Securities predicted Visudyne sales of $330 million U.S. by 2002, which would give QLT revenue of $140 million Cdn.

And since late 1995, Julia Levy has been president and CEO of QLT PhotoTherapeutics (earning $450,000 in 1998). It's one of only about two dozen of the continent's 350 publicly traded biotech companies to have such a likely blockbuster of a breakthrough drug in the final throes of testing. Within a couple of years of taking over, she not only initiated Visudyne's crucial clinical trials but also stage-managed an impressive equity financing—$73 million Cdn. raised domestically and in the United States—designed to assure QLT's long-term financial solidity (and in 1999 another $200 million, the second-largest in the Canadian biotech industry). The potential of success is all the more extraordinary given the fact that she is determined to keep her company in Canada, a country she came to as a young war refugee and continues to love passionately in her 63rd year.

This was the second time Levy had assumed the reins of QLT since its founding in 1981. The business has had a bumpy ride to its current respectability, with at least one dubious major investor—Vancouver's J. Bob Carter of gross-indecency infamy—and three allegedly lacklustre presidents. The best of the CEOs before her was cofounder Jim Miller, a UBC physiologist and the entrepreneurial dynamo behind the company. However, he left after ten years of wildly careering progress, following confrontations with American Cyanamid, QLT's heavyweight corporate partner in photodynamic therapy. The partnership is believed to have been the first-ever such strategic alliance between a small player and a giant in the North American biotech industry. Miller, who now runs a noncompetitive company in Vancouver called Inex Pharamaceuticals Corporation, respects his successor as both a researcher and a leader.

"She's an incredible scientist," he says. "If she had an idea, you knew it was well thought out and it would most likely work." If Levy lacks sheer business experience herself, he maintains, "she's put in a lot of support in the organization. Ken Galbraith is one of the better CFOs around from a business strength and from a concept strength in doing deals. And Julia's very good in the skill of listening to other people and taking what they have to say and then picking it apart and making some sense out of it. She has good people relations."

Levy herself says that while she wasn't ready to be CEO and president on the first occasion she filled in, this time she is, and has willingly left the laboratory to become the public face of QLT. She has a tight oval of a face and her slim, tennis-trim body is typically garbed in a black jacket over jeans. Thin-rimmed glasses covering intelligent eyes, dirty blond curls, and a prominent chin contribute to a kind-looking visage that bears virtually no makeup, or guile. It is a face that has become familiar to British Columbians recently through an aggressive campaign of newspaper advertising inserts from BC Tel ("When your business is saving lives, busy signals are not an option") and a *BC Business* magazine feature on prominent business executives and their pets—hers being a gentle 45-kilogram rottweiler named Lucy whose regular presence in her office is signalled by the dog-food and water dishes and ratty tennis ball dotted around her desk. Outside the province, Levy is gaining presence with her acceptance of honorary degrees from the University of Western Ontario, the University of Ottawa, and Mount St. Vincent University in Halifax.

This higher profile helps as she jousts with Johnny-come-lately competitors, some of whom don't play by the same rules. Miravant Medical Technologies of Santa Barbara, for example, announced in 1998 that the U.S. Food and Drug Administration had granted its own light-activated drug fast-track status, which would give it "a very significant competitive advantage" over QLT. As Levy retorted, "it's total bullshit"—her company was in final phase-three clinical trials with 600-plus patients, compared with Miravant's phase-one and -two trials with 28 patients. Miravant's drug, Purlytin, also causes sensitivity to light in patients for up to three weeks after treatment, which Visudyne doesn't. Miravant was the subject of a May 4, 1998, *Forbes* exposé advising: "There are plenty of near-miracles in medicine, but Miravant looks more like a penny-stock promotion than a magic bullet. ... Give this one a wide, a very wide, berth."

Levy says that as QLT comes closer to putting Visudyne on the market, "we're going to see more and more spoilers like this. There are other, more credible companies [than Miravant], but they're way behind us."

QLT now has 160 employees, among them Levy's husband, Ed, vice president of corporate development. They work in the crowded confines of two buildings just across the Cambie Street Bridge from downtown Vancouver. The company's original name, Quadra Logic Technologies, has been a fixture on the horizon, still boldly displayed along the wall of one brown brick structure. Anticipating growth and a move to larger quarters, Levy said, "We have to plan for success now. We have to plan for being a very different company [by 2000]." The planning process involved about 30 key employees, from administrative assistants to senior managers, and outside consultants. After nearly a decade and a half, QLT was acting on its president's belief in a well-proven corporate strategy.

Define your collective values in a mission statement

As Thomas J. Peters and Robert H. Waterman Jr. wrote in their groundbreaking book *In Search of Excellence*, the single all-purpose piece of advice they would offer companies is: "Figure out your value system. Decide what your company stands for. What does your enterprise do that gives everyone the most pride? Put yourself out 10 or 20 years in the future: what would you look back on with greatest satisfaction?" That is essentially what Julia Levy and her colleagues did at QLT, except they were taking a 50-year view, she said at the time. "The mission statement has to be durable," she insists. "We're trying to define what we want to go on to. It's very pivotal now because we're about to change enormously. What do we want to maintain? How do we see ourselves? There's a high bar here. There was a lot of talk about this being a company where you're not going to be punished for disagreeing with people, for failure if you're trying something new."

A healer in more than medical terms, Levy puts great store in an open door and a sympathetic ear for staff: "I'm very good at interpersonal things, which some of our managers are not. People come in my office and cry, but that's part of the thing a CEO does." Well, not necessarily, but perhaps they do at QLT, where two of the seven vice presidents and two of the seven directors are women and where the president describes herself as a solid, lifelong left-winger. "I feel I owe society," she says. "I've been very lucky, I've had a wonderful life. I wouldn't want to trade it."

Hectic as that life is today, she maintains her leanness—and sanity—playing tennis and exercising on a treadmill; walking her rottweiler on paths around Vancouver's downtown Granville Island, which the Levys overlook from their terraced 222-square-metre condo; and gardening on Sonora Island, where they share 40 hectares, almost two kilometres of oceanfront, and almost two kilometres of lakefront with 17 other families in a cooperative arrangement. "It's like owning your own national park," she says.

Julia Levy's lucky life and career so far are bookended by the inspiration and influence of her mother. The daughter's progress from scientific researcher to entrepreneur to CEO starts, if anywhere, with the British-born, well-bred Dorothy Coppens. Not that either she or her Dutch husband encouraged Julia to go into science. But their example of determination and independence proved powerful for the younger of their two daughters. She was born in Singapore, where her father was working for a big Netherlands trading bank until the family moved to Jakarta in the Dutch colony of Java. Just before the Japanese army arrived in 1942, Guillaume Coppens had the foresight to send his wife and preteen children to Vancouver, where relatives owned a small farm. An upper-middle-class woman who studied physiotherapy at university in England, Dorothy adapted quickly to the land where she and her family were illegal immigrants during the Second World War. She still had her dowry of 2,000 pounds to buy a house in the city. Taking a job as a physiotherapist with the Workers' Compensation Board, she managed to send her daughters to a private school, where they reluctantly boarded during the week. "My mother was the strength in the family," Levy recalls. "She was always very optimistic. I guess I inherited a lot

316

of her character. She never looked at the downside at all. She said, 'Well, let's get on with it.' She was a finisher, I'm a finisher."

Their father joined them in 1946 as a 43-kilogram survivor of a Japanese internment camp, his spirit broken along with his body. Before being imprisoned, Coppens had shipped a carved camphor trunk to his wife with cryptic instructions to keep it at all costs. She spent hours searching for false bottoms or other hiding places for valuables, finding nothing. Back with his family, he disassembled the chest's large brass lock in which he had secreted a cache of diamonds. Although never again demonstrating the dynamism of his wife, he tried to sell Fuller brushes and real estate before becoming a partner in a small accounting firm. "My recollection of my life was 'Don't upset your father,'" his daughter says now. "I was an unhappy child, actually. So many people I know in my adult life who are brighter than average are always miserable as children because you don't fit it. You can't fit in. You learn to survive by yourself. Once I was in high school, I was okay."

Levy considered being a concert pianist, a veterinarian, even a chartered accountant like her father. The Coppenses actively dissuaded her from accountancy, which in the 1950s wasn't considered a woman's profession. Deciding to pursue her passion for biology, she resented the fact that her parents considered her an anomaly for wanting more than a husband and children. She worked for a year after high school as a file clerk at BC Hydro, and with her own earnings and scholarships studied microbiology and immunology at UBC. "The consuming moment," she recalls, "was the first level of understanding the complexity of single cells—this is a microcosm, everything's going on, all the genetic material is in that single cell. ... I knew I was going to make research my life." It was a time of ferment in the field with the 1953 announcement by James Watson and Francis Crick of their discovery of the double helix of DNA, which would lead to the breaking of the genetic code in animal and human cells.

By 1955 Levy had her bachelor of science and a husband—a history and librarianship major—and a resolve to get her doctorate at the University of London's National Institute for Medical Research. As a woman doing graduate work, she was a minority. Her research was on the effects of stress on the immune system, and in 1959, aged 23, she had her Ph.D. "Those were the halcyon days of academia," she says. "I decided I wanted to come back to Vancouver and wrote to the head of the microbiology department at UBC and said I'd like a job, please, so I got one." She laughs at her naivete, which extended to her unawareness of any gender bias in academia.

While in hindsight it might have been smarter to do her postdoctrate elsewhere, her teaching and research on home turf never backfired on her. During the 1960s she made pragmatic, rather than theoretical, contributions in the field of immunochemistry: "We got into taking a whole molecule and finding out which part of it was the business end in terms of what the immune system saw, and then playing with it." Meanwhile she gave birth to a son and then became a single mother after her seven-year marriage ended. A couple of relationships left her despairing that she would find a man to match her mental checklist of necessary attributes. One liaison was with David Suzuki, the UBC geneticist who was about to win a fellowship as the best young Canadian scientist and launch a career as a science commentator on television and in books. "Dave comes bursting on the scene," she remembers, "and he's noisy, boyish, and larger than life, well connected, and science took on a much bigger scope. I was there working away in my lab and not really thinking of the big picture. He made me grow in that way. That was important for me."

Suzuki's whim that he and Julia should work in Russia led him to a UBC colleague who had done research there. Edwin Levy, a physicist with a degree in the philosophy of science, invited the couple to his home. "I was miserable that evening because I felt we were masquerading in some way that was not genuine," she recalls. "Ed thought I was a pretty crabby bitch." Nothing came of Russia, nor her relationship with Suzuki. But soon after, she met Ed Levy again to discuss an inegrated arts program he was teaching, they fell in love, and in 1969 were married.

During the next decade, molecular immunology hit its stride, and Julia Levy became engrossed in the possibility of harnessing the immune system to fight cancer cells.* It was about that time, too, that she discussed cow parsley with plant biochemist Neil Towers and urged

---

*Accepting her honorary degree at the University of Western Ontario, Julia Levy said: "I believe that the time between 1960 and 1985 was probably the best for someone to be an academic scientist in the life sciences. Research funds were readily available—one rarely heard of grant applications being rejected. The science departments in essentially all Canadian universities were in a growth mode and jobs were easy to find. All of us, I think, thought that this kind of situation would go on forever."

her graduate student to study photosensitive molecules as immunotoxins. But it was Levy's work in the area of monoclonal antibodies that would lead her to the private sector. Antibodies are human and animal proteins, and monoclonals can (as scientists would learn) target specific proteins, such as those on the surface of cancer cells—interfering with a tumour's ability to absorb growth agents from the bloodstream or actually carrying toxins that precisely kill malignant tissue.

Levy and her team were researching antibodies they believed had high potential in treating cancers, including leukemia. In the United States the first biotech companies were sprouting and, with government grants ebbing, she contacted UBC officials about the possibility of commercializing her work. The university had no industry liaison office at the time and no real interest in helping her (although it would later claim QLT as one of its successful spin-off companies). "I think they thought I was a shit disturber," she says. Unfortunately Canada then as now had no indigenous pharmaceutical industry to approach. Fortunately a colleague in the physiology department, John Brown, mentioned that he was talking with another UBC physiologist, Jim Miller, and two others about forming a company.

The lean-faced Miller talks with a slur, his speech full of colloquialisms, like a tout at the track giving you the odds on the next race. He figures he was an entrepreneur from boyhood. "I had the largest market share of any paperboy in Sept-Iles, Quebec," he once said. Later, he bought and sold hydroplanes, the speedboats he liked to race, putting himself through university on the proceeds. As a professor, he had long brainstormed about starting a business with a friend from the University of Western Ontario. Ron McKenzie had an M.B.A. and worked in Vancouver for Kaiser Coal and B.C. Buildings Corporation and later consulted for a medical company. On a table napkin in a pub in Victoria's Oak Bay, Miller and McKenzie drew up plans to launch their own company. One of their ideas was to supply research mice and rats to UBC for testing, but the university decided to raise the animals themselves. Miller had been evaluating medical technology for an American group interested in commercializing academic research and realized that his own university had some stars in the sciences, among them John Brown and Julia Levy. "The vision," Miller says, "was to take monoclonal antibodies, which were so exquisitely specific that you could use them for diagnostic tests. I said we could do tests for a variety of different diseases because it's important to figure out if you have the disease or not, using this technology. And gee whiz, we might even be able to use these as therapeutic drugs eventually. So wouldn't that be a nice sequence of events? Well, who knows anything about mono-clonal antibodies? Because I don't. And basically that's where Julia came in. She had been working with John Brown. She had identified or purported to identify some research activities, some antigens [sub-stances that stimulate the production of antibodies] that were related to lung cancer. And there was a large lung-cancer screening program going on. We said, gee, this fits right into this diagnostic approach and maybe we could use this as the starting point. And other than our own monies, we got a fair amount of government grant support to under-take the development of technology to do this lung-cancer diagnostics."

Levy was ripe for the plucking. "Geez, I might even be useful, not just doing science. Something here could actually benefit humanity," she says, paraphrasing her thoughts at the time. "I wanted to see it hap-pen, *but* I also wanted to have it here. I didn't want to sell it to a big company and let them do it." In 1981 Miller, together with Levy, Brown, McKenzie, and another old friend, UBC psychology professor Tony Phillips, founded Quadra Logic Technologies with investments of $50,000 apiece (the Levys mortgaged their house). Brown and Phillips were investors and directors but never went on staff; much later McKenzie spent about a year working for the company.

The first office and laboratory were on the second floor above a bakeshop and next door to a primal scream-therapist, whose clients howled into cushions. The partners had three employees developing monoclonal antibodies for possible diagnostic purposes. As lucrative as the government grant funding was, they realized the need for less-tar-geted money from private sources. Approaching sophisticated investors at the university, friends, family, and other contacts, they raised about $1.2 million in two rounds of financing. One early investor was Edgar Kaiser Jr., the son of the fabulously wealthy resource-conglomerate fam-ily whom McKenzie knew from working for the Kaiser coal operations in British Columbia.* Along the way, they were beginning to appreciate

---

*High-Tech entrepreneur Ed Fitzhenry also worked for Edgar Kaiser Jr. when he was employed at Ashland Oil Company in Calgary before founding Pelorus Navigation Systems *(see page 270).*

the different criteria for raising private and public funds—differences that Levy likes to pass along to other academics-turned-entrepreneurs.

Don't use the academic or government grant systems as a model for raising money from private sources

Forget the institutional granting process as a template for seeking funds from business people, Julia Levy warns. "Because that is not what investors want to see. They know you're smart. They know you can do good science. But they want a deliverable in a finite period of time. They want to know exactly where you're going to be 12 months from now. You never write a university grant that way. It's always pie in the sky. It's always looking forward to what new problem you're going to uncover. You don't really want to solve it because this is what you get your money for. You just want to keep on going," she says, laughing. As the partners tried to demonstrate the depth of their scientific capabilities, she admits, "We were outraged by the number of refusals we had. ... The first learning experience was that investors do not reward brilliance. They reward concise development planning with accurate time lines on when goals will be achieved. My initial reaction to the defined work plans were that they looked too thin. However, it soon became clear that there was no possibility for even starting to develop all the possible products we had."

Meanwhile the partners had moved to more reputable quarters near Vancouver General Hospital and were acting on advice to find a credible CEO to front the company, rather than trying to run it themselves while pursuing their academic careers. Their first executive was Dr. John Armstrong, formerly of the Canadian division of Pfizer, the diversified global health-care company. He came—and went—in 1984. "As a dress-up CEO, he was quite good," Levy says. "He was unable to deliver what we needed." Miller is less charitable: "He had no understanding of the technology, of running the business." The final straw was when Armstrong sent Levy to New York to describe the company's science to potential investment sources, who barely knew why she was

321

there. Returning, she called a meeting at a pub and suggested that Ron McKenzie fire Armstrong, since he had hired him. Miller immediately agreed to take a sabbatical year from UBC and lead the company, which was facing major financial problems.

One of his early duties was to dump J. Bob Carter as an investor. Carter and his people, some of them more respectable than him, had been casting about for opportunities in technology to complement their oil and gas ventures. While he had organized a record Canadian oil acquisition in 1977, his fortunes had been failing ever since. In late 1984, the 1.9-metre-tall, overstuffed deal maker used his drinking problem as an excuse in pleading guilty to gross indecency charges involving a whip-and-sex session with 14- and 17-year-old prostitutes. As a major investor in QLT, he had been throwing his considerable weight around in the boardroom. Until, that is, the meeting Miller enjoys recalling, during which Carter told him: "You can't do anything, you haven't got an opportunity to go anywhere, I'm writing the cheques around here, and that's all there is to it. We now own this company."

"Oh, no, you don't," Miller said, pulling a cheque from his back pocket and sliding it across the table. "You're out of here. Thank you very much—goodbye."

"That," he says now, "was just the most pleasant feeling I've ever had in my life." The cheque for $550,000 had come from a new investor, a low-profile but astute and imaginative local risk taker. Ray Maclean, intrigued with the blooming biotech sector, put in about $1 million on little more than a handshake and would do reasonably well with the growth of his low-priced shares.

At the time, however, the company was all over the technology map in trying to find a focus. Looking for a marketable diagnostic product, the partners decided to create a user-friendly pregnancy test. And after accompanying Vancouver Mayor Mike Harcourt on a trade mission to China in 1985, Miller came home enthused at the possibility of introducing such a test there, as well as trading in Chinese pharmaceuticals.*

---

*In 1987 Miller told *Maclean's* business columnist Peter C. Newman about a "unique cooperative arrangement" that within a year would "result in the Chinese and Canadian partners building a major British Columbia-based manufacturing plant that will process the imported raw materials into generic pharmaceuticals for sale throughout North America." And Quadra Logic planned to send 50,000 of its pregnancy and ovulation test kits to China. As it turned out, the company moved on to other ventures instead.

It was not to be. "Nothing ever happened," Levy says. "Certainly our experience in dealing with Asia in general is you're always at a big disadvantage because you don't really know what's going on. And I think the Chinese didn't have any money. And were their drugs up to good manufacturing practices? The answer was a resounding no."

Building on the China hype and a cornucopia of other possibilities, QLT became the first public biotech company in Canada, going on the Vancouver Stock Exchange in 1986 with a $3-million issue. Jefferson Securities were the underwriters, boasting of this "conceptual company with outstanding people that deserved to be capitalized like their American competitors."

Its principals, moving into a new building near the Cambie Street Bridge, were still dealing with Chinese products (including condoms that failed the blowup test) and researching areas where grant money was available, such as tests to diagnose viral and bacterial diseases of fish-farm salmon. In 1987, with a staff of 45, it continued to lose money—$739,000 worth. But the company was about to embark on a venture that would finally thrust it into the major leagues of biotechnology.

While Miller and other managers were pursuing the home run, Levy was out in left field. Working in UBC's department of microbiology, she had a $750,000 grant from the Medical Research Council of Canada to study light-activated drugs. She was collaborating with David Dolphin in the chemistry department on such a photosensitizer substance that could be used to treat cancer in animals. It was Verteporfin (now Visudyne), scientifically known as benzoporphyrin derivative, or BPD. Dolphin, who had created the drug, became QLT's vice president of technology development. However, there was already a more proven product in the same photodynamic-therapy field—Photofrin. Levy recalls: "I remember having a conversation with the other founders and saying, 'This is the home run. This is it. Discard all the other bumpf we've carrying around with us.'" She recalls recommending that the company buy Photomedica, a subsidiary of the Johnson & Johnson drug conglomerate handling that drug's clinical trials.

Miller and McKenzie flew to J & J's headquarters in New Jersey to put in a bid. "They thought we were a joke," Miller says, "because we were two guys from this company in Vancouver that didn't really know anything about this area at all." QLT would obviously need capacious pockets to afford to buy Photomedica, which had already invested $27 million in research. But Miller soon learned that the other serious bidder was American Cyanamid, whom he approached with a sly suggestion: Why not let QLT make the only bid at a low-ball price and then do a deal together later? That was a win-win situation, although not for J & J, and the subterfuge worked, Cyanamid dropped out of the race, while Johnson & Johnson agreed to sell worldwide marketing rights to Photofrin for a cut-rate $750,000 in cash, plus about $1.5 million in QLT shares when the drug was approved. After the sale, Cyanamid then purchased a $15-million equity in QLT, which essentially funnelled the investment back to its larger partner to handle the ongoing clinical trials of the drug that the smaller company wasn't equipped to do.

High-profile now, QLT went on the Toronto Stock Exchange in 1988 with a $10-million offering (and later on Nasdaq). That was the same year the founders agreed to take up philosopher/scientist Ed Levy on his suggestion that he join the company to deal with regulatory issues, including the deal with American Cyanamid. Miller was initially reluctant to hire his partner's husband ("Hey, this guy was in the philosophy department!" he pointed out). However, Ed had good organizational skills and the company had a trailer full of clinical records from Photomedica that needed processing. And, unlike Miller, he proved to be a quick study on the regulatory side, liaising with his counterparts at American Cyanamid.

Despite individual teams that worked well together, the partnership between the two companies would be troubled. As Julia Levy describes it, "The mouse in bed with the elephant—and the rolling over that goes on. And the fact that people in large pharmaceutical companies have very different agendas. You learn so much."

Partner with companies that have a similar corporate culture—and, if practical, partner with many companies

Recognize that the interests of big and little companies might be wildly divergent, Julia Levy cautions. "When a small company partners with a large one, they are always in competition with divisions inside that large company for R&D dollars—and they are always at a disadvantage. In the past few years, when

big companies have gone into restructuring and downsizing following mergers, it is almost always the outside alliance that gets
jettisoned first. This is rational—if Company X needs to cut its
budget, it would rather cut a project which does not involve lay-
ing off employees. Also competing internal R&D projects have
a great advantage in that they can lobby and promote their own
work on a daily basis. By partnering with a number of companies, the risk is significantly lowered that you will get hung out
to dry. A final condition we have learned in partnering is that
you should choose partners who have a similar corporate culture to your own as well as a partner who considers your project of great importance and not one of passing interest." Only
years later would QLT find partners that, while large in size,
had the flexibility and entrepreneurialism of a small company.

Levy speaks from the sad experience of the relationship with American
Cyanamid, which among many other things didn't understand the
importance of the lasers in Photofrin's clinical trials—evidenced by the
fact that these devices kept breaking down. "We were completely sitting
at the table learning at that point," she admits. "We met every three
months, a big group with their senior people in their clinical arm. And
we were so naïve. We just knew nothing. … They did a lot of things
wrong in the classic way of the big company. They took forever to get
decisions going. The thing that became apparent over the years was that
there were all sorts of internal politics. Me sitting there as a starry-eyed
idealist saying, 'This is a great therapy. It's a wonderful thing for people to have this alternative for cancer treatment, and how would anybody not want to make this go forward?' But you learn that there are a
lot of people who say, 'I'm here so I can get my next promotion and
how do I best get that? Is it by garnering all the funding for internal
projects? Is it by acting as the gatekeeper and if I think there's even a
whiff of a doubt that this won't get through FDA, try to kill it before it
even gets there?' … They were part of a big machine and looking at
where their next growth came from."

Over the next four years, the tension between the two companies
became electric, and Miller was the lightning rod for the antagonism.
With a risk-averse executive within Cyanamid trying to sabotage the

Photofrin project, the president of QLT engaged in what he calls "confrontational meetings between myself and some senior management that were not productive—yet we were standing up for our rights as a small company. It was our future." The battles grew so heated that Miller became the sacrificial lamb and quit the company in 1991. "The lesson," he says, "was that I could become more patient in the process. I'm no more patient today than I was, but I'm able to restrict my response pattern a little bit better these days."*

As Miller left, QLT's directors appointed a new chairman, Duff Scott, who had chaired Prudential-Bache Securities Canada and the Toronto Stock Exchange. Levy, who had her head down in the laboratory, was suddenly called upon to be interim president and CEO. The salary was inviting—$177,000—but she admits that "in '91 I was desperately unhappy. I had never been so tired in my life. I knew I had no confidence in my ability to do it at that time. I felt incredibly responsible for everything. We didn't have a cohesive management team. We were still very green. Also, I think the perception of the outside world was that I was an egghead."

She willingly ceded the responsibility in 1992 when the board hired William "Bud" Foran, retiring as head of Cyanamid Canada. It was a fence-mending exercise with QLT's major partner, but again the fit was less than perfect. "Bud was nicely corporate, a very effective CEO of a branch plant, and that was what his experience had been," Levy says. "He's an honourable, good man and was able to raise money because he looks the part and talks the talk. But when it came to operations, he was a fair arbiter but he wasn't used to the hands-on, small-company environment." In his year with the company, Foran's chief role—along with helping to raise a substantial $40 million in a public offering—was to find his successor.

Inevitably the relationship with American Cyanamid ended—for several reasons. One was that Cyanamid had been focused on the treat-

---

*These days Jim Miller is chairman of his own company, Inex Pharmaceuticals in Burnaby, British Columbia, which is "commercializing the precision of gene-based drugs with its proprietary drug-delivery system to target cancer, inflammation, and cardiovascular disease." With the recent acquisition of Lynx Therapeutics of Hayward, California, Inex claims to be a world leader in the area of antisense oligonucleotides, which regulate or block genes that produce an undesired disease-causing protein.

ment of bladder cancer and a tuberculosis vaccine emerged as a better product than Photofrin to treat it. Another reason was American Home Products' takeover of Cyanamid and the resulting disappearance of many of the people with whom QLT had been collaborating. Cyanamid returned the Photofrin rights to its junior partner for everywhere but Japan, where the drug had the most imminent payoff. But QLT, having been dropped by one major company, now had a hard time interesting other potential marketing partners. The company decided to go it alone in pursuing the long process of approvals for the drug, in this case to deal with cancer of the esophagus, a condition increasing more quickly than any other cancer.

By 1994 QLT was ready to appear before a public hearing of the Oncologic Drugs Advisory Committee of the U.S. Food and Drug Administration to seek approval for Photofrin as a new drug to treat esophageal cancer. The FDA had never supported a drug solely on the basis of clinical trials that showed only relief of symptoms, as Photofrin did. Alexandra Mancini, the company's director of regulatory affairs, had advised total honesty about its strengths and weaknesses—despite the counsel of a former FDA communications specialist to downplay the negatives. Integrity as a tactic worked: the ranking FDA representative swayed the rest of the committee, which voted 11-1 in favour of recommending Photofrin for restricted treatment of esophageal cancer. The company's joy soured when a reporter misinterpreted the decision as a rejection of the drug and filed a story that dropped QLT stock by four percent on the TSE. It did rebound, however, and has never fallen below double digits since.

It took another four years for the FDA to rule on the drug's use for the more common lung cancer, and when the decision came, it was much less than the company had hoped for: the regulatory agency approved Photofrin only as a potentially curative treatment for early stages of the disease (of 178,000 lung cancers diagnosed in the United States annually, no more than 30,000 are caught early). Only in December 1998 did the FDA approve the product for palliation (or alleviation of symptoms) of late-stage lung cancer—allowing QLT's U.S. marketing and distribution partner, Sanufi Pharmaceuticals, to launch the drug commercially in the first half of 1999.

Despite the snail-like approval process and the conservatism of the government agencies, the demand for honesty in corporate dealings continues to emanate from Julia Levy.

Sell the dream, but be honest about delivering it

"The community that's investing in biotech is very sophisticated and they'll see through hype," Julia Levy says. Her suggestion for how to sell a vision applies to any company seeking investments: "This is my plan and I believe in it and this is the potential for it, but there are a lot of go/no gos—if you're investing in me now, you're taking a risk because I can't assure you 100 percent that I'm going to deliver on the dream." She acknowledges that the approach depends on the type of investors you are selling to: "If you're talking to fund managers as opposed to their retail salespeople, you actually pitch things quite differently." Most of the biotech companies for whom she acts as a director take the high road, minimizing the hype, she says, and remain successful because the audience is more knowledgeable now. "They have long memories. We [at QLT] still suffer from some of the overpromises that were made. You can tell the truth 10,000 times and one time you don't, you're in a hole that you never dig yourself out of, because nobody ever knows if you're ever going to lie again."

For the two years leading up to the first FDA hearing on Photofrin, QLT had been in a delicate condition. Since its birth, investors had sunk nearly $80 million into a company that lost a major partner and had yet to put a product on the market. "This is when we could have tanked," Levy says. "Because what did we have? Not much." They did, however, have her research on Visudyne—BPD.

Today she credits two other researchers as the unsung heroines in developing the product. Anna Richter, a Ph.D. at Vancouver General Hospital who had escaped from Poland, approached Levy in 1986 to join the company and work on the photosensitizer drug. About the same time, Levy's mother had been diagnosed with age-related macular degeneration. Then an undauntable 82, still pruning her fruit trees,

Dorothy Coppens began slowly going blind. In 1992 her daughter attended a medical conference in Milan where a woman named Ursula Schmidt told her how much she wanted to work with BPD to treat this incurable eye condition in the elderly. QLT supported Schmidt's fellowship work on monkey eyes at Harvard University and then in Germany when she returned home.

It was tragically too late for her mother, who died virtually blind in 1996. But Julia Levy believed that her company had a product that could save millions of other elderly people from blindness. She knew instinctively, as well as intellectually, that together BPD and AMD spelled "blockbuster": "Because there's no competition in the field, it's a catastrophic condition, no alternative treatment, all the work so far looks so promising." As the clinical trials progressed, Levy realized the beauty of BPD, its user-friendliness: a patient receives a 90-second treatment and leaves 15 minutes later; the drug disappears from the body within a day and leaves no photosensitivity, as competitive drugs do. "If you start doing the arithmetic," she says, "it's scary. It's 500,000 new cases a year worldwide—and going up because the population's aging. ... And the other thing that just absolutely blows you away is the letters you get from the patients."*

Bud Foran left the company at the end of 1994. His successor as president had been with QLT since 1993, most recently as executive vice president and COO. Dr. Randal Chase came from Glaxo Canada, the brand-name pharmaceutical company, where he was senior vice president for technical operations. If Levy sounds critical of John Armstrong, she can't be contained about Chase: "Randal fooled us all. ... What became clear is that Randal is a nagger, an ankle biter. It works when you're COO, but when you're CEO, you've got to lead. He thought the board was his boss which, of course, is very bad for a company because you keep on calling board members and they become involved in operations—and they treated Randal with contempt." She was one of those board members, as well as being chief scientific officer. And when the embattled Chase decided to depart in his second year, she finally felt ready to accept a permanent position as president

*One such patient is Hinrich Schmeilan in Lübeck, Germany, who wrote: "My vision was getting worse and worse—I could no longer carry out daily activities like shopping or preparing meals. But after the treatment, the distortion went away and I could see clearly again."

and CEO. "What I've come to realize is that the CEO doesn't have to know everything," she says. "I thought I was not up to the job because of that. You have to be smart enough to hire people who do know what you don't know. I've never had the Christ complex."

By now QLT was into a strategic alliance with CIBA Vision Ophthalmics of Atlanta, part of the health-care division of Novartis, the world's leading life-sciences company. Levy found it remarkably entrepreneurial for a company that was then doing $700 million U.S. in annual sales. In return for 50 percent of the profits, CIBA Vision has been funding 60 percent of the development costs of Visudyne aimed at age-related macular degeneration. This is now one of many such alliances that QLT has forged with major partners. In the oncology field, Visudyne and Photofrin—in combination with the laser devices of photodynamic therapy—are targeting cervical, lung, and esophogeal cancers; precancerous Barrett's esophagus; and several autoimmune conditions. And the participation of Sanofi Pharmaceuticals, Beaufour Ipsen, Lederle (Japan), and Ligand Pharmaceuticals is crucial for a company like QLT, which has come to understand a humbling fact of business life.

Don't assume your great product will sell itself

Speaking to members of the B.C. Science Council (which had awarded her a gold medal in 1981), Julia Levy said, "I used to believe naïvely if you had a good product that would help humanity, you didn't need to spend a lot of time marketing it— it would sell itself. Not true. The marketplace is full of competing products and other companies actively working at cutting you out. Therefore, the biotech company that has successfully developed a drug still needs a partner to get the product onto the market." As she told me, "Who wouldn't use PDT (photodynamic therapy)? Well, a lot of doctors wouldn't. It's reality, and if you look at the examples in other biotech companies with products—where everyone's full of stars in their eyes and the product just kind of struggles along—it happens. If I were to start over ten years ago, I think I would have tried to understand the market a lot better than I did. None of us really understood what issues there would be in gaining the market in oncology."

What Levy has come to understand is the necessity of target-marketing specialists in the cancer field. "Photofrin is a surgical procedure," she says. "You go to the specialist who's going to do the surgical treatment—instead of going to the oncologist who takes all comers, be it ovarian or breast. What finally came into focus is that's how you build PDT business—you go by body parts. ... So a big company that has an oncology business, a sales force focused on oncology, they're not going to be able to sell PDT—it's the wrong audience. The penny dropped finally—we really don't want to have an oncology-business partner because the technology will die. They'll never sell a dime's worth of it."

Another realization has been the fierceness of competition in the biotechnology business. The most annoying has been Miravant, the California company that claims to be on the fast track, running neck and neck with QLT, in the race to put a PDT drug on the market to treat age-related macular degeneration. But as Christine Charette of Nesbitt Burns pointed out in mid-1998, "No clinical data is required to obtain fast-track designation [from the FDA] and it is fairly easy to obtain." She figured that Miravant's Purlytin was two years behind its competitor's drug. Rating QLT an attractive 5 as an investment, she said, "We expect the stock to continue to build momentum in anticipation of the completion of the phase-three BPD (Visudyne) for AMD trial and the release of the trial results." QLT is hoping for final FDA approval before the end of 1999. With the FDA's support for Photofrin and the continuing good news about Visudyne, QLT's stock became a high flyer on the TSE, reaching a 52-week high of $79.15 in March 1999.

With her brilliance as a scientist and her healing powers as a corporate leader, Levy has taken the company from an often mismanaged business in its development stages to a viable commercial enterprise—solidly financed, well partnered, poised on the brink of what promises to be staggering success.

As Jim Miller says of the venture he cofounded, "QLT helped to spawn an industry"—in British Columbia and Canada for that matter. "It created the crystallization and the spin-offs, [with others saying]

'They've done it. Why can't I?' In Ontario that just hasn't occurred. Venture capital is very significant in B.C. in supporting biotechnology companies. It's huge—and it's not going to stop."

TrendWatch

"We've led the way in biotech in Vancouver and now people are beginning to take the local scene quite seriously," Julia Levy says. "They have to—it's the fastest-growing biotech sector in Canada. We're way outstripping Toronto and Montreal. I was talking to a rep from Rothschild's—not a shabby organization— [and] they invest in some of the companies here. And she was saying she looks at maybe 20 companies a month in terms of the possibilities of investing and will invest in maybe four—and she says they're all in Vancouver. The quality of the science here is fantas- tic. It's wonderful to see it all happening here. It's just so exciting. And to feel like you're kind of a grandpar- ent, creating an environment which is critical-mass- dependent." This concentration of companies bodes well for biotech professionals looking to locate within Canada. "Our senior management can walk out the door at any time and get a job in any of these newer companies, who would kill to have them," Levy says. Laughing, she adds, with her typical directness, "I use that to get our board to give them bonuses."

Chapter Twelve

The Samurai's Daughter

Kazuko Komatsu, Pacific Western Brewing Company

The most astonishing fact about Kazuko Komatsu is not that she is the only woman to head a major North American brewery. True, her innovative Pacific Western Brewing Company of Prince George, British Columbia—the continent's most northern beer maker—is the largest Canadian-owned independent in the West and has the third-largest-selling product line after Molson's and Labatt's. It may also seem surprising that this Japanese expatriate, slight of build and soft of manner, once walked British Columbia's log booms and flew into its fishing camps carrying hundreds of thousands of dollars in a suitcase. And that with no formal business training, this former mathematics teacher has been a successful land developer and an exporter of a gamut of Canadian goods to Japan, from french fries to log homes. Yet what is even more astonishing is that nearly 20 years ago she was diagnosed with cancer and underwent radiation treatments and an operation, which together were so traumatic that she says she lost her memory of everything to that time—nearly lost her ability to communicate in either Japanese or English—and that she fought back so tenaciously to accomplish all of the above.

However, perhaps it isn't so extraordinary, after all, when you hear her history, the ancestral stories that she has been retold in the years since the details of the first three decades of her life were apparently swept away like cherry blossoms in the wind. For this deceptively gentle woman not only comes from an old sake-brewing family but she is also a proud descendant of the samurai, Japan's aristocratic warrior class. The samurai, even as they became bureaucrats and judges in the 19th century, retained the right to bear swords and to decapitate insolent commoners.

Of course, as statesmen and businessmen, they helped build the modern Japanese economy, and it is their strengths in these callings, as much as their martial tendencies, that form a vital part of Komatsu's heritage and character. The man in her life, Harry Mayor, who is Pacific Western Brewing's operations manager and a feisty personality himself, says, "Kazuko [pronounced "Kass-ko"] is very dainty, very demure, but she's lethal. She's told me her family have always been strategists and they've been involved in war for 400 years." He also quotes her as saying, "For people to respect you, there should always be an element of fear."

She has, however, won respect as a Japanese-Canadian entrepreneur for the enlightened management of the privately owned brewery she took over in 1990 and as a philanthropist for the community involvement she accepts as a responsibility. Komatsu initiated a bonus system for employees, which was active until a couple of years ago, when the Japanese downturn shrank the company's substantial export sales. She also turned Pacific Western into the first brewery in North America to get ISO 9002 certification for the quality of its operation. As for giving back to the community: even though she is based in the Lower Mainland city of Burnaby, she is a governor of a Victoria college and a Prince George university, and her charitable donations go to higher education and provincial hospitals (the hospitals she has feared ever since her operation). And to help the ailing Prince George economy, her brewery has begun to buy local products more aggressively and for every dozen of its beer purchased there is contributing 25 cents to a community fund.

All this has earned Komatsu the Order of British Columbia and a Canadian Commemorative Medal for outstanding contribution to country, community, and compatriots. The Federal Business Development Bank has given her a B.C. Entrepreneur Award for business-management excellence and the Vancouver Junior Board of Trade declared her Business Leader of 1998. That same year international trade minister Sergio Marchi named her to his Team Canada Inc. Advisory Board; in 1999 she accepted a federal invitation to serve for three years on the Canadian Agri-Food Marketing Council. A director of the Brewers Association of Canada and the Western Brewers Association, she has been involved in contentious industry issues, including the unsuccessful fight to have Ottawa restore antidumping duties on imported American beer.

In that battle she was in league with Molson and Labatt, normally her mortal enemies. Of the dozen or so brewing companies in the province, the two majors control more than 90 percent of the market; hers has a mere four percent. Her annual production of about 140,000 hand-brewed hectolitres (with 300 bottles per hectolitre) is less than a fifth the volume of Molson's thoroughly computerized Vancouver plant. When the B.C. Liquor Distribution Board introduced a minimum-pricing policy to effectively discourage cheaper American imports, that decision hurt lower-priced Pacific Western, as had the LDB's positioning of its products in less-than-prominent places. Combined, these developments have cut the company's market share in half, spurring Komatsu to launch her first ambitious advertising campaign and to offer free samples on Canadian Airlines domestic flights. Meanwhile she is considering legal action against the provincial-government body to force a higher profile for her beers in the liquor stores. In early 1999, British Columbia's NDP government did give Pacific Western a tax break worth about $500,000 a year by creating a new, lower regional-brewery tax rate that applies only to her company (Prince George is home to two NDP members of the legislature).

Given their relative anonymity, you may well ask exactly which brands she brews. The 13 domestic products run from conventionally named Pacific Pilsner and Traditional Light to such oddities as TNT (Totally New Taste), an amber nectar with a mild hop flavour and strong alcohol volume of six percent, and LimeLite, a four-percent blend of lager and lime juice.* That last beverage is one of Pacific

---

*The Canadian product list includes: Amber Ale (five percent), a mellow ale from premium two-row barley, hops, and the brewery's own pure spring water; Traditional Lager (five percent), a smooth, light golden-hued brew; Ironhorse (6.4 percent), a full-bodied medium gold; Pacific Dry (5.5 percent), with a finish hinting of citrus and grain; Traditional Light (three percent), very light gold with fewer calories; Traditional Cream Malt (5.5 percent), full-bodied with a bittersweet aftertaste; LimeLite (four percent), traditional lager and lime juice; TNT (six percent), amber-coloured, stronger, and slower-brewed; Pacific Genuine Draft (five percent), a cold-filtered, clean-tasting draft; Pacific Pilsner (five percent), flaxen in colour, longer-aged, with a sweet, citrusy start; Canterbury Dark Mild (five percent), richly toned, with an earthy, slightly chocolaty aroma; Pinnacle Dry Ice (5.8 percent), a deep yellow and very mellow; and NatureLand Organic Lager (5 percent), a light, refreshing brew made from 100-percent organic Harrington malt from Saskatchewan and 100-percent organic Hallertau hops from Lower Bavaria, Germany. "Organic certification ensures that no pesticides, fungicides, herbicides, dessicants, chemical seed treatment or conventional nitrate and phosphate fertilizers have been used in the cultivation of the barley or hops used in your beer," consumers are informed. A 14th beer, a lager, is due in 1999.

Western's many innovations under Komatsu's ownership. The brewery was the first in North America to make dry beer (fermented to complete dryness, with less sugar and an alcohol level nearly double light brews); the first in Canada with dry ice beer (filtered with ice) and organic lager (a delicious brew from 100-percent organic malt and hops); and the first anywhere with the lager-and-lime mix and a low-malt herb beer for export called King Solomon. Between 1991 and 1996, the brewery was the trailblazer in exporting Canadian beer to mainland China (1991), Argentina (1992), and Russia (1996). And it was the first to introduce beer in Quebec liquor stores that had been brewed outside the province.

A reviewer for *Montreal's Gazette*, trying a trio of Pacific Western beers, said "they are enjoyable summer drinking and perfect for those who find the bitterness and intense flavours of most beers heavy going." Several years ago a *Toronto Star* critic wrote: "Although none of the Pacific brands offer anything more or less than expected from mainstream lagers, the traditional brews do have a bit more in the way of character than your standard, commercial beer." In particular he liked the Traditional Cream Malt, which had "a full and creamy caramel body and even elements of rooty hop showing up toward the finish." Perhaps the praise the brewery most appreciates came recently from John Winter, the former president of Molson's western division, who said Pacific Western had differerentiated itself in the market with beers that are "imaginative and innovative"—particularly LimeLite and NatureLand Organic Lager.

NatureLand is the only one of her brews that Kazuko Komatsu can imbibe. She is allergic to most alcoholic beverages. "Make me sleepy. And my heart start beating fast," she says in her truncated English, which remains uncertain after more than two decades. Certainly she has the figure of someone who shuns beer. As slim as a bamboo stalk, she maintains her form with the aerobics she does daily while meditating. Exercise and working in the capacious garden at her West Vancouver home are among the few escapes from business she allows herself; she hasn't taken a vacation in ten years. Her gracile frame shows well with her tasteful, low-key wardrobe, quiet gold necklaces and bracelets, and long, well-manicured nails. She appears a nicely preserved 50, which is what both Harry Mayor and I guess her age to be. Guess, because she isn't telling: "When you start saying about your age, you start realizing where you are standing and you start acting like that age."

That is only one of the secrets that tantalize her interviewers. Another is exactly which sort of illness Komatsu endured in 1980. She was diagnosed with cancer, but what kind? "Gynecological," she says. But there is some doubt whether she actually had the disease, after all. Mayor says he has heard that she was misdiagnosed and perhaps didn't have the ovarian cancer for which she was being treated. But he suspects the resulting operation is the reason she has never had children. The other hidden aspects of her life are shrouded by the memory loss Komatsu says she sustained after her illness. The amnesia has embarrassed her when she couldn't recall old friends from Japan. At first she asked me not to mention any of this "because it's impossible telling everybody, explaining [to] everybody. When they get to know where I come from, more people start contacting me and I don't remember. ... I don't want to cause too much problem for me and for other people." When I suggested that it was unlikely anyone in Japan would read this book, she agreed to keep things on the record.

But anything she can relate about her beginnings, and her ancestry, is apparently all secondhand—stories that she says her father, brother, and relatives have fed her since her pre-1980 memories were shocked away by the trauma of her treatment and operation. Which is a shame, because the hints of the past she presents are fascinating.

Her forebears were members of the samurai warrior class that crystallized in Japan during the Tokugawa period of the early 1600s. The shoguns of this feudal system closed the country to foreign influences and eventually entrusted the knightlike samurai to govern the lower classes. A year after the Meiji Restoration of 1868 displaced the shoguns with an emperor and began embracing the techniques of western civilization, the uncle of Komatsu's grandmother was one of the first few Japanese to enroll at Oxford University. He returned to become the first speaker of the Diet, the Japanese parliament. Overseas he had studied the Bible, which led to his conversion to Protestantism, and had brought home a stiff-papered, substantial edition of the classic Oxford dictionary, which was read by the young Kazuko. In the years leading up to the Second World War, a granduncle of hers studied medicine in

Germany. "So I grew up with foreign ideas, foreign materials," she says. Her Oxford-educated ancestor became a brewer of sake, and the rice-wine business remained part of the family fortune before the war. A grandfather was a professor, her father a chemist for an oil company whose essential work kept him out of the armed forces.

Kazuko, born in Kobe after the war, has heard about her childhood in a family complex amid the rice-paddied countryside near Kochi, on the southern island of Shikoku, where she went to school. "But *I* don't know about Kochi," she says. Does she recall anything about her education? "I don't remember. Funny thing is, in dream I could see friends. Sometimes I realize that this is a dream and during dreaming I'm saying I should remember this. But next day I forgot—too busy." She attended university in Tokyo—which one she would rather not say, for fear of inspiring fellow students to look her up and being ashamed when she can't remember them. There she majored in mathematics and then taught high school. (About a decade ago she was invited to a reunion of the school and "according to the letter I get, they really respected me, they were inspired by me. But I couldn't be there because I don't remember.")

After a year—or two?—of teaching, Komatsu decided to come to Vancouver, for some reason she can't conjure up now. Although she has said publicly the year was 1975, she tells me it was probably a year later. She can't recall having any goal of starting her own company, but that was what she did. When I ask if she had help from family in Japan, she holds her head in her hands and says, "I'm not sure." What made her go into the business she named Kowa Canada? I ask. "Probably—I *think*, not I *thought*—I should be independent. So I should do something. This is a mystery, I'm not sure about. *Now* I *think* I should be independent—that's what I'm telling people, but I'm not sure. I think I should be independent so I made a company. I was sending copper artwork and handbags, Canadian leather purses, for export."

Those were predictable products for a woman to handle, but Komatsu also believes she had already started to bring Japanese buyers to Canada to acquire raw logs. In that role, she had to take her clients directly to the source along the West Coast. And so clients could judge the quality of the wood firsthand, the diminutive agent became fearless in walking with them on the logs lashed together in booms on the water. Obviously emboldened by that venture into natural resources, she communicated with an uncle in Japan: "I think he was sick, retired from Mitsubishi. He got leukemia from atomic bomb." Years later she heard from a cousin that she had asked this uncle if he could help develop her embryonic business linking Canada and Japan. A friend of the uncle was a major shareholder of a Japanese industrial gas company, which was interested in importing helium, a relatively rare and costly constituent of natural gas. A Canadian friend of Kazuko had an uncle living in Alberta with contacts in the petroleum industry. Through him she met the dynamic chairman of Dome Petroleum, Jack Gallagher, but he had just made a deal with another Japanese company.

She continued to pursue the idea of sourcing helium from North America, but it was about this time—1980—that a doctor delivered the horrific diagnosis of cancer. As her radiation treatments began, she felt she was near death. "I was getting treated for a long time, but then went to hospital," she says. "Before I get the operation, terrifying. When you start getting treatment, it makes it too hard to do anything. You don't remember, facing every night or day. Maybe that time was a long time. … but now to me that's a very short time. It's gone, see?" She says the turmoil of the treatments and a major operation, the fear of dying, wiped out the details of her life. What she was left with was her warrior's will: "I have a strong mindset that didn't go away. The emotional thing, mental power, they don't go away—that you don't lose." During this time, she suggests she could hardly speak her native tongue, never mind the English she had studied for a year in Vancouver and had been practising ever since. Although her mother was dying in Japan, her father came to be with her and reassured his daughter: "After the sickness, he told me, don't worry. I have very high IQ I can memorize from now." He had read his great-uncle's Bible as a child, as had Kazuko, and now she turned to it for comfort: "Our family is Buddhist, but since I got sick, I start believe in God."

However, she admits, "it was *real* hard to recover." Especially if, as Harry Mayor now says, there was some knowledge that she had been given the wrong diagnosis and had not really had cancer. But with the help of her father and a new religious faith, her mental and emotional resources resurfaced and, as they did, Komatsu resumed her search for helium. "Even after I came out from hospital," she says, "I went to

United States with a buyer. I went to Air Products, which supplies helium gas to NASA." She tells of accompanying her Japanese client to Omaha, Nebraska, for a meeting in an impressive boardroom and dinner at an exclusive country club as she facilitated the introduction to the American supplier. The two companies then dealt directly while she was paid a fee for services. The North American oil industry was booming as the Organization of Petroleum Exporting Countries shocked the world with dramatic price increases. She went on to source other helium producers, including Union Carbide and Northern Products. Her company, Kowa Canada, also continued to find logs for export, sometimes shipping 80 containers at a time to Japan.

In 1983 Komatsu entered another resource industry, once again where women were considered fish out of water. It would be one of the most painful experiences of her career—one she can't forget. A group of Japanese approached her to run a fish-processing company to be based in the Greater Vancouver municipality of Delta. Her job as president of Pisces Trading would be to acquire salmon and the delicacies of herring roe and herring roe on kelp for sale in Japan. She wasn't interested and told them so. "It was after the sickness. It consumed too much energy." Although she introduced the financiers to other Japanese Canadians, they insisted that Komatsu was the best choice. Reluctantly she accepted their offer—against her better instincts. The bitter experience that followed would underline a belief she has hewn to through much of her life.

Always pay close attention to your intuition

"No significant advance could have been made in civilization without intuition," the Canadian physician Daniel Cappon writes in *Intuition: Harnessing the Hidden Power of the Mind*. "No lasting work of art, no startling discovery, no wizardly piece of science, no delicious recipe, no successful business. ... could have been wrought without intuition." While it is a philosophy Kazuko Komatsu shares, in this case she ignored it: "I didn't want to do this. ... Sometimes I ask questions and [ask for] advice, and because I know I should listen to people, and I should take advice, sometimes I put my intuition aside. I ask friends and business people"—but not family members—"and nobody said not to do." So, acting against the instinctual insight she had registered immediately upon hearing the offer, she decided to accept the position. Since then Komatsu has relied on the intangibles of instinct to help make hard business decisions, such as whether to buy a faltering brewery. She is in good company. Researchers at the New Jersey Institute of Technology did a study that showed 60 percent of the companies that had a doubling of profits in the previous five years were operated by executives with above-average ratings for intuition, which fortunately is a trait we all have and, once identified, can develop with practice.

If she had listened to her intuition, Komatsu would have avoided a net load of grief in the few years ahead. In her own understated words, she says: "I did so many things women never did." She had to round up as many as 40 packer boats at a time to supply fish to a mother boat. That required her to take a chartered floatplane to the fishing grounds up the coast as far north as the Queen Charlotte Islands and bargain with fishermen. "That's interesting, carrying $1 million cash in suitcase," she says. Sometimes she had a Mountie beside her for protection. Jumping into boats, she had to decide—quickly—how much to pay for a haul of fish. If her bid price stopped going up, the fishermen might get angry. "This is dangerous, risky business, fishing," she says. "Many dishonest people. So I tried to establish my reputation." Her father had reminded Komatsu of a discipline the family tried to instill in her as a child, which could be summed up in the phrase "Yes, no, or I'm not sure." As Komatsu explains: "When I promise, I will do. But 'No' means 'No.' And 'I'm not sure' *means* 'I'm not sure,' or 'I don't remember.'" To apply that slogan now, she demanded written agreements with the fishermen so they couldn't claim she had promised something she hadn't or that she didn't know English well enough to understand the deal that was made.

Early on she also began asking about the worst-case scenarios that could occur on the fishing grounds. More of her father's advice rang in her ears: From the beginning, ask *why* things happen and *how* the system works from start to finish. Her investigations led her to arrange with an underwriter to insure the huge amounts of cash she carried. It was a smart move: in the middle of one night, she got a telephone call that a packer boat had caught fire and, while everyone was safe, all the money aboard had burned; another time a boat had supposedly sunk and taken the cash down with it. "It's a good thing I don't have to worry so," she says today.

By now, Komatsu had someone to share her worries with. Not long after becoming president of Pisces, she was with a male friend at a party on Vancouver's North Shore when she met a ruddy-faced, stocky—and outspoken—Englishman. Harry Mayor had escaped his family's coal-mining past to become an electrician like his father. Immigrating to Canada in 1964, he worked as a superintendent for a pulp company on northern Vancouver Island and for Noranda in Montreal. He married a Belgian woman there and moved to Windsor as a foreman for Ford and then to Toronto as a transportation superintendent for Dominion Bridge. His marriage breaking down, he left his wife and took their son to live in Vancouver, where he was working in the field of workplace health and safety for the Burrard-Yarrow Shipyard. At the party, his interest in the attractive Japanese woman was so obvious that her boyfriend wanted to fight with him. Mayor began to date Komatsu and one day went with her to Pisces Trading, where she casually told him to use one of the staff cars to take his son on a trip out of town. Thinking she was an employee, he told her she couldn't go around handing out company vehicles like that. "That's when she told me she was president," he says. "She was in jeans and a pair of runners—not exactly my idea of a Japanese president." They eventually bought a house together, where she lived with Mayor and his son. Today, when he asks her why a samurai's daughter with a university education was attracted to a coal miner's son with street smarts, she tells him, "You shouldn't push the issue."

Mayor was some comfort as the stress of Komatsu's work discouraged her: "This business doesn't suit me, doesn't inspire me." In 1986 she was ready to quit after three years of dealing with the vagaries of the fishing industry and the allegedly unsavoury practices of the owners of Pisces Trading. "I felt they are not 100-percent honest with me," she says. "And they are taking benefit of profit to Japan, leaving debt in Canada. I have to fight." One important battle took place in the lounge of Vancouver's Holiday Inn Harbourside. She was meeting with one of the Japanese principals and a Japanese-Canadian accountant representing him. Those two suggested that they could declare the company bankrupt and walk away from its debts. Speaking loudly in English so others could hear, Komatsu said, "This is planned bankruptcy, I cannot accept that." The accountant asked her to switch to Japanese. "I will talk to you in Japanese one by one, not one against two," she replied, and the accountant left. Komatsu then told the owner that he had borrowed money from the Royal Bank and he must repay it; but, whatever happened, as president she wouldn't allow the company to go bankrupt.

In fact, he let go all the fish-processing staff and sold the plant to pay back some of the loan, but left with about $100,000 outstanding. Harry Mayor, now working as a private health and safety consultant, had helped Komatsu in the negotiations, but as he says, "the guy conned me—he left town the next day." She told the bank she would make good on the debt, which she did, while also shouldering some of the cost of offices and warehouse she had to sublease for a year. "That time was very hard, 1986," she admits.

Her sympathetic bank manager agreed to lend her money to reestablish her entrepreneurial career. She started a company called Nika Marketing, which over the next few years exported hay from Alberta, peat moss from New Brunswick, and log homes from British Columbia to Japan—"anything," she recalls. On her regular trips home, Komatsu was aware that beer had long since replaced sake as the most popular Japanese beverage. She knew about a small brewery in Prince George and began shipping a lager made by Pacific Western Brewing to her Japanese contacts (who were less than thrilled by its crude label design: a large red heart with a bold "Beer" on a tan background). The import sold for a 20-percent premium over domestic brands. Because Japan was having a love affair with so-called dry beer, she worked with Pacific Western to adapt the recipe for a crispy brew she called Dragon Dry. It was good enough that not only did the Japanese begin ordering it in volume in 1988 but the brewery also asked to market the brand as Canada's first dry beer.

Within two years, Pacific Western was no longer a safe source of supply. Its owners were talking seriously of shutting it down if they couldn't find a buyer for the failing business. The brewery had a yeasty past, going through the ferment of half a dozen owners, none of whom could make it work. The most colourful was Ben Ginter, a German-born entrepreneur who had made his name—which was often "Mud"—in British Columbia's pulp and construction industries, employing more than 9,000 at the peak of his career. He was known for currying favours with the Social Credit politicians of the day and often refusing to pay his many creditors. As biographer Jan-Udo Wenzel writes in *Ginter*, "People either admired him, saying he was a great man, or hated him, saying he was the biggest scoundrel that ever lived in the North." His notoriety grew in 1962 when he bought the abandoned Cariboo Brewing Company in Prince George, a city that had the highest per-capita beer consumption in British Columbia, a province that led all others in beer-drinking. The plant had been built five years earlier by private investors who soon sold the struggling brewery to John Labatt Ltd., which briefly produced brews there under its national label and then closed the operation down.

Ginter rechristened it Tartan Brewing and produced European-style, more bitter beers using wonderfully pure spring water that came from aquifers beneath the brewery. After various incarnations, his brand became known as Uncle Ben's, and he put his bearded mug on the label.* Among his innovations in the brewing industry as he fought the majors were the first pull-tabs for cans and ring-pulls for bottles— and even a dime taped to every case of a dozen cans to protest the provincial liquor board's decision to increase the price of canned beer. When the board ordered him to stop the instant refund, Ginter became British Columbia's first brewer to pay for the return of cans. Despite these tactics, and his opening of breweries in Manitoba and Alberta, his beer sales went flat over the years. In 1975 a strike led to a union's "hot" edict against his products and the closing of the B.C. plant. Early the next year all of his holdings were placed into receivership and he never recovered; Ben Ginter died six years later.

---

*At first Ben Ginter branded his beer with names like Budd and Paaps, crudely disguised versions of popular American beers that weren't being sold in British Columbia yet. After the U.S. breweries objected, he resorted to yet another ploy when he introduced the province's first beer can in 1966: this brand he called PILcan and this time a Canadian brewery, Carling's, forced him to pull it off the market for infringing its "Pil" trademark.

The consortium that bought the B.C. brewery for $1.55 million was led by a no-less-controversial character, Nelson Skalbania (the same Skalbania partnered with Century 21 chairman Peter Thomas in various deals). The Vancouver real-estate flipper, who as a World Hockey Association team owner had signed Wayne Gretzky to his first major-league contract, was riding high at the time. But he was too busy hyper-speculating—buying and selling buildings, sports teams, and pricey pieces of art—to focus on some little beer plant up north. While the unsubtle Skalbania had called it Canadian Gold Brewing, the business turned to brass in 1981 when his empire began collapsing and he was forced to sell the brewery to a group led by W. R. Sharpe, formerly of Canada Dry. The new owners ran it as Old Fort Brewing and later Pacific Western Brewing until 1986, when it was merged with Potter Distillers. The Langley, British Columbia, company produced various liquors and wines with such names as Bag-in-a-Box Blanc de Blanc. An early president of the new enterprise, International Potter Distilling Corporation, was playboy entrepreneur Herb Capozzi, the scion of a B.C. wine making family. Within two years, a Vancouver Stock Exchange rogue had taken over as chairman: Harry Moll had owned nightclubs on the coast before going bankrupt in 1976 and rebounding to hawk shares in a stock-play company that made plastic tire chains and to chair a junky junior oil-and-gas venture. International Potter claimed to have spent $1 million on trying to modernize the Prince George plant, but any renewed marketing efforts never came to a head—and in 1990 the perennially money-losing Pacific Western Brewing was again for sale.*

For sale—or for the dumpster. The principals of ailing International Potter announced that if new owners couldn't be found, they would close the brewery. Among potential buyers approached was Kazuko Komatsu, who had been selling her Dragon Dry, made by Pacific Western, in Japan. She had already been tangentially involved in one failed deal for a brewery when she tried to broker the sale of Vancouver Island Brewing to Japanese buyers. Initially she was intrigued enough

---

*The overreaching International Potter, while selling its distillery site in Langley, also bought Granville Island Brewing, a cottage brewery in Vancouver, built another medium-size brewery in St. Catharines, Ontario (which wasn't included in the deal with Komatsu), and paid $16.9 million for British Columbia's Calona Wines.

by Pacific Western to consider the acquisition. But her interest waned when she learned that its employees, most of them members of Brewery Workers' Local 300, were desperately attempting to buy the company themselves, with the help of the B.C. government. Some of them had even stood outside local liquor stores pleading with customers to buy their brands, which impressed Komatsu. "If I compete with employees, on bidding and takeover, they're not happy," she explains. But the hoped-for assistance from government didn't happen, an alleged agreement with Labatt never materialized, and suddenly International Potter came calling on Komatsu to close a deal quickly.

A little too quickly, as it turned out. She needed time to have the books analyzed and the plant inspected. Meanwhile, almost everybody she talked to, from accountants to a couple of well-placed lawyers in Prince George, advised her not to buy. She soon realized the lie implicit in the parent company's prediction that the crippled Pacific Western would make $1.5 million in the next fiscal year.* For one thing, the figures she saw claimed the operation would earn more in the winter than it had in the summer, an unlikely prospect in the beer business. But Komatsu also was going with her intuition that the brewery could be turned around—intuition, and her banker's more tangible agreement that there was substantial waste and inefficiency in its operation, as well as lack of maintenance. Harry Mayor visited the operation to do due diligence and remembers: "The plant was really run-down. In the last year alone, there hadn't been any money for maintenance. To get spare parts for the air compressor, you literally had to get in touch with a museum in England."

Negotiations with the large International Potter team of legal and accounting staff began in September 1990 and (borrowing a phrase from a sheet of background information from the current owners) "rapidly detriorated into unpleasant conditions." Komatsu fired an industrial-accountant consultant when he failed to notice anomalies that she was uncovering herself by asking—as her father had taught her—how and why things worked in this industry so new to her. For instance, International Potter tried to charge her for the bottle deposits

---

*And, in fact, Kazuko Komatsu still smarts at media reports that later quoted International Potter as saying that Pacific Western, far from being the moneymaker described to her, had actually drained $8 million from the parent company in the previous year. "I could sue them," she says of the dissembling.

for which it had already been paid and which she would have had to refund to the Liquor Distribution Branch. She was highly insulted by the negotiators' antics, says Mayor, who was in the meetings. "They made her feel dirty, and she didn't want to talk with them. She said, 'I don't want to be in the same room with you anymore.'"

One of her concerns was that they had no sympathy for the unionized employees. Mayor contends, "The previous owners were desperate to sell and said, 'We can throw the union out and the employees would accept that because they're desperate to keep their jobs.'" Although he himself thought she might avoid re-signing with the Brewery Workers' local, Komatsu was adamant: "She said the employees have worked a long time to get those benefits and the company is only as strong as its employees—and if you take away what they've got, why should they help you?" It was a lesson she had learned from her family.

When starting a business, invest in your greatest asset: people

When Kazuko Komatsu launched her own company, an uncle in Japan advised her that even if she didn't have a lot of capital, she could and should count on the less obvious asset of people. At first she would rely on business associates, but in seriously considering the acquisition of Pacific Western Brewing, she realized the existing staff could be her strength. "Today PWB's asset is employees," she says. And, in her eyes, to have destroyed their bargaining rights—an opportunity at hand many entrepreneurs might have seized—would have been callous and perhaps even stupid. As she told a journalist not long ago, "The union is very important. People need a job and you cannot do business with hatred. You also need experienced employees who are concerned about the company." Operations manager Harry Mayor says it is more than lip service: "She feels a heavy responsibility for feeding a hundred families when times are tough."

Komatsu finally agreed to pay $4.3 million for Pacific Western Brewing. Half the funds came from an individual investor she had cultivated in

Japan, who offered her a ten-year term on the loan. The rest was a combination of bank financing and her own money from the export business, furnished through her Pinnacle Investments, in which she was the sole shareholder. But even before she took over the brewery in February 1991, her investment in people continued. When the deal was signed at the start of the year, International Potter announced it would immediately stop operating the plant, throwing the staff out of work until the new ownership took over. Komatsu leaped in to assure the employees the brewery would stay open, they would keep their jobs, and she would pay an extra $140,000 to cover the interim wages. Not all the staff were retained, however. When International Potter's negotiators had said the 20 or so managers on staff would be her responsibility, she retorted that "the union people are my employees" and kept only four of the upper echelon, among them a veteran plant manager, who is still there. After the deal closed, grateful employees took inventory and hid such items as office supplies up in the plant's roof, away from the previous owners' eyes—"that's how much they hated them," Mayor says.

Aside from the commitment of its staff, and the purity and freshness of its own natural spring-water supply (important because beer is 95-percent water), Pacific Western Brewing was drowning in problems. The first thing the new owners replaced was the brewery's antique air compressors. It would take $2.7 million over the next 18 months to upgrade the interior. "No use having good makeup if it's not beautiful inside," Mayor quotes Komatsu as saying. "If we made any money, she put it back into the company. I objected. But she's the boss—it's her company—and she's right. For a chauvinist, that's hard to say."

Her first move was to cut operating costs by controlling purchases—instead of buying without thinking—and controlling waste. "Wasting products, like packaging materials, and wasting time, too," she explains. "And damaging products becomes waste—damaging raw material to make finished product. Or putting wrong beer into wrong cans. But after that, when you don't read well, when you don't ship out accordingly, beer will get stale. That's waste, too. I told them, 'Waste is your enemy.' They don't realize it eventually [can cost] their jobs."

The staff were working to a game plan that Komatsu had implemented soon after taking over. She is a strong believer in setting a company's goals for all to see, especially when the goalposts have been too low for too long. "The major point was to restore the confidence of the employees," Mayor says. "Their morale was shot." She assured them that they had an open phone line to her office, which was nearly 800 kilometres to the south, and distributed envelopes addressed to her that they could use to send suggestions and communicate problems. Her first five-year plan stressed equipment upgrades and renewal (which would cost $4.2 million in all, including pollution controls), the revamping of product packaging, new product development, expansion of export markets, and quality—of ownership, service, and product.

The biggest problem was the poor reputation of the various brands, which had suffered from years of neglect. For several weeks, with a view to improving their taste, Komatsu imported a German brewmaster with an engineering degree. "At the beginning, our employees are not happy," she says, "because he was very tough, German-style." However, she also empowered her employees to be guardians of quality by authorizing them to hold up an entire shipment for export even if they found one defective can: "If they have doubt, do not ship." Mayor says this presidential edict caused some concern among managers who weren't used to such grassroots action. But Komatsu was firm on her goals: "I wanted to change the company image and the product image in five years." She still wasn't satisfied with the steps being taken. That was when Pacific Western took a giant step toward achieving a shift in the public perception of her company.

Investigate the possibility of having your company's management systems ISO-certified

Harry Mayor says Kazuko Komatsu kept asking, "How can we differentiate ourselves from the competition? How can we improve quality?" He went to the library and came across a book on the ISO benchmark developed by the Geneva-based International Organization for Standardization in 1987 to facilitate global trade. The standards of ISO (from the Greek *isos*, for "equal") are a way of identifying exactly what a company does—whether it provides services or manufactures products—and having management systems in place to measure performance, report problems promptly, and communicate the actions taken to solve them efficiently within an organization. In effect, it deals with processes and attitudes related to quality control. ISO consultants do an initial audit and then follow-ups every six to 12 months. A small firm may take only half a year to get certified; it took Pacific Western about three years. Although the process wouldn't directly affect the taste of its beer, Mayor says, "Everybody becomes more aware of quality. Our quality is more consistent. In actual fact, it's reduced our costs because you make fewer mistakes. The impact of the system is that everybody is doing their job properly the first time." And it allows the brewery to put the ISO sticker on its products, which proved to be a good marketing strategy in quality-conscious Japan. Pacific Western got its preliminary ISO 9003 certification for manufacturing in 1994, an upgrade to 9002 two years later, and now it is going for 9001 status, which covers product design and development.

Amazingly Komatsu's moves stopped the financial hemorrhaging within six months. Based on the losses the brewery experienced in the first couple of months, if she hadn't implemented the changes it would have lost $8 million over the year. The improvements led to continuing small profits that allowed her to repay her Japanese investor within five years, half the term of the loan. The success was due to new products and expansion of existing export markets. Like British Columbia, Japan was one of the few areas in the world where beer consumption wasn't falling. In 1993 the brewery introduced the first dry ice beer in Canada and a year later signed what was described as a $20-million deal to produce the brew for Nihon Shurui Hanbai, Japan's largest alcohol-beverage distribution company.* NSH's trade manager said that along with the taste of the beer, the manufacturer's ISO certification was a deciding factor. For the past two years, the brewery has been supplying 400 Harvester Restaurants—a sit-down chain operated

---

*Actually the deal was worth a lot less to Pacific Western—the $20 million total was what the 500,000 cases of beer would be worth when sold at the retail level in Japan.

by KFC Japan—with NatureLand Organic Lager. These agreements helped cement Pacific Western's position as the third-largest exporter of beer to Japan, after Heineken and Budweiser.

Even in 1995, Komatsu felt the Japanese economy wouldn't keep growing as relentlessly as it had. They had to develop a product that couldn't be benchmarked on price, she told Mayor. Small Canadian breweries like hers can't compete on price alone. As Japanese beer-drinking began to decline, the nation's breweries were lowering their prices and offering favourable financing to domestic distributors. In 1995 Pacific Western produced the first-ever malted herb beer aimed at the Japanese market, where it is known as *happoho* (pronounced ha-posh-oo). Because this King Solomon brand had a lower malt content, it avoided one of the alcohol taxes there. "It was a rip-roaring success because it knocked 12 bucks off a case," Mayor says. "Domestic brewers complained and got it reclassified as a sparkling wine, which put the tax back on. Then Canadian authorities intervened and we won." He even went on television in Japan as a *gaijin* extolling the virtues of the brew—"but by then there were another 23 low-malt beers on the market." The company has since relaunched the brand as Super King Solomon with a slightly stronger flavour. "This certainly taught us a valuable lesson," Komatsu says. "To have a clean, first-mover advantage is critical success factor for our company."

Fearful of putting all of its brews in one barrel, Pacific Western has been targeting other countries. It was the first to export Canadian beer to mainland China, in 1991, and the first in Russia, five years later. While neither investment has paid any real dividends yet—the company has been meeting with new Chinese buyers, but the Russian market collapsed along with the ruble—it keeps trying. Some of its brands sold briefly in the United Kingdom, but no real distribution is expected there until this year (one brand, LimeLite, shared its name with a British toilet-bowl cleaner). It hopes to approach buyers in France with its NatureLand Organic Lager (which until recently had run into problems in Japan, where a company that trademarked the word *organic* was trying to extract royalties from Pacific Western's distributors). To access these countries, Komatsu and Mayor are fans of both domestic and foreign trade shows, but advise caution.

Be highly selective in the trade shows you attend—research as much as you can ahead of time

Industry trade shows *can* be ideal vehicles to broaden markets, Harry Mayor says. Last year the company successfully launched its NatureLand Organic Lager in the American market at the Food Marketing Institute's Supermarket Industry Convention in Chicago. In the past, Kazuko Komatsu's companies might participate in about 16 such events each year in Japan alone. But Mayor warns that a potential exhibitor should qualify a show well before signing up for a booth. "It's not enough to say a trade show is for beverage buyers," he says. "Are they alcohol, soft-drink, or water beverage buyers? The government of Canada might bring buyers in from foreign countries and they don't have alcohol licenses. The government doesn't qualify them properly." Sometimes, he points out, a show will introduce a product to possible end users yet have no system in place to link exhibitors with business contacts such as distributors. The best trade shows can assist a company in market research of factors like taste and packaging by allowing a new product line to be sampled by a target audience. However, he investigated one show in the United States that he had planned to attend, only to find out he couldn't do a beer-tasting there—which made the event useless for his purposes.

While Japan, despite its economic gloom and overall decline in drinking, will remain a key market, the United States is Pacific Western's prime growth area. The brewery is amid its second five-year plan, which has among its objectives the expansion of exports to both the United States and South America (although with the low currency values in Brazil and Argentina, Komatsu doesn't expect to sell large volumes there). She feels the vaunted trade between Canada and the United States isn't terribly free in her industry, where a Canadian brewery requires an "import licence, distribution licence, approval of design—like 100-years-ago rule." Mayor says they have been working for three years to get into the American market with a good distributor and will probably not succeed until sometime in 1999. However, he says, "I think we will end up putting more [beer] into the U.S. than we do in Japan—or an even split."

Expanded markets are crucial for the company as its share of the domestic beer-drinking audience has dwindled—in large part, Komatsu believes, because of the way the liquor boards across the country handle beer from the small breweries. As Mayor describes the B.C. situation, "they decided to place our products in deemphasized positions" in the stores in relation to the major breweries. "We've said to the LDB, 'What you've done with Molson and Labatt is wrong.' We're getting lip service—they implement changes that piss off the store managers with PWB." Pacific Western, he told me in late 1998, will soon have to decide whether the situation should become a public war.

If it does, Komatsu says, she will have the support of her employees. She has asked them what they want her to do—"because if I make wrong decision, they will lose jobs." They have sent letters of protest to provincial politicians and wanted to follow up with pickets at liquor stores and the Liquor Distribution Branch offices, but she dissauded them from that. "They said they will back me up 100 percent. Even when I was in Prince George last trip, some employee come to talk to me, holding my hand, and say, 'I've been here for 16 or eight years,' and they like working for me. That gives me energy. Then I feel, *Oh, I should fight for them.*" Could she see herself taking legal action against the LDB, for example, I ask her. "Yes, if it's necessary, I will take action because"—she pauses, weighing her words—"the present system is for benefit of big breweries. ... LDB means Liquor Distribution Branch of British Columbia. That means for people in British Columbia—not only two big breweries and their employees."

The truth is, Pacific Western Brewing has been hurting recently (1998 volume was likely down from the previous year, when the retail value of exports was $32 million and the wholesale figure for domestic sales was $20 million). The brewery closed for a week in the summer of 1998 and hasn't made money in the past couple of years. Its president has never drawn a salary from the operation and won't, Mayor says, "until the company is 100-percent secure." Staff production bonuses haven't been awarded since 1996, but the company has a new Gainshare committee that promises to give employees half the savings the company makes in cost reductions that they identify. Already one side benefit of this policy, written into the union contract, has been environmental—a lessening of effluent produced by the plant. In the next contract, the hope is to have an accident-reduction program tied to the provincial Workers' Compensation Board, which would give employees all the money returned under a WCB bonus system.

Given the pressure of returning the brewery to its profitable recent past, it would be understandable if its president retreated from the public duties she has assumed. Industry affiliations are expected, but she is also on the Vancouver Board of Trade, Prince George Chamber of Commerce, Canada Japan Business Committee, and Canada Japan Society. She continues on the board of governors of the University of Northern British Columbia in Prince George and recently became a governor of Royal Roads College in Victoria. UNBC and Prince George's College of New Caledonia are prominent among the beneficiaries of her donations. The desire to donate springs from a deep well.

Give back to the community—in good times and bad

The uncle who told Kazuko Komatsu that good people could be her asset also said that she should be a resource in return. "Now people help you, but one day you should be asset for people," she quotes him as saying. In her mind, being a valuable asset means to be reliable and helpful, to develop a reponsible pattern of behaviour that others can depend on. Her family had a history of donating to education in Japan, and she believes that proper schooling is the bedrock of Canada's future. "Some people say, 'When I have money, I will donate, when I have time I will do volunteer job.' When people say, 'When I got money I will give'—you never, ever give money. You never have enough money and not enough heart and not enough time to give away. In that sense, *we* don't have money, we don't have time, PWB is having a hard time." Yet she still donates to higher education and hospitals. "This donation is coming through all my employees' heart. I hope they understand each of employees are giving charity—not the company, not me. ... Giving things, you get sometimes millions more back. Mentally you feel better. But you shouldn't buy comfort because of your giving. That should just be natural."

For the moment, not only is Pacific Western Brewing in a slump, but Komatsu's other companies are also mostly on hold. Nika Marketing—"a one-stop shop—anything the Japanese wanted we would find," Mayor says—evolved into Royal Canadian Homes, a manufacturer of log houses and building materials, including a window designed specifically for the export market. For a while, it even operated a school in Nagano to train Japanese in the art of building with the North American two-by-four construction materials it was exporting. "We caught the boom at the best time," says Mayor, who was one of 11 employees. "Royal Canadian Homes started doing very well. Possibly in our next year we did $7 million. [In 1998] the volume is almost zero because the Japanese can't get mortgages." Beginning in the late 1980s, Komatsu's Mayor Development Corporation profitably built expensive homes on 40 lots amid eight raw hectares in West Vancouver and still has land available for housing when conditions improve. She also owns the 1,857-square-metre building that houses her head office on about one hectare in a well-positioned industrial park in Burnaby.

Komatsu isn't visibly suffering. She drives a Mercedes and lives in one of those lovely West Vancouver homes she developed, which she shares with Mayor, a Japanese Akita dog, and a half-blind cat. She once had two cats, who were always scuffling, and Mayor tells the story of how their mistress took them by the scruff of their necks, put them face-to-face, and then banged their heads together three times while saying, "You will not fight anymore." Which, he says, they never did.

There is a Japanese word Kazuko Komatsu relates to: *kizen*, which means "continuous improvement." She isn't about to give up the fight to keep her brewery viable and its employees working. Nor is she going to stop planning for expansion of her enterprises. She is introducing a new brand, aimed at the B.C. market: PWB 360 Lager, with a label that is expected to feature a tough-looking little penguin against a mountain backdrop. And last year this quietly aggressive descendant of the samurai reported she was hoping to build a $30-million bottled-water plant in Prince George, capitalizing on the natural springs beneath the brewery, which she had already been canning and selling on a custom-order basis for seven years. A Métis group might be a minority partner in the new venture.

When we met, however, this typically self-assured Maverick entrepreneur, an immigrant with a strong sense of place and possibility, was floating yet another prospect. It is one that could have great potential for the northern half of the province she has adopted as her home, a province hoping to recover from recession and regain its place in the West as a nourishing incubator of risk-taking entrepreneurs. It will build on what she sees as more than a mere vogue among North Americans.

TrendWatch

"My business ideas come from going back to philosophy," Kazuko Komatsu explains. "Basically what do people need and where is the world moving?" People want, as well as need, to become more health-conscious, she says, and are demanding a better life (not *lifestyle*, a word she equates with wealth). They are seeking the ongoing self-improvement of *kizen*. And one way to better themselves is through sensible eating and drinking. Prince George, she points out, has a climate close to northern Europe's, which has productive herb-growing land. What if she were to bottle her pure water as a value-added product with the addition of healthful herbs? Visiting Europe, she has discovered similar beverages, which are tasty and drinkable on a daily basis. And it is the European herbs, rather than Asian ones like ginseng, that she foresees for her bottled-water products. Her dream reaches beyond her own interests: if the provincial government encouraged the growing of herbs in northern climes, residents could lessen their dependence on industries such as mining that draw on non-renewable resources. What is needed, she says, her voice rising slightly in a controlled excitement, is a specific plan and government guidance to sell the development of that half of the province as a specialty-agricultural region. "Then you see, 100 years later, all northern British Columbia is the best place for herbs in the world. Right?"

Index

Advice. *See* Business tips
Aellen, Werner, 77
All Aboard: the Canadian Rockies by Train, 144, 196n
Allard, Tony, 60
Almaraz, Mark, 164
Altner, Sandy, 13
Anatomy of an Entrepreneur, 20, 299
Andre, Brenda, 307n
Andrew, Mark, 201, 202
Antonson, Rick, 197
Armstrong, Beverley, 194, 195, 200, 202
Armstrong, Charles, 195, 196
Armstrong, John, 321, 322
Armstrong, Peter, 143, 144, 177–205
Ashton, Barry, 230
Asper, Izzy, 25
Asquith, George, 162, 163, 167, 169, 172, 173
Atherton, Murray, 191n, 203
Atlantis Submarines, 149–176
Bad ideas, 154, 155
Baird, Tina, 61
Ballard Power Systems, 257, 258
Banks, 297, 302
Barbee, Gene, 224, 225
Barnett, Peter and Jeffrey, 42
Barr, Gordon, 198n
Barron, Dave, 207
Bartlett, Art, 43
Bates, Harold, 125, 133
Baxter, Don, 191
BCIT Entrepreneurial Skills Training Course (BEST), 18
Beamish, Mike, 264, 278, 282
Beck, Nuala, 232
Bellchambers, Barry, 161, 164
Bennett, Bill, 128
Berton, Pierre, 24
BEST, 18
Biomira Inc., 258
Bioriginal Food & Science Corporation, 259
Biotechnology, 311–332
Birch, David, 125
Bolton, Ken, 13, 99–105, 107, 109, 110
Bonner, Robert, 190

Boom, Bust & Echo (Foot), 207, 232
Brancato, Chris, 62, 78
Branson, Richard, 180n
Brewery, 333–357
Brown, John, 319, 320
Browning, Richard, 194, 200
Building a Dream (Good), 11
Busby, Don, 71
Business tips
  bad ideas, 154, 155
  banks, 297, 302
  cash flow, 294
  charitable donations, 354
  cheerleader for employees, 111
  client whims, 68
  communications program, 169
  competitor analysis, 137, 138
  consultants, 225, 226
  control of suppliers, 171, 172
  corporate/personal strengths, 73, 74
  customer education, 109
  directness/honesty, 38
  do-or-die issues, 199
  due diligence, 48, 49
  family business (orderly succession), 35, 36
  family/relatives, as investors, 160
  focus on business, not share price, 228
  fun-generating game, business as, 290
  global business relations, 276, 277
  going into business with friends, 215
  government programs, 101
  government regulations, 129
  ignorance about business issues, 188, 189
  income-tax filing, 79, 80
  industry involvement, 134, 135
  innovations, 238, 239
  intuition, 340, 341
  ISO certification, 349, 350
  know your customer, 221, 222
  leverage, 274, 275

manufacturing process, 241
marketing, 165, 166, 249, 330
mentors, 218
mission statement, 315
negatives of life, 51, 52
new product lines, 93
partnership expectations, 105
partnerships, 324, 325
passion, 125, 265, 266
patents, 238, 239
peer groups, 200, 201
personal relationships, 185
provincial government experts, 246, 247
public relations, 61, 62
raising money from private sources, 297, 302, 321, 328
regulatory reporting, 79, 80
relationships with employees, 347
salesmanship, 122
share vision with employees, 181
start-up capital, 157
strategic alliance, 280, 281
style of doing business, 40, 41
suppliers (credentials), 245
sustainable products, 68
teaching, 268, 269
too good to be true, 104
trade shows, 251, 252, 352
undersell, then overdeliver, 299
visualization, 63, 64
Butler, Michael, 44
Cannell, Stephen J., 75n
Capozzi, Herb, 345
Cappon, Daniel, 340
Cariou, Len, 2
Carter, J. Bob, 313, 322
Cash flow, 294
Cash, Martin, 286
Century 21 Canada, 29–56
Chan, Charlie, 309
Charette, Christine, 313, 331
Charitable donations, 354
Charlwood, Albert, 36
Charlwood, Christopher, 33–35, 38, 50, 52–55
Charlwood, Martin, 33, 34, 49, 50, 53, 54
Charlwood, U. Gary, 29–56

Chase, Randal, 329
Cheerleader for employees, 111
Clark, Glen, 81
Clark, Joe, 179
Clelland, Rocky, 209
Client whims, 68
Coleman, Deborah A., 125
Coleman, Gwen, 119
Collingwood, Tom, 44
Communications program, 169
Competitor analysis, 137, 138
Consultants, 225, 226
Controlling Interest: Who Owns Canada? (Francis), 25
Coolidge, Calvin, 182
Coombs, Ann, 181, 203, 204
Coppens, Dorothy, 316, 317, 329
Coppens, Guillaume, 316, 317
Coppola, Francis Ford, 78
Creo Products, 258
Crooks, Malcolm, 295, 298, 300
Cruise, David, 3n
Cruise-ship business, 176
Cuff, John Haslett, 79n
Cunningham, Randy, 20
Customer education, 109
Dane, Barry, 193n
DeFehr, Art, 12n
Dennis, Frank, 48
Dent, Roger, 75n
Diamond, Ephraim, 10
Differential GPS, 257, 261
Directness/honesty, 38
Do-or-die issues, 199
Dolphin, Dave, 323
Downing, Gordon, 190
Drever, Michael, 34
Drever, Mike, 54
Drysdale, Kathy, 20
Due diligence, 48, 49
Duncan, Murray, 67, 70, 71, 74, 80
Educational opportunities, 18, 19
Elliot, Mel, 241
Elliott, Darrell, 80
Ellipse Spatial Services, 256
Empire makers, 23–27
 Charlwood, Gary, 29–56
 Gamble, Tim, 57–82
Enns, Peter, 11
Entrepreneur 30, 18
Entrepreneurship camps, 19
Family business (orderly succession), 35, 36

Family/relatives, as investors, 160
Farais, John, 168
Farentino, Deborah, 210
Fast, Tamara, 20
Fattouche, Michel, 256
Field, Brad and Lori, 209–232
Fitzhenry, Ed and Shirley, 261–283
Food. *See* Palate pleasers
Food Fight: Truth, Myth and the Food-Health Connection, The (Mowbray), 96
Food processing, 85–87
Foot, David K., 207
Foran, William "Bud", 326, 329
Ford, Glenn, 134
Francis, Diane, 2, 24
French paradox, 116, 117
Friends, going into business with, 215
Friesen, David, 11, 12n
Fry, Doug, 163, 165
Fun-generating game, business as, 290
Galbraith, Ken, 314
Gallagher, Jack, 270, 339
Gamble, Tim, 57–82
Gates, Bill, 178n
Gender pioneers, 305–309
 Komatsu, Kazuko, 333–357
 Levy, Julia, 311–332
Gibran, Kahlil, 38
Giles, Jack, 44
Ginsberg, Larry, 157
Ginter, Ben, 344
Giustra, Frank, 72
Global business relations, 276, 277
Global Commerce Development, Inc., 86n
Global positioning system (GPS), 255–257
Goldberg, Michael, 84
Goldie, Susan, 288
Goldsmith, Russell, 76
Good, Walter, 11, 12, 20, 51
Government programs, 17, 18, 101
Government regulations, 129
GPS, 255–257
Graves, David, 10
Great Canadian Railtour Company, 177–205
Great Game of Business, The (Stack), 290n
Griffiths, Allison, 3n

Guerrilla marketing, 109
Guiney, Bert, 193n
Hainle, Tilman and Sandra, 85
Hainle, Walter, 85
Hamilton, Robert, 195
Harcourt, Mike, 322
Harley, Dave, 216–218, 224, 226, 227, 230
Harris, Brian, 78
Harrison, John, 169
Haseloh, Dan, 205, 206
Hawthorne Moutain Wineyards, 115–141
Helps, Kathy, 98n
Heritage Foods, 85, 86
High-tech entrepreneurs, 255–259
 Fitzhenry, Ed and Shirley, 261–283
 Loewen, Charles (Chuck), 285–304
Hill, Anne Chong, 86n
Hill, Fred, 25
Hill, Michael, 211, 212, 228, 263
Hockin, Tom, 197
Hollingshead, Audra, 307
Holmes, Harry, 192
Honesty/directness, 38
Hope, Bob, 183
Hopper, Bill, 270
Hopper, Grace Murray, 129n
Houston, James, 194, 195, 200
Hughes, Jesse Willard, 85
Hungerford, George, 195
Hunky Bill's House of Perogies, 86n
Hurd, Dennis, 149–176
Hurd, Roy, 12, 155, 158, 160, 162, 164
Hurd, Susan, 159n
Ignorance about business issues, 188, 189
Income-tax filing, 79
Industry involvement, 134, 135
Innovations, 238, 239
Internet commerce, 253, 254
Intuition, 340, 341
Intuition: Harnessing the Hidden Power of the Mind (Cappon), 340
ISO certification, 349, 350
Ivany, Terry, 202n
Iwamoto, Robert, 173
Jackson, Dave, 269

Jackson, Murray, 192–194, 199, 200
Jacobs, Andreas, 99n
Janca, Phillip, 159
Jim Scharf Holdings Ltd., 233–254
Johannson, Clark, 20
Johnson, Chester, 124
Johnstone, Lucy, 160n
Jones, Juliet, 74
Jones, L. Bruce, 166n
Jones, Yvonne, 96
Ka-Shing, Li, 16
Ka-Shing, Victor, 16
Kaiser, Edgar, Jr., 270, 320
Kane, Marion, 91n
Keen, Bill, 163
Keizer, Dorothy, 249
Kellogg, John Harvey, 95
Kelowna, 210n
Kendall, Ken, 162
Kenny, David, 163
Kenny, Peter, 160
Ketchum, Jess, 194–196, 202, 203
Khosrowshahi, Hassan, 10
Klawe, Maria, 14
Klein, Chips, 218
Klein, Ralph, 207n
Knittel, Werner, 206
Know your customer, 221, 222
Komatsu, Kazuko, 306, 307, 333–357
Konyk, William, 86n
Kotler, Mel, 230
Kulow, Rick, 259
Lambert, Garrett, 17
Lawby, Don, 31, 32, 45, 51
Lawrason, David, 139n
Lee, Wellington, 66, 67
Leone, Mike, 167
Lessons, See Business tips
Leverage, 274, 275
Levy, Edwin, 318, 324
Levy, Julia, 305, 306, 311–332
Levy, Michael, 34, 42, 45, 47, 53
Li Ka-Shing, 16
Lift-Off, 18
Light, Terry, 288
Lindquist, Jack, 173
Little, Joe, 230
Loewen, Charles (Chuck), 285–304
Loewen, Eleanor, 291
Loewen, Ray, 9, 285n
Lorent, André, 130, 227, 230
Lougheed, Evans, 124

Lounsberry, Fred, 166, 167
Ludwig, Wally, 102–104
Lwowski, Ezra, 313
Lyttle, Howard, 196
MacDonald, Tom, 187, 188, 191, 192
MacIlroy, Doug, 155, 163n
MacKenzie, Lewis, 211, 213, 227, 230
Maclean, Ray, 322
Magee, Christine, 307n
Makowecki, Walter, 85–87
Malo, Shelley, 287, 289
Mancini, Alexandra, 327
Manek, Raj, 252
Manufacturing magicians, 205–208
  Field, Brad and Lori, 209–232
  Scharf, Jim and Bruna, 233–254
Marketing, 165, 166, 249, 330
Martin, Douglas, 20
Masson, Paul, 127
Maverick mindset, 11–14
Max, John, 94, 95
Mayor, Harry, 306, 334, 337, 339, 342, 346–353, 355
McCarthy, Grace, 189, 191
McCartney, Linda, 92
McCartney, Paul, 92
McClelland, Jack, 312
McIntosh of Dyee, 86, 87
McKenzie, Ron, 319, 320, 322
McLeod, Bill, 188
McWatters, Harry, 115–141
McWatters, Kathy, 130
Mennonite entrepreneurs, 11, 12n. See also Loewen, Charles (Chuck)
Mentors, 218
Mesiti, Jay, 279
Metzger, Darrell, 154, 155, 159n, 172–174
MicroBio Rhizogen Corporation, 259
Miller, Jim, 161n, 313, 319–322, 324–326, 331
Miller, Merv, 217
Miller, Mike, 183, 184, 186
Mines, Robin, 84
Mission statement, 315
Mitchell, David J., 144, 196n
Mitchell, Peter, 60
Modha, Ash, 21
Molendyk, Gordon, 209
Mondetta Clothing Company, 21

Money Rustlers: Self-Made Millionaires of the New West, The (Grescoe), 3, 12
Moore, Roger, 36
Morrison, Rod, 202n
Mowbray, Scott, 96n
Murrills, Angela, 92
Negatives of life, 51, 52
Neufeld, Dave, 294, 295, 297
Never Fight with a Pig: A Survival Guide for Entrepreneurs (Thomas), 30, 43
New product lines, 93
Newman, Peter C., 24, 322n
Nichum, Oli, 178n
Norris, Mac, 195, 196
Nutraceuticals, 259
Nuytten, Phil, 150n, 151n
O'Connor, Matthew, 75
O'Rourke, Richard, 195
Okomoto, Sam, 107
Online Business Systems, 285–304
Pacific Safety Products, 209–232
Pacific Western Brewing Company, 333–357
Page, Nicole and Jeremy, 17
Palate pleasers, 83–87
  McWatters, Harry, 115–141
Potvin, Yves, 89–113
Partnership expectations, 105
Partnerships, 324, 325
Passion, 125, 265, 266
Patents, 238, 239
Pattison, Jimmy, 1, 2, 25, 44
Peach, Jack, 217
Peace Arch Entertainment Group, 57–82
Peer groups, 200, 201
Peer Resources Network, 218n
Pellatt, George, 160n
Pelorus Navigation Systems, 261–283
Penner, Bruce, 295
Perrault, Jennifer, 63
Personal relationships, 185
Peters, Thomas J., 315
Pevsner, Donald, 143
Phillips, Michael, 199, 200
Phillips, Tony, 320
Philom Bios Inc., 259
Pollock, Ann, 195
Poole, Tom, 86, 87
Potvin, Claude, 104
Potvin, Francine, 104

Potvin, Yves, 89–113, 201
Preview, 2
Price, Dulcie, 20
Provincial government
  experts, 246, 247
Pryor, Rob, 256
Public relations, 61, 62
QLT Photo Therapeutics,
  311–332
Rader, Tom, 193, 194, 201
Radloff, Laurie, 48, 53
Regulatory reporting, 79
Relatives/family, as investors,
  160
Renaud, Serge, 117n
Richmond, Bud, 133, 136,
  138
Richter, Anna, 328
Roberts, Tom, 161
Rogers, A.B. "Hell's Bells",
  196n
Rosen, Al, 92
Ross, David, 19
Rovinsky, David, 5
Rowe, Tom, 75
Ruffel, Terry, 122
Sa'agd, Don, 169
Saari, Bob, 207n
Salesmanship, 122
Saul, John Ralston, 145
Sawchuk, Craig, 65, 67, 69,
  72, 74, 80
Scharf, Clarence, 236, 239,
  245
Scharf, Jim and Bruna,
  233–254
Schmeilan, Hinrich, 329n
Schmidt, Alan, 132
Schmidt, Lloyd, 127–129,
  131–133
Schmidt, Ursula, 329
Schreiner, John, 117
Schulz, Bernie, 207n
Schwartz, Gerald, 202
Scott, Duff, 326
Search of Excellence, In
  (Peters/Waterman), 315
Sebazco, Maria Isabel, 52
Segal, Joe, 190
Sepp's Gourmet Foods, 86,
  87
Sharpe, W.R., 345
Sheen, Martin, 72
Siemens, Tim, 297–299, 301
Sirsley, Christena Keon, 193n
Skalbania, Nelson, 30, 42,
  345
Slater, Sandy, 198, 199

Small Business, Big Money
  (Ginsberg), 157
Smed, Mogens, 23, 24
SMED International, 23, 24
Smith, Nelson, 75n
Soar, Roger, 227, 231n
Soft-adventure tourism, 145
Southern, Ron, 25
Spratt, Derek, 74n
Springfield Remanufacturing
  Corporation, 290n
Stack, John P., 290n
Step Ahead One-on-One
  Mentoring Program, 218n
Sterlinger, Sepp, 37
Stern, Eli, 69
Stoddart, Darcy, 21
Strategic alliances, 280, 281
Strategies. *See* Business tips
Strauss, Peter, 72
Strengths, 73, 74
Strong, Maurice, 269, 270
Sturgeon, Arnold, 195
Style of doing business, 40,
  41
Sugar, Larry, 57–61, 64,
  76–78
Sumac Ridge Estate Winery,
  115–141
Suppliers
  control of, 171, 172
  credentials, 245
Sustainable products, 68
Suzuki, David, 318
Tanchak, Dave, 17
Teaching, 268, 269
Thomas, Peter, 29, 30, 42,
  43, 46, 50, 51n
Thomspon, Bonita, 70n
Tips. See Business tips
Too good to be true, 104
Tourism impresarios,
  143–147
  Armstrong, Peter, 177–205
  Hurd, Dennis, 149–176
Towers, Neil, 318
Townsend, Ray, 46, 49
Trade shows, 251, 252, 352
Trice, Allan, 158, 159
Trinh, Hien, 106
Undersell, then overdeliver,
  299
Uniglobe Travel
  (International), 29–56
Van Horne, William, 196n
Venture, 18
Vision, share with
  employees, 181

Visualization, 63, 64
Voltaire's Bastards (Saul), 145
Walker, William, 165
Wall, Brad J., 15
Walsh, Memory, 119n
Wareham, Bob, 118, 119,
  127, 135, 138
Wasserman, Jack, 183
Waterman, Robert H., Jr.,
  315
Weiner, Michael, 98, 99, 112
Weintraub, Jerry, 76
Wenner, Paul, 108n
Wenzel, Jan-Udo, 344
Wessamann, Johan, 275, 276
Western Canadian culture,
  11–17
Western Economic
  Diversification Canada, 18
Western Youth Entrepreneur
  Program, 18
White, Cam, 60, 61, 64, 70,
  75–77
White, Dan, 220
Wine industry, 84, 85
Winemaking, 115–141
Winter, John, 336
Witney, John, 161, 165
Women. *See* Gender pioneers
Women Business Owners of
  Canada, 307n
Women Entrepreneurs of
  Canada, 307n
Wong, Milton, 6n
Woodward, Robyn, 158, 166n
Worthington, Reg, 26, 62,
  65–69, 70n, 71, 74
Wright, Bob, 144, 145
You BET!—Youth Business
  and Entrepreneurship
  Training, 17
Young, Doug, 264
Young Entrepreneur
  Financing Program, 18n
Young Entrepreneurs'
  Organization, 200n
Young Leaders Committee,
  20
Young Presidents'
  Organization, 200
Youth Entrepreneurship
  Camp, 19, 20
Yves Veggie Cuisine, 89–113
Zaghloul, Hatim, 256